CW01647795

FILM MAKER'S GUIDE TO SUPER-8

The "How-To-Do-It" book for beginning and advanced filmmakers.

by the editors of
SUPER-8 FILMAKER magazine

Sheptow Publishing
San Francisco, California

Curtin & London, Inc.
Somerville, Massachusetts

Van Nostrand Reinhold Company
New York Cincinnati Toronto Melbourne

Copyright © 1980 by SHEPTOW PUBLISHING

Library of Congress Catalog Card Number 79-9606

ISBN 0-442-23344-2 cloth
ISBN 0-442-23319-1 paper

All rights reserved. No part of this work covered by the copyright hereon may be reproduced or used in any form or by an means—graphic, electronic, or mechanical, including photocopying, recording, taping, or information storage and retrieval systems—without written permission of the publisher.

Printed in the United States of America

Published in 1980 by Sheptow Publishing, Curtin& London, Inc., and Van Nostrand Reinhold Company
A division of Litton Educational Publishing, Inc.
135 West 50th Street, New York, NY 10020, U.S.A.

Van Nostrand Reinhold Limited
1410 Birchmount Road
Scarborough, Ontario M1P 2E7, Canada

Van Nostrand Reinhold Australia Pty. Ltd.
17 Queen Street
Mitcham, Victoria 3132, Australia

10 9 8 7 6 5 4 3 2 1

Library of Congress Cataloging in Publication Data
Main entry under title:

Film maker's guide to Super-8.

1. Cinematography. I. Super 8 filmaker.
TR850.F55 778.5'3 79-9606
ISBN 0-442-23344-2

INTRODUCTION

You don't need a cigar to be a producer or a beret to be a director. You don't even need sunglasses to be a star. In the world of Super-8 filmmaking, you can be all these things—all by yourself—and throw in scriptwriter, cameraperson, editor, make-up artist, production designer and grip. With Super-8 camera in hand, you can make films for fun or money, to teach yourself a craft or capture the moments of your life.

Super-8 was born in 1965 in Rochester, New York. The small, black plastic cartridge of film revolutionized the home movie industry and sent camera manufacturers scurrying to bring new designs to the market. But most folks buying the new format didn't think of themselves as *filmmakers*. They were just fooling around, shooting family and friends.

Any group of "most folks" contains a special few with a larger vision and these "fooling around" filmmakers looked at their footage and saw fantasy, documentary, comedy, drama—in a word—art! Artistry tempers a medium, working it toward strength and sensitivity. Filmmakers since 1965 have expanded the Super-8 medium enormously, demanding better cameras, faster film, longer-running cartridges, sound and more sound; and their demands for information were the loudest of all.

So, in the winter of 1972, a magazine was born to spread the word about the latest techniques, ideas and equipment. In the pages of SUPER-8 FILMAKER, Super-8 users found their forum. Letters and articles, tips and queries poured in. The enthusiasm of these pioneering filmmakers, their incredible creativity and eagerness for knowledge, has been phenomenal.

We've taken the most useful and informative articles from the first five years of the magazine to create the FILMMAKER'S GUIDE TO SUPER-8. These stories will tell you how to do a range of filmmaking techniques, why to do them and what equipment to do them with. We've included articles on building your own equipment and a chapter on turning your film hobby into a money-making business. Other chapters cover sound, special effects, animation, scripting, teaching with film and more.

The writers represented here are working Super-8 filmmakers from around the world who have chosen their medium not only because it is economical and accessible, but also because it is so personally and profoundly a part of the future of art itself. We thank them for sharing their experience and expertise with us.

Our thanks to those who helped make this book a reality; magazine editors Joyce Newman, Tiiu Lukk and Bruce Anderson; designer Tony Naganuma; editorial consultant Dennis Duggan; indexer Chet Roaman; typesetter Jean Graphics; production artists Lynne August and Cathy McAuliffe; production consultant Marsha Mim; and publishing coordinator Alexandra Grant.

—The Editors

CONTENTS

EQUIPMENT

SOUND

SCRIPTWRITING

FILMING TECHNIQUES

PROCESSING AND PRINTING

EDITING

ANIMATION

SPECIAL EFFECTS

HOW TO SHOOT A...

THE DOCUMENTARY

MONEY AND MOVIES

EDUCATION

BUILD YOUR OWN

EQUIPMENT

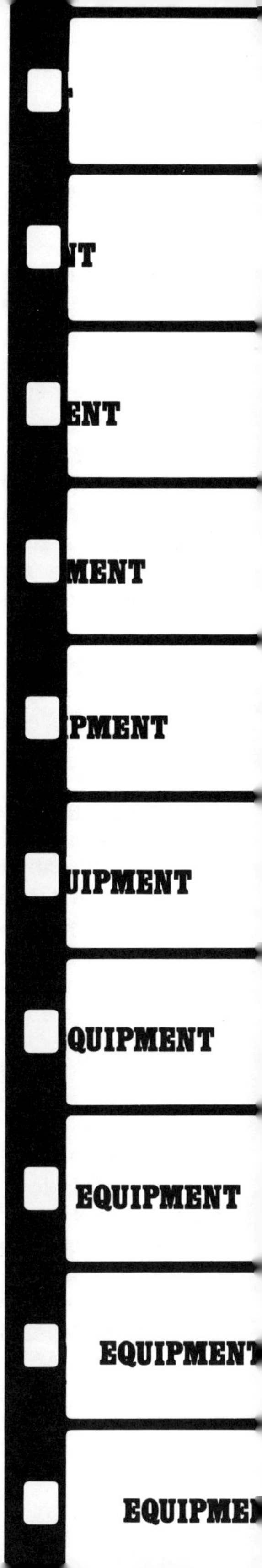
NT
ENT
MENT
PMENT
UIPMENT
QUIPMENT
EQUIPMENT
EQUIPMEN
EQUIPME

CHOOSING A SUPER-8 SYSTEM

Stephen Aubery

Perhaps the most difficult question facing a filmmaker going into serious Super-8 production is "What kind of equipment should I buy?" Since the applications of Super-8 are countless, it's impossible to give a simple answer to this question. I have found, however, that certain types of gear are more suitable for use in a given application.

Film Format

Within the realms of Super-8, there are three basic format subdivisions: cartridge Super-8, Single-8 and Double Super-8. Since the three types of film are *not* interchangeable in their respective cameras (although they are in projection), the "Professional-8" must make a choice of format before purchasing a camera.

Cartridge Super-8

This is the most familiar and available Super-8 format. It is most suitable for professional applications requiring maximum speed.

Advantages:

1) Removing an exposed film cartridge and inserting a new one takes literally seconds. If you've ever worked in TV news filming, you'll know that you generally run out of film at the beginning of the most important statement. What cartridge Super-8 can do for you in this situation is reduce the time lost to about 60 seconds for 16mm magazines. 2) Magnetic striped film is available in Super-8 cartridges, allowing single-system sync sound production. This is an advantage not only for TV news reporting, but also for producing in-house industrial sound films. 3) The notches on the cartridge automatically set the camera for ASA and filter. This helps when you have someone less experienced doing some of your shooting. For example, suppose you are making a film in a chemical research institute. You need to have footage of the ongoing progress of various experiments, as well as a record of any findings that are made. It's unfeasible for you to be on hand every day, waiting for the magic moment. With a little training, the researcher could easily roll the cartridge camera at the right moment and get the necessary footage. 4) The Super-8 cartridge can be removed from the camera anytime and replaced later, with only about a dozen frames of picture being exposed (fogged). This makes changing from a low ASA film (for outdoor shooting) to a high ASA film (for indoor filming) very simple. 5) Super-8 film in cartridges is very easy to find in stores, so it only takes a few minutes to replenish your supply. 6) The ASA 160 films available in Super-8 cartridges, coupled with one of the new "XL" (existing light) cartridge

cameras, make available light filming a reality. 7) With the arrival on the market of a new Kodak film, SM 7244, and a new processor (the Supermatic 8), cartridges of this film can be processed and screened within 15 minutes from the time you finish shooting. (There's an aid for TV news!)

Disadvantages:

1) The pressure plate, which maintains the correct film position and alignment in the camera, is plastic, mass-produced and contained in a disposable cartridge. In other professional cameras, the pressure plate is precision machined and built into the camera itself. The result of using nonprecision pressure plates can be soft focus. Some say the plastic pressure plate has nothing to do with the soft focus; I can only speak from my own experience, and I've found some cartridge Super-8 footage to be slightly soft. 2) Two important considerations in film are contrast and grain. If you're planning to edit and release the original, then most cartridge films will provide quite acceptable grain and contrast; but if you plan to duplicate your original, there are few available cartridge films that have low enough contrast and grain to reproduce with good results. The increased grain and contrast may or may not be acceptable, depending on how critical your client is. For instance, if you're just documenting some research and need to make another print, then duplicating a cartridge film will probably provide adequate quality. However, if you're making a promotional film for a travel club, then a grainy, contrasty cartridge duplicate won't impress your client or prospective customers. Again, the kind of work you plan to do determines how sophisticated your methods must be. 3) In-camera effects are very limited. The Super-8 cartridge was never designed for backwinding, and although several methods have been devised for backwinding a Super-8 cartridge, they are all limited to short lengths, generally 100 frames.

French film director Jean Luc Godard using a Beaulieu with interchangeable lenses.

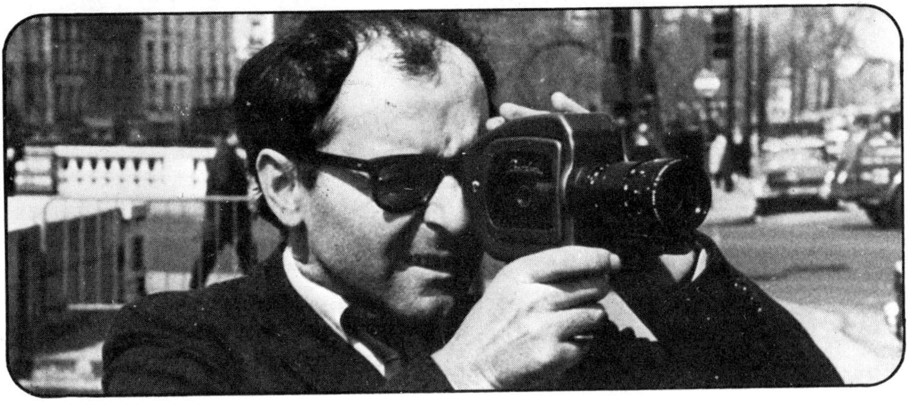

CENTRE NATIONAL DE CREATION ET DIFFUSION SUPER-8

Single-8

Single-8 operates with an entirely different cartridge design. Instead of the supply and take-up spools running in a coaxial configuration (that is, side by side, as in cartridge Super-8), they are mounted in a displacement cartridge, much like the design in an audio cassette.

Advantages:

1) The pressure plate for Single-8 is contained within the camera, unlike cartridge Super-8. Therefore, the focus should be consistently sharper. 2) Fuji (the only manufacturer of Single-8 film) uses a polyester-based film. Polyester is more durable than the acetate that is used for many Super-8 films. 3) Due to the design of the Single-8 cartridge, backwinding the entire 50-foot length is easy, making extensive in-camera effects (dissolves, double exposures, etc.) quite simple. 4) Since Fuji's recent introduction of a Single-8 color film with an ASA rating of 200, Single-8 available light filming has become much easier.

Disadvantages:

1) When purchasing film for a Single-8 camera, you are limited to only Fuji film stocks, of which there is not a great variety. 2) Single-8 is not as popular as cartridge Super-8, so there are many stores that don't even stock Single-8 film, requiring you to special order—which can be time-consuming and aggravating. 3) Single-8 films are available only in 50-foot cartridges, thus limiting your running time. 4) Only one manufacturer, Fuji Photo Film, U.S.A., makes Single-8 cameras and film, so the choice of camera models is very limited.

Double Super-8

Double Super-8 (DS-8) is not contained in any sort of cartridge, but is supplied on daylight-loaded spools. As the name suggests, Double Super-8 is 16 millimeters wide, and has Super-8 perforations along each edge. The film is run through the DS-8 camera, exposing one half of the width. Then the film is turned over, reloaded in the camera, allowing the remaining half to be exposed. The film is then processed, slit and the ends of the two pieces of Super-8 film are spliced together.

Advantages:

1) In my opinion, one of the greatest advantages of DS-8 is the availability of Kodak Ektachrome Commercial film (ECO) for use in DS-8 cameras. ECO, long used in 16mm production, is known for its low contrast and grain, and prints made from ECO look very good. If optimum image quality is of importance to you or your client, then ECO is necessary for production. 2) The standard length of DS-8 rolls is 100 feet, meaning that you can run continuously for 6 minutes and 40 seconds (at 18 fps) or 5 minutes (at 24 fps), then turn the film over and run those same lengths of time without interruption. Some DS-8 cameras are

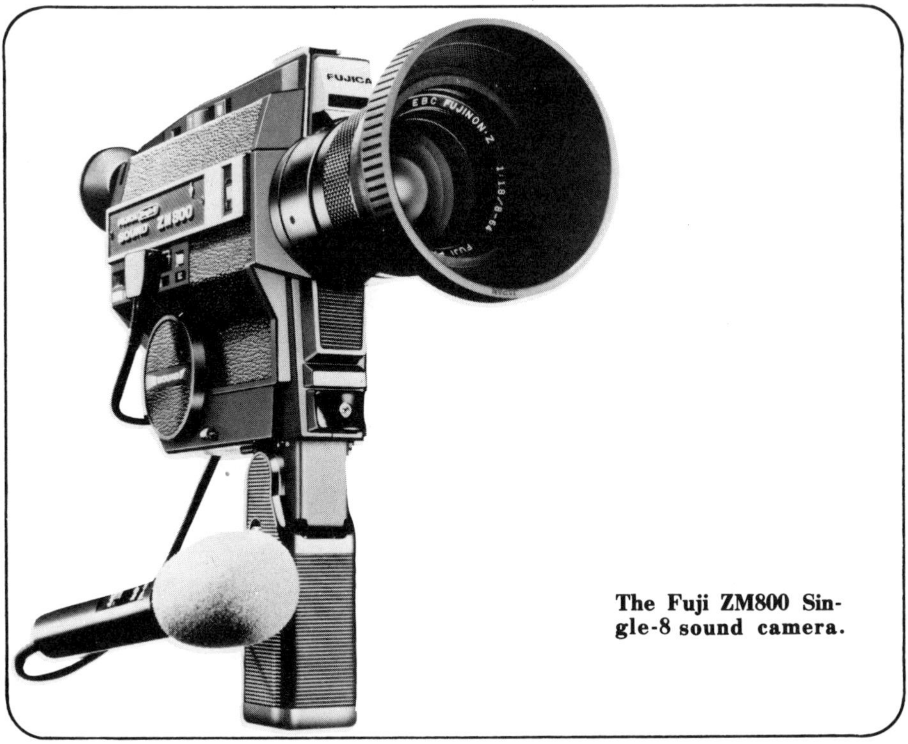

The Fuji ZM800 Single-8 sound camera.

FUJI

even capable of accepting 400-foot loads of film, giving you about 26 minutes of uninterrupted running time. 3) Since DS-8 stock is produced in larger quantities and doesn't require cartridges (or loading into cartridges), it is less expensive. Processing costs less, too. 4) Because DS-8 cameras are redesigned 16mm cameras, they are usually of sturdier construction than many other Super-8 cameras. 5) As with Single-8, DS-8 cameras have a built-in precision pressure plate which helps account for the very sharp focus attainable with this format. 6) DS-8 also has unlimited backwind capability, so in-camera effects are no problem.

Disadvantages:

1) Since DS-8 film is not contained in a lightproof cartridge, removing the film from the camera partway through a roll would result in fogging about 6 feet of the film. So if you wanted to change from a high ASA film to a low ASA stock for shooting outdoors, you must be prepared to sacrifice a little. 2) Changing film in a DS-8 camera takes longer than with either of the other two formats. And when the new roll is in the camera, you must run 2-3 feet into the film in order to avoid using the head footage that was fogged during loading. 3) DS-8 film is also a special order item in many cases, and is made only by Kodak; ordering ahead so that you don't run out is a necessity. 4) Although ECO is an excellent

duplicating film with an ASA of 25 (tungsten) and 16 (daylight), it is unusable in low available light situations. 5) The only high speed film available for DS-8 use is Ektachrome EFB 7242 (ASA 125 tungsten) which reproduces with considerable grain and contrast. There are labs, however, that will postflash DS-8 EF (that is, expose the film to a weak light before processing), which reduces the contrast and brings out detail in the shadows. You'll have to live with the grain, though. 6) DS-8 cameras are larger and heavier than other Super-8 and Single-8 cameras, and so are less adaptable to situations where you're trying to be inconspicuous. 7) The choice of DS-8 cameras is limited.

Filming Speed

Super-8, unlike other motion picture formats, has two sync sound speeds for filming: 18 and 24 frames per second. It all began when Super-8 was first introduced to the home movie market and 18 fps was accepted as the standard filming speed. It was only natural that the first amateur sync sound systems should also operate at 18 fps. But, as people started reducing 16mm films (shot at 24 fps) to Super-8 for release in various cartridge projectors, a second sync speed emerged—24 fps. Since some cameras run *only* at 18 fps, an important question to consider before purchasing is "Which sync speed should I use for filming?"

18 Frames Per Second

Advantages:

1) If you film at 18 fps you have 33 percent more running time than you would have for the same amount of film at 24 fps. This means lower costs and fewer film changes. 2) At 18 fps, there are fewer shutter openings per second, meaning that each opening of the shutter lasts a little longer than at 24 fps. With a longer exposure time, you have the ability

The author filming with the Canon DS-8.

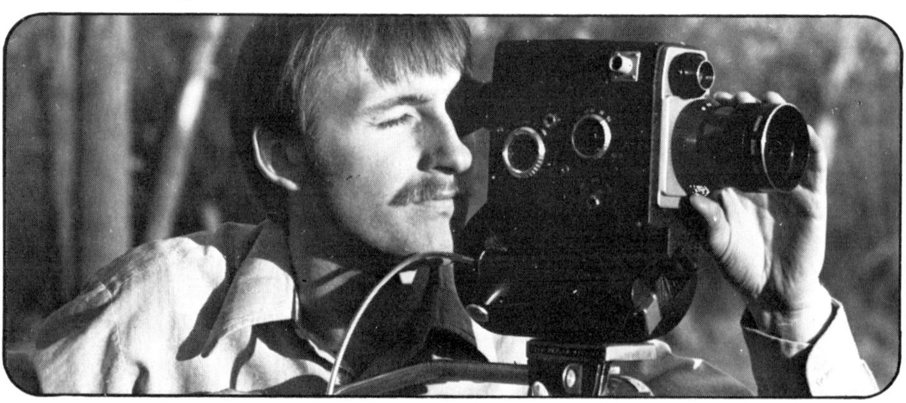

to shoot in lower light. It works out that you gain about half an *f*/stop in exposure. 3) A camera runs slightly more quietly at 18 fps.

Disadvantages:

1) A fast moving-subject will have a greater tendency to appear blurred on the screen when filmed at 18 fps. This is because the shutter, being open longer, allows time for the subject to move farther per frame, thus registering a blurred image. 2) Blowup to another format is very difficult when your Super-8 is shot at 18 fps. Since the standard rate of other formats (16mm, 35mm, 70mm) is 24 fps, an 18 fps Super-8 blowup must be step printed. In step printing, every third Super-8 frame is printed twice. The result is often an unsteady, unacceptable image. 3) Sound recorded at 18 fps suffers in quality. Specifically, the signal to noise ratio (designated S/N) is low. That means that the noise (hiss and hum) that is inherent in electronic systems is increased in relation to the volume of program material at this lower speed. Also, the frequency response (the ability to record or reproduce all sounds at an equal volume) is poor, meaning that high frequencies reproduce poorly, making *s*'s sound like *f*'s, and cymbals sound mushy. The greatest loss of

A single-system camera, the Sankyo Sound XL 300S.

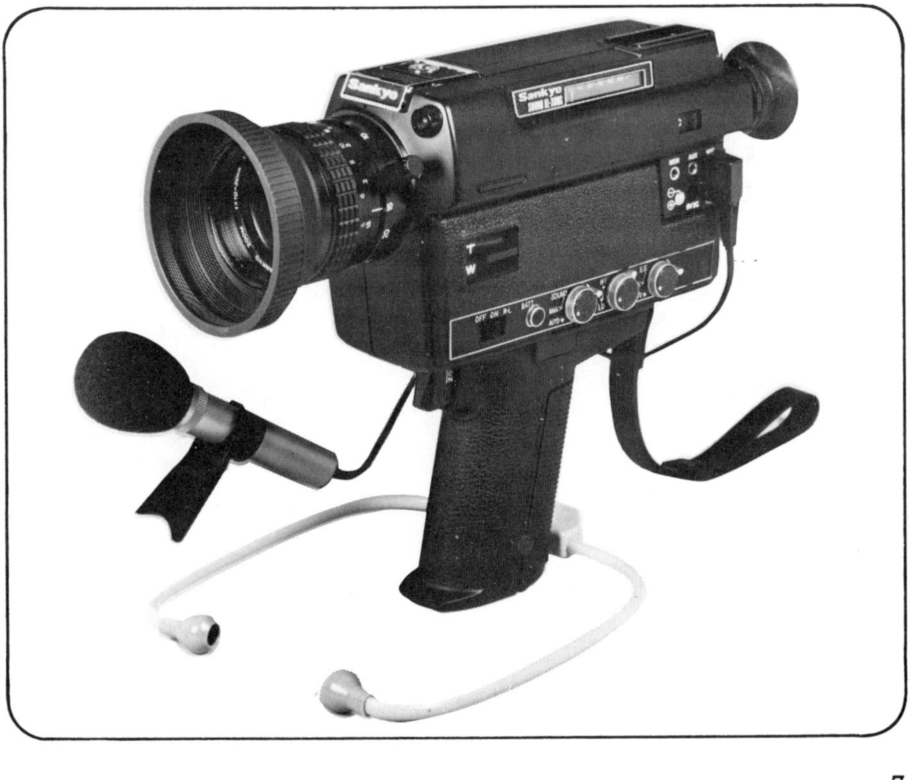

SANKYO

quality is noticeable in music recording and playback. 4) Many Super-8 cartridge projectors, since they were designed to show prints reduced from 16mm (at 24 fps), will not run at 18 fps. So if you're planning cartridge projection, it would be wise to investigate the projector you're considering before you start.

24 Frames Per Second

This has been accepted as the standard sync speed for most motion picture formats.

Advantages:

1) The most important consideration in filming at 24 fps is the sound quality. For some reason, the same technology used to improve the quality of the audio cassette over the past few years (at a tape speed of only 1 7/8 inches per second—ips) has not yet been applied to matching the quality of 18 fps sync sound (at 3 ips) with the improved response of sound recorded at 24 fps (4 ips). Maybe in the not-too-distant future that will change, but for right now shooting at 24 fps is a sound decision (pardon the pun). To check the difference simply record a short section of music on a fullcoat recorder at 18 fps. Then, immediately following, record the same piece of music at 24 fps, with no changes other than the speed. The playback results can be quite surprising. 2) In the event that a blowup is desired, 24 fps is compatible with other formats. 3) Prints at 24 fps are compatible with most cartridge projectors.

Disadvantages:

1) A camera running at 24 fps is slightly noisier than at 18 fps. 2) Using more film costs more money.

Production Sound System

Since the introduction of magnetic-striped Super-8 film by Kodak in 1973, there have been two basic methods of shooting Super-8 sync sound: single or double system.

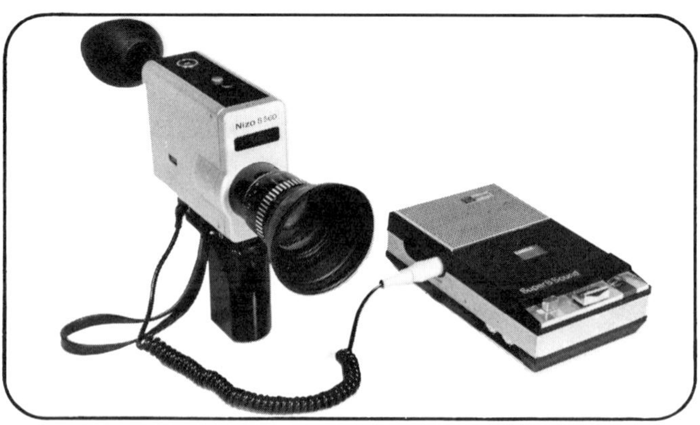

A double-system setup featuring a Nizo S560 synched to a Super8 Sound recorder.

Single-System Production

This system utilizes the striped film just mentioned. The basic components of this sytem are a single-system camera, magnetic-striped film cartridges and a microphone. A single-system camera not only records the visual image on the film emulsion, but also records the sound on the magnetic stripe. Recording the *picture* requires intermittent movement of the film (that is, the film advances, then stops while the shutter opens and exposes a frame, then the film advances again); recording the *sound* requires a smooth continuous motion. For this reason, the two cannot take place at the same time and at the same point on the film. As a result, there is an 18-frame separation between the film aperture and the sound record head; this space houses a drive capstan and flywheel to smooth out the intermittent motion.

Advantages:

1) Both sound and picture are contained on one piece of film so you don't need to worry about synching the picture to a separate piece of sound tape. 2) Single-system production is compact and very portable since the camera performs two functions. 3) One-person single-system operation is quite easy, since both light and sound levels are usually visible in the camera viewfinder, and the touch of one button starts and stops both operations.

Disadvantages:

1) Super-8 mag-striped film is available *only* in Super-8 cartridges. Therefore, if you want the advantage of Single-8 or Double Super-8, you can't shoot single system, and *vice-versa.* 2) ECO film is not available with a magnetic stripe. 3) The quality of single-system sound is generally poor. Although voice reproduction is usually acceptable, music sounds poor due to low signal-to-noise ratio, poor frequency response and wow and flutter problems. (Wow is the objectionable dragging, and flutter is the obnoxious wavering of sound in some recordings.) The wow and flutter are caused by the capstan and flywheel not being able to smooth out the motion of the film completely before it reaches the recording head. 4) Editing single system is difficult due to the 18-frame sound and picture separation, but if you're careful about shooting your scenes, it can be done. An easier way to edit footage that is shot single system is to transfer the sound from the stripe onto Super-8 fullcoat, then edit it on a double-system bench or table.

Double-System Production

This system requires the use of a tape recorder which is separate from the camera. Sync is maintained in a number of ways, the most common method making use of a camera that emits a sync pulse (a continuous tone, a tone burst per frame or simply the closing of a switch once per frame known as 1/F) which controls the speed of the tape recorder via a camera connecting cable. Some recorders merely record the sync pulse on a separate channel which is then used to control the speed of the recorder during playback. A double-system camera doesn't need record electronics or a head since it does no recording. Another method of producing double-system sync sound is often called "cableless" sync. Both the camera and recorder are slaved to identical external references (*e.g.*, a crystal control as in crystal sync) and no cables are needed.

Advantages:

1) The quality of sound that is recorded double system is much better due to four basic reasons. First, the recorders designed for this type of work generally have better electronic systems, making them capable of producing finer quality sound. Second, there is no intermittent movement in a tape recorder, cutting down even more on the already low wow and flutter. Third, the quality of the magnetic oxide on a good quality reel-to-reel cassette tape is superior to the oxide on magnetic striped film. Fourth, on many double-system recorders you have a much wider sound track than on magnetic striped film (.082-inch for half track quarter-inch tape or fullcoat; .027 for mag-striped film). All these reasons may seem negligible, but when you consider that your release print can be as many as four generations from the original recording, and that sound quality degenerates with each generation, you can understand why getting the best results possible in your original recording is important. 2) Many currently available Super-8 cameras are already equipped with a sync output of some form. Even if the camera you wish to use doesn't have a sync output, it takes just a few days and a few dollars (about $75) to modify it for sync. 3) You don't need to use prestriped film for double-system production. In fact, due to their larger size, Super-8 sound cartridges will not fit in non-single-system cameras.

Disadvantages:

1) You need more equipment to shoot double-system sync sound, including a recorder and connecting cable, or crystal controls for both the recorder and camera. This extra equipment can make one-person operation more difficult. In order to film a scene, the camera/sound person must start two pieces of equipment instead of just one (although in some cases the recorder start/stop is remote controlled by the camera), watch the lightmeter through the camera viewfinder and keep another eye on the sound VU meter on the recorder. This can be an awkward situation, especially if you're in a hurry. 2) Since the picture and sound are separate, a common start mark must be recorded on them simultaneously, so that they can be played back later in sync. The most common method of doing this is by using a clap-slate.

So far we've discussed three important choices to be made before venturing into the realms of Professional-8. *You* have to determine how these options apply to your specific needs in order to come up with the facility that gives you the flexibility and quality you need.

HOW TO BUY A CAMERA

Dennis Duggan

You want to buy a camera. You've read every review and report you could lay your hands on. You've talked to other filmmakers, and you've separated the facts from the hype in the camera ads. You've weighed all this information against your bank balance, and now you're ready to take...

The Multiple Choice Test

Super-8 abounds with choices. Does the convenience of a single-system (sound recording) camera outweigh the advantages of automatic lap dissolves and other refinements found on the more sophisticated double-system (silent) cameras? Will I shoot at 18 or 24 frames per second (fps)? Do I need an XL or a normal shutter? Will a short but fast (6 to 1 zoom, *f*/1.2) lens serve me as well as a longer but slower (12 to 1 zoom, *f*/1.8) lens? These are some of the questions you ask yourself and anyone else you can get to listen. And to help you make your decisions, some "expert" is always willing to tell you the "best" choice. It seems to me that it's always best to leave yourself an alternative. If the camera you select has many options, you're free to choose each time you film. Automatic everything is great, but manual override options give you more flexibility.

Your choice of camera, of course, should reflect *your* individual needs and be built to withstand *your* normal usages. It doesn't need to be built to last 20 years. Super-8 technology is improving at a tremendous rate; automatic focus and instant movies are almost upon us. Five or 10 years from now, the magical marvels of today will probably look like primitive antiques. Imagine 1 to 10 second "Dial-a-dissolve" or automatic color correction in any kind of light, minute-long zooms, or voice command controls.

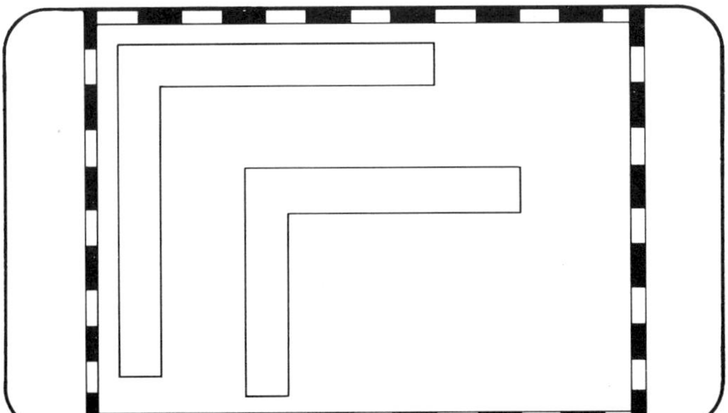

Reproduce this chart on 8½-by-11-inch paper. With camera on tripod, film the chart on a wall for 5 to 10 seconds. When film is processed, compare the projected image to the image you saw in the viewfinder.

Your camera should have every single feature that you anticipate needing, and probably a few more. Favoring extreme close-ups of wildflowers should lead you to look for a lens that has a macro capability over most, if not all, of its zoom range. If you plan to shoot indoor dialogue scenes with actors, you'll need a very quiet camera, or one that can easily be quieted with a soundproof "barney," without making the controls inaccessible. If you see yourself directing action films with fights and car chases, you may require a speed like 12 fps to make it all look fast without getting anyone killed.

A friend who's new to Super-8 proudly showed me a new camera with all the features he's heard me tout—but it also had an eyepiece that stuck out a full inch. This protrusion wouldn't have upset me so much if he weren't making a sports film. Handheld. Skiing in downhill races. The first time he falls with that camera up to his eye may be the last time he skis with a camera. And that's too bad.

Getting What You Want

You've given it a lot of thought, and now you know what features you want in a camera. But how do you tell a superb optical instrument from a plastic and glass gimmick box? Even more difficult, how do you tell a good camera from a so-so model? The answer is to pay a visit to your local camera store and put your top choices to the test. Eventually, you'll have to pay for a few cartridges of film and processing, but it's worth a few dollars to know if your chosen camera can make the grade. Buying a lemon can cost you plenty in ruined film, repair bills and aspirin. And if you suspect your current camera is a lemon, see how it scores on our tests.

Niceness Counts

You'll need cooperation at your friendly, neighborhood camera shop. The kind you won't get if you sail in some busy Saturday afternoon, push everyone aside and start pinning up test charts. On the other hand, if you're sensible and considerate, you'll probably get the help

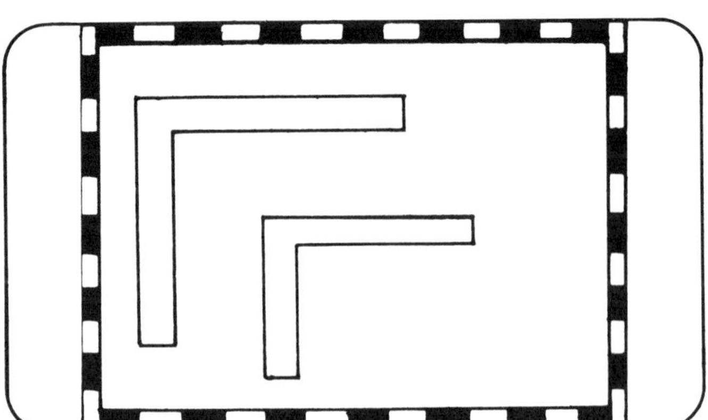

Figure 1: Image as seen through the viewfinder and produced on film by a few extremely exacting cameras. This level of accuracy is necessary for tightly cropped copy work and animation.

you'll need. First, you should have a pretty good idea of which camera you want. Then talk to the salesperson and explain what you want to do. Try to set up an appointment to make your tests when the store isn't busy. Some stores are reluctant to let you step outside the door without an armed guard, while others will let a familiar customer take a camera home overnight. Having cash or credit cards on hand for the store to hold can usually relax the tensions.

Tactile Maneuvers

The heft of a camera pressed close to your face. . . the way your fingers naturally reach out to the right controls. . . the ability to follow focus with moving action by feel as well as by eye. . . all are important and often underrated considerations. Filming should be as smooth and graceful and natural as playing a musical instrument or making love. Case in point: I bought a Bolex Rex4 Regular-8 camera and had it converted to Double Super-8 to use on my J.K. Optical Printer. Although I put its workings through rigorous testing, I ignored its "feel." This Bolex is one of the finest cameras ever made in terms of quality construction. It has excellent registration, ground-glass focusing, multiple speeds and total backwind. I thought I'd probably shoot my next film in Double Super-8. I was wrong. After working with well-balanced Super-8 cameras with big, bright, clear viewfinders, easy cartridge loading, long zooms and automatic everything, I just couldn't, or wouldn't, readjust to the cumbersome product of a bygone era. The Rex4 stays on the optical printer. Case closed.

The Dry Run

Before you check out a camera, adjust the viewfinder for your eyesight. This is usually done by turning a little wheel, called a "diopter," on or near the viewfinder to a plus or minus position, depending on your particular vision. If you normally wear glasses, leave them on while you make this adjustment and use the eye that feels most natural. Many of us are right-handed but left-eyed. The simplest way to

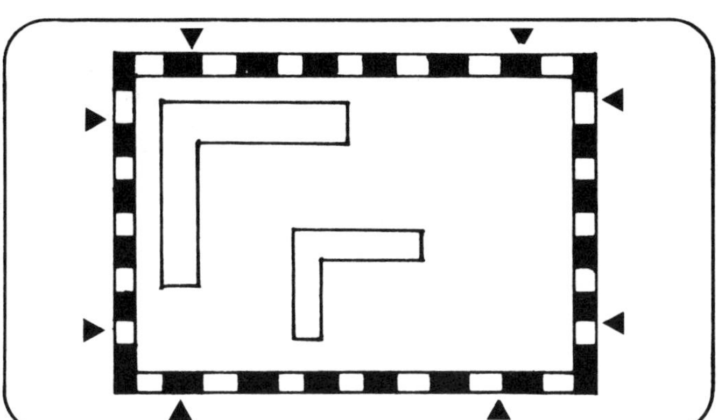

Figure 2: Image as produced on film by most acceptable cameras. Shows more than you see in the viewfinder, but most projector gates mask this part of the frame, so the inaccuracy is not critical. However, be careful not to let a light or mic intrude on the edges of the frame.

make this diopter correction is to view a plain piece of white paper through the camera and turn the wheel until the focusing grid itself (rangefinder, microprism, *etc.*) comes into sharp focus. Forget about focus or zoom settings. Only the lines that make up the focusing grid matter. There are many myths floating around about how to make this adjustment. They usually start with "Pick a subject at infinity," wherever that is. Forget them. Use the plain white paper and be close enough so that it fills your viewfinder. Failure to take this basic step properly is responsible for most of the out-of-focus footage I've seen.

Now set the zoom at its longest focal length (highest number and narrowest field of view), and turn the focusing ring (usually the front portion of the lens) until the rangefinder or other focusing aid indicates proper focus. If you did everything right, your subject should also look in focus and the distance set on the focusing ring should agree with your estimate of the actual distance.

Now work the zoom back and forth, both manually and automatically. Is the movement smooth over the entire range or does it have sticky places? Is the manual control capable of doing fluid zooms, or only good enough for changing focal lengths between shots? Here again it's a matter of what *you* need. The manual zoom movement on my Nikon R10 is so free that it might annoy other filmmakers by its lack of resistance, but for me it's perfect.

Aside from changing focal lengths between shots, I use it mainly to zoom very quickly between actors' lines in sound takes. That way we don't have to stop and use the clapboard every time I move to a close-up or a long shot. Of course, the 4 or 5 frames of zoom are later cut out, along with 4 or 5 frames of magnetic recording tape (fullcoat). It's a great time saver.

Try all the speeds and controls. Does everything work consistently and without strain? Pan across areas of different light levels. Does the meter respond instantly to light changes? As you go into or out of instant slow motion, does the meter compensate for the different speed *immediately*? If it doesn't, the dynamics of this feature will be ruined

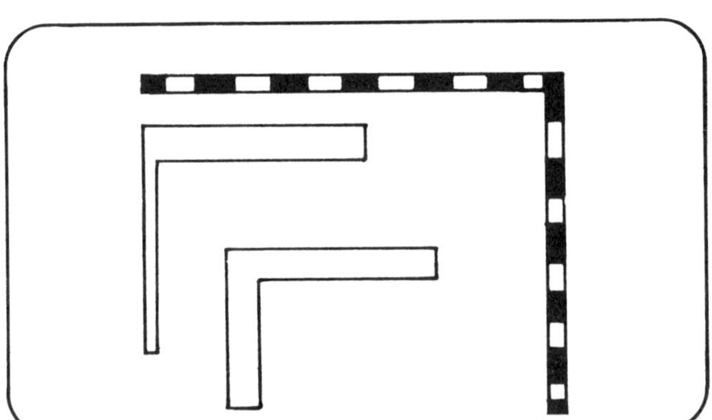

Figure 3: Poorly positioned image is intolerable for all but the most casual filming.

by a few inches of improperly exposed footage at the beginning or end of the effect. Just how easy is it to fade while you zoom, or to use any other combination of effects you might want simultaneously?

If the camera you're considering is single-system sound, how quiet is it indoors? Use a good (optional accessory) mic and put on a pair of earphones matched to the camera's impedance, then listen to the response. How quickly does the automatic gain control respond to changes in the sound level? Does the camera bring the amplifier up to strength before shooting film? Is it possible to monitor sound between shots? Does it have a flash sync attachment in case you want to do some double-system recording of music or something that's outside the range and capabilities of the camera's own sound system? Does it handle silent cartridges and shoot them at the same speed? Or does that matter to you? How about the light-emitting diodes (LED) and other indicators in the viewfinder. Do they give you all the information you'll need, or are some of them just distracting nuisances that you'll never learn to live with? After you've answered all of these questions for yourself and you feel familiar with the workings of the camera, it's time to give it. . .

The Final Exam

Check the battery condition. Load the camera with a film cartridge. Set the filter key or switch for tungsten lighting (assuming you're inside a camera store). Set the lens at its longest focal length (telephoto). Focus. Now move the zoom back to its shortest focal length (wide angle) and begin shooting. While you're shooting, zoom to telephoto and keep filming for a few seconds after you get there. Go outside the camera store (with permission, of course), and run the same test, being sure to switch the filter to the correct position. Now use each of the camera's features and potentials one by one while you record the results on film. Test the camera's low light limits with high speed film, and keep shooting even after the indicators say it's hopeless. For sharpness and color rendition tests, use Kodachrome 40 in daylight (with the filter in place) or under lights that have a Kelvin temperature of 3400° (movie lights). Photograph skin tones and nature, if there is any in sight. If the camera allows an automatic exposure (+ or —) adjustment, try a test at about a half stop underexposed. You might like it better than the manufacturer's idea of "normal" exposure.

Century Precision Optics (10659 Burbank Blvd., North Hollywood, Calif 91601) will let you have a poster-sized zoom lens focus test chart free. Get it and film it. When your film is processed, you can judge just how sharp the contending cameras are. Use a tripod for these tests to make sure that any unsteadiness you see is not your own fault. If you hold your shots to about 10 seconds each, you can run 20 individual tests on a single cartridge.

Of course, if you're looking at a sound camera, you'll also want to run some sound film through. Again, these tests should be made both inside and outdoors, but this time don't be too concerned about the visuals. Concentrate on what you hear. Does the camera sound louder with film running through it? Does the mic pick up camera noise or vibrations from its top-mounted position, and does the extended mic boom make the camera unbalanced or unwieldy? Is what you hear through the headphones reflected accurately by the blinking LED or the VU meter?

If you plan to purchase a better mic later, try it now. It may not match the impedance of the camera you've chosen, or, on the other hand, it might radically improve the response. Either way, this is the time to find out. You can't expect miraculous sound in a camera shop, but with close miking, it should be more than intelligible.

Graduation Day

In a few days your film will come back from the lab. If you don't have your own projector, go back to the camera store to screen the results. They should be delighted to show you a projector.

Does the lens stay in focus over the entire zoom range? If it goes out of focus as you zoom up to telephoto, you probably didn't set the eyepiece diopter correctly, or else you didn't focus accurately. If an object that's in focus at the telephoto setting slips out of focus as you zoom to a wider angle, the lens elements are probably set improperly and the camera should be avoided.

Whether or not the in-focus shots are really sharp and sound is of high quality, is something you'll have to judge for yourself. Fortunately, most popular brands of Super-8 equipment produce better than acceptable results for people who plan to show their original footage. If you intend to have your work printed, you should be looking for top optical quality (which usually—but not always—costs a few extra bucks).

The Happy Ending

If the camera flunks, you'll have saved yourself a lot of money and heartache, while learning more about equipment in general and your needs in particular. If you're happy with the results, on the other hand, you'll have gotten some worthwhile practice with the camera and confidence in its abilities. Buy it. You've found a friend.

ALL ABOUT SOUND CAMERAS

Dennis Duggan

What a drag it is to find out that you can't film a special shot because your camera doesn't have that one essential feature. It's especially aggravating to realize you could have bought a camera with that option, if you'd only known what it was and how you might have wanted to use it. Let's go over some of the features that are common to the current sound cameras. Let's see what the manufacturers had in mind when they included certain features, and some ways inventive filmmakers can use these same features.

The Zoom Lens

Fortunately, in Super-8 we have a choice of optics far beyond what was previously available to even the most sophisticated professional filmmakers. Do you crave the reach of a 13-to-1 super zoom? Or will a short 9-27mm focal length answer your needs? How fast should the lens be? You alone can make these decisions, but you should know that, at least theoretically, the shorter zooms will tend to be sharper. An *f*/2 maximum aperture will not allow you to shoot in as low light as an *f*/1.1, but here too, quality is often sacrificed for greater speed. As I said, though, these generalizations are theoretical. A fairly long Nikkor, Schneider or Elmo lens will still outperform many shorter, slower versions. A good rule to follow is to settle on the shortest focal length and slowest aperture that will *not* limit your cinematic expression. For most of us, something between a 5-to-1 and 10-to-1 zoom ratio with an *f*/1.4 to *f*/1.8 lens speed will fill the bill. On the wide-angle end, there is a considerable difference in range between 6mm and 8mm. While on the telephoto end, there is hardly any difference between 70mm and 80mm. It is also true that anything longer than 50mm is almost impossible to handhold steadily. A powered zoom that takes 10 seconds to traverse an 8-to-1 distance will *appear* to have greater zoom length than a motor that gets you there in half that time.

Macro Focusing

When the whole frame is filled with the image of something that's too small to get a good look at in real life, we are usually impressed. Macro capability, now common to so many Super-8 cameras, allows and encourages these dramatic close-ups. In practical terms, macro can show the small print on a map for a travel film, or let us know precisely where a tiny spring is inserted in the movement of a Swiss watch for a training film.

Zoom capability must be relinquished whenever you want to film in macro, since the zoom ring is used for focusing in the macro setting.

There is, however, an alternative to the macro lens that allows focusing extremely close to the lens while retaining full zoom capability. Separate and inexpensive close-up attachments (which are rated in +1, +2 and +3 strengths) can be screwed onto the front of a camera lens like filters. These attachments will give you the option of zooming from a close-up to an ultra close-up.

An offbeat but worthwhile side effect of being able to focus right up to the front lens element, as many macro cameras can, is being able to check the lens for dust particles. While this dust might not be noticed by the naked eye, its presence nonetheless degrades image quality.

Variable Speeds

Most sound cameras do not, at this time, offer a great variety of shooting speeds. With sound, it's more important to have an accurate 18 or 24 frames per second (fps) motor than a "wild" motor that can give you fast and slow motion at the possible sacrifice of precision. Many sound cameras offer extra speeds, such as 36 fps—slow motion, but only with silent cartridges. If 18 fps is your normal shooting speed and you have the option of shooting at 24 fps, you can introduce "kinesthetic" slow motion. This is not usually perceived by the viewer as an abnormal speed, but it does have an arresting effect subconsciously. Many serious filmmakers today use a multi-speed silent camera for all their effects, and a sound camera with one or two speeds for lip sync scenes. This may be the most practical solution.

Fades and Dissolves

Some people never use them, while others of us can't think of filming without them. Professionals have the lab create their effects optically

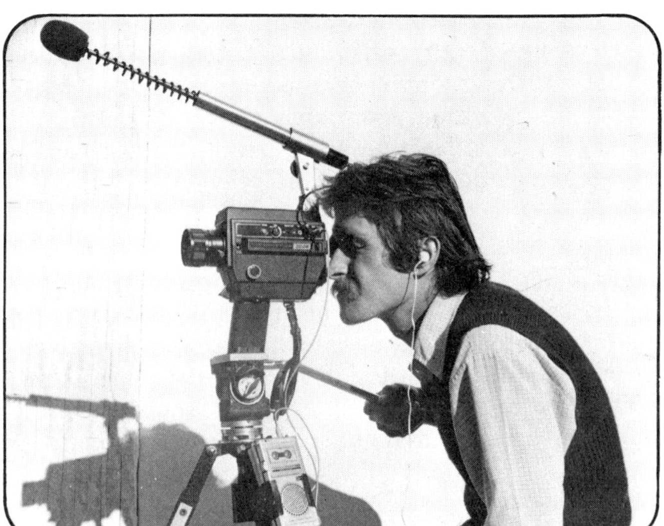

This filmmaker has rigged a small cassette recorder to his camera's monitor jack in order to check the quality of his sync sound track right after shooting.

or from a contact print made from an A and B rolled original. The logic of waiting until the post-production stage is that you have a choice of introducing (or not introducing) the effect to suit the development style of the film as it's being edited. There is also the possibility that one action might best be dissolved into a scene taken months later at a different location. But optical effects are usually expensive and introduce another print generation with its attendant quality sacrifices. The more spontaneous, free-flowing style of Super-8 tends to make in-camera effects a more natural choice.

PC Contact Switch

This little socket, so common to still cameras, has found its way onto many Super-8's. It allows firing an electronic flash in sync with the single frame mechanism of the camera, and it is commonly used with interval timers in situations where it would be impractical to leave hot floodlights on for several hours. Some smart Super-8 people put this switch to a more important use. Since it closes once for each frame of film exposed, it can be made to send 18 (or 24) signals to a tape recorder each second, thereby producing an accurate record of the actual running speed of your camera. This widely used method of double-system sync sound is known as the *digital* or *once-per-frame* system. If the sound camera that you choose offers this feature, you have the option of shooting single- or double-system sync sound—the best of both worlds.

Shutter Angle

Many sound cameras carry the now-familiar letters "XL" in their names. The XL stands for "existing light" or available low light filming.

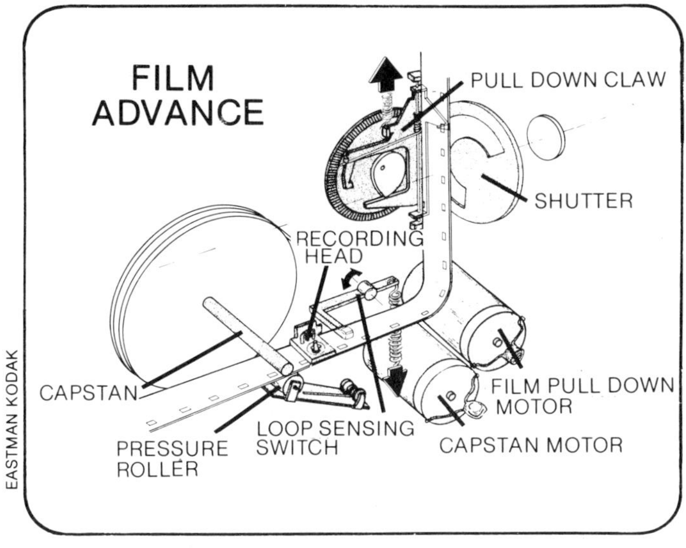

A typical sound movie camera has two motors. The capstan motor and associated recording mechanisms are inoperative when a silent cartridge is in the camera.

To qualify for the XL designation, a camera should have a fast lens with a maximum aperture of $f/1.1$ or $f/1.2$ ($f/1.4$ at the maximum). The lens must also have a shutter angle of between 200 degrees and 235 degrees, as opposed to a normal shutter angle of, say, 170 degrees. The wider angle simply lets more light through. The metering system should be able to handle film with an exposure index of at least ASA 160 as well. This combination of fast lens, wide shutter angle and fast film capability allows filming in most light situations without use of additional lights. The XL camera is a practical approach for the home moviemaker who doesn't want to drag out hot lights every time he or she wants to shoot indoors. It is also valid for the documentarian who wishes to keep everything natural and avoid making the persons filmed self-conscious.

Filmmakers interested in creating, rather than simply recording, might do well to look at a camera's XL capabilities in a different light. High speed films are just not as crisp or grain-free as most slower films, and a normal shutter angle of 150 to 170 degrees will produce less blur in fast-moving actions and in pans.

A soft cover or "barney" such as this designed by Super8 Sound can reduce camera noise by as much as 10 decibels.

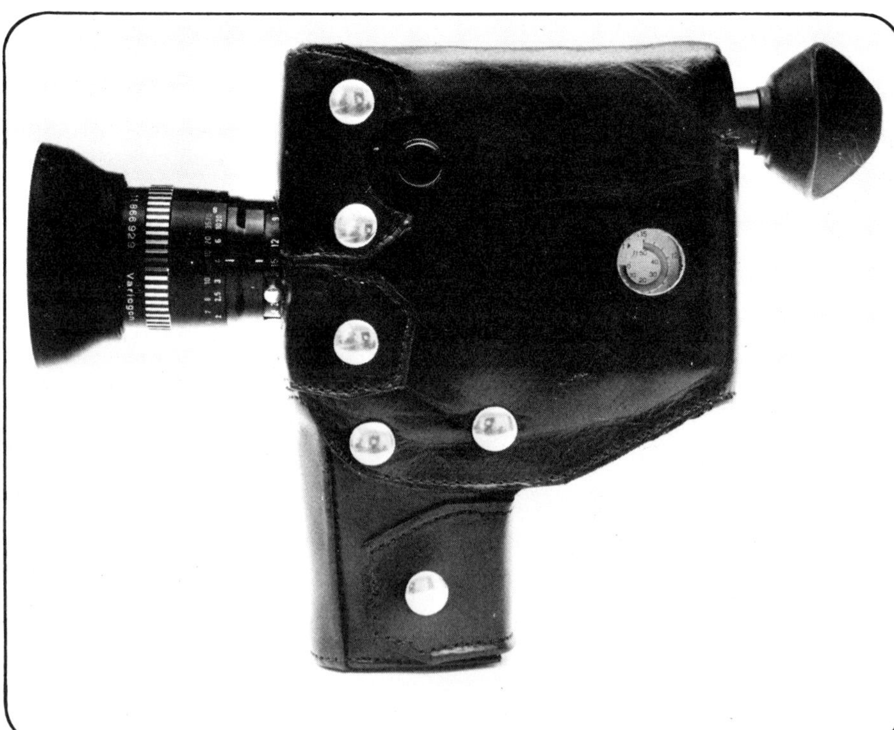

Featurettes

There are many other less basic features that should not be overlooked. How many microphones can you plug into the camera simultaneously? Does the camera have an auxiliary input for recording from a tape recorder or other source? Can you monitor sound without filming, so you can rehearse and arrange the best mic placement? Will the lens zoom without running film through the camera? And, most important if you're trying to meet professional standards with your work, how noisy is the camera, and how easily can it be soundproofed with a "barney" (soft cover) or "blimp" (hard casing)? Since none of the Super-8 sound cameras even approach the silent operation of sound stage standards, and only a few are quiet enough even for acceptable amateur ventures, a camera's "blimpability" is an especially important feature.

If you're planning to buy a single-system camera, but actually plan to use it for double-system recording with the much less expensive silent cartridge, think twice. *Most* sound cameras film on silent cartridges at 20 fps (rather than 18 fps). Since no sound projector has a setting for this speed, you must choose carefully.

Filter Size

The size of the front of a camera's lens, and the size of filters it will accept might seem like a strange thing to emphasize. However, if you already own filters for a movie or still camera, you might consider buying a sound camera that can use those same filters. A sound camera with a front element that is the same size or smaller than your present lens can accommodate your old filters, either directly or with a lens adapter.

Control

Many serious filmmakers are anti-automatic. I do not share this feeling. I wouldn't want to own a sound camera that didn't offer automatic exposure as well as automatic sound level control, and I look forward to the day when we will have automatic focusing, too. On the other hand, I wouldn't go for a camera that didn't offer manual override of these features. My philosophy is "automation replaces the assistant I can't afford." But neither do I want to be my assistant's slave.

Response

Sound frequency response figures can be determined in many ways, and while they can sometimes offer a general idea of sound quality, your own ears should be the real test of fidelity. This holds true for meter response and lens sharpness as well, and above all for the camera's ability to respond to your commands.

Quality is the most important feature any camera has to offer. The camera that can film with consistently sharp pictures and good clean sound is the main course. Everything else is gravy.

HOW TO SELECT THE RIGHT SCREEN

Elinor Stecker

You can project film on almost any surface—on a giant balloon or a piece of sculptured styrofoam. You can even project film on the human body. These are exciting if you're looking for experimental surfaces and weird effects. But nothing can beat showing your film on a good, conventional movie screen.

Choosing a screen isn't as bewildering a task as choosing a camera or a projector—there aren't that many options you have to consider. On the other hand, you don't want to walk into a dealer and fall for the first screen that meets your eye. Before you invite that screen home to meet your projector, make sure it meets your needs

Screen Size

How large a screen do you need? Good question. Many projectors like the Kodak "Moviedeck" series come equipped with a little built-in screen, and this is adequate for one or two people huddled a foot or so away. It obviously won't do if you're showing films to a group of friends in your living room or the entire fourth grade in the school auditorium.

An accepted rule of thumb is that the last row of the audience should be no farther away than six times the width of the projected image. You can also calculate this distance by taking eight times the height of the image. Since the height to width proportion of the Super-8 image is 3:4, the distance will be the same calculated by either method. Because movie screens generally come in square shapes, we'll consider only the long dimension or width for our calculations. With this in mind, my little pocket calculator and I worked out a table indicating the minimum screen size needed in order for the person farthest away to view the picture comfortably (see Figure 1). If the farthest away from the screen in your viewing room is 25 feet, for example, you'll need a screen at least 50 x 50 inches.

Viewing Angle

Several different types of projection screen surfaces have been developed, because all viewing situations are not created equal. A screen's job is to reflect the light from the projector back to the audience. Most screens do the job equally well, reflecting nearly all of the light the projector sends out. So what's the fuss?

The fuss is that different screens have different light distribution characteristics. There are surfaces which will reflect most of the light in a narrow cone, while others will distribute it over a wide angle. And since there is just so much light to be reflected, the wider the angle over which the light is spread, the less bright the image will be. Of course, you want to have the brightest possible image the screen is capable of giving, especially since the light thrown by many Super-8 projectors is dimmer than we'd like it to be. But we may have to sacrifice brightness in order to have an angle of view that will include the poor guy crouched off on the side of a very wide room.

In selecting a screen, it's important to know how people will be sitting in relation to the projector-to-the-screen axis (see Figure 2). If the viewers are right in line with the projector beam, bending to keep their shadowed silhouettes from being cast on the screen, there is no problem—almost anything can be used as a screen, from the side of a refrigerator to the back of an old poster. These are okay for emergency situations, but you'll need something better for regular screenings where more than one or two people will be viewing the film. The following screen types vary in their ability to reflect light at angles suitable for viewing.

Matte screens will give an almost unlimited angle of view. The brightness of the image will play no favoritism between the person in the center of the room and someone who is far off to the side.

However, the image becomes distorted when you're seated at an extreme angle, so try not to have viewers more than 30 degrees from the lens axis (Figure 2). Matte screens have a surface similar to a smooth plaster wall. In fact, the white plaster wall you may have been using is really not a bad substitute for an actual screen. Although matte screens are the least bright of all the surfaces, the brightness is adequate, and the color fidelity and image resolution are superior to any other type of surface.

Lenticular screens have more directional light patterns and are the

Figure 1: The minimum size screen you'll need for your viewing room is determined by the farthest distance people will sit from the projector.

Figure 2: The angle at which viewers sit in relation to the projection axis is important for bright, undistorted images. About 30 degrees from the axis is generally best.

Screen Size Chart

Distance from Screen	Screen Size
15 feet	30 x 30 inches
20 feet	40 x 40 inches
25 feet	50 x 50 inches
30 feet	60 x 60 inches
35 feet	70 x 70 inches

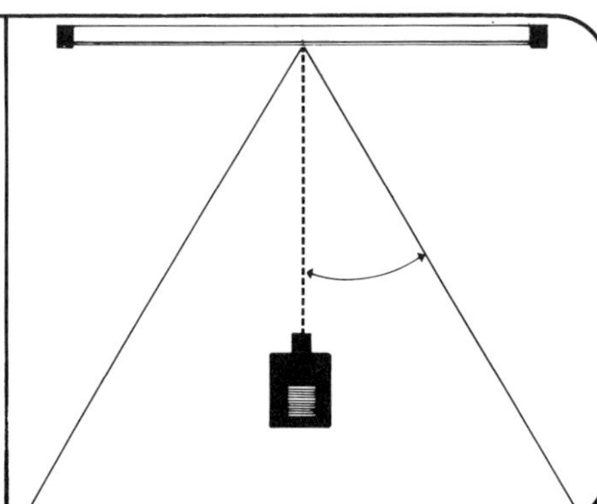

best choice if viewers do not have to be seated at extreme angles to the screen. These screens have a pattern of rectangles, stripes, diamonds or ribs embossed on them, which act like mirrors or lenses to reflect the light. When you look at the screen close up, it has a corduroy-like appearance which is not visible when watching a film from normal viewing distances. (Viewers should always be a minimum distance equal to two times the height of the image.) Some lenticular screens are metallic—that is, the embossing is done on an aluminum coating. These have a narrower angle of view than the non-metallic lenticular type, and so are a little more brilliant. Although the actual angle of view varies from manufacturer to manufacturer, generally metallic lenticular screens will have the brightest viewing area within 25 degrees from the projection axis, while non-metallic screens should give good visibility within 35 degrees.

Beaded screens used to be the most popular type, especially for home projection, and they still are a good choice for long, narrow rooms or for use with a projector having an especially poor light output. These screens have thousands of little clear glass beads which are bonded to a white material and concentrate light in a narrow path. At five degrees from the projection axis, the image is extremely bright, but brightness falls off quite quickly at wider angles. As with lenticular screens, there is variation from one screen manufacturer to another.

Brightness and Reflection of Stray Light

How dark can you make the viewing room and how bright an image your projector throws are factors that should affect your decision in selecting a screen. A *matte screen* presents the least bright picture of all, but the brightness is constant over the entire area. No other screen

Screen Shopping Guide

	Screen Surface				
Screen Characteristics	Matte	Beaded	Metallic lenticular	Non-metalic lenticular	High gain
Best viewing area	Unlimited	10°	25°	35°	30°
Room illumination	Quite dark	Completely dark	Partially dark	Partially dark	Light
Brilliance in main viewing area, compared to to matte screen		Up to 4 times	2 to 4 times	2 times	12 times
Can be wall or ceiling hung	Yes	Yes	With added tension	With added tension	On rigid support
Can be rolled for storage	Yes	Yes	Yes	Yes	No

Figure 3: This chart will help you select the best screen for your viewing room.

can make that statement. The room, however, must be fairly dark since any stray light creeping in will degrade the image.

The brightness in the viewing area of a *lenticular screen* is about double that of a matte screen, and some metallic lenticular screens may go as high as four times the matte screen in brightness. Remember, though, the greater the brightness, the narrower the viewing angle. The room doesn't have to be pitch black, since some of the viewing area will be reflected back outside that area.

Beaded screens are brighter yet. Within their narrow viewing area, they can produce an image up to four times the brightness of a matte screen. This image brightness falls off rapidly outside the viewing area, and for anyone seated beyond 25 degrees from the projection axis, it is unsatisfactorily dim. Beaded screens must be used in a completely darkened room, since stray light originating both inside and outside the audience area can dim the image.

High gain aluminum screens are unbelievably bright. Kodak's "Ektalite" and Prima's "High Gain Projection" screens are made of thin sheets of specially processed aluminum foil, permanently laminated to a lightweight frame. The screen reflects an image that is about *12 times* as bright as a matte screen in a 30-degree viewing angle. Outside of the viewing area no image can be seen. The principal advantage of these screens is the visibility they give to an image in a well-lit room. Any light not originating near the projector will be reflected away from the viewers. The cost of these screens is more than for other types, and the largest size available is only 48 x 48 inches.

Mounting, Carrying and Storing Your Screen

How you are going to mount, transport and store your screen is a practical problem. All except the high gain screens can be had with tripod mounts that allow them to be rolled up neatly for storage or transporting. There are screen cases available, too. Hanging the screen from the wall or ceiling is a great convenience, and is fairly unobtrusive, even in a living room. Many matte and beaded screens are available for mounting this way. Lenticular screens must be stretched to eliminate all wrinkles and waves before use. This is done automatically with a tripod mount, but you'll need to devise additional tensioning for lenticular wall screens.

Another interesting screen is the Eberhard "Faber-Board Visual Aid Panel." This self-adhesive panel, with a non-metallic lenticular surface, can be pressed onto any smooth surface. Additionally, you can write on it with special felt markers (takes the place of a chalkboard), and some models will accept magnetic characters.

Everything we've been talking about is listed in chart form on the "Screen Shopping Guide" (Figure 3). Take the chart along when you go shopping for a screen. It should help you find the best screen for your particular viewing situation.

GOING STEADY: USING A TRIPOD

Elinor Stecker

One of the joys of using a Super-8 camera is the ease with which it can be handheld. Whether you're maneuvering through crowds or shooting in cramped locations, Super-8 allows you to move about quickly and unobtrusively. In many cases, it's just easier and faster to film without bothering to set up a tripod.

But if that's really the case, then why should you even consider giving up the simplicity of handholding the camera? Well, there are a number of filming situations that really require a support to smooth out camera wobble:

1) *Filming at long focal lengths:* Most people can learn to hold a camera steady at focal lengths of 25mm and less. At the longer focal lengths, the image becomes magnified and so, too, does every bit of vibration from the camera motor and the person holding it.

2) *Zooming:* If the zoom starts or ends at a long focal length, the quivering will be obvious unless the camera is on a tripod. In addition, manual zooming can be executed more smoothly with the added stability of a tripod.

3) *Panning:* For unrivaled smoothness, use a tripod with a good pan head, especially a fluid head. A tripod is doubly helpful when you're combining more than one camera movement, such as panning and zooming simultaneously.

4) *Macro photography:* There's no way of avoiding the need for a camera support when filming subjects that are close to the lens. Titles, still photographs, dew drops on a spider web—all will be pretty jumpy unless filmed with a rigidly supported camera.

5) *Animation and time lapse:* The very nature of stop action cinematography is based on the premise that the camera will not move between shots.

6) *Special effects:* Many tricks and special effects require a rock steady camera. A quick glance through the chapter on special effects will give you some idea of just how important a stable camera is in the successful execution of these tricks.

7) *Long takes:* Some shots, especially when you're doing sync sound, may last longer than you can hold your breath. If you inhale during a shot, your body movement will be transferred to the camera. In addition, your arm muscles may start to tire, so you may not be as steady at the end of the shot as you were at the beginning.

8) *Talking while shooting:* If you give oral instructions to your subjects while the camera is running, your body movements will shake the camera. Try to give all your directions before you press the run button, or immobilize the camera on a tripod.

9) *Physically handicapped persons:* Tripods and other camera supports can be used or modified to be used by people who otherwise wouldn't be able to hold a camera.

10) *Remote control:* If your camera has provision for remote control, you can mount the camera on a tripod and include yourself in the shot. Remote control is also frequently used for filming wildlife, where a person's presence may be detrimental.

11) *Aesthetics:* The use of a tripod adds a special quality of precision, a different "look" to the film. It's not good practice to intermix hand-held and tripod shots in the same sequence, as the difference between the two may be quite noticeable.

Tripods come big and tripods come small. You'll get the most use out of those that are sturdy, extend to eye-level height, and have pan heads that operate very smoothly. The smoothest operating heads are fluid heads, and they are sold separately from the tripod. Miller and Bilora both make them for Super-8. A tripod can be made maneuverable by attaching a dolly. This set of wheels attaches to the base of the tripod, allowing the camera to follow the action (Welt/Safe-Lock makes one). Small tripods are advantageous for low-level and close-up shooting. The Bolex Minipod, with its spider-like legs, is extremely versatile and lets you film indoors or out, on any kind of terrain. Little table-top tripods are easy to pack in a camera case.

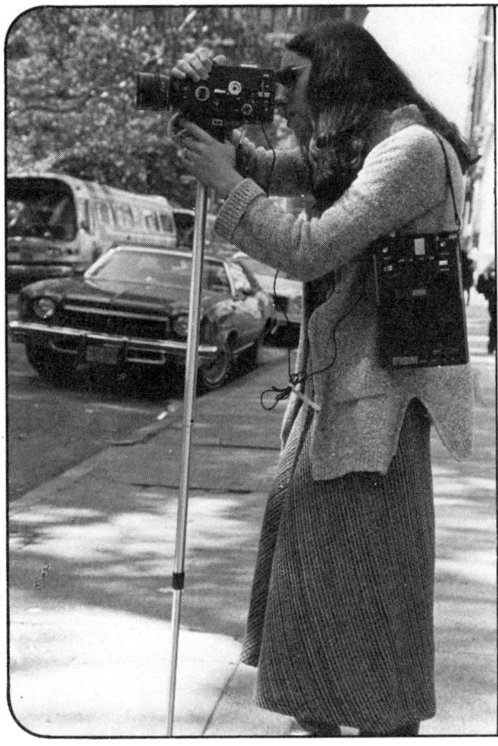

ELINOR STECKER

Tripods come big and tripods come small. A monopod is a good alternative when travelling light.

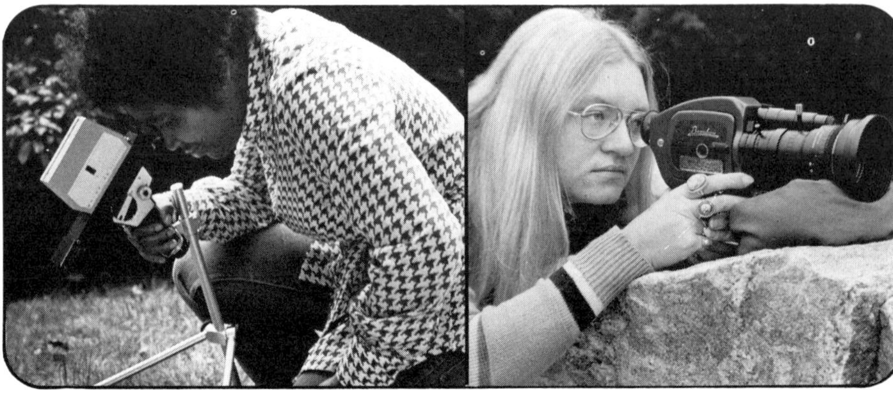

ELINOR STECKER

You can do macro and low-angle shooting with a minipod. A beanbag is the most portable of all camera supports.

There are other camera supports that add stability to your shots under a variety of circumstances.

The monopod, for example, is less steady than a tripod, but it's collapsible, lightweight and can be used in tight quarters. It may be permitted in locations that have restrictions against tripods.

Pro-Jr. Sta-Sets are helpful in preventing a tripod from slipping on an ultra-smooth surface, and if you want to shoot from the top of your car, get some Camart tie-down clamps.

For optimum maneuverability, even shooting while walking, use a brace. A belt pod, chest pod or shoulder pod has a rod to support the camera at one end while the other is braced against the body. The Cine 60 Combi Pod was one especially developed for Super-8 cameras. You'll also want to look into the P & L Stedi-Pod, an inexpensive, lightweight chest pod that has a ball-and-socket panhead.

A practical solution to stabilizing your camera is to rest it on any convenient object: a fence, the branch of a tree, the back of a chair. To improve this support, cradle the camera in a beanbag. You can make your own or buy one from Omnipod. Theirs is filled with almost weightless beads, which can be removed via a zippered opening for compactness when traveling (fill it with whatever's available at the site). Clamping the camera to a supporting object is yet another alternative. Camera clamps have jaws that tighten around poles or other objects. Some even have little tripod legs, and Bogen's Super Clamp is the basis of an entire system of accessories. Whatever and wherever you're shooting, there are lots of devices available to support your camera. Using them at the right time can add a professional touch to your filmmaking.

BUYING AND USING MICROPHONES

Gunther Hoos

If you're already adding sound to your films, or are about to start, you should examine the microphone you're using before you record another syllable. It may not be the right mic for the sound you want. The type of mic you choose and how you use it will determine how good the dialogue, music or effects will sound on your final track.

Here then is an evaluation of mics I've found most useful in Super-8 work, and some miking tips that should enable you to get the cleanest possible sound for your film track.

Dynamic vs Electret Condensor Microphones

There's really no controversy between the two; they just function differently. Dynamic microphones produce their own electrical current and as such are self-powered. Incoming sound vibrates the microphone diaphragm which, in turn, causes a coil to move through a magnetic field. This movement produces a small electrical current corresponding to the frequency and intensity of the original sound. Because the current is relatively weak, you shouldn't run cables from these mics for more than 25 feet without amplification.

The sound quality of good dynamics is excellent with a tendency towards more mellow or soft sound. Most dynamics are extremely rugged and not subject to breakdown. In adverse situations (where both microphone and sound person are in danger of being trampled, for instance) the dynamic would be the microphone of choice. Because dynamics require no batteries, they would be your best bet if you plan to

Lenny Lipton filming "Revelation of the Foundation" with a Beaulieu 5008S using an omnidirectional mike.

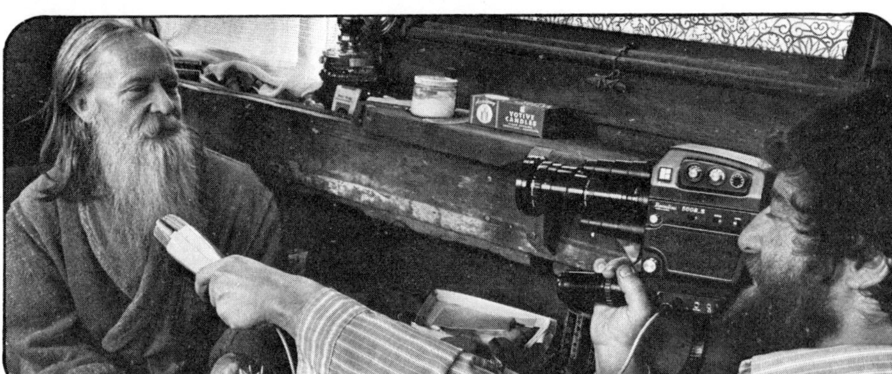

film in remote areas. You'll find dynamic mics tend to be somewhat bulkier and heavier than electrets, and are also less sensitive to handling. Good dynamics are usually more expensive than good electrets.

Electret microphones contain a diaphragm that maintains a permanent electrical charge. Microphones of this type require such a small diaphragm mass that they can rival more expensive electrostatic condensor microphones or dynamic mics in frequency response while costing a fraction of the price. Electrets require power to operate, and even though batteries tend to last for hundreds of hours, you must keep spare batteries on hand. Without batteries, these microphones won't operate. Electrets are more sensitive to high frequency sound than are dynamics. The increased sensitivity makes cleaner sound possible—sound that is pure with its frequencies and harmonics intact. On the other hand, greater sensitivity to sound that you *do want* also means greater sensitivity to sound that you *don't want*, such as camera noise and mic handling or people breathing.

Physically, electrets are more fragile than dynamics, and you must take greater care in handling them. They are also liable to distort high intensity sounds more quickly than dynamics. Electrets are excellent for use where long cable runs without intermediate amplification are required. Runs of 75 feet or even 100 feet present no problems in high frequency loss. For the same given price, electrets tend to have a greater range than dynamic microphones. That is, they can more easily reproduce without distortion sounds from a whisper to a shout.

Microphone Pickup Patterns

Omnidirectional: As the name implies, microphones with this pattern pick up sound in a 360-degree sphere—even up the wire of the microphone. For film use "omnis" are far from the ideal microphone since cameras are still very noisy. However, there is one variation of the omni that is very useful. This is the "lavalier" or "tie tack" microphone. Because the lavalier mic (attached to clothing or worn around the neck) is usually less than 12 inches from the mouth, other sound sources, no matter what their direction, have very little influence on the primary sound.

Cardioid: The cardioid pattern is somewhat pear-shaped. It is designed to favor sound pickup from the front and to reject sound from the rear. Consequently, if you position it correctly (pointing away from your camera), it will not pick up camera noise or other sound from behind the mic. Because its pickup pattern is more directional, it can be used at a greater distance from the sound source. This sound pickup pattern is the most useful for film work.

Hypercardioid or shotgun: This pattern differs from the normal cardioid pattern in that it is even more directional. In addition to sound from the rear, the shotgun mic also rejects much of the sound from the sides. It does this by having a specially designed and perforated tube ahead of the diaphragm which effectively cancels out sound from the sides. A shotgun mic permits working at much greater distances from the subject. Even though shotguns are among the most expensive microphones, their sound quality rarely matches that of a closely positioned and cheaper cardioid. These microphones are superb in situations where it is difficult or impossible to get close, such as in cinema verite and newsfilming.

Parabolic Reflectors: The ultimate in directionality, if not sound quality, is achieved with a parabolic dish and almost any type of microphone. The principle of the parabolic microphone reflector is to gather sound coming from a distant source and focus it all into the microphone. The microphone points into the center of the reflector which bounces the sound back to the mic head. This type of system greatly extends the recording distance from the sound source. It's not impossible to record the talk of football players from the stands. Don't expect miracles, however. When you use a parabolic reflector, you sacrifice some fidelity and sound volume simply because the sound has to travel all that distance. The range and quality of the sound you get depends on how well you "focus in" on the sound surface.

To illustrate the variety of high quality but moderately priced microphones, I've chosen the products of three manufacturers as representative. There are other equally good microphones made, but the following have been in constant use at the Super 8 Film Group, giving me a chance to test their overall performance.

Chinon Wireless Microphones

The wireless microphone unit is a combination microphone, FM radio transmitter and receiver. The microphone picks up the sound and transmits it to a carefully tuned receiver. The output of the receiver is then plugged into the input of your recorder or sound camera. This eliminates the need for a cable between the microphone and the recorder. Since you don't have to follow the action with a mic (the wireless microphone is usually mounted on the subject), you can record sync sound while your subject is in motion.

Chinon makes a set of radio microphones, including a lavalier, a cardioid and the receiver, for under $175. But before you rush out to buy one, consider the following. Radio mics are specialty mics, and sound people use them only when they have to. This is because they are subject to interference, which can come from anything that is capable of producing some sort of radio frequency noise. The Chinon Wireless Mic 103 works very well and with astonishingly good sound quality, and though interference is sometimes a problem, Chinon has improved the mic since it was introduced to the point where it is very reliable in almost all situations.

Although the Chinon wireless is designed to work with Chinon cameras, you can use it with any recorder or single-system sound camera as long as you have the right adapter. The microphone has a low impedance (200 ohms) and a specified range of 65 feet. In practice, 50 feet is about tops for the best sound.

Sony Electret Microphones

Sony produces a series of high quality and moderately priced microphones which are excellent for film use.

The *ECM-16* is a very small tie tack microphone with an excellent frequency response. It has a built-in bass roll-off filter to compensate for sound recorded so near the chest cavity. Because of its small size, it's easy to conceal under jackets or sweaters. These mics are sensitive to rubbing and, therefore, require careful mounting on the speaker. You might try taping gaffer's tape to the subject's chest and then taping the microphone to the gaffer's tape. The ECM-16 has low impedance (250 ohms) and works very well with all Super-8 cameras and recorders. At $34.95, the ECM-16 or one like it is a must for any sound equipment arsenal.

The *ECM-250* is a good bargain-priced cardioid microphone with a built-in windscreen. Its directional pattern does a good job of rejecting most sound from the rear. Its sensitivity is a little limited, so for best results you should use it within about 4 feet of the sound source. The ECM-250 works well with a boom that can hold the mic close to the sound source. For most film work, a roll-off filter is recommended because of the mic's sensitivity to handling noise (Sony does not supply these—see "Accessories" under Sennheiser). Like all electrets the ECM-250 is battery powered. Its impedance is compatible with all cameras and recorders. The list price is $59.95.

The *ECM-280* is one of the finest all-around microphones for the money (about $100). If you can only afford one microphone, this may be it. ECM-280 is an extremely sensitive and directional microphone and contains a switch that activates a built-in roll-off filter to help reduce handling noise. Used with a windscreen on a boom, this mic will work well even if you can't get in close. Sony also makes a portable parabolic reflector, the *BPR-400*. You can mount your own microphone at the focus of the dish. The list price of this unit without a mic is $59.95.

Sennheiser Electret Microphones

This name in microphones has always been synonymous with high quality and high price. Their series *415* and *805* condensor microphones have long been the workhorses of filmmakers across the world. Unfortunately, the price of a fully equipped Model 805 usually exceeds the cost of most Super-8 cameras.

Feeling the competitive sting from Sony no doubt, Sennheiser introduced an outstanding series of microphones with consumer prices. The basic electret microphone set consists of a common powering module and three interchangeable microphone heads. The powering module

K2U costs about $80. The microphone heads are the omni (*ME20*) at about $60, the cardioid (*ME40*) at about $80, and the shotgun (*ME80*) at around $110. There's also a telescopic boom (*MZS802*) for under $60 that mounts on top of your camera. The whole set may be purchased as a unit, or you can buy each module separately. I've found very few applications for the omni head. I've used the shotgun head extensively outdoors and use the cardioid primarily for interior studio and narration work. The microphones produce clear, sharp and clean sound and are more sensitive than any of the Sony microphones. As excellent as these microphones are, there are a few drawbacks to their use. One of these is the high cost of required accessories, and another is the lack of information provided with the microphones.

Accessories: Although this series of microphones is consumer oriented, all the accessories are drawn from Sennheiser's professional equipment and are disproportionately high priced. The windscreen costs about $18 and a simple pistol grip/shock mount costs around $90. Because the microphones are so sensitive, they will tolerate almost no handling without passing noise on to the recorder. Consequently you must purchase a roll-off filter to attenuate base frequencies below 200 Hz. The Sennheiser filter costs about $83. You can shop around and buy shock mounts for around $50 from Super8 Sound (95 Harvey St., Cambridge, Mass. 02140) and for about $18 from Shure. Shure also makes a roll-off filter that costs less than $25.

These Sennheiser microphones are also sold without a connecting cable. The cable can cost you an additional $30. Also, the wiring and use booklet shipped with the microphones is pure Greek to the average Super-8 filmmaker.

That said, however, these units are still highly recommended. They will work exceptionally well with all Super-8 recorders and single-system cameras. They are battery powered by a 5.6 volt mercury battery (hard to get, so buy two). Don't try to use either the shotgun or the cardioid head outdoors without a windscreen and a roll-off filter. These sensitive heads will pick up all kinds of unwanted noise. How-

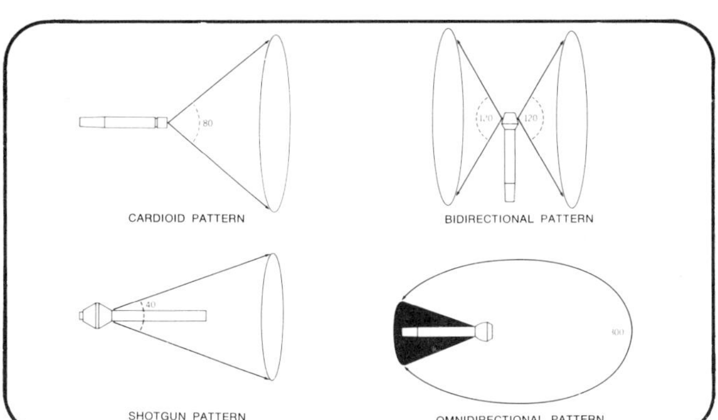

The type of mic you choose and how you use it will determine the sound on your final track. Here are some microphone pick-up patterns: cardioid; bidirectional; shotgun; omnidirectional.

ever, both the shotgun and cardioid head are virtually deaf to sounds from the rear and consequently are ideal with noisy cameras.

Some Other Microphones

Here are some other microphones that I've not used extensively but are of high quality (prices are approximate). AKG offers an electret microphone system similar to Sennheiser's. It's based on the *SE-5* powering module ($60) which can be used with the *CE-2* omni mic head ($45), the *CE-5* cardioid head ($55) and the *CE-8* interference tube to make a mini shotgun ($85).

The *Electro-Voice DL-42* Cardiline dynamic shotgun is an excellent microphone with a frequency response of 50-12,000 Hz. For the list price of around $345, you get a shock mount, windscreen and cable. The *Shure SM82* unidirectional condensor microphone is one of the most rugged condensor mics made. It features a built-in "pop" and wind filter and includes a windscreen and locking stand adapter for about $178. Shure's low priced *SM61* omnidirectional dynamic microphone (around $80) has good noise isolation and good frequency response with a built-in "blast filter" that cuts wind, breathing and pop noises very effectively.

The list could go on, of course, but the sampling here should more than cover your filmmaking needs. Just as important as choosing the right microphone is how you use it when you're recording on location.

Tips for Sound Recording

Whether you own a very expensive or a very cheap microphone, much of the quality of sound depends on how you do the miking. In film situations where the action is usually fluid and often uncontrollable, the best system is to use a sound boom with a shock mount.

Booms can be made of many materials. Some people have used bamboo fishing poles, and others have cannibalized lightweight light stands. One of the most useful booms can be made from tubular 12-foot extendable painter's or window washer's poles which can be purchased

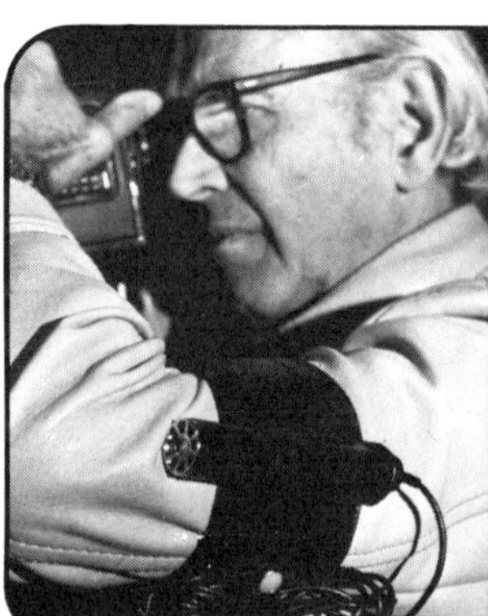

Invention is the mark of a filmmaker. An ingenious method of microphone use is this form of "one-man band."

at many hardware stores. These extend from three feet to 12 feet and cost less than $25. You can mount your microphone to the boom with a shock mount, such as the Shure mount mentioned previously. Run the mic cable along the boom pole and extend the pole to whatever distance is needed for best miking.

In most miking situations, the sound person holds the boom overhead, between 12 and 36 inches from the subject's mouth, and locates the mic just outside the frameline. Unless framing dictates otherwise, the mic is best above the subject. This generally gives the cleanest sound. Of course, you should always face the microphone away from the camera.

You should always monitor sound recording with headphones. The headphones should fit well and isolate you from the sound of the surrounding area. Keep the volume good and loud so you can hear every sound being picked up by the mic. Only in this way can you position the microphone for optimum sound. Unfortunately, most Super-8 single-system cameras have miserable monitoring facilities. For the most part, the sound is barely audible, and qualitative judgments are impossible. A solution is to buy a small pre-amp from an electronics store (such as Radio Shack) and connect it into the headphone line. These small microphone amplifiers cost less than $20 and are a good idea if the sound from your monitor is a problem. You can throw away those tiny earphones that are supplied with many sound cameras, and get a set that covers both ears. They need not be expensive. Sony makes an earphone set for around $10 (Radio Shack also has one).

Always use a windscreen outdoors and even indoors—it never hurts. Windscreens do not affect the quality of the sound. All they do is isolate the microphone from high velocity moving air and eliminate wind noise and popping "P's." In a pinch, you can always place a sock over the microphone or cut a piece of foam rubber to fit.

There's one last important matter, and it can't be overemphasized. You must train yourself to listen. You must listen critically to not only the subject sound, but to every other sound as well. Which sounds are acceptable and which are not? What can you do to improve, change or modify the sound? Is the sound appropriate to the situation being filmed? If you're recording dialogue with a lavalier (tie tack) microphone, make a note to record ambient location sound as well. Mixing this sound in later will give life to the dead sounding lavalier sound. If there are effects in the scene such as doors shutting or car engines revving, record them separately. Then, if you want later to emphasize these sounds, you can mix in the separate effects to match the action.

Whenever possible go for the cleanest sound. Later, during the sound transfer or during the mix, you can manipulate the sound as desired. If the original sound is poor, your choices will be limited. With sound, control is the key—always leave yourself options.

GUIDE TO FILM STOCKS

Dennis Duggan

How much choice does the Super-8 filmmaker really have when it comes to original camera film? There was a time when film stocks varied a great deal, and photographers and filmmakers chose the brand and type of film to suit the aesthetic needs of the job at hand. Ansco-chrome film, for example, might bring out the autumn colors in a wood-land scene, while Ektachrome would enrich the blues in a seascape. Hollywood companies would order a particular emulsion to suit the style of a production. Emulsion runs were so distinctive that each major film had a look uniquely its own. But this has changed.

Technology in film manufacture has led to more accurate, consistent and dependable emulsion stocks. Films can now render colors with astounding fidelity, and less expensive brands come very close to the front runners in general appearance. This might be looked upon as a mixed blessing. Today's films offer more, on the surface, to the realist than they do to the impressionist. But if you think about it, you'll probably agree that it's the manufacturers' job to produce film stocks that are accurate and consistent, and our job to use or alter this accuracy to lend individual expression to our films. Let's look at the available Super-8 film stocks to investigate our choice and to see how these choices serve our particular needs.

Fujichrome Film Stocks

People shooting in Super-8 who want the advantage of a metal pressure plate built into the cameras and a cartridge that offers unlimited backwind usually opt for the Fuji system of cameras and films. At this time, Fuji offers two emulsions or film stocks, both of which come unstriped in silent cartridges or striped in sound cartridges, for use in Fuji cameras.

Fuji offers two films: *Fujichrome R25* for daylight shooting and *RT200* for tungsten lights. R25 has an ASA or exposure index of 25. (By the way, *exposure index* or *EI* indicates a film's sensitivity to light, and is often referred to as the film's "speed." *ASA* is the American Standards Association's rating of the film's speed. The two terms are often used interchangeably.) Fujichrome R25 is equal to Kodachrome 40 (with an EI of 40) in terms of light sensitivity when used in daylight, because R25 doesn't require a #85 daylight conversion filter. This filter, built into most Super-8 cameras for daylight shooting, cuts back some of the light that would normally reach the film. Of all the films I've tested, I would rate Fujichrome R25 among the top three for color fidelity, resolution and grain structure.

It is difficult to describe the look of this film, other than to say that

R25 has "psychological integrity." Places, people and things filmed on this emulsion don't look *prettier* than they really are. Rather, there's an impression of "truthful" reproduction. This seems especially suited to the needs of documentary filmmakers. As is the case with most high resolution films intended for direct projection, Fujichrome's contrast is slightly harsh for reproducing high quality duplicate prints. If you plan to have this film printed, you might look into Tiffen's low contrast filters.

Fujichrome RT200 is the only emulsion offered by Fuji for use under artificial or tungsten light, since they no longer make *RT50*. As the name indicates, this film has an exposure index of 200 in tungsten (3400°K) illumination, and it can be exposed in daylight with a #85 filter over the lens at an EI of 125. I was sorry to see the RT50 film discontinued. Even though it's easier to light a scene for the faster 200 EI film, high speed films usually appear significantly grainier and have lower resolution. Nevertheless, RT200 is a surprising exception to this general rule, with less grain and better resolution than some slower films. Although it falls a *little* short of the R25 standards, it's a most acceptable choice for indoor work, and cuts well with the slower emulsion without creating the feeling that you're suddenly watching a different movie. Of the high speed color films, I'd say Fujichrome RT200 is the best.

Fujipan black-and-white film stocks are no longer available, but B&W devotees can always shoot in color and then have their work printed in black and white.

Kodak Film Stocks

Kodak—a word that to many people is synonymous with film, and even with photography itself. It's impossible to imagine life in our media-oriented society if there had never been a George Eastman and there were no Eastman Kodak Company. Super-8 itself is a product of Kodak. No wonder then that most of our films are Kodachromes or Ektachromes of one kind or another.

Ektachrome 160 (E/160) is the highest speed color film stock available in the familiar yellow box. It was introduced by Kodak along with XL cameras, so that any amateur could make color movies almost anywhere without the inconvenience of hot, cumbersome movie lights. But unless you *must* work in a low light situation, you will be much better off with a slower film. The graininess of E/160 is apparent in almost any viewing situation. Although grain can be beautiful in a still photograph and can even be used artistically to enhance a particular film, you'll find the constant dancing of a grain pattern annoying and distracting for general use.

While E/160's resolution has much improved over the years, it is still noticeably inferior to many slower films. This lack of sharpness and increase in grain appear to be *doubled* when this film is printed. For certain situations, like underwater filming where you need every bit of film speed possible to compensate for low lighting, Ektachrome 160 is a godsend. It can even be "push-processed" by a lab to achieve an effective film speed of 320 or even 640. But such emergency situations are a far cry from normal shooting situations.

There is also Ektachrome 160 *Type G*. This film stock is intended for the same use, but the folks in Rochester went a step further and eliminated the need for the #85 filter and its companion filter key, screw or switch. If you're the kind of person who has trouble remembering whether you're sitting in a softly lighted room or bathing in the rays of the afternoon sun, Type G might be the film for you. Type A films such as E/160 are balanced for accurate color rendition in (3400°K) tungsten illumination. Daylight films show their true colors in average daylight (approximately 5600°K). Either can be used in the other's domain with proper filtration. Type G, however, is balanced for light somewhere in the middle of these color temperatures—in other words, for neither light condition. In my tests, the artificially lighted scenes were warmer, more orange than they should have been, and daylight footage was cooly blue. A straight lab print (without color correction) further exaggerates these inaccuracies. Together with grain and resolution on a par with E/160's, this makes Type G film a poor choice for general applications. It might come in handy for a shot lighted by both daylight and tungsten bulbs, or maybe under fluorescent bulbs. But unless you're willing to sacrifice quality for convenience, forget Type G.

Ektachrome EF7242 is another fairly fast film, with a 125 EI in tungsten lighting and 80 EI in daylight (with the #85 filter in place). Since there is no notch on the cartridge for a film of this speed, your camera thinks it's exposing E/160 film. I don't know whether labs give EF7242 a little boost in the developer or whether the film's latitude compensates for the slight underexposure provided by automatic metering systems, but test exposures seemed accurate. The grain and resolution fell right in the middle between the 40 EI and 160 EI films, so it's a much better choice when you need its extra speed. Although only ½ stop slower than 160 film, EF7242 is noticeably superior. I expected it to cut well with Ektachrome 40 (E/40), which it did, but I was surprised to find that it also matched well with Kodachrome 40 (K/40). When I used K/40 for outdoor scenes and EF7242 for interiors, the transition was not at all jarring. EF7242 is a "Type B" emulsion, which means it is balanced for 3200° Kelvin lights. Amateur type photoflood bulbs are rated at 3400°K, and professional film lights are 3200°K. Anyone who uses pro lights with Type A films should use a #82A (pale blue) filter over the lens. (Many filmmakers don't bother, because the slightly warm look without it is not unpleasant. By the time the film is printed, though, people start to look like burn victims, unless, of course, you have scene-to-scene color correction done in the printing.) With EF7242 and professional lights, there is no need for the #82A

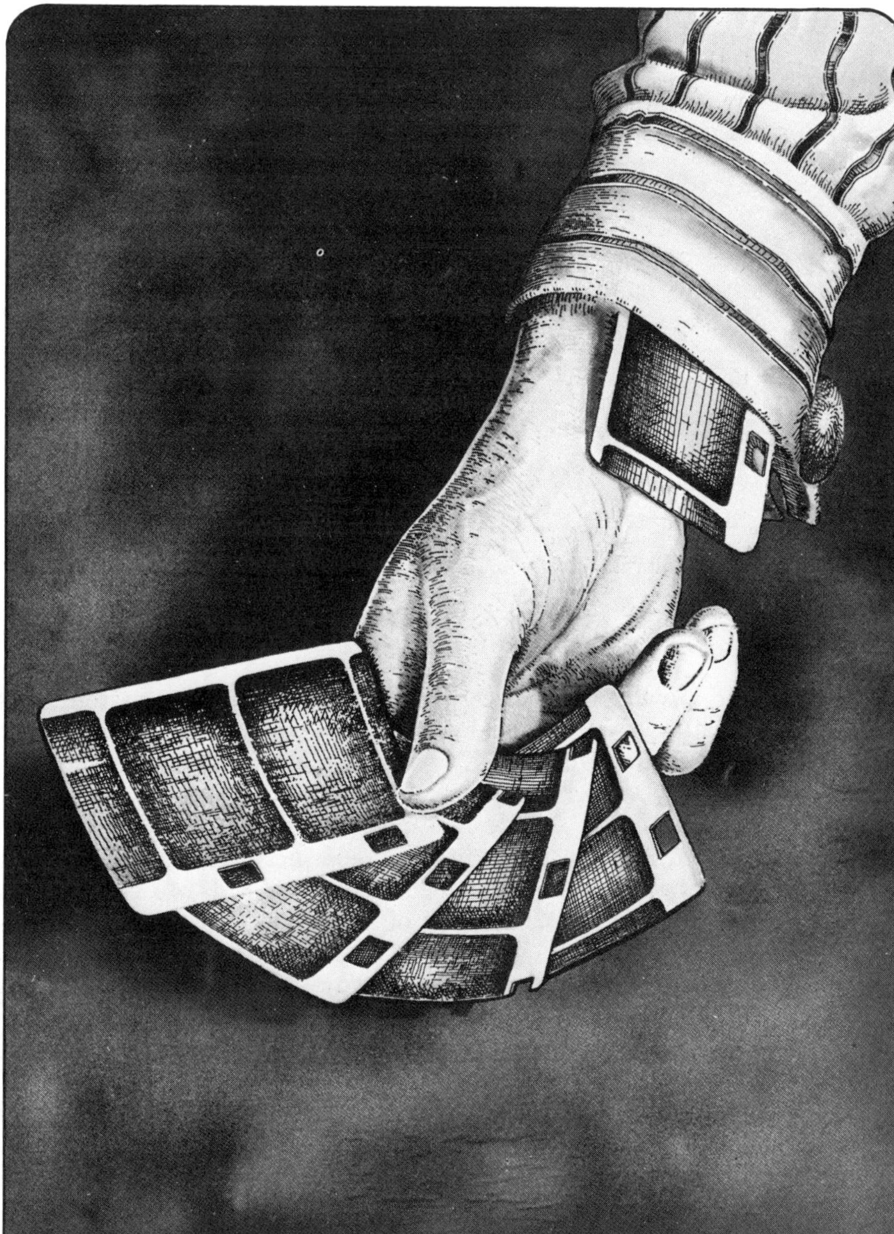

Pick a film stock, any film stock, then test it to judge its qualities for your own use. Note that each film brand is unique, i.e., Kodachrome 40 gives a rich, warm tone with little grain, Ektachrome 160 is the highest speed color film stock, though it tends to be grainy, Fujichrome R25 has superior fidelity and high resolution, etc.

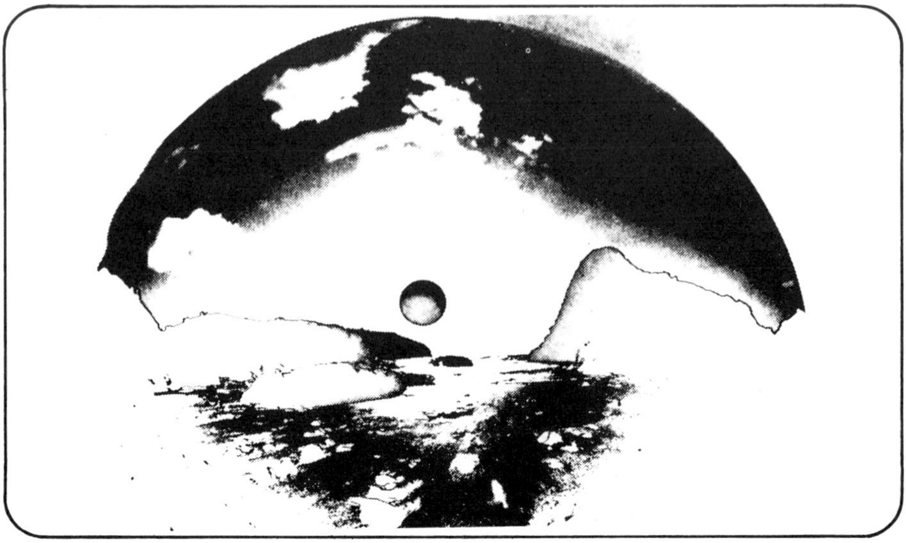

With black-and-white film and do-it-yourself processing, you can do effects like the solarization above.

filter. Another advantage is that it's often processed by custom labs that offer "postflashing" (exposing the film to additional light) to reduce contrast. When your 40 EI film just can't cut it, then Ektachrome EF7242 (Type B) is a decent choice.

Ektachrome SM7244 is a little faster again, with a 160 EI for tungsten lighting and 100 EI in daylight—a speed increase which seems to have been made with minimal sacrifice in quality. SM7244 is the most unusual of all the films I tested. First of all, it was designed to be processed in Kodak's wonder machine, the Supermatic 8 processor. This processing machine produces a ready-to-project, 50-foot length of film in less than 15 minutes, and is reputed to be trouble-free and easy to use even by totally untrained personnel. The trouble is, there aren't too many Supermatic 8 processors around. SM7244 can, however, be processed by some custom labs with another chemistry in more usual processing times.

The most unique aspect of this film is not its processing, but the end result on the screen. It has a moody ethereal quality that seems to transcend the naturalness of a mundane scene. In some of my garden shots, flowers took on a breathtaking luminescence that was almost unreal—yet colors seemed accurate. Even the grain, which was noticeable, had a Van Goghish feeling that was not at all hard to take. I'm sure that if a Supermatic processor were at my disposal, I'd shoot a great deal of Ektachrome SM7244. Even with the ordinary wait for results and my inclination toward slower films, I'm not through exploring the almost magical possibilities of this unusual film.

Ektachrome 40 (E/40) is a sharp, fine grain film with a color rendition that is subtly different from Kodachrome 40. The quality level of this film is very high, so the choice between it and K/40 is mostly a matter of personal taste. Rumor has it that this film is being taken off the market by Kodak. If that's true, it's a loss for all of us. If the people at Kodak who make these decisions looked at some of Lenny Lipton's 3-D footage shot on Ektachrome 40, they might reconsider their action. If you are unfamiliar with this emulsion, you owe it to yourself to try some before it's all gone.

Kodachrome 40 (K/40) is, in my opinion, the state-of-the-art. No other film has ever been able to capture the world around us with the visual hi-fidelity of Kodachrome. No wonder Paul Simon wrote a song about it. It has the finest, almost talcum-like grain structure, and a resolving capability second to none. Blacks are deep, rich and black, and grays and whites reproduce without color casts. I've even copied black-and-white film onto K/40 without picking up any traces of color.

If it's your habit to shoot K/40 and project the original, you have an edge on the big Hollywood film companies. None of their original stock is as fine as Kodachrome, and what they release to theaters is a second or third generation print.

But most of us are not interested in showing unedited films on a small screen to amuse ourselves and our immediate families. In a world where we are constantly fed on visual imagery, we want to express ourselves in an unlimited way through the medium of film. To take part in this visual communication with a relative amount of success, we must be able to edit our work, mix a sound track and make a *print* of the end product. This is the Achilles' heel of Kodachrome 40.

The qualities that make K/40 so good in its original form make it very difficult to print. The rich saturated colors and full, hard-edged contrast that give it clear definition as a projection medium, render it muddy in the final print. This is not to say that the other film stocks I've mentioned would print better. They are, in fact, worse because their graininess and lack of resolution also become exaggerated in the print. All of them also have the contrast problem that is inherent in all reversal films designed for projection. I cite the problem in relation to Kodachrome because it is the only film that is sharp enough to weather the losses of printing and still be well defined in large screen projection.

You can do much to reduce or eliminate the saturation and contrast of Kodachrome, and, with extreme care, very acceptable prints can be achieved. It would still be easier if Kodak helped by putting out either a version of K/40 that was a little softer to begin with, or if they offered postflashing or some chemical method of reducing contrast and saturation at the processing stage. Kodachrome 40 is still the best possible choice as a general purpose film stock in Super-8. And it works equally well in XL cameras and is cheaper than the 160 stuff.

When GAF dropped out of the film business, Agfa-Gevaert

dropped in. At this time, only Agfa 40 silent film is available in the U.S., but old-time Agfa fans are hoping for a chance to try the full range of stocks now sold in Europe. Especially tempting is Agfa 40 Plus, prestriped film in a silent cartridge.

Black-and-White Film Stocks

Black-and-white Super-8 film, thankfully, is still with us. The films that impressed me most as a child, that made me want to become a filmmaker, were almost all black and white. Even as an adult, I've found films like *The Pawnbroker, In Cold Blood* and *8½* more heavyweight than I think they could have been in color. Major Hollywood films in black and white are now almost extinct, and there is a strong possibility that it will demand the dedication of interested Super-8 filmmakers to keep this exciting and challenging medium alive.

There are three black-and-white film stocks available from Kodak at this time. As well as being as expensive to work with as color film, *none* of them are available prestriped, and you usually have to find a custom (more expensive) lab for processing. If you can get past these initial problems, black and white has much to offer.

Plus-X 7276 is the slowest, finest grained and sharpest of the black-and-white trio. Its exposure index is 40 for tungsten lighting and 32 for daylight with the #85 filter in place (although the automatic exposure keying in Super-8 cameras exposes Plus-X at 25 EI in daylight). It has been my habit to leave the filter key in (filter out) at all times with Plus-X. It seems pointless to balance color for a black-and-white emulsion. Unless you're shooting at high noon on the salt flats, the extra speed without the filter should not be a problem. Initial results with Plus-X can be a little discouraging, particularly if your lens isn't extremely crisp. The film's lower contrast casts a gray look over everything. Prints made from Plus-X original, however, are beautiful, with rich blacks and sparkling whites, and a good tonal range between them. Working properly with light, be it daylight or artificial, takes discipline, as does working continuously with rather dull looking footage with only the promise of a fine print to keep you going. Having a "work print" made of black-and-white film by a lab will preserve your original and provide an on-going preview of your end product. Black-and-white prints from Plus-X original projected 20 feet wide through an arc lamp projector have been technically the most impressive footage I've seen in Super-8.

Tri-X 7278 film offers many of the same advantages, plus a higher film speed. The daylight speed of Tri-X is 200 EI, but the automatic keying of Super-8 cameras will expose it at 160 EI, which is well within the tolerances of this film's latitude. Under artificial light, the exposure index is truly 160. Tri-X has evolved over the years to such a state of perfection that it is almost indistinguishable from Plus-X, even though it is four times as fast and very easy to use. It is as convenient for low light shooting as Ektachrome 160, Type G, but without the color balance problems. And you can use it outdoors without having to worry about filters. You can even film with it in bright sun, if your Super-8 camera stops down below *f*/22, if you have a variable shutter or if you shoot with a neutral density filter over the lens.

The minimal graininess of Tri-X is more than tolerable, and results look crisp. If you don't want or need to use Tri-X as an exclusive universal black-and-white stock, it cuts in beautifully with the slower and finer grained Plus-X. Since the film is so fast, it doesn't take a heavy investment in lighting equipment to get professional looking indoor results.

4-X 7277 black-and-white film stock will turn even cameras with the slowest lens and narrowest shutter into XL's. With a 400 EI for daylight shooting and 320 EI for tungsten, you'll have enough light to explore the secret passageways of a mummy's tomb.

This extreme speed exacts its toll, however, in terms of grain and general reduction in quality. 4-X should be thought of as an emergency film, and used only when there is no other choice in an extreme low light situation.

Kodak does not offer processing for any of these black-and-white film stocks. Your camera store should be able to suggest a local lab that will. You should know that it's not too difficult to process your own black-and-white film if you're on a tight budget or at some distance from a custom lab. Do-it-yourself processing also makes available "solarization" and other neat effects that are not normally done by labs. Chemical color toning of black-and-white films is also very easy, and the results can be both beautiful and unique. Each scene can be colored differently to match the mood of the piece.

I'd like to take a moment to mention some of the choices that we *don't* have in our film stocks. First of all, there is no negative emulsion available to Super-8 filmmakers. And infrared color film has never been offered in a cartridge. (This is an exciting 35mm still camera film that gives you red grass and purple grapefruits, if that's your style. Or almost any color combinations you might desire.) And there is still no high contrast black-and-white material for making mattes and counter mattes. These films are available in 16mm and 35mm. If these gaps aren't filled by Kodak or Fuji, someone else may come along to close them.

As much as we don't have, there is still quite a bit of choice in the film stocks we can use in Super-8. Now that you have an idea of the camera films available, you should try some of the various stocks before settling on one. That's a sure way to know that what you pick will be a winner.

SOUND

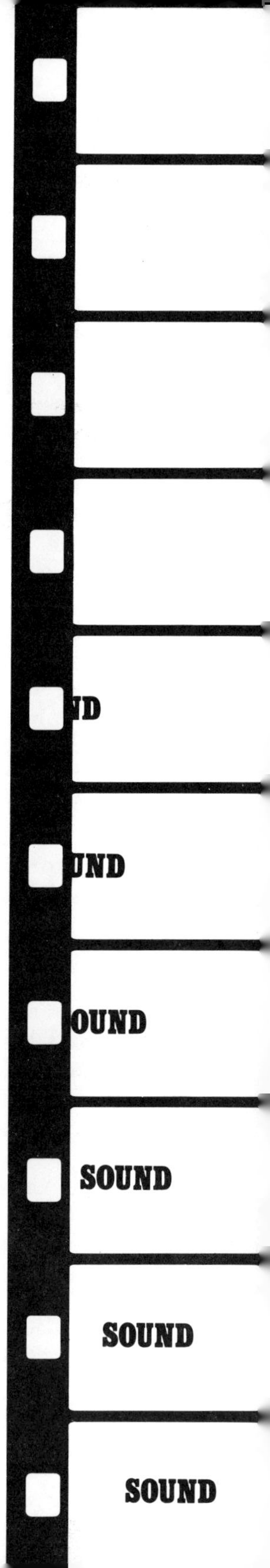
ND
UND
OUND
SOUND
SOUND
SOUND

SHOOTING AND EDITING SOUND-ON-FILM MOVIES

Rod Eaton

When you can't think of any more scenes to shoot, you have to face the fact that 27 50-foot rolls of Super-8 sound film lurk in a box beneath your bed—haunting your nights with their refusal to magically edit themselves into the 20-minute film you envision.

One way to edit single-system film is to convert it to double-system, using Super8 Sound, Optasound or similar equipment. But such equipment is expensive, and besides, not all of us would want to work with that kind of exotic equipment. It seems to defeat the simplistic intent of single system, anyway. So use what is readily available—a good viewer, a wet splicer or tape splicer such as the Guillotine, which leaves the mag stripe free, and a sound projector. The sound projector is a must at the editing stage, since it is necessary to view each shot a number of times to become familiar with the sound track.

If you can swing it, a viewer with a magnetic sound head is a real asset. Not only will it save you the frustration of trying to lip-read an actor in a long shot, it will also save your family and dog from your frustration. There are viewers on the market with sound-reading capability but with some ingenuity, a few dollars and a Sunday afternoon you could add a magnetic head to your own viewer. Problems in cutting single-system film, of course, are caused by the 18-frame picture-to-sound separation. In the camera, film traveling at 18 fps passes over the sound-recording head one second after it passes through the gate assembly. This means that the sound is located 18 frames ahead of the picture, and you are forced to cut off one or the other—usually the picture—when editing.

In the Kodak Ektasound camera, this business is additionally complicated (or simplified, I suppose, depending on your point of view) by the fact that Kodak has built a capacitance gizmo into the recording circuitry. A capacitor is a little electronic component that, when a signal reaches it, hesitates before it passes the signal along. In the Ektasound camera, the time it takes for the capacitor to make up its mind is one second. What this means is when you start the camera there is a one-second delay before sound will be recorded. This one second of "dead" time is also the time it takes for the first frame of a new shot to reach the sound head. In other words, the capacitance circuit prevents sound from a new shot from being recorded on the last 18 frames of the previous shot. Thus, for the first second of each shot, there will be no sound. What's important to remember is that because of those silent 18 frames, it is necessary to allow a second or two at the beginning of a shot before you cue your sound to start.

Other single-system sound cameras have done away with the capacitor in their design, and thus eliminated the dead time. This is a good idea if you don't plan on doing any editing on your films, because that sound drop-out is hard to get used to every time a scene change appears on the screen. However, if you will be cutting your film, you will still need to allow a couple of seconds at the start of each shot before your dialogue or vital sounds begin.

The secret of being able to match creative camera work with single-system sound is meticulous pre-planning and careful scripting. You don't have the luxury of waiting until you reach the editing stage to decide how you want your film to look. Everything must be planned in advance before you even put film into your camera. The result of all that planning will be a film that doesn't tell whether it was shot single or double system.

When editing, always remember that the sound is 18 frames ahead of the picture. If your viewer lets you edit from left to right, the sound is to the right of the picture. Let's say your first scene is a man speaking. On the viewer screen locate the first frame in which he begins speaking

When the sound cartridge is inserted in the camera, the film is automatically positioned between the sound-recording head and loop-sensing switch, and between the capstan and pressure roller.

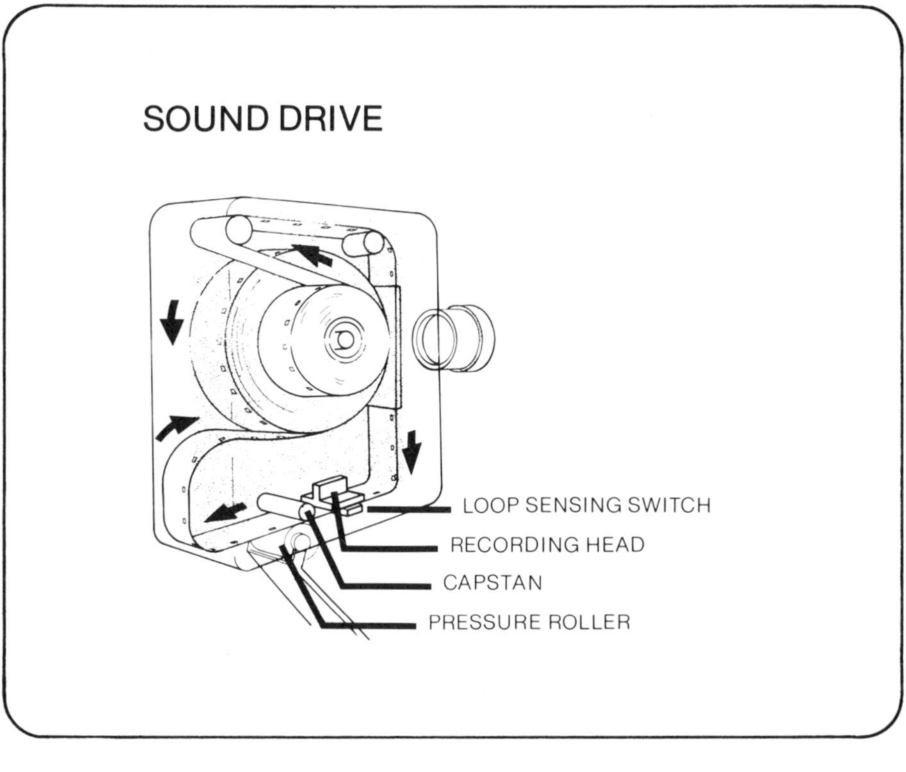

EASTMAN KODAK

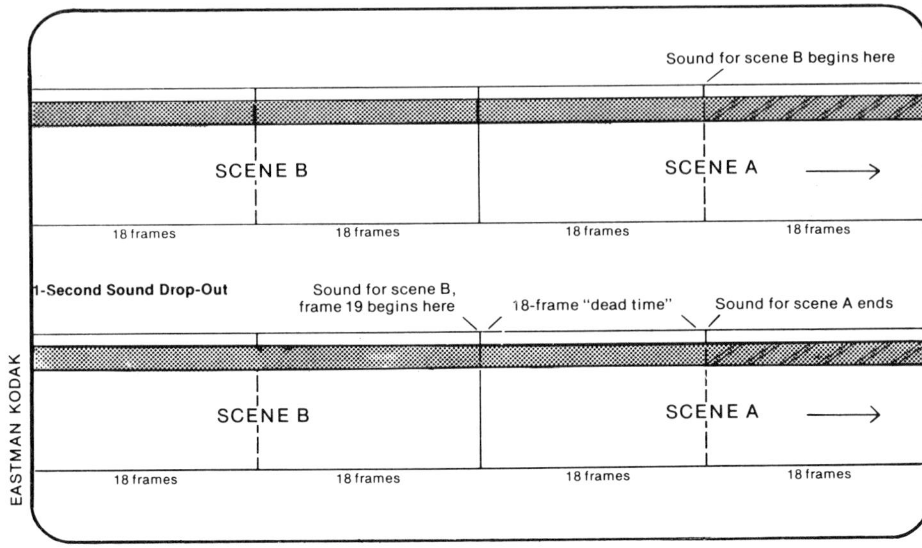

Figure 1: Typical 18-frame sound and picture displacement.

and mark it. Now count ahead—to the right—18 frames. That's where his first word begins. You would have to cut 18 frames ahead of your first shot or you will cut off the beginning of his sentence. The end of the shot is easier to cut. Since the last word he says is 18 frames ahead of the corresponding picture, you simply cut visually at the scene's end.

A dialogue sequence between two people shot in individual close-ups will require some pre-planning. If you put two shots together—person A speaking in the first shot, person B answering in the second shot—you end up with a one-second pause between the end of A's line and the start of B's line. This may be acceptable in many instances, especially if the dialogue provides for thoughtful silences, but at other times it can destroy dramatic content. To eliminate this problem, you can cut the first shot at the end of the sound—18 frames before A stops moving his lips visually. The end of his line will carry over the splice and be heard during the first instant that person B is on the screen. What's important when shooting this sequence is for B to look as though he is listening to A before he speaks. To be on the safe side, always have actors "act"—hold a facial expression or perform some action—during those extra seconds at the beginning of each shot.

If, in this dialogue sequence between A and B, you plan to cut away to B reacting while A is still speaking, shoot it like this. First, shoot A's entire line. Then shoot the cutaway of B, but have A repeat his line into the microphone off-camera. With these two shots, which have the same dialogue, you can cut from A to B's reactions without losing a word. If you don't have a sound head on your viewer, this can be tricky. However, with repeated viewings on a sound projector, you begin to notice slight visual cues—a hand movement, a nod of the head, even a blink of an eye—that you can use for cutting references. You locate that reference frame on the viewer, count ahead 18 frames, and then make your cut.

If you require a sequence in which you intend to change the camera angle during an actor's line, shoot the first angle and have the actor go through all the action, getting up out of a chair, for instance. After you've changed your camera angle, have the actor repeat his action as well as that part of his line with which you want to begin the second shot. You will end up with two pieces of film with overlapping action and sound, and you shouldn't have trouble finding a place to cut where both can be matched.

You may have shot some parts of your film without sound—titles and credits, establishing shots, etc.—with the idea of adding sound to them later. Although these sections could be filmed on non-striped film which could be striped before editing into the rest of the film, it may be wiser to shoot them on prestriped stock anyway. You can record sound on these sections of film before editing them into the rest of the film, or you can edit them in and add sound at the end of production. The method you use will be determined in part by the sound projector you use to record with. Some machines go in and out of the recording mode easily and quietly, making it fairly easy to put sound on a section in the middle of the film. With other projectors this could be a risky business—there is always the chance of erasing part of your pre-recorded track by entering the recording mode at the wrong time. One solution is to abort the erase head. The erase head is the first one the film passes over (most sound projectors, in fact, every one I have ever seen, have two heads—erase and a combination play/record). You may be able to cut into the wiring to the erase head and put an on/off switch in to control "erase," if you're mechanically inclined. A more primitive but much easier method would be to put a small piece of masking tape over the head. Use an expendable piece of sound film to make sure the erase head has been thoroughly thwarted, and be sure to clean the head after you remove the tape.

Granted, working with single-system sound is a lot more work than shooting pictures without sound. But it's also a lot more rewarding. You don't have all the flexibility of double-system editing, but you don't have the complexity or the cost, either. Editing single system allows many creative possibilities to the filmmaker who has an interest in making good films at a reasonable cost.

SIMPLE SOLUTIONS TO SINGLE-SYSTEM SNAGS

James Gustafson

If you've ever filmed with a single-system (sound-on-film) camera, you know how easy it is to shoot sound in perfect sync with picture. In fact, the term *single system* means you are using one machine—a camera that records sound on the film's magnetic stripe—instead of two machines—a camera and a separate tape recorder. The latter is called *double system* and requires an expensive sync recorder and elaborate editing set-up. While single system is easier and much less expensive, there are problems to solve before you can edit your film.

In Super-8 sound cameras, sound is recorded on the film's stripe 18 frames in advance of the image that corresponds to that sound. Sound projectors have the same 18 frame advance and, thus, will play back image and sound in sync. However, when you edit out some of your picture, say 18 frames that you don't want, you'll also be removing the sound track for the next 18 frames *you do want*. Also, with single system you can never play back sound immediately after you've filmed to check the quality of the recording. And you can't record continuously when you're not shooting.

I've used several tricks to solve these problems for my own sound shooting. They're not as costly or complicated as shooting double system. Let's look at some of the problems and ways you can solve them.

Problem #1

You've just completed a very difficult lip-sync shot, in which you had to pan, tilt, zoom and dolly with your camera. Your concentration on camera moves and composition was superb. A terrific shot! Then your actor has the nerve to say, "Did I sound all right? I felt like I sounded a little stilted."

"Did you *sound* all right? After that beautifully complex visual move I made, you tell me you may not have said it right?!"

What can you do? There's no way to play back the sound and see if your actor is right. With double-system sound where you're recording in sync on a separate tape recorder, you just rewind the tape and check it. But not with a single-system sound camera. You must wait until the film is processed.

Solution #1

This can be avoided with "instant replay sound." If your camera has a monitor jack for an earphone plug, you can run a cord with the appropriate plug from the monitor jack to a portable tape cassette's auxiliary or microphone input. You may have to experiment to find which input on the recorder matches the camera output. You can buy a cord with the right plugs on either end at any electronics supply store such as Radio Shack. Then you plug your earphone headset into the cassette's monitor jack. (While you're in Radio Shack, buy an inexpensive set of headphones. The earphones that come with cameras are virtually useless.) Put the cassette in record, and shoot the scene. On some cameras, you'll have to depress a monitor switch on the camera to make the monitor jack "live."

The result is that you have instant audio replay. If you have any questions about your sound, rewind the tape and play it back just like double system. The sound you hear is the same sound recorded on the camera's film—through the same microphone. This way you can check your audio for wind noise, camera noise and actor's accuracy and inflection. The advantage of this over just running a separate cassette with its own mic is simple. The cassette's microphone cannot be placed exactly where the camera's microphone is. A few degrees away can make a big difference. Also, the cassette mic and camera mic may not match up in sensitivity or directional response characteristics. So the cassette's recording may not be the same as on the film. Recording from the monitor jack solves this problem.

Problem #2

You've just shot a "talking head" interview at a parade, with a band playing in the background. For variety in visuals, you stopped the camera several times to change your camera angle. When you edit your footage, you want to connect these abrupt angle changes with "cutaways" to other action such as portions of the parade that you filmed at a later time. Since your "cutaway" segments were shot at a different

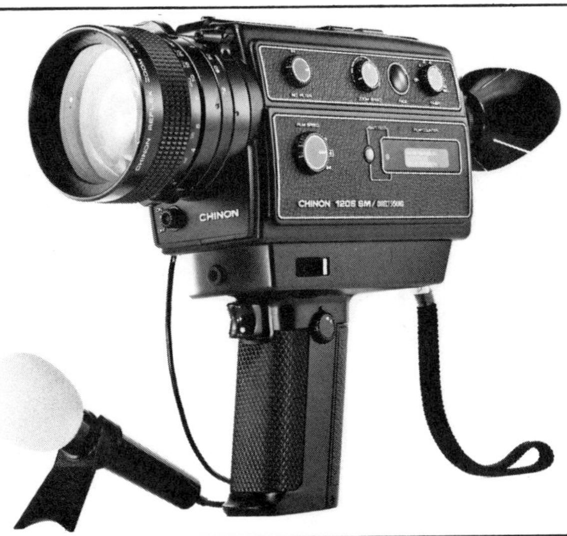

CHINON

There are many good single-system sound cameras. Here is a Chinon 1206 SM/Direct Sound.

time, there are distracting jumps in the background sound between interview and cutaway. How do you make them sound like they were shot at the same time and give the interview a smooth, professional appearance?

Solution #2

To maintain a continuity in background sound throughout the interview, hook up your cassette as you did in Solution #1. As you shoot your first shot, start recording on the cassette. When you want to change angles, stop the camera but let the cassette continue to run. You may have to keep a monitor switch depressed in order to keep the microphone "live." Repeat this procedure until your interview is complete. Visually you'll have a start/stop picture, but you will also have a continuous audio track recorded at the same time, through the same microphone. This track can be recorded on your cutaway inserts to give sound continuity as you switch camera angles. In fact, you may want to shoot the cutaways silent with this in mind.

When you've edited your film and inserted the cutaways, you can add the continuous background sound from the cassette on to the "blank spaces" in the cutaway sequences using the sound-on-sound control on your projector. Just listen for a cue word at the end of a sync sequence, find that word on the tape and mark the tape. If you have a projector of the Eumig type, you can cue your cassette to the mark where you want the inserted sound to begin, and start the projector. When you hear your cue word on the film, punch the projector into

Shooting with two sound cameras can give you the ability to do quick-cut visuals and still have a continuous sound track.

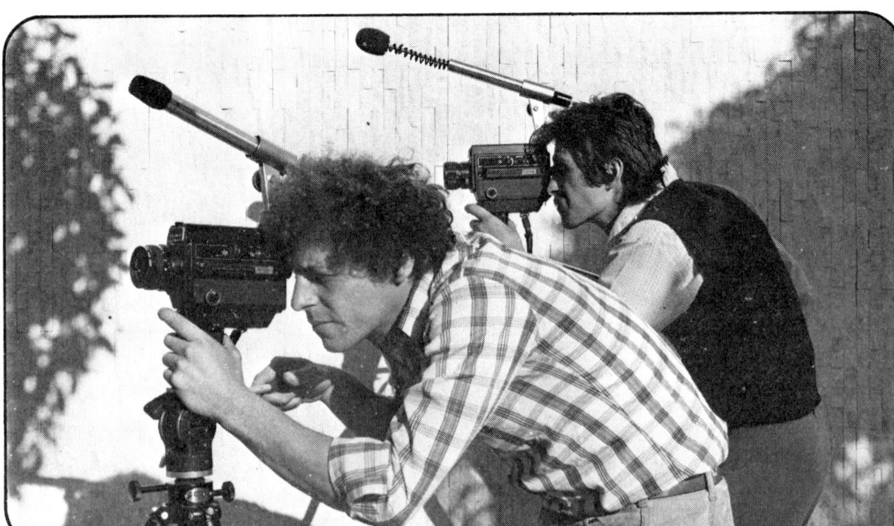

"record," start the tape and turn up the sound-on-sound volume. At the end of the insert, turn down the sound-on-sound control, and stop the projector. Repeat this procedure until all sound inserts are transferred.

This also works on a film in which you plan to have a rather long interview cutting away to illustrate what is being said. In the end, you'll have your full audio track and sync visuals when you need them. You can shoot your inserts and cutaways at another time.

Problem #3

You want to shoot a sync sound film. Both you and a friend have single-system sound cameras, silent editors and a sound projector. You don't have any sound equipment like a sync recorder. Your script calls for several quick cuts which the 18 frame sound advance won't allow you to do without making a mess of the sound track.

Solution #3

You can solve this one by using two cameras to shoot the scene that calls for quick cutting or montage. When you plan this scene, plan it as though you were directing cameras for a TV special. Work out your shots so you can alternate from one camera to the other as you shoot the continuous action. By overlapping camera runs, you will film the beginning and end of each shot twice, once on each camera. When editing these overlaps, not only will the action match perfectly but the 18 frame sound advance won't be a problem. The sound on the tail of the first shot will match with the visual on the head of the second shot.

In theory, both cameras have to be run synchronously for this to work. But in fact, "wild" cameras will run accurately enough so your sound and picture will appear in sync from one camera to another. If you want to make sure both sound cameras are well matched for this, shoot some test footage and edit it together.

To really make this dual camera shooting look good, you must be sure that both cameras have the same exposure reading so image brightness and contrast will be consistent. When you plan your alternating shots, remember to keep the overlap shots at least 1 second long. Of course, the more overlap you provide, the more editing options you'll have. Using two viewers can make locating the exact frames to cut easier.

These suggestions can make using single-system cameras almost as versatile as a double-system sound set-up, and they will cost you a lot less money.

HEAR'S THE WORD ON DOUBLE-SYSTEM SOUND

Stephen Aubery

So you've decided you want to shoot double-system sync sound. Now you've got to figure out what *kind* of double system to use.

Sync Pulse Type

Until Super-8 sync sound came on the scene, the motion picture industry had basically one standard synching system, known as *pilotone.* By using modern electronic technology, however, a new method of synching a camera and recorder was devised called *digital.* This method not only reduced the cost of sync generators, but also miniaturized them, making it easier to install them in compact Super-8 cameras.

Pilotone sync conventionally makes use of a continuous sine wave (60 Hertz in the U.S. and 50 Hertz in Europe and some other countries) generated by the camera, and recorded on the sync track of the tape recorder. (Hertz, abbreviated Hz, stands for the international unit of sound frequency, equal to one cycle per second.) One picture frame is equal to 2½ pulses in the 60 Hz system, and 2 pulses in the 50 Hz system. *Advantage:* Pilotone is the standard for the other motion picture formats (e.g., 16mm and 35mm). Therefore you can adapt your existing sound equipment for use with pilotone Super-8 cameras. This is especially useful for a 16mm production house interested in getting into Super-8 production, since the sound equipment they already have would be compatible. *Disadvantages:* 1) Although a few Super-8 cameras are equipped to give a pilotone sync pulse, most of them are not. Most of those that are, however, have also been wisely fitted by the manufacturers with a digital sync output. 2) Pilotone sync generators are more expensive than digital.

Digital sync utilizes one sync signal per frame (rather than the 2½ or 2 per frame pilotone). The signal usually consists of either a contact switch, which merely closes a circuit, or a tone burst (generally 1,000 Hz) once per frame. Because one sync pulse is sent to the recorder for each frame of picture exposed in the camera, digital sync is often called "once-per-frame" or 1/F sync. *Advantages:* 1) Many Super-8 cameras now come equipped from the factory with some sort of digital sync outlet, often in the form of a flash synchronization (PC) socket. Since this type of sync output is inexpensive, it is increasingly becoming standard equipment on Super-8 cameras. 2) A camera without a sync output can be modified for digital sync at little cost. If you already own a non-sync camera, it won't become obsolete when you decide to shoot sync sound, but will merely require a simple modification. 3) There are electronic interfaces available today which match the 24 pulse-per-second sync signal from a digital camera with the 60 cycle-per-second tone needed for pilotone recorders, so that digital and pilotone equipment can be used together. *Disadvantage:* Digital systems are not universal. One system utilizes a tone burst, and another merely closes a contact switch once per frame. Sync sound equipment designed to work with Super-8 cameras must be capable of synching to either system.

Synching Systems

In this discussion we will refer to each piece of equipment (either camera or recorder) as a master or a slave. A master runs at its normal speed (governed only by its internal speed controls) and a slave runs at a speed governed by some other source, generally a master.

Camera master, recorder slave: In this configuration the camera maintains its normal speed, and the recorder (connected by a cable) records a pulse (or modifies its speed) dictated by the rate of the camera. *Advantages:* 1) Any camera fitted with a sync output can be used as a master without modification. 2) Most sync recorders are designed to be slaves, and to operate as such without modification. 3) Since modification is unnecessary for either the camera or the recorder, this is the least complicated synching system. *Disadvantage:* Since the speed of some Super-8 cameras is fairly unstable, you can end up with wow and flutter in the sound track.

Crystal Control

Camera slave, recorder slave: In this system the camera and recorder need no interconnecting cables as in the preceding method. Instead, each piece of equipment is slaved to a separate but identical reference source—a crystal control in the case of a crystal sync, or a 60 Hz reference from the AC line, in the case of AC line sync. *Advantages:* 1) There are no cables connecting the camera and recorder. In fact, cameras and recorders fitted *internally* with crystal need no cables at all, while equipment utilizing *external* crystal control must have a short cable between the crystal control and the camera or re-

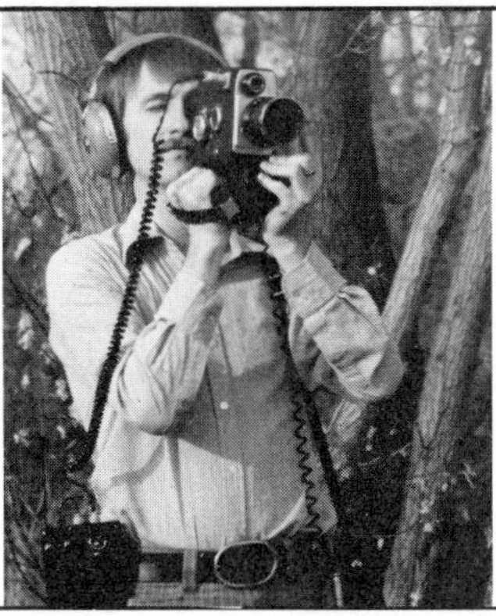

One-man-band shooting with the Canon DS-8 and a Uher tape recorder using the Cine Slave for sync.

corder. With AC line sync, both camera and recorder must be connected to the AC line. 2) Both the camera and the recorder are slaved to identical *accurate* sources, so that wow and flutter aren't dependent on either piece of equipment. 3) If you need to shoot sync sound of the same scene with more than one camera or recorder, there is no need for cables to interconnect all of the equipment. This can be a great advantage if you have two or three cameras 100 feet apart since it eliminates the need to bring and set up yards of extra cable, along with the chance that someone will trip over a cable and interrupt sync. By eliminating cables, you cut down the possibility of one of the connectors making a faulty contact, creating loss of sync. 4) With most of the currently available crystal controls, there is some form of sync readout to show if you are filming at sync speed. With some, if your batteries are too low to run at the correct speed, your camera won't run. With others, a light or meter indicates the lack of sufficient power for sync shooting. Thus, the traumatic experience of arriving back at the studio and finding that your sync sound really isn't sync at all is practically eliminated. *Disadvantages:* 1) The major drawback is that this is the most expensive of the systems. 2) Another drawback is that crystal is not available for many unmodified cameras and no Super-8 camera (yet) has built-in crystal control.

Sync Recorders

Two types of sync sound recorders have traditionally been used in motion picture production: fullcoat and quarter-inch tape recorders. In the early days of sound filmmaking, bulky, cumbersome and noisy recorders which ran expensive fullcoat film (*i.e.*, sprocketed film which is coated on one side with a magnetic emulsion for sound recording) were dragged from stage to location for sync recording. In the last few years we've seen quieter, more portable quarter-inch tape recorders put into use in the industry for sync recording. Now, with Super-8 producers demanding even more portability and lower costs, cassette recorders have been adapted to function as sync recorders.

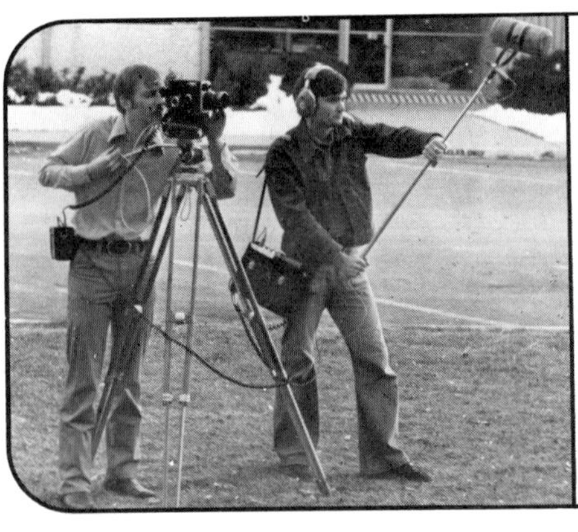

Shooting double system with the Canon DS-8 and the synched Uher recorder. The Cine Slave can be seen on the author's belt.

Sync cassette recorders in use in Super-8 today are often audio-visual recorders which were originally designed to operate with slide-change equipment. The control track, which was intended to carry slide projector command tones, readily lends itself to the task of recording a camera sync pulse. Other sync cassette recorders available include stereo models in which one of the stereo tracks carries the sync pulse (making the recorder mono when used in the sync mode), and a stereo recorder modified to record a sync track in addition to two program tracks, thus giving sync stereo. *Advantages:* 1) Fairly good quality sync cassette recorders are relatively inexpensive and won't deplete your equipment budget. 2) Tape cassettes are inexpensive, and they are readily available. If you run out of tape on location, it's simple to buy more from a nearby store. 3) Changing cassettes takes very little time since there is no threading involved. 4) Because cassette recorders are generally small and easy to carry around, they are suitable for documentary shooting, and very useful when you're doing one-person filming. 5) This may sound sordid, but because of their low cost, many cassette recorders are more expendable than other sync recorders, so a filmmaker can take the recorder places he or she was previously afraid to go for fear of damaging the equipment. *Disadvantages:* 1) Sync cassette recorders can only be used in recorder slave applications. (NB: The recorder *speed* does not actually slave to the camera, but the recorder slaves in terms of recording the pulses as the camera—the master—dictates them.) 2) The sound quality of a cassette recorder (running at 1-7/8 inches per second) is generally lower in terms of frequency response and signal-to-noise ratio than quarter-inch or fullcoat recorders. However, the quality is generally better than single-system cameras.

Quarter-inch sync tape recorders have been available and widely used for many years in the motion picture industry. *Advantages:* 1) They can run at higher tape speeds (traditionally 7½ ips and sometimes 15 ips), giving you increased frequency response and a better signal-to-noise ratio. 2) Some quarter-inch sync recorders can be used in recorder master applications, further reducing wow and flutter in sync recordings. *Disadvantages:* 1) Quarter-inch sync recorders are larger, heavier and more expensive than most sync cassette recorders. 2) Tape stock is more expensive than cassette tapes.

Fullcoat recorders used in Super-8 differ from the 16mm and 35mm decks in many ways. First, they don't use sprocket teeth to transport the sprocketed fullcoat at sync speed, but rather use an electronic sensor to determine the rate at which the perforations are moving. If they are advancing too quickly with reference to the sync pulse, the electronic "brain" tells the motor to slow down. If they are too slow, the "brain" speeds up the motor. This eliminates the need for the enlarged transport system found on 16mm and 35mm fullcoat recorders, since a large flywheel assembly (which cuts down the wow and flutter caused by the sprocket transport) is no longer necessary. Also, since Super-8 fullcoat is only slightly wider than quarter-inch tape, Super-8 fullcoat recorders have been manufactured economically from redesigned quarter-inch recorders. *Advantages:* 1) Fullcoat is the medium with which you generally edit double-system sound Super-8; therefore there is no need for transferring or resolving. You merely sync up the fullcoat with the picture and proceed with editing. 2) Since no transfer has taken place, you edit first generation sound. *Disadvantages:* 1) If the original sound is edited and you make a mistake or a wrong cut in editing, the original recordings could be destroyed. For this reason, if you record your original on fullcoat, you should make a safety copy (generally on quarter-inch tape with a sync reference original) before you start editing the original. Then, if you make a mistake in editing, you can retransfer your safety copy to fullcoat and continue editing. 2) Fullcoat stock is *much* more expensive than the best cassette or quarter-inch tape. If you intend to do original recording on fullcoat, both good and bad takes must be recorded, but if the original recording is done on either cassette or quarter-inch tape, you need only transfer the good (print) takes to fullcoat, saving money. 3) Since most Super-8 fullcoat recorders are redesigned quarter-inch recorders, they tend to be larger and heavier than cassette recorders. 4) Fullcoat stock is available from relatively few outlets, so it can be very hard to get in case of emergencies.

Editing System

Single-system editing can be done with a simple viewer fitted with a *sound reader* (a playback head connected to an amplifier and speaker). For more complex editing functions, however, most single-system editors prefer to transfer the original recordings from the magnetic stripe to fullcoat for double-system editing. Regardless of whether the original was shot single or double system, when you edit double system you are faced with several options when choosing editing equipment.

Vertical editing benches basically consist of a pair of rewinds, a viewer, sound readers (one for each sound track) and a synchronizer (often called a sync block). They have long been used in 16mm production as a inexpensive way to edit double-system sync sound. The vertical benches that have been designed for Super-8 use, however, have had several features (such as third hand rewinds, sliding sound readers for locating sync, differential adapters and synchronizer outriggers) built into them that make the operation of a Super-8 vertical bench much easier than its 16mm counterpart. *Advantages:* 1) Compared to other editing systems, a vertical bench is relatively inexpensive. This makes vertical benches ideal for the production company or film school on a tight budget. (And these days, who isn't?) 2) Most 16mm filmmakers are familiar with this form of editing, so if you convert or add Super-8 to an existing facility, a vertical bench will more than likely fit right in with current procedures. *Disadvantages:* 1) The sound playback quality of a vertical bench is relatively poor, even if the bench is motorized (which is highly recommended). 2) Take-up on the reels must be accomplished by hand winding. This usually poses only a slight inconvenience, especially with the newly modified Super8 Sound third hand rewinds or differential adapters.

Horizontal editing tables (often called flatbed editors or postproduction consoles) have basically "come into their own" only within the last few years in 16mm and 35mm production. While they were designed to make editing easier and more convenient, the price of the larger format units has been quite prohibitive. Most Super-8 horizontal tables have been developed with the lower budget requirements of Super-8 in mind, and are much less expensive. *Advantages:* 1) Since take-up is accomplished by using electric torque motors, there is no need for hand winding, and as a result, operation is more convenient. 2) It takes a surprisingly short time for a filmmaker familiar with a vertical bench to get used to the different operating procedure of a horizontal table. And once you're acclimatized, it takes a lot less time to edit. 3) The editor can concentrate on the creative aspects of editing, since most of the mechanical functions are taken care of by the table, not the editor. *Disadvantage:* The disadvantage is that horizontal tables generally cost two to three times more than the vertical benches.

Sync Sound Mixing

Mixing is the process by which dialogue, music, sound effects and narration are combined for a desirable balance, and unwanted sounds are filtered out (also referred to as dubbing or rerecording in professional circles). If more than one kind of sound is to be heard at any one time in the film, this becomes an important step in the preparation of a final sound track. For example, adding background music to a narrated training film requires a sound mix of some sort. Traditional methods of sound mixing in other motion picture formats cost thousands of dollars

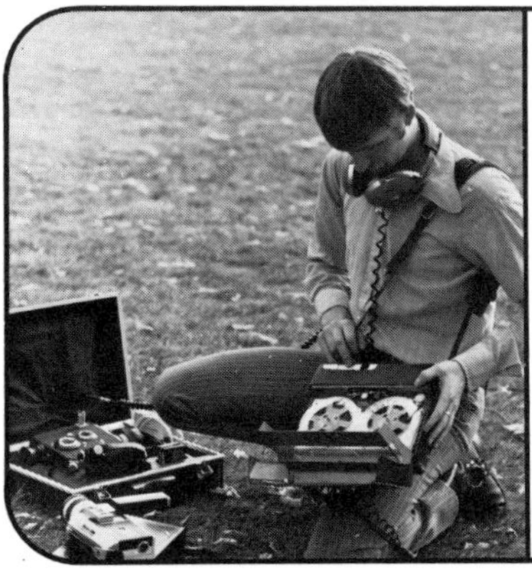

On location, the author checks the recording before shooting the next scene.

since they require a bank of fullcoat playback decks and a fullcoat recorder. Selsyn motors keep all of them running in perfect sync with each other and a projector. Since 16 and 35mm fullcoat decks and Selsyn interlock systems are very expensive, the price of such a set-up is extremely high. So, in keeping with the basic economic philosophies of Super-8 production, other less expensive methods of sound mixing have been devised, utilizing modern stereo hi-fi developments to economize in terms of both cost and size. Some horizontal editing tables, which we will not cover here, can be modified or adapted for mixing, and some electronic editing systems are also adaptable.

In-projector mixing is the method often used to add music or sound effects as a background on an already existing mag-striped print. This is often called *sound-on-sound* mixing. *Advantages:* 1) You only need a projector capable of sound-on-sound recording, thereby keeping equipment purchases to a minimum. Some projectors are even capable of mixing two external sources simultaneously without added equipment. 2) You can watch the picture during the mix, which helps to correctly position sound fades over picture transitions, and to keep the correct sound perspective. *Disadvantages:* 1) With sound-on-sound mixing, you are generally restricted to mixing only two sync tracks. 2) Since a mix of this type usually requires recording directly on the release print, each print must be mixed individually. However, you could mix onto fullcoat on your projector, then transfer the mixed fullcoat from a fullcoat recorder to the magnetic stripe of a release print. 3) With sound-on-sound recording, you are erasing part of the original recording as you overlay the second track. If you miscalculate a level, you could easily erase too much of the first recording, forcing you to start all over with your first recording. If your first recording happened to be the original single-system stripe recording, then—oops!

Multiple fullcoat decks utilize a group of Super-8 fullcoat recorders all running in AC line sync. Starting them together calls for some sort of common-start device or procedure, such as plugging them all into an AC extension cord (once edit sync has been established on each recorder) which is then inserted into the wall receptacle. *Advantages:* 1) The edited track is played back on the fullcoat deck, eliminating the need for a further transfer (and loss of sound quality) before mixing. 2) If you have a large force of location filming units, you may already have several fullcoat recorders on hand without having to purchase added equipment. *Disadvantages:* 1) Although it is much less costly to purchase several Super-8 fullcoat recorders than either 16mm or 35mm fullcoat decks, nevertheless, it is still rather expensive. 2) If a mistake is made during mixing, you can't back up in sync and correct the mistake. You must start the mix from scratch.

Multitrack quarter-inch tape recorders became popular on the consumer level with the interest in quad sound. Hi-fi enthusiasts requested good quality four-channel quarter-inch recorders at a price lower than the professional lines. As a result, several manufacturers produced versions of the four-track decks, many of which fit extremely well into the ideologies of Super-8 production. *Advantages:* 1) Compared to some of the other systems, multitrack quarter-inch recorders take up a small amount of space. 2) Many four-track quarter-inch recorders are less expensive than fullcoat recorders with the same capabilities for mixing. 3) Once the tracks are transferred to the four-track recorder, you can return to head sync any number of times and they will all still be perfectly in sync without any adjustments. 4) With some multitrack recorders (such as those modified by Inner Space Systems), you can run in the forward mode with a projector in lip sync. *Disadvantages:* 1) In order to mix with a multitrack deck, you must transfer each edited fullcoat track on a separate channel of the recorder, necessitating an extra generation of sound quality loss. 2) You can't back up with the picture in sync. In order to correct a mistake, you must return to edit sync and start over. 3) Pick-up recording (the ability to back up a few feet and record over a mistake without going back to the head of the film) is only available on the more expensive professional line of

Here is a setup for transferring sound from fullcoat to stripe. The film should be a splicefree print with a magnetic edge stripe and balance stripe applied by the laboratory.

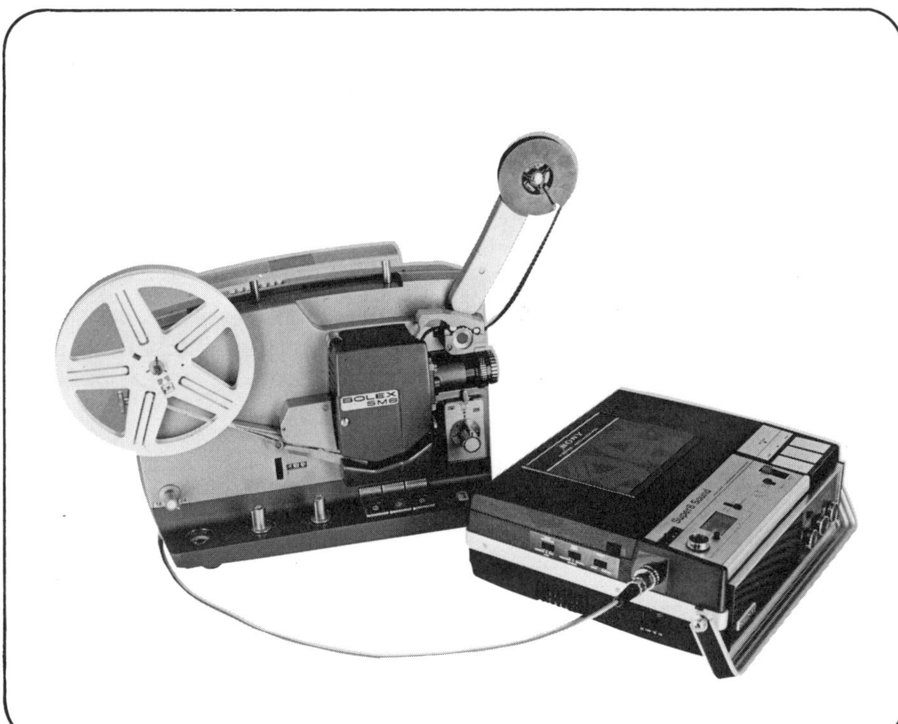

multitrack recorders (*e.g.*, the Ampex 440 series and the 3M professional line).

16mm Fullcoat Mixing Systems

It may seem a little odd to find this heading listed under Super-8 mixing systems (especially after what I said earlier about the expense of such a set-up), but there's reason to mention it. There are a number of 16mm production houses that are gearing up for Super-8 production in addition to their 16mm work; and I have found that existing 16mm mixing equipment is readily adaptable for use in mixing Super-8 films. All that is needed is a transfer from the edited Super-8 fullcoat to 16mm fullcoat, and the mix can proceed. Since Super-8 fullcoat recorders can lock to the AC line for sync, and most 16mm transfer decks also lock to the AC line, your transfer will stay frame-for-frame in perfect lip sync. *Advantages:* 1) For a production company with existing 16mm mixing facilities, this can be a very inexpensive method of mixing Super-8 sound. All that is required for mixing with picture is the purchase of a Super-8 projector modified for Selsyn motor operation. 2) Since most 16mm mixing set-ups are capable of pickup recording, you no longer need to return to the head of the film to correct a mistake. You simply back up a few feet, then record over it. 3) This kind of facility allows the mixer to go either forward or reverse at any time with both the picture and sound maintained in frame-for-frame sync. 4) Greater use of existing mixing facilities would reduce a production company's overhead costs. *Disadvantages:* 1) If you don't already have access to a facility of this kind, the equipment would cost tens of thousands of dollars. 2) A transfer is required from Super-8 to 16mm fullcoat, causing the loss of one generation of sound quality as in a multitrack quarter-inch mixing set-up. 3) The final mix would be on 16mm, not Super-8 fullcoat. This could create problems if you planned to make your own transfers to the release print magnetic stripe. However, the lab that makes your release prints will most likely be geared up for transfers from 16mm fullcoat to Super-8 release prints, since many labs were reducing 16mm prints (and hence transferring 16mm fullcoat to Super-8 stripe) long before original Super-8 production became popular.

MIXING WITH A SOUND-ON-SOUND PROJECTOR

Tony Plesman

Interested in mixing sounds onto your striped film, but lacking the fancy equipment to do it? You might try transferring sounds directly onto striped film via the sound-on-sound component built into many projectors. Unsophisticated as it may seem, if you know some of the ins and outs of the process, you'll be amazed at what you can accomplish—if you don't start out expecting a 16-track studio mix.

In order to see for myself what could and could not be done with such a method, I purposely chose an inexpensive but solid projector having a limited frequency response of something like 75-7,500 Hz. This is still superior to the range of most single-system sound cameras, and about the same as an optical sound track on 16mm film. The projector I used was the Eumig Mark S 802.

My first project involved simply recording a music track against visuals of the sea smashing against rocks along the California coastline. The film shows various angles of rocky cliffs and low, shrublike vegetation. A violent sea is churning below. Some shots are static wide-angle "stills," while others utilize a constantly moving camera (including zoom and dolly shots).

Because of its dynamic range and color, I chose Bartok's *Concerto for Orchestra* for my music track. The piece was also moody enough for certain passages where the fog begins rolling in. I connected Eumig's universal re-recording lead between my amplifier and the projector's line input. (Different hi-fi amplifiers accept different jacks, so make sure you've got the right one for your set-up.) The procedure for recording the music in this simple manner is pretty straightforward. With everything properly connected, run your projector until just before the first scene disappears into the top of the threading channel. Stop the projector and cue up your record to the passage you need. Keep the volume of your amp turned down. (It helps to have a cueing lever which allows the tone arm of your turntable to ease down gently.) Now, punch the red recording key to the rear of the Eumig and turn the main function switch past "threading" to "forward projection" and immediately bring up the amplifier volume.

Since the Eumig 802 is one of those basic machines without a volume level indicator, you will have to literally play it by ear. Another shortcoming on such a projector is the lack of a manual recording volume control. All recording is regulated by what Eumig calls their AGFC (automatic gain and frequency response control). But if you're aware of these limitations, I've found you can easily work around them for really impressive results.

After recording the entire music track for the film, I ran the film back to the beginning and cued up to the first scene again. While the music certainly did its job in providing a solid background for the visuals, something was missing: the sounds of the sea. Probably the most authentic recorded sounds of the sea are to be found on Environmental's sound series recorded on the Atlantic label. (These are not the usual hokey sound effects records, but meticulously recorded sounds of nature.)

I had previously timed my music so that one minute into the film, the music would crescendo to a climax at the same time the sea rose to a climactic roar. Now I needed the sound of that roaring turbulence. I set up my sea record as I had the music, dropping the needle just before the dramatic moment and setting my amplifier volume. Right next to the volume control on the Eumig sits another knob for mixing in subsequent tracks. What it actually does is partially erase the previous track in favor of the new track being laid down on stripe. I turned the mix knob completely left to 0, where it has no effect on the previous recording—even while in the *recording mode*. With the sea record already spinning and my film approaching *the moment* of climax, I quickly

Figure 1: The mixing knob on the Eumig Mark S802.

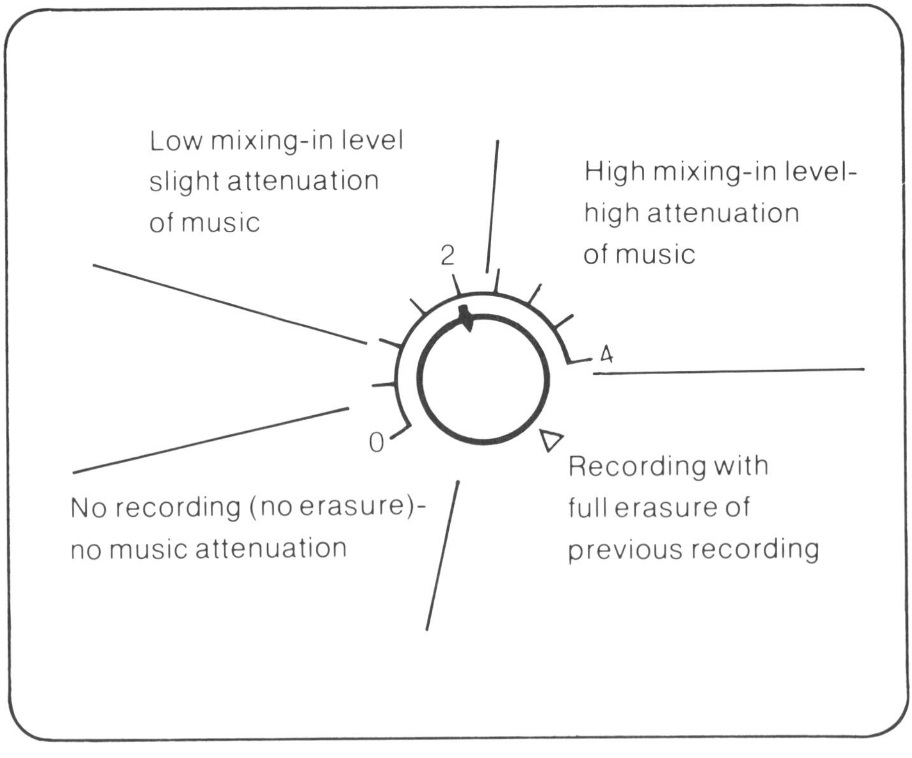

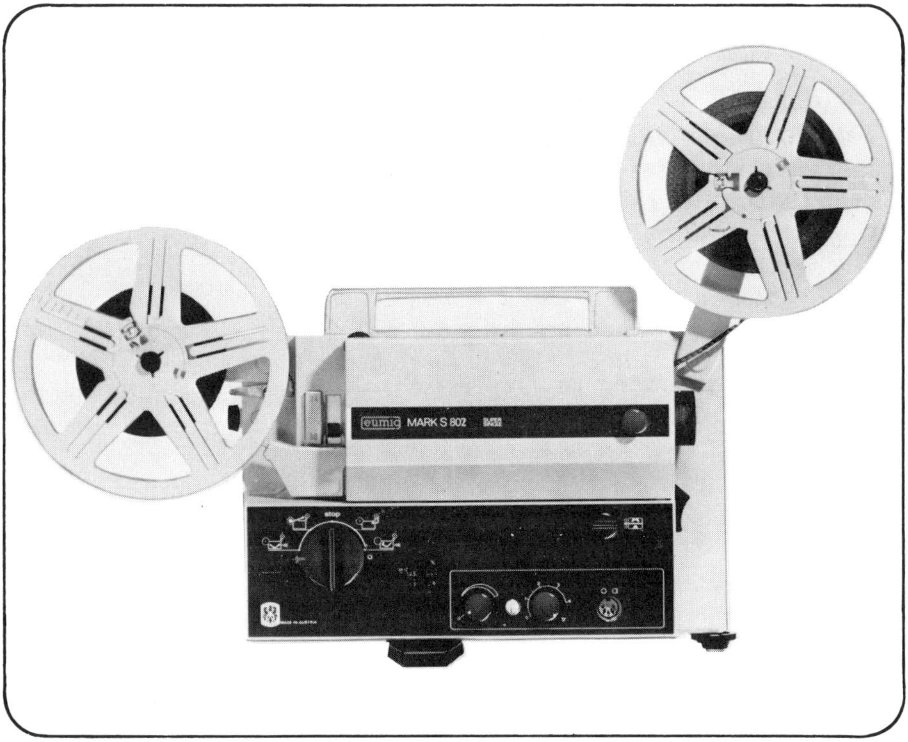

The Eumig S802 projector with magnetic sound recording capability.

turned the mix knob up past the number 2 point. This effectively subdued the music without squashing its vibrance altogether, and allowed the sea sounds to predominate. As the tide ebbed, I slowly turned the mix knob down to number 1 for a few moments, then faded the sea out completely in favor of another music lift. This mix knob was now on 0, and the music, at full volume, played out to the end.

I wondered if a third track would damp down the others to such a degree as to render them muddy and unacceptable. Another thing came to mind: if I goof on the short narration, I'll have to erase the entire business and start from scratch. Is this any way to make a multitrack mix? Yes and no. Yes, because I wanted to see how the Eumig would respond if I made an acoustical "live-voice" track; that is, if I recorded my voice directly into the Eumig microphone which was plugged into the projector. On the other hand, you might prefer to record narration on tape first (isolated from projector noise), then transfer this prerecorded narration to fit the timings of your various shots.

Since this was simply a test, I chose the direct method and recited the first part of Hemingway's *The Old Man and the Sea*. There is something about those simply-put but singing words that smack more of poetry than prose. Even though there was not a boat in sight, the words fit my ghostly fog-shrouded sea perfectly: "He was an old man who fished alone in a skiff in the Gulf Stream. He had gone 84 days now without taking a fish..." and was ..."definitely and finally *saleo*, which is the worst form of unlucky...." I tried it, and without *saleo* I squeaked through without a hitch. But how was my mix? And what happened to my other sounds of music and effects?

Even though I had determined that turning the mix knob slightly up to the 1 or 2 position results in only slight erasure, turning it to 3 or 4 produces considerable erasure of previous tracks. Overall, I was amazed at the outcome. While it wasn't absolute perfection, it was acceptable. When I refined my techniques further—boosting here, and toning down there, it became even more acceptable.

The only problem with the AGFC is that you must "set it up" to the level of your voice before actually recording. So you press the recording button, turn the projector's function switch all the way to "forward" and say one word like "ready" into the microphone. This suppresses room noise during the mix and favors the signal from your voice. You do this before operating the mix control, but you don't stop the projector after this cue word. You set your mixing in level (my position was between 3 and 4) and sail right into the narration.

At this position, I was able to reduce the music and sea sounds considerably so that my voice was clear and dominant. The music didn't become muddy but the sea sounds were less specific. This didn't really matter that much, since they were meant to be low during the narration. When I faded down this third track so that the sea and music could return to their normal level, everything came in with clarity.

The great thing about experimenting in this manner with sound-on-sound is that I don't have to bother calling in two or three other people to assist me in controlling the portable mixer while simultaneously feeding in taped effects and recorded music, and juggling with live narrations. On the other hand, the great thing about a separate mixer and manual volume settings is that ultimate control remains in your hands, not in the hands of the projector manufacturer. But I'll say this: For those of you doing one-person mixing sessions with a maximum of three tracks, automatic volume settings and sound-on-sound devices are a great asset.

CREATE YOUR OWN SOUND EFFECTS

Elinor Stecker

One of the most effective and powerful ways of creating mood or adding realism to a film is through the use of sound—not only dialogue or narration, but also sound effects and music. While film is primarily a visual medium, the addition of appropriate and creative sound can add another dimension to what you see on the screen. Imagine this scene: a ship is leaving the harbor and moving out onto the ocean. The picture would be pretty bland and lack reality without the sounds of the harbor and the gentle slapping of water to accompany the movement of the ship. Or visualize a man placidly eating his dinner: he stops suddenly, and a look of terror covers his face. Why? The sound preceding his startled look will explain—it could have been the crash of a car, the beat of marching feet, even a telephone ringing or a door slamming. How can you produce these sounds? Well, creating sound effects such as these is a simple task for the inventive filmmaker.

Sounds of Everyday Life

Let's start out with some common everyday sounds, such as the sound of a door slamming or a telephone ringing. Recording the actual sound on location seems to be the obvious way to capture these sounds. The sounds of a door being slammed, a telephone ringing, a water faucet dripping, water being poured into a glass, dishes breaking, wood being sawed, or nails being hammered are all easily recorded with a microphone placed near the source. But frequently it's not practical or possible to record the real thing. You don't want to smash up the family car to get the noise of an off-screen car crash. And how are you going to get the sound of crunching dry leaves when it's summer? Not to say anything about trying to get your cat to meow on cue!

Theater people and radio people are extremely adept at devising artificial means to produce all kinds of sound effects. You'll find the descriptions in texts on radio and play production. You'll discover that by crumpling a ball of cellophane in your hands, you can make the sound of fire, and by blowing through a straw into a pan of water you'll get a sound similar to a bubbling brook. Rain can be simulated by letting a stream of salt fall on the appropriate surface (wood if the location has a wood roof, for example). But the most unusual device I found was a diagram of a rain machine that I found in a radio textbook. Here's how it works: Bird seed is poured into a large funnel. When the bird seed comes out of the spout of the funnel, the stream of seeds hits against a ping-pong ball, which disperses the seeds. Some of this bird seed, in turn, bounces off a blown-up paper bag and falls into a wastepaper basket filled with crumpled paper!

Rather than trying to simulate "real" sounds, you may decide that recording natural sounds is the best way to go. Unfortunately, recording actual sounds may not always give you exactly what you want or expect. The reason is this: The ear is a selective device, but a microphone isn't. For example, if you are listening to the surf, you will be aware only of the sound of the surf, and you will tune out everything else. A microphone, on the other hand, will pick up the sound of an airplane, thruway traffic, a dog barking, somebody laughing, the refrigerator motor or other irrelevant sounds.

After several attempts at fighting with nature and the environment while trying to record actual sounds, you may decide to stay in your own living room and take advantage of the many sound effects recordings that are available commercially. There are a number of companies that sell long playing record albums containing hundreds of different sound effects. If you get a catalog from these recording companies, you'll find a list of sounds from A to Y—from an adding machine to a yawning man—just about everything you might need in the way of simple direct sounds.

Mixing Sound Effects

Sometimes you'll want to alter the sounds or mix several sounds together. Take that ship-going-out-of-the-harbor scene. On the recordings you'll find harbor noise and surf; you'll have to mix these two together. You can add a few sea gulls to that, and if you want to get really fancy, a couple of buoy bells. If the scene takes place at night, you can even put in a foghorn. As the boat moves out of the harbor, the harbor sounds should fade out and the water sounds should fade in. Later, you can add some wind to that to help give the impression of going from the harbor into the open sea. You can create this effect by mixing one sound behind the other to give it continuity.

Although there are a seemingly infinite number of sound effects available on commercial sound recordings, you still might not find exactly what you need. Let's take wind: You might find a recording of a little breeze with the rustling of leaves, a blizzard, wind with rain, and a nice moderate wind. But what if you want an eerie whistling wind for a graveyard scene? You can create it by taping that moderate wind sound from the disc at a normal volume level. Then play it back at a lower volume at *half speed*. If you vary the volume while playing it back it will sound like the wind gusting in and out. You'll end up with the wooooo of a spooky cold winter wind. You can alter a surf noise in a similar manner.

Do-it-yourself Sound

Lots of times the only way you can get the sound effect you want is to create it yourself. Although commercial recordings may give you the best quality sounds, they are limited to the more commonly heard

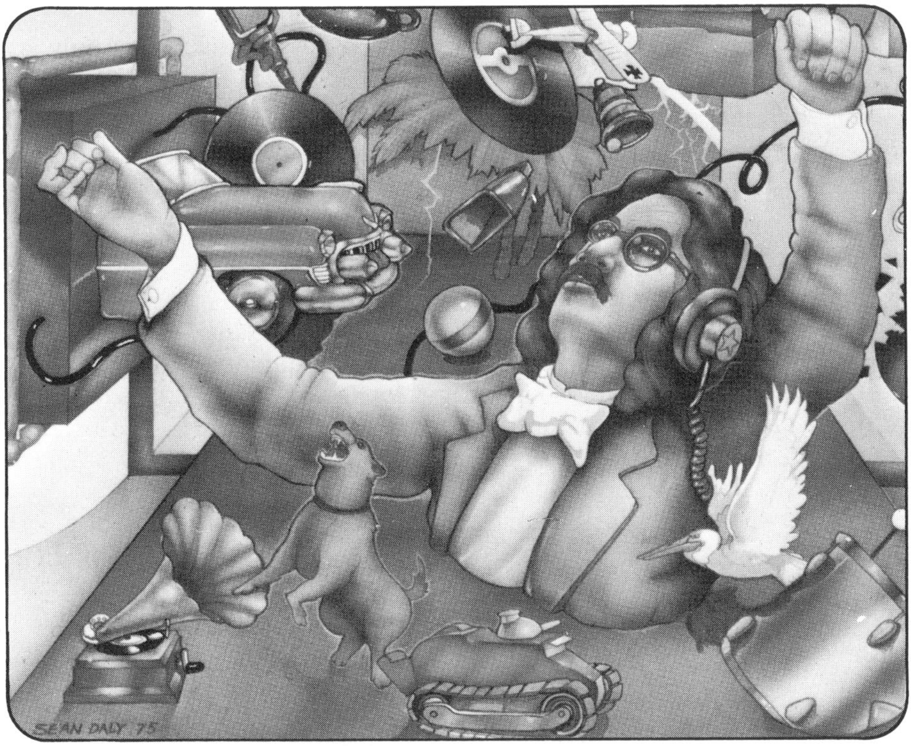

SEAN DALY

The creation of sounds is as unlimited as your imagination.

human and environmental noises. You may want to add certain sounds that are neither music nor sound effects (in the same sense of representing specific sources), but are sounds that will create moods unto themselves. You can, for example, get beautiful electronic effects by putting rubber erasers between the strings of a piano, and then either playing the strings or rubbing them with your fingers. You can get other fantastic electronic sounds by recording a child's merry-go-round music box toy, and playing it back at half speed, backward. Another idea is to drip water into a large empty tub and record it at a very loud level; then play it back at half speed or double speed, backwards. Take a guitar and slide your fingers up and down the strings, then play the tape at different speeds. Or record tiny wind chimes or several different types of wind instruments being played out of tune; then play them back at the speed at which you think you get the most interesting results. Or you can record two of these effects at different speeds on different recorders; then play one forward and one backward at different speeds against each other. You'll wind up with a really weird electronic effect. Have fun! Experiment by manipulating your tapes, and you can create some unusual and fantastic effects.

Sound and Picture

As a filmmaker, you control where the audience looks, not only by where the lens is pointing, but also by which sounds are dominating at the moment. Even with many things going on simultaneously, attention is directed by the loudest sound.

Keep in mind, however, that sound volume depends on the visual perspective. For example, the sound of a child bouncing a ball should be louder in a close-up than in a long shot. This does not mean that you have to change the volume level every time you change image size—frequent and abrupt changes would be disturbing—but there should be enough change between shots taken from noticeably different perspectives to be consistent with reality. If you zoom in from a long shot to a closer one, the volume level should get louder as you get closer to the subject. This level change can be made at the time you do the original recording, or it can wait until you mix onto a separate effects track or onto the film's magnetic stripe.

Consider that long shot again. Are there lots of children on the playground—swinging, playing baseball, laughing, yelling, splashing in a pool? In a wide-angle shot, you should have all of these sounds, without any one sound predominating. Then, as you zero in on that bouncing ball, all the other sounds should be reduced to background noises, and the sound of the bouncing ball brought up so that it will predominate. Or suppose you start off showing a bulldozer clearing one part of the playground. At first you would hear only the noise of the bulldozer in operation. In the next shot you pan away from the bulldozer, until the camera comes to rest on the child. As the camera moves, the focus of the audience's attention changes, and the sound should move accordingly.

None of these "rules" for creating sound effects is absolute. But understanding the relationship between image and sound effect is important when you want to break the rules to create a specific effect. Imagine, for example, panning from the bulldozer to the boy, while maintaining the sound of the bulldozer at its original level. The audience would be annoyed or disturbed when they saw the boy's lips moving, but couldn't hear him talking. This handling of sound would establish a certain relationship between the bulldozer and the boy, and would result in building tension in the viewer. By creating tension, sound effects keep the viewer's interest. The viewer, in turn, seeks an image that will resolve the tension. In the case of the long shot of the playground, for example, you could make the sound of the bouncing ball very loud to start out with. The viewer will not rest until he's located the source of the sound, which he will discover in the next shot, a close-up of the ball. Even more disturbing is sound without a corresponding image to explain what is causing it—unseen sound sources can be mysterious or even frightening.

One extremely effective device is the complete cessation of sound. Cutting off sound creates fear and anxiety; used judiciously, it can have

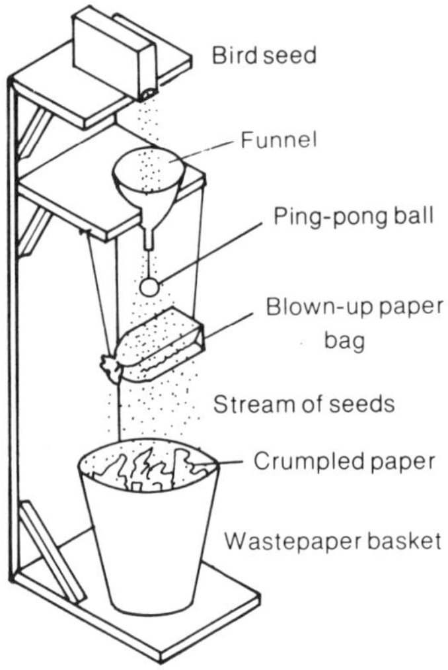

Rainmaking machine: Illustration from Waldo Abbott's "Handbook of Broadcasting," McGraw-Hill, New York, 1957.

a powerful effect. In a scene from *A Man for All Seasons*, after the ax falls at the execution, the screen goes black and there is absolute silence on the screen for almost thirty seconds. The effect is powerful. You feel as if you're going over the edge, as much as the victim. In another film, where a person was being hung, the whole world dissolved into slow motion. Everything became pink, then red, then very dark red, and finally melted into blackness, while the sounds slowly faded into dead silence. It was a slow dissolve effect rather than an abrupt cut-off, but it was devastating as well.

Setting Scenes and Moods with Music

Along with sound effects, music is often used to help set a mood. Very rarely is only a sound effect used. Almost always, there's music coming in and out that tells you the mood of the protagonist in the film, as well as when and where the action is taking place. Big cities are hard to identify immediately unless you see one of the great landmarks; but the right music can make the location apparent to the audience.

A quiet pastoral scene would require music that is quite different from a scene with a rapid-fire automobile chase. The former would probably need something soft and slow, while the latter would be aided by louder and very fast, possibly discordant, music. A tired man trudging home in the snow obviously needs a slower accompaniment than an energetic skier zooming down a snow-covered mountain slope. The speed or tempo of the music has to be carefully chosen, and so does the rhythm. A marching beat might be appropriate for kids walking home from school, the post-op patient ambulating down the hospital corridor, or ducks following their mother. A waltz rhythm sometimes works out well with a moderately fast-moving vehicle, and you might want to find a very pronounced beat to accompany a train ride.

Music can be playful or foreboding; tranquil or exciting; romantic or angry; and there are compositions that express all of the gradations between the extremes. Look at your visuals and decide what mood you want to convey; then find music that will reinforce and complement it.

Try a little experiment. Take a film and project it several times, each time playing a different piece of orchestral music with it. Pick some compositions that even seem inappropriate. Note the effect different compositions have on the mood and feeling of the film. You may be surprised at the effects that occur when you add music (or sound) that is in contrast to the picture's mood or actions. If you need a nondescript background music to set a mood, get acquainted with composers whose work achieves this effect. Look for music that is calm, without sudden blasts of sound that will jar you. Most important, do not use music that has a prominent, well-known theme. If you're playing the latest Elton John hit, the audience will start listening to the theme of the music and be distracted from the film itself.

What you *should* use is always hard to define. What you *shouldn't* use is easier to pinpoint. It's usually best to avoid violin, clarinet or piano concertos; their solo lines will almost always interfere with the spoken word, and they'll trip all over each other. Try not to use something that has loud (crescendo) passages followed by very soft (diminuendo) passages, especially if you're using the music behind the voice. Another thing to avoid is music by brass ensembles, unless you want it to stand out front. Even then, you should establish it and then fade it down.

The music doesn't always have to be behind the narration. It can come in loud, rise a little bit, then fade down. When it drops to a certain level, the voice can come in and the music can then fade out behind the first few sentences. That's nice for setting a mood. Later, when the mood of the narration changes, you can fade in another piece of music. Another technique that can give your track professional sound is the use of a *segue* (pronounced segway). That involves going from one piece of music to another, without a pause between the two. A segue is a type of overlapping fade: one piece of music fades down, and when it gets to a level which is almost inaudible, the other piece of music fades in. They overlap each other, like a film dissolve. When you segue, you've got to be careful that the two pieces of music you're butting do not clash. Avoid going from one key to another if the keys are radically different, because an abrupt change in tonality can really assault your ears.

Copyright Laws

There is a discordant note when using recorded music or sound effects in your film—the matter of copyright. All recordings (with the possible exception of some foreign ones) are protected by copyright and *may not be used* in a film unless you have secured written permission in the form of a license, and in most cases, paid a fee. In fact, you actually need two licenses to use a recording in your film. You must request a *synchronization license* from the copyright owner (the publisher of the music) and *dubbing rights* from the record company. The synchronization license allows you to use a composition, and the dubbing right lets you transfer a particular recording of that music to your film. If there is a soloist featured on the recording, you may even have to obtain additional permission from the artist. The cost of obtaining these licenses varies, depending on how your film will be used and where it will be shown. You can get world-wide rights, or clearance just for the United States. You can request rights for non-theatrical showings, commercial showings or for television broadcasting, and to some extent, these rates are negotiable.

If all of this sounds complicated, time-consuming and expensive—it is! That's one reason why music libraries have sprung up. If you purchase their music you can obtain the rights to use it just by applying to the library and paying them one fee for each "needle drop." ("Needle drop" or "needle down-needle up" designates each selection or part of a selection you use. If you use the same piece more than once, you pay for it each time you use it.) The fees vary, but can start at $25 for a tune used in an educational film.

There is at least one music library, Filmoods Company, that includes all rights with the purchase price of their recordings (about $20 per disc). Thomas Valentino, Inc. has sound effects records that are licensed for use in films without additional permission or royalty payment needed.

Take heart. There is a way to avoid paying any licensing fees. Select public domain music and have a musician friend or friends play it while you record it on tape yourself. Many music students are also able composers, and they might be delighted at the opportunity to compose and perform for your film. Be sure to give the person a title credit.

How sounds and images work together to affect an audience is a complex and exciting subject. You undoubtedly understand that the impact of a film is the result of many individual effects, both visual (the content, pacing and editing of each shot in every scene) and aural (including music, dialogue, narration, incidental sounds and silence). The coming together of these elements is the essence of cinema. The best filmmakers know how these elements work together and use them to create the total effect they want.

SCRIPT-
WRITING

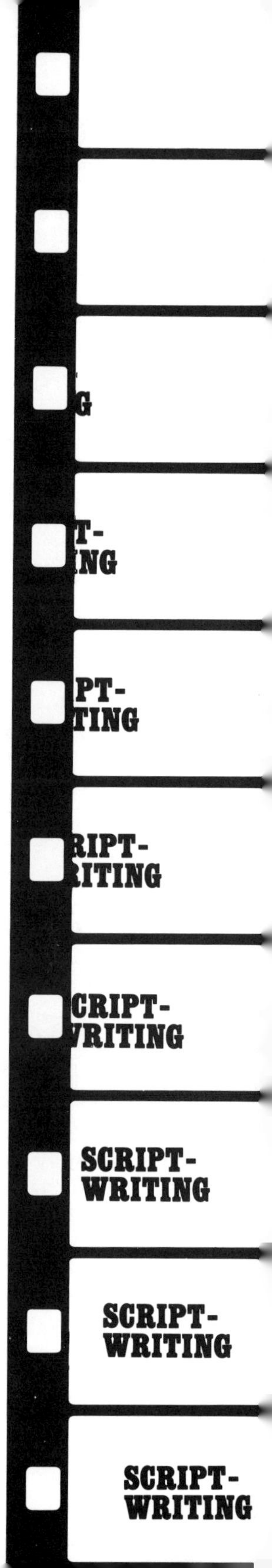
SCRIPT-WRITING
SCRIPT-WRITING
SCRIPT-WRITING

WRITER'S CRAMP? STRETCH YOUR FILM IDEAS

Mik Derks

Hollywood has always been more than happy to show us how movies are written. Remember that lonely screenwriter, pacing back and forth past his idle typewriter, kicking at the wads of paper that litter the bare wooden floor of his unheated garret? Then, as the deadline approaches and all seems hopelessly lost, it happens: INSPIRATION. The writer sprints to his desk, crams a piece of paper into the carriage, and begins to tap away, hesitantly at first, then faster as ideas and pages virtually fly through the typewriter. Two dissolves later, the script is finished, and you can tell by the satisfaction smeared across his exhausted face that it's going to set the movie world on its ear.

Well, you shouldn't be too dejected if that *Fabulous Idea* hasn't come along and grabbed you yet. Actually, the inspiration involved in writing a film script is so dispersed that if you don't watch carefully, you'll miss it altogether. The professional screenwriter is not a mystic who has discovered some secret for snatching brilliant ideas out of an ethereal void. He or she is a craftsman who understands how to put together an appropriate concept systematically, then develop that concept into a motion picture that will hold people's interest and leave them satisfied that they have seen something worthwhile.

Judging Your Ideas

You'd be surprised at the high percentage of movies that sound simply wonderful when the filmmaker explains them, even though they make absolutely no sense at all when viewed on the screen. It's easy to take an essential piece of information for granted when you write your script and then discover that people are totally confused by what you thought would be so obvious. Make it a firm rule never to expect an audience to reach conclusions that are not clearly spelled out for them, either visually or aurally. For those of you who don't have sync sound capabilities, this rule becomes particularly critical because you are forced to explain everything visually.

Simplicity: Example No. 1

A little preschool girl, like all of us at some point during our childhood, yearns to be an adult. At a party thrown by her parents, viewing grown-up shows on television, out for an evening at the theater, and so on, she watches and mimics the adults, doing everything possible to be just like them. Then one day, the little girl stumbles upon her father preparing snails as a special surprise for her mother at dinner. One look at the slimy little creatures adults eat, and she is once again content to be a little girl.

Now that seems simple enough, doesn't it? But if you ever attempted to make that movie, you would find that it isn't so simple after all. To begin with, there are all kinds of complications inherent in the production itself, such as getting people together for the party sequence, locating a theater to shoot in front of, trying to keep all the other theater patrons from looking at the camera, *etc.* Even if you managed to solve the production problems, you'd still have trouble telling your story. For one thing, the concept demands a lot of whomever plays the little girl, and finding children who can manage anything more than not looking like they're "in a movie" is a rarity. So without the help of her acting, how do you *show* that the little girl wants to be an adult? How do you *show* the change when she decides that she is happy just to be a little girl? And how do you *show* that the very thought of snails is enough to motivate that change? There *are* ways to answer those questions, but the time and footage it would take to do it are probably more than the basic idea could sustain. Thus, you would be left with the choice between a confusing movie and an unsatisfying one.

Simplicity: Example No. 2

A small boy and girl are walking hand-in-hand down the sidewalk when a second girl steps out from behind a hedge to intercept them. The "eternal triangle" replayed in miniature, the new girl begins to show off by working her yo-yo and making faces at the same time. Able to stand no more, the first girl drops the boy's hand and charges her competition head on. The boy watches patiently as the girls scuffle at his feet and eventually struggle to a stalemate. Then, the panting girls climb back to their feet, take a good look at the boy they are fighting over, and sprint off down the street together. A most perplexed little boy stands all by himself watching them disappear.

All you need to make this movie are three children and a single exterior location. Furthermore, the children aren't asked to do anything that doesn't come naturally to them. Indeed, what better way than wrestling to get a couple of girls relaxed in front of the camera. Best of all, there's no way you could be confused by the characters' actions in this little film. That's the kind of simplicity you should be looking for.

Another criterion by which to judge your ideas is that of feasibility. Remember that you're one person with one camera, and unless you're planning on getting some help, that means you have to put your idea on film all by yourself.

Feasibility: Example

Your party's presidential candidate has decided to make a campaign stop in your hometown. It's the biggest thing that's happened there in years, so you decide to document the event with a movie. You'll capture the whole affair from beginning to end, including the gathering of the crowd, the candidate's arrival, his speech, his departure and any aftermath that might prove interesting.

Now this idea may seem within the capabilities of any filmmaker, but unless you're one of the organizers of the event, and privy to certain information and freedom of access that would not otherwise be afforded you, there's not much chance that you could manage it. Why not? Because it's impossible for you to be in more than one place at a time. To begin with, things happen very quickly at a campaign appearance, but never when they're supposed to. If you *are* lucky enough to be in a position where you can cover the arrival of the motorcade, you'd never be able to fight your way to a new position in time to shoot the speech. In the second place, you would need a nice high place that gave you an unobstructed view to film the candidate with a long lens, because neither the packed crowd nor the Secret Service men would allow you close enough to get a clear view with a standard lens.

You could perhaps cover the event by concentrating on the crowd of people: their arrival, the gathering momentum of their cheers and sign-waving, their reaction to the candidate's arrival and speech and finally their abrupt departure, along with the eerie stillness that always characterizes an abandoned location. But to do that, you'd probably have to forget about the candidate altogether. That might make the movie considerably less interesting (or *more* interesting, depending on how well you did your job), which brings us to the final criterion for judging your ideas.

Interest Potential: Example

After years of planning and saving, your new house is finally being built. You've decided to record the building process in weekly installments from excavation to the day you move into the house.

That's certainly a movie you and your family will never grow tired of watching, and a movie most other people will be completely bored with the first time they see it! The movie's only draw is a personal one in that it is *your* house being built. Take that away, and all you have left is a progressing series of construction scenes.

But don't give up on using your new house in a movie. After all, it's not every day that such a nice prop happens along. So try to think of ways to modify ideas instead of simply scrapping them when they don't pan out. For instance, it *would* be interesting to watch a movie about a family who leads a normal life inside a house composed of nothing but studs and rafters.

Where to Find Ideas

Now that you know how to check out an idea once you come up with it, let's talk about how to go about looking for them. An idea is like a diamond in the rough—it only gets sharp-edged and shiny after you've had a chance to work on it. But to find them in the first place, you have to be able to recognize both the diamond and the idea in their rough natural states.

If you've decided to make a dramatic movie, here are some sources of inspiration you might consider:

Newspapers and Magazines: Every kind of story imaginable shows up in these publications, with a brand new crop coming through every day. You'll probably have to alter the locations and characters to suit your own purposes, and maybe even the story itself, but it's an excellent place to begin.

History Books: A lot of the stuff that ends up recorded for posterity does so not because it's particularly important, but because it's a good story. If you don't have the means to do a period piece, modernize it.

Folklore, Legend and Tall Tales: Fantasy and legend have always made a big hit at the movies. You'll have to cut through all the regional embellishment to get to the basic plot, but try to preserve the colorful characterizations that are so much a part of these stories.

Personal Experiences: Without fail, we all look back over the things that happen to us and think of how they could have been improved upon. This is your chance to make things turn out the way they should have instead of the way they did!

Your Environment: Open your eyes to the world around you and you'll be amazed by the number of stories that are taking place there. Of course, you'll have to supply a lot of missing information to make those stories complete, but that's generally an improvement.

If you're more interested in making documentaries than dramatic movies, you should naturally look at your sources of ideas with a different perspective. Here's some places you might look:

Special Events: Local annual events, such as street fairs, carnivals, air shows, Fourth of July celebrations, *etc.*, are especially good because you're already familiar with them and can plan ahead. Unplanned events like natural catastrophes are more difficult, but still possible if you're fast enough on your feet.

Your Private World: What makes your family, your town, your friends or your way of life unique?

The Compilation Film: We all know how much fun it can be to explore an old family album of photographs, so why not compile the same kind of visual history with movies. You'll be shooting "segments" instead of individual movies, but when you put them all together you'll have documentation of your family's expansion, coverage of the year's major events, a history of vacations or whatever.

Wherever you search for ideas, the key is not to push yourself too hard. If you sit down with a blank sheet of paper in front of you, determined not to quit until you come up with a movie, all you're going to get out of it is lots of frustration and a stomach tied in knots. If you come across an idea, give it time to develop in the direction you want it to go. The idea will let you know when it's ready!

The Secret of the Script

Make it an absolute rule never to go into production without a complete shooting script to work from. For one thing, a script is the only way to gather and organize all those production considerations that make the difference between an organized shoot and a nightmarish fiasco. For another thing, only by preparing a script can you previsualize your movie thoroughly enough to insure that your original idea makes any sense when it gets to the screen.

You could learn to write movies by trial and error if you worked at it long enough, but that's a pretty expensive way to go about it. Especially when you can learn to write scripts for practically nothing from people who do it for a living. A good place to begin is with a published script, preferably one from a movie that you have seen enough times to remember some of the scenes in detail. Another good approach is to read a script and imagine as vividly as possible what every scene should look like. Then go see the movie, if you can find it playing anywhere, and compare what you visualized to what the director actually put on film. Be careful when you pick out a script to study, though, and make sure that it describes all the action in detail. Some give little more than dialogue, which isn't much help in visualizing a picture.

Another good place to learn about scripting is television, but you should stick with the movies and commercials rather than the regular series. The weekly shows won't teach you very much about scripting because they're shot by formula, using dialogue to tell the story and visuals just to keep your eyes occupied while you're listening.

The nicest thing about television is that it gives you a chance to really pick things apart so you can see how they're put together. A common mistake made by beginning filmmakers is that they take too long to get to the point they're trying to make in a shot or scene, wasting critical time on unnecessary action. As a result, their movies turn out ponderous and slow. To see just how fast things should happen on the screen, watch a movie carefully and make note of absolutely everything that goes on in a 60-second segment. During an "opening" sequence you'll find lots of information to get you ready for the rest of the movie, like settings, character introductions, personality indicators, plot elements, *etc.* They'll all be delivered in the most exciting way possible because the movie has to draw you in right away so you'll keep watching.

Even in what seems like a "quiet" sequence, you'll find lots of subtle things going on. It may be only a change of expression here, or a slight pan of the camera there, but enough is happening to hold your attention and keep things moving. "Action" scenes, on the other hand,

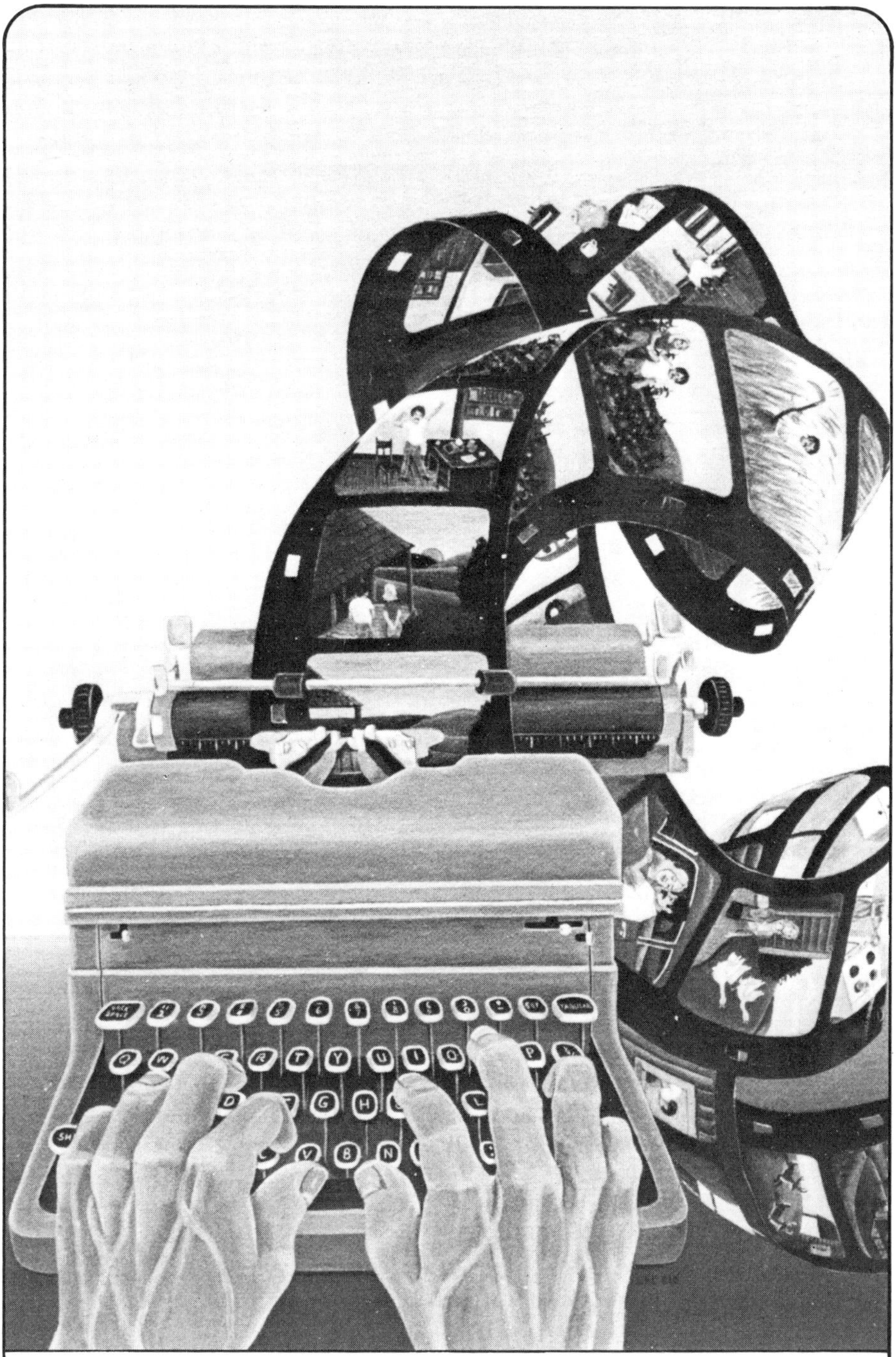

RAUL DEL RIO

The perfect machine for a screenwriter: a typewriter that turns a screenplay into celluloid in one easy step.

actually become less complicated when you watch them carefully. What seemed like everything happening at once becomes nothing more than a rapid series of not very complicated shots showing people moving around a lot. Notice, also, how the very special action sequences that come at the climax of a movie draw on the emotions and sympathies that have been building in you since the beginning.

Next, try writing down what you see in script form. Describe the action and copy the dialogue as accurately as possible, so that when you read it over, you can visualize that bit of the movie just as vividly as if it were happening right there in front of you. What have you got after you've written it all down? Action! No explanations. No fancy interpretations. No single-sentence concepts. Just lots of action. That's because you're writing what you see instead of what you think.

Now that you have a better idea of *what* happens in a movie, let's concentrate on *why* it happens that way. Every single scene in a movie has a valid purpose for being there, playing its part in the overall dramatic development. Watch a movie and see if you can determine the purpose of each scene, whether it is there to say something about a character, establish tension, provide comic relief or whatever. Observe how the movie maintains *continuity* as it progresses from shot to shot and scene to scene. Make note of all the transitions, *i.e.*, the match cuts, dissolves, fades, straight cuts, *etc.* What does each one tell you? Keep track of the *pacing*. See what happens when the pace picks up, and why. Note how long one pace is held before the movie shifts into another one, and try to get a feel for the overall rhythm established by the changes in pace. Finally, identify the *mood* of each particular scene. Is it gloomy? Gay? Foreboding? After you've got it, figure out how that mood was created. Was it with music? The position of the camera? The dialogue?

Obviously, you can't study all of these cinematic elements at the same time, but it is important that you familiarize yourself with each of them because they are the tools that enable the screenwriter to tell a story in the most dramatic way possible.

But before you start working on your script, there's another exercise that will help you become still more comfortable with the form. And you can practice this one anytime, anywhere! Take a good look at yourself occasionally, just to see what you're doing. Imagine that you are the star of a movie, and the world around you is a set. Now observe those movies you've been studying. Of all the things you do and say, which are the most revealing of your character? What would it take to cinematically establish where you are and what you're up to at any particular moment? When something interesting happens to you, write it up as a movie scene, keeping it as concise and simple as possible. Then revise that scene to make it even more interesting. When you've finished, you may not be able to recognize yourself as the central character, but you'll know how to write something to be seen instead of read.

WHAT COMICS CAN TEACH YOU ABOUT MOVIES

Steve Gerber

One of the best and most entertaining textbooks on filmmaking is available in almost a hundred new editions every month at your favorite newsstand. But you won't find it among the film and photography publications. And you may have to wade through a mob of unruly teenyboppers to get to where it is displayed. Moreover, once you've located it, you may find yourself embarrassed to purchase it, especially if you're over, say, 18 years of age and your reading habits up to this point have been rather conventional. So prepare yourself to be snickered, squinted, and even pointed at.

You should also be aware that this textbook goes by some rather strange names, such as *Amazing Spider-Man, Creepy, Conan the Barbarian, Justice League of America, War of the Worlds, Man-Thing,* and *Tomb of Dracula,* to mention but a few. Generically, these weirdly titled four-color pulp-paper pamphlets are called, of all things, *comic books*. And though it's likely you've never thought of them as instructional material, others definitely have.

Consider the fact that William Kuhns and Robert Stanley produced an introductory cinema text entitled *Exploring the Film* (Pflaum/Standard, Dayton, Ohio), in which the chapter devoted to "Camera Angles" features 20 pages of Spider-Man battling the villainous Rhino. And another new film text, *Moviemaking Illustrated,* by James Morrow and Murray Suid (Hayden Book Co., Inc., Rochelle Park, N.J.), consists entirely of comic-book drawings accompanied by text to illustrate virtually *every* aesthetic property of film.

Mere flukes? Coincidence? Stuff for beginners at best, you say? Uh-uh. . .No less a personage than Federico Fellini has dropped in to visit the offices of the Marvel Comics Group (for which I spend most of my waking hours writing such strips as *Daredevil, Tales of the Zombie, Man-Thing,* and so on) to swap stories and theories on filmmaking.

Insanity, you exclaim: What has Spider-Man in common with *Satyricon?* How can the aforementioned Rhino, a seven foot-tall human being encased in grey artificial hide complete with horns, who goes smashing through the walls of the nation's lending institutions, be compared to Bonnie and Clyde, who simply rob banks? And why is Fellini visiting comic-book publishers instead of film schools, anyway?

Look at it this way. On the most basic level, the creators of comics and of cinema are faced with an identical task: *telling a story in a series of still pictures designed to give the illusion of motion.* Visual narrative and movement are at the heart of both. And the similarity doesn't end there. Even the mechanics of the creative process are remarkably alike for the two media. Much of the terminology is the same. Indeed, the only major differences between comics and film—with regard to storytelling, at least—are technological ones.

Otherwise, a comic book is essentially a film. . . in shorthand. And what comics teach about movies is something all filmmakers, whether their interest is documentaries, sports reportage or biblical epics, need to know: how to construct a dramatic event in pictures; how to make the pictures move.

Comics Writer as Screenwriter

A comic book begins as a typed synopsis in which the writer describes the action of the story page-by-page, often even panel-by-panel, for the artist. Every relevant detail is noted: what each character is thinking and feeling, the expression on his or her face, what they're doing with their hands, their physical appearances, and the settings, costumes and props. Diagrams and sketches of these items may be attached to the synopsis. And snatches of dialogue are often included, along with ideas and suggestions for unusual artistic approaches and special effects. Fight scenes are choreographed. The need for an establishing shot here, a close-up there, is specified. And perhaps most importantly, the writer includes his estimation of how much space (one panel, one page, more?) each scene should require.

Thus, in form, style and content, the writer's synopsis for a comic book bears a distinct resemblance to a story treatment for a film. In the case of a silent Super-8 short, it could even suffice as a shooting script. Chances are a film will require *more* separate shots than a comic book, but consider the advantages of planning your shooting on paper as tightly as I plotted the following sequence (shown in Figures 1 and 2) for a comics story called "The Return of the Mummy."

Scene One: Four-panel opening page with sequence as follows: (1) A wooden crate resting on the floor of the Egyptology Room of a New York museum; the room is dark except for moonlight streaming in from a skylight in the ceiling. (2) Same shot, but a bandaged arm is smashing out from inside the crate. (3) Entire crate flies apart as Mummy breaks out. (4) Large panel; long shot of Mummy looking around him, seeing the various Egyptian art objects, *etc.*

Now let's look at the techniques involved in creating these panels. A picture of a wooden crate in a dark room (panel 1) is not particularly exciting in itself, but it poses a mystery immediately. And the lighting, a single shaft of cold silver from above, casting stark, shifting shadows, at once establishes a mood. Without a word of dialogue or sound effects, we've made it clear that whatever is inside the crate poses a threat.

To create the same mood in a film, you might open with a long shot of the Egyptology Room, with the crate standing upright in the center of the shot. (Actually, the panel shows you where to position the crate

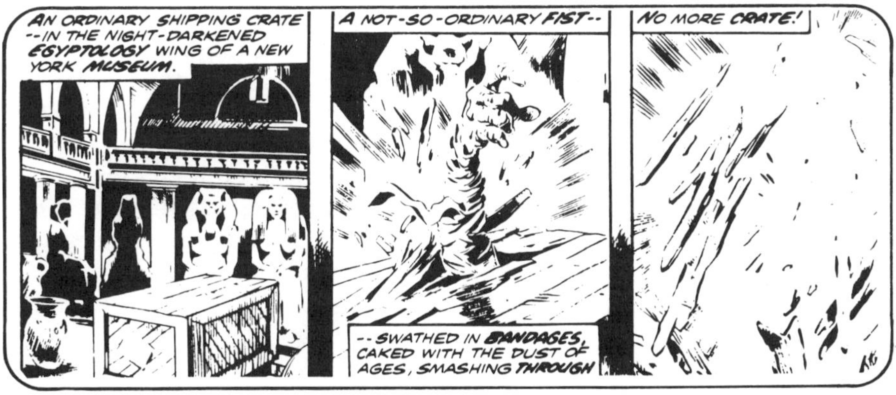

Figure 1: Comic-book as shooting script acts as visual "shorthand."

and your camera.) You might dolly in slowly, silently, until the crate dominates the scene. Then you halt, holding the same shot for several seconds. Next, the crate itself rocks ever so slightly, creating the first sound of the film. Suddenly, one arm smashes out, splintering the wood; then you cut to the other arm, as it comes through the opposite side of the crate; then a foot, a knee—each shown separately in a series of quick cuts. Then you take a long shot as the entire crate flies to pieces, revealing the full, fearsome figure of the Living Mummy.

The point here is that the storytelling techniques of comics are directly translatable into cinema *if* you, the screenwriter, remember that the comic book is presented in visual "shorthand." That "if" cannot be overemphasized because the image on the movie screen is constantly changing. The viewer isn't able to flip back a page or reread a panel to see if he's missed something. This means that the "information gap" between panels in comics can be much wider than the gap between shots in film; every action need not be detailed in comics. Nevertheless, the technique of getting from "point A" to "point B" in the plot is virtually identical.

Comics Artist as Filmmaker

Working from the writer's synopsis, the comics artist draws the story in pencil, breaking down each page into an arrangement of panels, composing each individual drawing, deciding which panel, if any, should dominate the page. In so doing, the artist also contributes to the overall rhythm and continuity of the story, and performs functions similar to those of the filmmaker.

The *size* of a panel drawn by the artist, for example, is roughly analogous to the *duration* of a shot—but only roughly. In this respect, comics are somewhat more flexible than film. The artist is not bound to a rectangular frame of predetermined size for his panel; the filmmaker, obviously, is. Then too, the effect on the audience of certain approaches to a scene are different in comics. For example, a page consisting of, say, nine small panels, may either elongate a scene, if the content of those panels is calm, or produce a staccato effect, if the content is rapid-fire action. A series of short, quick shots in a film is almost always likely to produce the staccato effect, regardless of content.

Aside from these differences, though, the function of the artist is like that of the filmmaker who does all the shooting, as well as directing and editing. The artist, in effect, sets up the shots, blocks the actors' movements, and generally provides the print equivalent of shooting and cutting. Dialogue and captions are added later by the comics writer, much the same way background music and voice-overs might be added to a silent film. As a rule, the tighter the writer's synopsis, the more likely it is that the artist will draw what the writer had in mind.

This principle can be applied to cameramen and screenwriters, too. Take, for example, the 3-panel sequence shown here in Figure 3. Matt Murdock—the blind attorney who is secretly Daredevil—hears a voice from "off-screen." We cut immediately to the source of that voice as Matt perceives it with his radar sense, the unique power that com-

Figure 2: Take a long shot as the entire crate flies to pieces revealing the "Living Mummy."

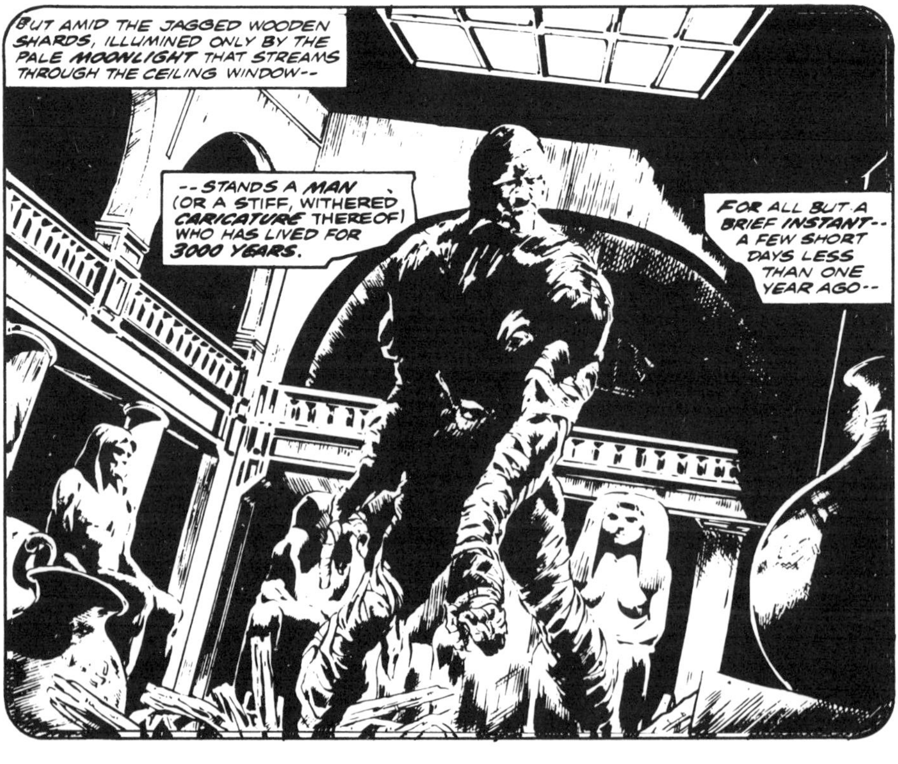

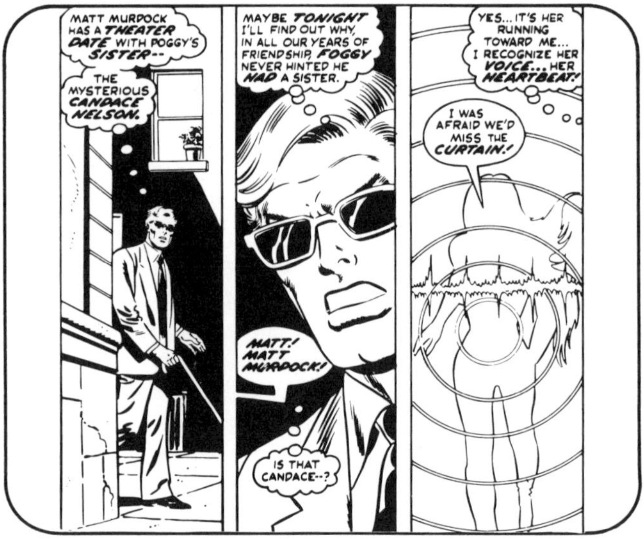

Figure 3: Comic-book version of off-screen voice, special effects and matched cuts.

pensates for his lack of sight. For the comics artist, Sal Buscema, each of these panels required written description down to the last detail. The direction from which the voice is heard, the "radar sense" special effect, the matched action from the "real" shot to the "radar" shot, and, of course, the urgent emotions and movements of both characters—all had to be carefully written out for the artist to render the sequence correctly. For the cameraman/filmmaker the same tightly written directions are useful. If you construct your shooting scripts meticulously, the chances of making the film you set out to make are greatly enhanced.

At the same time, a certain flexibility is desirable. Just as the comics artist may visualize a shot differently than the comics writer, you-as-cameraperson may discover possibilities that you-as-screenwriter never anticipated. For example, take a look at Figure 4, which shows the final comic-book scene of a drama about a clown who commits suicide in a swamp. The monster you see is Man-Thing, here returning to his home. The scene is composed of three panels (note the vertical dividing lines that do not completely separate the panels), and is the comic-book equivalent of a "tracking shot." The idea for this scene was entirely the creation of artist Mike Ploog. My own unimaginative little ending for the story had Man-Thing wander off into the marshy sunset in a typical "wide-angle" type panel. Mike, on the other hand, created a more powerful image by depicting the monster in two stages of movement: standing fairly straight, and then slouching deeper into his swamp.

The monster seems to lumber towards the reader. If you were filming him, he'd be moving closer to the camera even as you move it, tracking him from left to right. Meanwhile, the characters who are delivering their final lines about the clown's suicide, seem to recede in the background. Of course, this type of scene should be carefully planned *before* it is shot on location, but you should also give yourself room to maneuver once you get there. Lots of good ideas come at the last minute from unexpected sources.

Besides sharing responsibility with the writer for visualizing the overall flow of the story, the comics artist shares a concern for using a variety of panels. Nothing is duller in comics than a page made up entirely of close-ups (or long shots, or medium shots). In breaking down a page, the artist again plays the role the filmmaker and film editor play in shooting and cutting a scene—all the same rules apply. The shots must be varied, but they must come together to form an integrated whole. And just as the overuse of "trick shots" is to be avoided in film, overly fragmented layouts are shunned in comics. If the cinematic technique is to be effective, it must be "invisible." It must not distract the viewer or it defeats its own purpose.

We turn to Matt Murdock again—this time in his Daredevil outfit (see Figures 5 and 6)—for some ideas on placing diverse shots together. Gene Colan drew this fight sequence using several separate panels arranged to present a coherent picture of the action. First you see the scene from street level (low-angle shot); then from the air (vertical dolly shot); then from the points of view of the villain, the hero, and the spectators. The result is a fast-paced action sequence (it *had* to be fast paced, we ran out of pages), in which the reader alternately sees the fight as if he were a participant and an observer. Comic books are filled

Figure 4: Equivalent of a tracking shot, the monster is shown in two stages of movement across three panels.

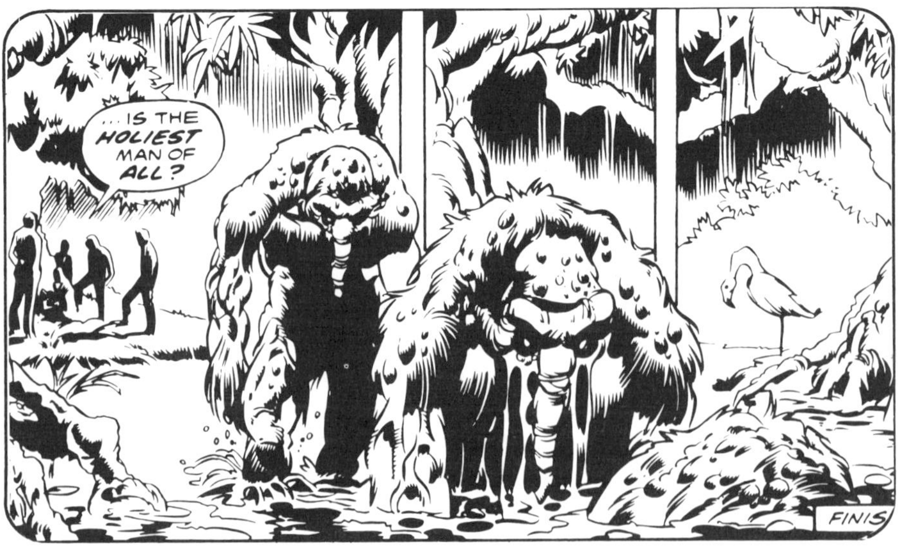

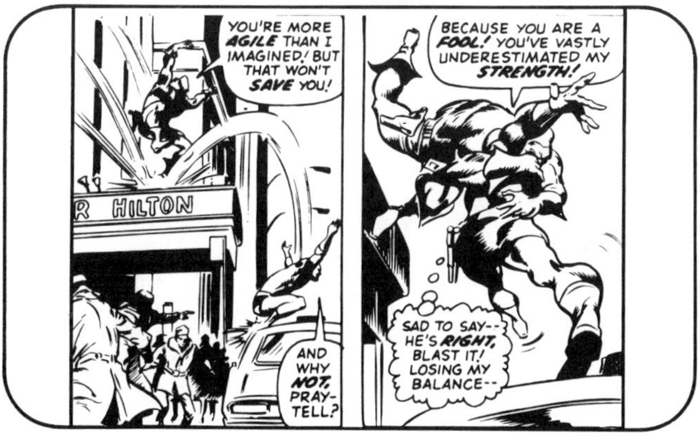

Figure 5: A low-angle shot and a vertical dolly shot for a fast-paced action sequence.

with sequences like this one; for the filmmaker, they are the perfect guide to new framing techniques and the provocative use of various camera angles.

Summing up, then, it seems clear that the problems to be solved by the comics artist and the filmmaker are very nearly the same. How best to tell the story? Convey the mood? Follow the action? To find answers to these questions, you can study the work of the best comics artists: Jack Kirby, John Buscema, Rich Buckler, Jim Starlin, Will Eisner, as well as those whose work is displayed here. Their names are usually listed in the credits which appear at the beginning of each comic-book story.

How Comics and Movies Differ

Despite all the parallels, comics are not movies, and understanding their dissimilarities is equally vital to learning about one from the other. First, and perhaps most crucial, even though the goals and the creative mechanics of the two media are analogous, the technologies involved are vastly different. Given a little imagination and a sharp pencil, the comics writer-and-artist team can tackle anything from a sock hop to an intergalactic war. Most Super-8 filmmakers, it's safe to assert, will probably have to content themselves with the more mundane end of that spectrum. So it's wise not to let yourself be influenced by the subject matter of the comics, enticing though it may be. Don't attempt the sequel to *2001* as your first film—or even your second.

But realize, too, that it would be far more difficult to portray the sock hop scene in comics than it would be in movies! The finite areas of space on the comic-book page, the limited number of pages in each book, and the relative unsophistication of the four-color printing process, make subtleties extremely difficult to achieve, both in dialogue and illustration. Generally speaking, the artist gets only one chance at each panel. The printer has a range of only 32 shades. If the writer writes too much copy, he covers up the picture.

The filmmaker has a far greater range of moods, textures and colors

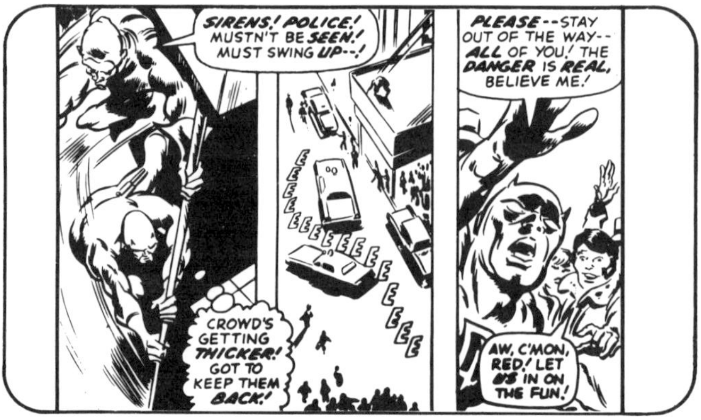

Figure 6: These panels demonstrate different camera angles and points of view.

to work with. He need not rely on archetypes and stereotypes as substitutes for real characterization. (True, the comics are maturing, coming out of that phase, but it's still possible to tell the hero from the villain by the color of their respective longjohns.) The themes that film can explore are much richer, much more complex. And they can be dealt with, even by the novice, with a pretty fair degree of success.

Comics are forced by their nature as a medium to work on a mythic, cosmic, larger-than-life scale. The rule for writers in comics is never to attempt *too little*, nor too much. The more spectacular and otherworldly the settings and characters are, the better. Real people are almost dull in the context of the comics. Monsters have to be bigger, more powerful; the destruction they wreak more immense and unthinkable, just to create the aura of mystery and danger such stories require.

Movies can go the cosmic route, too, but they can also provide real drama as opposed to melodrama. They can look at humanity as it is. And, of course, the reason for this is that you, as a Super-8 filmmaker, can *select* the audience you wish to please, even just yourself!

A Personal Note

I am not an experienced filmmaker. My unabridged filmography consists of three Super-8 shorts: *Stricken*, a series of surrealistic blackouts built around the theme that the world is essentially dysfunctional; *Ego, Passion and the Zombie*, a comedy about the walking dead; and . . . *And the Birds Hummed Dirges*, directed by Howard Tockman, and based on my short story about a suicide pact gone awry. That's it. And none of them exactly set the world on fire.

On the other hand, during my past two years with Marvel, I've authored almost 100 comic books—100 "screenplays." And in doing so, I've learned an awful lot, I think, about film. We'll find out. I'm currently at work on the script for a theatrical horror film that may just make *The Exorcist* seem tame by comparison; a film that will put to use all the techniques I've discussed in this article. If it scares *me*, I'll know I was right about what comics can teach you about the movies. I hope you will try the comic book approach, too, and let me know what you discover. In the meantime, take the word of a self-proclaimed non-expert. Pick up a copy of *Thor* or *Black Panther* or *Fantastic Four* or *Dr. Strange*. Take it home. Read it. When you've finished, you'll be 20 minutes older, maybe a little happier, and you'll have experienced a lesson in filmmaking you couldn't get anywhere else.

FILMING TECHNIQUES

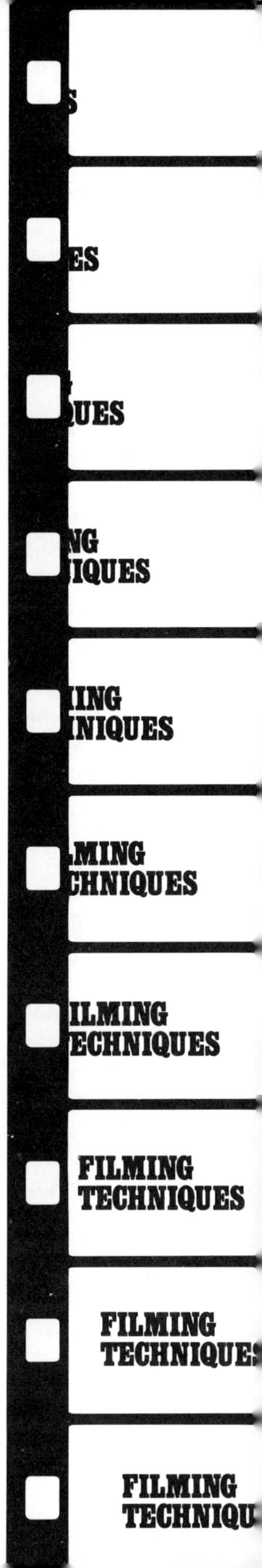
FILMING
TECHNIQUES

ZOOMSMANSHIP

Jerry Yulsman

Filmmaking, like writing, has its own form of punctuation. A pitfall common to both media is the too frequent, and usually meaningless use of the exclamation point. In the film medium, the quick *zoom* is analogous to an exclamation point. This is certainly the case in Super-8 filming where many cameras have a smoothly operating power zoom lens, some having monstrous 13 to 1 zoom ratios. These zooms are too often used by their proud owners as magical little toys. It is just so satisfying, so effortless to operate that little rocker switch. The kinetic results turn you on. You are omnipotent; in total command. Your eye soars out to the horizon on optical wings. And zooming back is like riding the tail of a rocket, watching the world widen out and recede. Through the viewfinder, it can be terribly exciting.

On the screen, however, the long zoom in either direction is meaningless *unless* it has a specific purpose. It propels your audience (who is just sitting there, minding its own business) through space, toward what you are leading them to believe is a specific target. They take it for granted that something of importance is about to be revealed, or some valid, filmic point is about to be emphasized. If, however, you have hurdled your audience forward only to confront them with something having no relevance to your total cinematic statement, then you have misled them, and frustrated their expectations.

Just as zooming in tends to emphasize the subject, zooming out tends to de-emphasize it. Therefore, to zoom one way and then another is contradictory: it creates confusion in the ranks. Zooming out places the subject in perspective. For example, if you zoom back from a close-up of a broken down shack, you slowly (or quickly for that matter) place it in its context or environment. If the shack looks incongruous relative to its environment (let's place it in the center of a very modern and expensive real estate development), then zooming creates a long socially descriptive sentence—it reveals more and more of the incongruity as the shot progresses. The appetite of the audience for more visual information on the subject is being continuously satisfied until, finally, they see the shack in a wide-angle shot surrounded by its rich neighbors. You've started with an isolated slum dwelling and, in the course of the zoom out, you have completed a valid social statement without one word of dialogue.

Zooms in either direction should be used with discretion. As a dramatic device, zooming loses most of its impact when overused. There are exceptions, of course. To emphasize the frenetic quality of a political demontration, a monstrous traffic jam, or a fast, rough sporting event, the employment of a series of quick zooms in to specific targets is an exciting rhythmic device which hardly ever fails to involve the audience in the frantic activity on the screen. But, and this can't be stated too often, the zooms must be meaningful in terms of the subjects and their actions. Each close-up that results from a zoom must symbolize the general action. And the quick-paced zooms, naturally, should all be in the same direction.

When using a series of rhythmic zooms, it is almost always more effective to cut the shot *before* it is resolved. In other words, you should end the shot before the zoom is completed. The next shot should then begin with the lens well into the next zoom. The effect on the screen is a single continuous inward or outward movement which carries the audience from one exclamation to another. As many as ten fast, pulsating zooms can be laid end to end in this manner. However, if you're going to *zap* your audience with this sort of thing, you'd better make damned sure that the subject matter justifies your efforts.

Another, more sedate use of the rhythmic zoom can evoke an entirely different audience reaction. For example, a series of slow, unresolved zooms connected by lap dissolves can create a poetic feeling. Flowers, fall foliage, landscape components, animals, pretty girls, children, sailboats, can all look incredibly serene. With the proper choice of music, the results can be breathtakingly beautiful. In particular, the slow repetitive zoom connected by long lap dissolves is a very useful device for travelogues.

So, to sum up: the main function of a zoom lens, more properly called a variable-focal-length lens, is to provide an infinite number of focal lengths within its range. It is a magical device which can perform the functions of a host of wide-angle, normal and telephoto lenses. Consider its zooming function a bonus. Only when it is used meaningfully and sparingly can the zoom itself add much to your film.

EIGHTEEN RULES FOR PANNING

George G. Siposs

How many times have you sat through an amateur film only to feel a slight case of vertigo or motion sickness? The film had too many dizzying blurs and wavering pans. What was wrong? The cameraperson had fallen into one of the most common errors in amateur filmmaking—using the camera to *create* action instead of *filming* action.

You can avoid this pitfall in your own films by keeping in mind the few basic rules for panning. The "panning shot" where the camera scans a scene from a fixed point (such as a tripod mount) is often misused to create a false sense of action. It's so easy to handle a Super-8 camera, that filmmakers can't resist swinging the lens back and forth to cover their subject. This rapid, freewheeling movement is not only disturbing when viewed, but in most cases is unnecessary.

In order to avoid the temptation to pan, it's best to simply move the camera back far enough so that its field of vision will take in the entire scene without having to scan it back and forth. Imagine yourself sitting in a judge's seat at a tennis match or in an orchestra pit of a theater. In order to watch the action, you have to crane your neck and look from side to side. Isn't it easier to move back a few rows?

Proper panning technique is surprisingly easy. Once you acquire the habit of supporting the camera on a tripod instead of waving it back and forth like a garden hose, your movies will look a lot smoother. If there is no tripod available, you should rest the camera on a railing, rock ledge or other sturdy object. If such a rest is not available, try holding the camera against a broomstick or tie it down with a piece of string. Tie one end of the string to the camera while you stand on the lower end. This provides versatility of movement as well as a surprising amount of steadiness. If you support the camera by hand, take a deep breath before starting the shot, exhale part way and hold your breath during the entire pan.

This way your breathing won't jiggle the camera. Hold your elbows against your sides and generally relax in a sharpshooter-like stance. If you grip the camera firmly and pan slowly, you can get acceptable results without a tripod.

18 Basic Rules for Panning

1) Don't pan if there is any possible way to avoid doing so. Move the camera back far enough so you can take in an entire scene. If you're filming a group of people, have them stand close together so you won't need to move the camera to keep everyone in the scene. The less you pan, the more your shots will be rock steady and have a surprising professional quality.

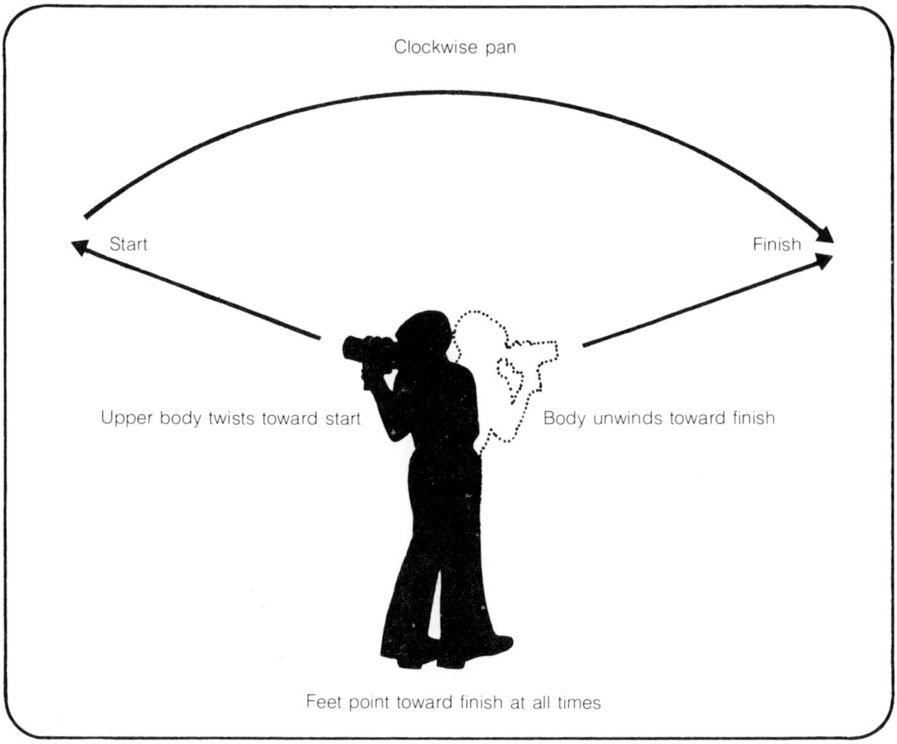

HIDEO IWATA

Plant your feet in the direction you will be facing at the end of the shot, twist your upper body toward the beginning of the pan and unwind as you shoot.

2) When you do pan, use a "pan head" mounted on a tripod. Most tripods for film come equipped with pan heads. Loosen the handle on the pan head just enough to permit smooth movement. Pan no faster than the sweep second hand of the wristwatch. This means you would only pan 90 degrees in 15 seconds, or a full 180 degree pan in 30 seconds. The slower, the better.

3) If you use a pan to make the establishing long shot at the beginning of a movie (*e.g.* to show the landscape and surrounding area where the action will eventually take place), start filming but don't begin to pan for a few seconds. This will allow the viewer's eye to get used to the scene. When you finish the pan, keep filming for a few seconds without camera movement to bring the scene to a conclusion.

4) Don't pan for more than 180 degrees. If you want to cover the action of a roller derby, for example, don't position yourself in the middle of the infield. Move your camera to the outside where it will only have to swing in a small arc.

5) When you approach the end of a pan, stop the camera while it is aimed at an interesting object. Try not to end your panning shot on a blank space or meaningless object. If the camera has moved too far,

you can always cut the unwanted part of the pan later during editing.

6) Before you begin to pan, sweep the camera (without running the motor) through the entire arc and check for proper exposure. If the camera is equipped with automatic exposure, it should be capable of adjusting to varying light conditions. For manual cameras, you may need an assistant to adjust the *f*/stop as you pan. Do not pan from very light to very dark areas suddenly. Instead, stop the camera, select a new location and start a new shot. You'll find this is more satisfying to the eye.

7) It's best not to pan vertical objects horizontally. For instance, if you make a horizontal pan of a picket fence, the vertical rods rushing across the screen may disturb the eye. They may even show up as a stationary fence due to synchronism effects (like moving tank treads appearing stationary in military movies). Similarly, avoid panning up or down on a series of horizontal lines like a rattan curtain.

8) Never counter-pan a moving object. For instance, if a procession is moving from left to right, don't pan from right to left. It's best to lock in on one object and follow its movement at the same speed. This will keep the relative position of the object, on the screen, stationary. This is called a "follow shot" and is much more pleasing than panning on a stationary object.

9) It's usually best to pan from left to right because our eyes are used to reading in that direction. A left-to-right pan, thus, seems more natural.

10) A telephoto lens records only a very small and condensed part of any scene. For this reason, panning with a telephoto lens produces an extremely fast blur. You should use a normal lens or wide-angle lens for panning.

11) Don't switch from a horizontal to a vertical pan in mid-pan. Keep your pan on one plane or the other. In other words, don't use the camera like a paintbrush or garden hose.

12) Make sure that the camera swings in a level arc during horizontal pans. If your tripod has a built-in bubble level (similar to the surveyor's level), you can use it to set your camera on a level plane. Or use a simple carpenter's level placed on top of the camera. Extend the tripod legs to compensate for uneven levels.

13) Pan in one direction only, never back and forth in the same shot. If you wish to return to a subject, begin a new shot.

14) Once the rate of panning is established, don't change it. Keep the speed of the pan constant—don't slow down or speed up in mid-pan.

15) Never pan in a circular motion (*i.e.* left to right, then up, then to left, then down). This can be quite disturbing to watch and is hard to follow.

16) Avoid panning beyond an object in the scene that will arrest the viewer's eye. If the object is moving or attracts attention to itself, the camera should rest on it and examine it. If it is irrelevant, it can easily

be passed by. Stopping the pan to dwell on an irrelevant object will only confuse the audience.

17) "Wind up" your body before the pan and let it unwind as it moves the camera. For instance, if you are following a race car, stand with your lower body and feet pointing in the direction where the car will end up at the conclusion of the shot. Twist your upper body towards the car at the beginning of the shot and slowly unwind as you shoot. This technique will avoid jerkiness during the pan.

18) If you're panning with a handheld camera, rotate from the waist only. Don't try to move your entire body. Let your feet be a steady rest.

By now you should be aware of all the pitfalls that can spoil an otherwise good shot. A good pan is smooth and unnoticed. It is an integral part of the story, a tool and not the goal of filmmaking. A good cameraperson never pans for panning's sake. So remember rule 1: Don't pan if you can possibly avoid it.

CREATIVE CAMERA ANGLES

Carole Kahn

A single shot may not make a film, but it can help. If your films sometimes lack the impact you want, the problem may be in your choice of camera angles. Whether you're doing a documentary, theatrical or industrial film, careful attention to camera angles can make the difference between a dull film and one that grabs and holds the audience's attention. Take a look at effective TV commercials. Chances are they're the ones that use unusual camera angles for dramatic effect. Even something as mundane as fabric softeners can have visual impact through clever camera angles. Imagine plastic bottles of fabric softener gently falling like rain from on high into a basket full of diapers!

In theatrical filmmaking, camera angles can be as effective as dialogue in showing the relationship of characters to each other. Angles can create frenzy or humor or doubt. In fact, camera angles are some of the most powerful tools the filmmaker has for telling a story—whether that "story" is designed to entertain, educate or sell. All film, whether documentary, industrial or theatrical, has one purpose: to make the audience react in certain ways. Camera angles can heighten the dramatic visualization of the story, or they can distract and confuse the audience.

But before we continue, let's define our terms. According to Joseph Mascelli's *The Five C's of Cinematography*, a *shot* is a continuous view filmed by one camera without interruption. A *sequence* is a series of shots, complete in itself, and can occur in a single setting, or in several settings. And a *camera angle* is defined as the area and viewpoint recorded by the lens—every time the camera moves, the audience sees the action from a new point of view.

What Makes a Camera Angle?

Three factors determine the angle of your shot: the size of the subject in the frame; the viewpoint from which the camera films the subject; and the direction in which the subject is angled within the frame. All of these factors depend on the choice of camera position and the focal length of the lens used for the shot. This requires careful planning before you shoot. Whether you use a script, a storyboard, "shot" cards or any combination of these, you will need at least a rough idea of what you want to achieve in the sequence being filmed; you also have to know what you want with the individual shots in that sequence. You will have to be aware of the context of the sequence in the film, and its significance to the story. That should help determine how detailed your coverage will be of that portion of the storyline. In other words, will you be covering the action in four shots, or 20, or will you decide, like

Alfred Hitchcock in *Psycho*, that you need 70 different shots to convey the intensity of a stabbing scene that covers just 45 seconds in the finished film!

Each shot should serve a purpose. Every time you move the camera, you lead the audience to expect additional information. Are you changing the shot to bridge a gap in time, to show a reaction to a previous shot or to create a special effect? Do you want the audience to be shocked, feel awed by or out of sympathy with the characters in the shot? Once you know the purpose of the shot, your choice of camera angles becomes easier.

The first thing to consider in choosing camera angle is image size. Do you want to show a large part of the action, a detail, or something in-between? This will depend largely on what part of the action the shot must cover, and on the mood the shot should convey to further the story. Close-up shots, for example, tend to involve the audience in the action more intimately than long shots. But, depending on the action, even a very long shot can get the audience involved. Imagine a shot of a tiny speck of a person stumbling across a seemingly endless desert.

Choosing an Image Size

Basically, there are three image sizes to choose from: *long shots*, *medium shots* and *close-ups*. Each has its own variations and uses. The so-called *extreme long shot*, for example, is most often used as a scene opener because it conveys things on a grand scale: an aerial view of a city, a fleet of ships at sea.

The *long shot*, while not so grand, can help add perspective and set the scene. The long shot covers the entire area of action in a particular scene. For example, the sequence in *Ninotchka* where Greta Garbo checks into a hotel began with a long shot of the entire hotel lobby and the people in it. The long shot enables the audience to get acquainted with the setting and figure out where players are located in relation to each other. In terms of creating a mood, the long shot can be effective for depicting the vulnerability of man against nature, since it makes people look small against the landscape.

It is also used for deliberately distancing the audience from the on-screen action—whether to put the audience in the position of know-it-all observer, or to protect the audience from a scene that may be too violent to watch close-up.

The *medium shot* makes up the bulk of theatrical filming. The characters are framed from just below the waist. Medium shots place the audience at a middle distance and are commonly used after a long shot which has just set the scene. In a medium shot, the figures are close enough to exhibit details of facial expression, yet far enough away to show any action.

Perhaps the most dramatic use of a medium shot is the *two-shot*, in which two people are seen talking. The positioning and lighting of actors is particularly important for establishing mood in this kind of shot. Who is the dominant figure in the scene? Not a word of dialogue should have to be spoken for the audience to know the answer to that question. Is one person standing, and the other sitting? Is one person lit more dramatically than the other? Is one person positioned to face the camera more directly than the other? The angle and direction of camera tilt is also significant, but more about that later.

A *close-up* puts the audience at a conversational distance from the actor, and is, in fact, often used after medium two-shots to show each actor in turn. Such face-to-face confrontations help make the audience a part of the on-screen dialogue. The most commonly used close-ups are the medium close-up, a shot from about mid-chest up, and the aptly named head-and-shoulders shot. More dramatic is the choker close-up which frames the face from just above the eyes to just below the chin. Anything closer than that is called an extreme close-up and is usually reserved for tiny objects that have been magnified so they fill the screen.

Changing the Image Size with Lenses

The filmmaker has two ways of altering the size of the image in the frame. You can move the camera closer to the subject, or you can change the focal length of the lens you are using. In general, the longer the focal length of the lens, the larger the image size will be on screen. In Super-8, a 12mm lens is considered normal; higher numbers, such as 24mm, are considered telephoto; and anything under 10mm is called wide angle.

Wide and long lenses not only change image size, but they also change perspective. They can make near and far objects in a scene seem closer than they really are, or farther apart. And they can make any movement in the scene seem faster, or slower. The scene in *The Graduate*, in which the hero runs furiously in an attempt to stop the wedding ceremony of his girlfriend, was shot head-on with a long lens. The result is that, like Alice in Wonderland, Dustin Hoffman runs very hard but appears to stay in one place. The reason is that the long lens tends to foreshorten, that is, to compress the apparent depth of the scene. As a result, objects which are farther away from the camera don't appear as small as they should. The same technique is used in filming horseraces. The distances between the horses do not seem as great as they actually are, so the horses seem to be running neck and neck, thereby increasing the viewer's sense of excitement.

A wide angle lens, on the other hand, exaggerates the distance between the foreground and the background. This is a useful device for making a small room look larger than it actually is, but it can also cause some weird distortions if anyone in the scene reaches or moves toward the camera. You may remember the TV commercial in which a person walks down a narrow corridor toward the camera. As he nears the

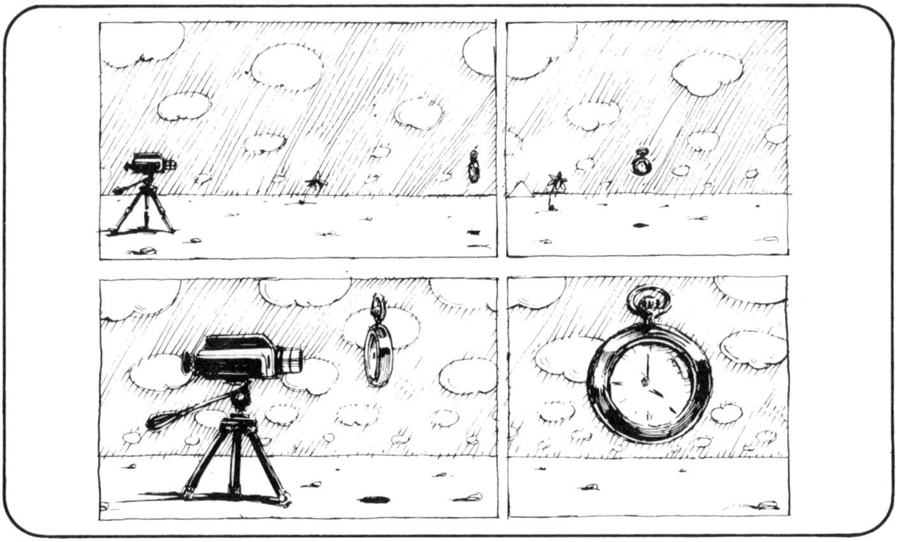

Figure 1: The long shot can help add perspective and set the scene or can be used for deliberately distancing the audience from the on-screen action.

Figure 2: In the medium shot, the one most commonly used in filming, the figures are close enough to exhibit details yet distant enough to show action.

camera, his face flattens out and his nose grows huge, until all you see is a caricature of a human being. This may be a very useful device for filming things such as dream sequences, or the way a dope addict or a psychotic experiences reality. But be careful when you're filming movement with a wide angle lens. The lens will make people and vehicles appear to move much faster than normal. Special effects like these can add enormously to the interest of a film, but they must be used sparingly, and only when they directly advance the film story.

Wide and long lenses also are useful when you are doing handheld shooting, and want a steadier image than you would normally be able to get. With a long lens, you can get a close-up of the subject, while throwing the background completely out of focus. If you want to include the background, you could instead use a wide angle lens and move the camera in closer. The wider the lens angle, the less hand movement will show. Because of their greater depth of field, wide angle lenses are also useful for maintaining focus when the camera is tracking (following) a moving person. Since the lens covers a larger area than a normal lens, it also enables you to keep the person within the frame—a real advantage when the shot is unrehearsed, as in a documentary. Of course, there are times when a handheld look is desirable. A shaky, occasionally out-of-focus camera filming a street fight can make the audience feel very much a part of the action.

Creating a Sequence

In choosing image size, you must not only keep in mind the action and the mood of the shot, but also how it will edit with the shots that immediately precede and follow it. Pay particular attention to the opening and closing shots in each sequence. If the film is to work as a whole, these shots must be composed to cut in easily with adjacent sequences, both technically and aesthetically. Mood can be heightened in the editing room, provided the filmmaker has the right mix of long, medium and close-up shots. You can, for example, create a feeling of urgency, of action moving to a climax, by cutting a series of progressively closer shots, each on the screen for a shorter time than the previous shot. If you want to create a "you-are-there" feeling, you might contrast an extreme long shot of a missile launch, with an extreme close-up of the firing button.

Sometimes you may want to create your own editing rhythm in the camera by changing the image size *during* the shot. You might zoom in from a group shot, for example, to the main character. Or you might dolly back (move the camera back) from a head-and-shoulder close-up of a terror-stricken child to a medium shot that reveals a man and a woman fighting in the same room. In any case, the filmmaker must keep editing in mind while shooting. A film, after all, is a series of sequences that work well together, so a sequence must be a series of shots that work together.

Point of View

Image size, however, is just one facet of camera angle. For a shot to work, it must also have a point of view. When we speak of point of view we're referring to that of the audience, not of any individual in the film. An objective point of view, for example, is when the audience views the action from the sidelines. The players act as if they are unaware of the camera. If objectivity is to be maintained, the actors must never look into the lens. If an actor *does* look into the lens, the audience will feel it has been discovered peeking through the keyhole, and objectivity will be lost. Once a player looks directly into the lens, the audience is forced to relate to the character on a one-to-one basis. The actor seems to be speaking directly to each person in the audience, and the point of view then becomes subjective. Subjective technique is often used in television news and documentaries to maximize viewer involvement, to "eyeball" the viewer into listening.

In theatrical films, subjective treatment is usually restricted to a more indirect approach. The audience is momentarily put in an actor's place to view the action. For example, the audience may take a harrowing ride on a roller coaster in place of the actor. All it takes to effect the transition is to shoot a rear view of the actor on the roller coaster in the preceding shot. When the next shot shows the downhill ride, the audience will assume it is seeing the ride as the actor sees it, experiencing each nerve-wracking turn as the actor experiences it.

The subjective approach is particularly useful for filming flashbacks. Since a flashback is an impression of a past reality, the audience is prepared to view that reality through the eyes of the performer. In the Hitchcock movie, *Spellbound*, for example, Gregory Peck relives an incident in which he accidentally kills his brother. First you see a close-up of the adult Peck, staring straight ahead. Then you see a close-up of Peck as a child, also looking straight into the camera, and shouting. Next there is a long shot. The camera looks up at the two brothers sitting on the near and far ends of a bannister, the spiked tips of a gate looming up across the bottom third of the frame. Then a shot "through" Peck's eyes, looking past the top of his shoes to his brother, who is sitting on the bottom edge of the bannister, with his back to Peck, perched just above the spikes. Next, a shot of Peck's shoes about to slam into his brother, who, at that moment, turns partly around to scream. Finally, an extreme close-up of the brother's hunched-over back, a corner of his sweater caught on a spike. It is a powerful sequence.

Camera Height

There is another aspect to camera angles: the height of the camera in relation to the subject. You can change the entire mood of a shot just by adjusting the height of your camera. Consider this scene: a woman is ironing in a small room, with a child tugging at her skirt. Film the scene with the camera positioned high above the woman and she will look small, trapped in a room with walls closing in on her. Shoot the same scene with the camera positioned below the woman, looking up at her, and she will look powerful and authoritative next to the child. If you film the scene again, but with the camera stationed just about eye level with the woman, the scene will look ordinary, a normal domestic scene with no unusual psychological overtones. These three scenarios cover the basic choices for camera height available to the cameraperson: *high angle, low angle* and *eye level.*

A *high angle* simply means that the camera is above the subject being filmed, looking down. The "angle" doesn't have to be very high. It can be a mere "nod" to look down on the cover of a book, or an extreme high angle to show a "bird's-eye view" of a city, as seen from an airplane. If there are people in the shot, a high angle will make them look smaller than they really are. This, in turn, can have a belittling effect, as in a shot of a jailer "looking down" on a handcuffed prisoner. Or, it can simply reflect a difference in the real height of the people being filmed, showing the scene from each person's point of view.

A *low angle* is shot from below the eye level of the subject. This shot will increase the height of the subject, causing the person to loom up on the screen. It can be used effectively to inspire awe, or to symbolize authority and power: as when you "look up" to a judge. A low angle can

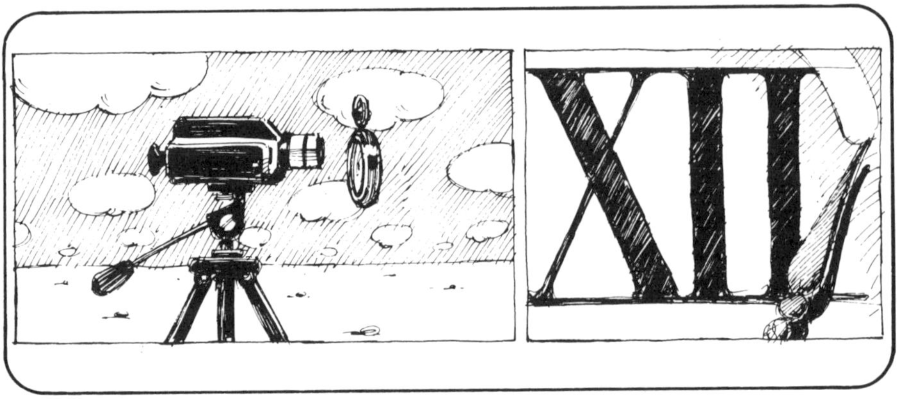

A close-up is often used to present face-to-face confrontations thereby helping to make the audience feel they are part of the on-screen action.

also be used to cut off part of the foreground or background so that the action is framed more dramatically. Or it can be used to relate the background to the subject; such as in a low angle shot of a senator against the backdrop of the Capitol dome.

This shot, however, can turn into a political caricature if filmed with a wide angle lens, since the lens would exaggerate the low angle effect. The senator would look like a "Shmoo" punching bag—a tiny head on a fat body. Because low angles, like wide angles lenses, make objects that are closer to the camera appears much larger than objects farther away, the Capitol dome would look like it was very far from the blown-up Senator. If political satire is not your bag, you might limit yourself to the low angle, and forget the wide angle lens. One other important use for a low angle camera position is when it is used to film a subject moving toward the camera. A fast-moving car filmed from a low angle position will grow larger and higher in the frame as it approaches the camera. It will seem to move faster and faster because the background will appear to recede rapidly at the same time the car moves closer to the camera.

Eye Level Camera Position

The least distorting camera position is at *eye level.* When you film a person at eye level, you maintain the illusion of eye contact with the audience, or with other people in the film—a technique that helps the audience become involved with the characters on screen. Although not normally as dramatic as high or low angles, eye level shots can be thrilling if used to film cars rushing headlong toward the camera.

The Tilt

Still another way to change the mood of a shot is to *tilt* the camera on

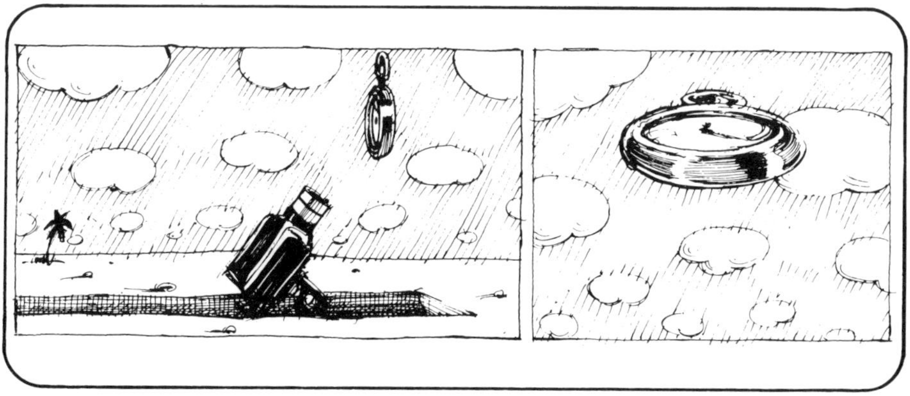

In a low angle shot the camera is positioned below the eye level of the subject. This increases the height of the subject, causing it to loom up on the screen.

a sharp slant. Such angles are usually reserved for a violent or unstable effect, such as filming a scene from the point of view of a drunk, or portraying panic or confusion. If you edit a number of sharply angled shots together, you can build a kind of time machine sequence that shows the audience glimpses of a larger event, condensed into a short period of time. TV commercials frequently use this technique because of the very short amount of time they have to tell their "story." The direction of the tilt can be very significant to the mood of the shot: a sharp slant to the right will seem more forceful than a sharp slant to the left. The most violent tilt effects are those shot with a wide angle lens from a low camera position.

Camera Direction

The final determinant of camera angle is the direction of the camera in relation to the subject: is the camera directly opposite the subject, or is it a little off to one side? Generally speaking, a subject filmed straight-on will look flat, while one filmed at about a 45-degree angle will look solid and real. Similarly, a landscape filmed at an angle will have a greater sense of depth than one filmed straight-on. The reason is that when you view something at an angle, you see the same scene (or subject) from at least two perspectives. By lowering or raising the camera, you add a third dimension.

On location, there will be additional factors to consider, such as the terrain, the angle of the sun or the size of the room in which you are filming. All this can be rationally dealt with if you know in advance exactly what you are trying to achieve in the sequence, and you have learned how to "play" with the various aspects of camera angles to achieve that effect.

If you plan the sequence shot by shot, you will be ahead of the game,

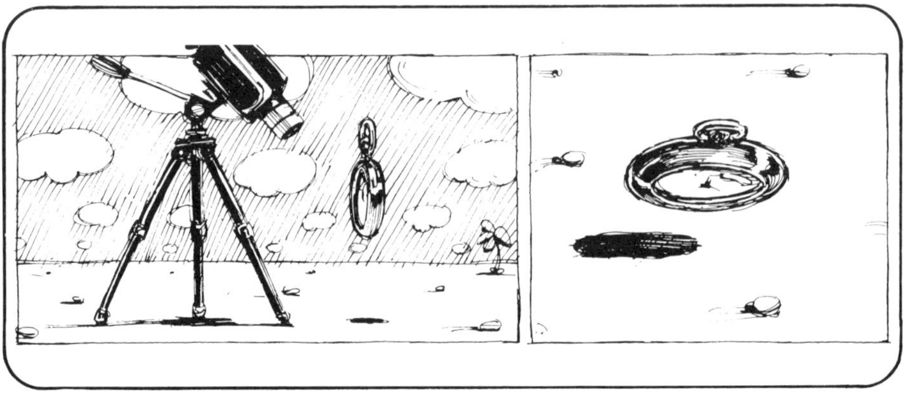

In a high angle shot the camera is positioned above eye level of the subject, making it appear smaller.

even if you have to change your plans during the shooting. At least, you will have worked out the effect you want from the sequence, and one way of getting that effect. For people familiar with the language of camera angles, there are always alternatives. As we said at the outset, a single shot may not make or break a film, but it sure can help.

SHOT CONTINUITY

Elinor Stecker

One of the reasons "home movies" have a bad name is that they too often lack continuity. Every film, whether it's based on fact or fantasy, should have a smooth, logical, *continuous* flow of visual images. The object of *continuity* is a realistic portrayal of events. Without it, your film will just be a hodgepodge of unconnected shots. With good continuity, your viewers can forget about the filmmaking process and concentrate on the story you're trying to convey.

As a home moviemaker, you are a documentarian. You have some very important stories to tell, and you don't have to wait for the big events—the gathering of the clan at Christmas, the long-anticipated vacation or the Fourth of July picnic—to document them. Even your everyday activities can make interesting movies if you do it right. One secret is to shoot enough scenes so that you can edit them to show a sequence of events where the images flow smoothly and naturally from one scene to the next. If you can, try to make the film tell a little story. This doesn't mean it has to have a momentous plot, but it should have a beginning, middle and end. Shoot several sequences so there is some sort of introduction (*e.g.*, parents give their child a new bike), the main activity (child riding the bike) and a conclusion (child puts bike away in garage).

The raw material you're working with are the basic shots: the long shot (LS), the medium shot (MS) and the close-up (CU). Of particular importance in maintaining continuity is the *establishing shot*. As the name suggests, its function is to establish the locale of a sequence. A long shot or an extreme long shot can be used to establish the scene. Without the establishing shot, the audience will be disoriented—they won't know where the action is taking place and who is involved.

The customary progression of shots in a film is the way in which a person actually looks at a scene. Suppose you saw Robin with her new bike. Your eyes would take in Robin, the house, the sidewalk, the bike, and her sister Lauren standing next to her, helping her get on the bike—in other words, an establishing shot. Then you would probably focus on Robin as she gets on the bike—translated to camera language, you'd use a long shot. But your interest would quickly move your eyes in closer for a medium shot. You would start noticing details—lots of close-ups: hands on handlebars, a smiling face, feet on pedals. And then, once again you'd be aware of Robin's entire body as she rides down the street—another medium shot. Robin's sister runs over to her, and you watch the two girls—long shot. So we've gone from a broad view to a closer look, then pulled back for another overall look. In order for your movie to have continuity, you, as filmmaker, should duplicate this progression of images with your camera.

For the sake of clarity, an establishing shot is needed every time the location changes; without it, the audience will assume that all of the action is taking place in one place. Suppose you are shooting in your backyard. You take a close-up of your friend Dick. Then you go into the kitchen and shoot a close-up of Dick's hand holding a coffee cup. When the audience watches this on the screen, it will seem as if all of the action is taking place in the backyard. The confusion could be avoided by shooting an establishing shot when the camera moves indoors. Another time you'll need an establishing shot is when a person enters or leaves a scene. For example, suppose you've established your location and followed with some interest-provoking medium shots and close-ups; then you show a close-up of a new face. Who is she? When did she arrive? We need an establishing shot to show Ms. X coming into the room. The same holds true when someone leaves, otherwise it will seem as if the person simply disappeared. The audience also periodically needs a reminder of the setting they are in. After a succession of medium shots and close-ups, another long shot or medium long shot—called a re-establishing shot—is needed to re-establish the scene of the action.

A frequent cause of lack of continuity is the ubiquitous jump cut. This abomination is a shot in which a piece of the action is missing. Let's say you're filming Robin riding her bike down the street; you press the shutter release for five seconds; then you decide it's not exciting, so you stop shooting for two seconds; but then you change your mind and start the camera again. When you project this on the screen, you'll see Robin move along nicely, then suddenly jump several feet down the road. Whenever you stop the camera and start it again, while filming the same subject, the result will be a jump cut.

There's a simple way to avoid jump cuts: *whenever you stop the camera, change the size of the image, your shooting angle, or both.* These changes, if they are significant, will distract the viewer and allow the scenes to move smoothly into one another. To illustrate, take a long shot. After you stop the camera, move or zoom in closer, and frame the subject in a medium shot before you press the trigger again. Or move around to the side or shoot from a low angle. A combination of a different-size shot combined with a different angle will be even more effective in preventing the jump cut. The change in angle or size must be significant, or the technique won't work.

In the excitement of shooting, you may still have some jump cuts that you won't notice until you see the film on the screen. But even if you didn't *prevent* them, you still can *cure* them in the editing room if you filmed a number of "cutaways" and "cut-ins." This might be a shot of a detail in the scene (a cut-in), such as hands holding bike handlebars. Or it might be a shot of something related to the shot but not visible in it (a cutaway).

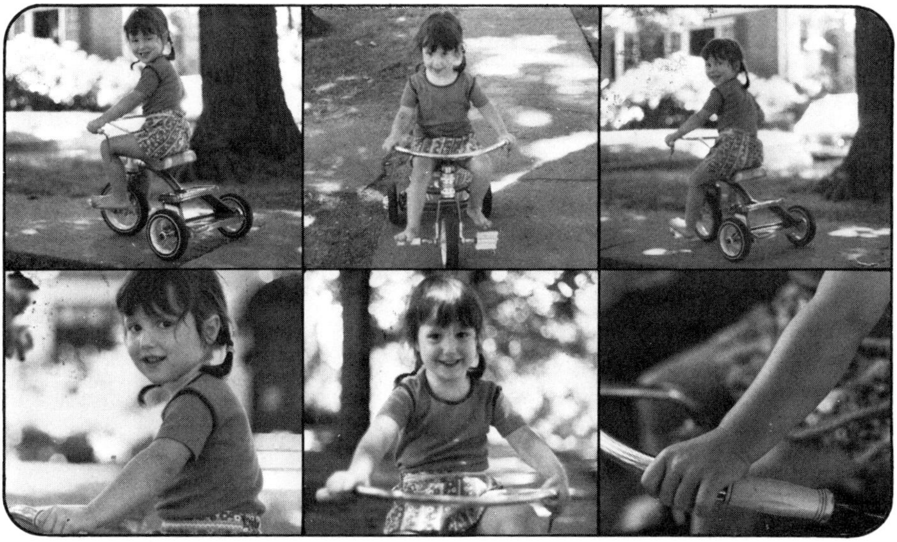

Figures 1, 2: If the camera doesn't run continuously through a scene, the subject will appear to jump across the screen.

Figures 3, 4, 5, 6: Avoid the "jump cut" by changing the size of the image . . . or changing both the image size and camera angle . . . or by interjecting a cut-in.

Why all this fuss about continuity? Well, you could shoot three or four random shots of the kids on their bikes, but you will have missed the joy of creating a continuously moving story of an event. Follow some of the basics of continuity and you'll find that any home activity can be built into a film that will be satisfying to watch.

CONTINUITY OF SCREEN DIRECTION

Elinor Stecker

To most of us, the word "continuity" conjures up an image of a script secretary (or "script girl," to use the pre-women's liberation term) busily jotting down notes about a scene being filmed: Is the book in the actor's right or left hand? Did he put his gloves on the table or the chair? All this seeming trivia becomes extremely important in a feature film, since consecutive scenes may be shot days apart. The viewer will be disturbed to see an actor who was wearing a hat in a long shot, without a hat in the following close-up. Such inconsistencies can also creep into the home moviemaker's casual filming of family and friends.

Suppose you're at a picnic, taking pictures of a badminton game. You leave for a few minutes for some refreshments and then return to the game, never noticing that one of the players has removed his jacket. But you and your audience will notice it when you project the film. Fortunately, an audience's memory is short, and you can rescue the scene during editing. All you have to do is insert a "cutaway" (*e.g.*, a close-up of a hand on a racket, the shuttlecock going over the net, or a spectator reaction shot) between the two problem shots and your audience probably won't notice the difference in clothing. The way to *avoid* the problem is to make mental notes or write things down when you shoot a scene that will be continued later—and always film lots of cutaways.

Another type of continuity that must be considered is that of screen direction. If a person moves from left to right in one scene, he should move from left to right in the next scene; otherwise he will appear to have turned around. You'd think that this would be no problem to shoot, but it is. The camera must always stay on one side of the line of action, otherwise you will violate the continuity of screen direction and your subject will appear to be going in the opposite direction. You can insure continuity by following the 180° rule (Figure 1). That places an

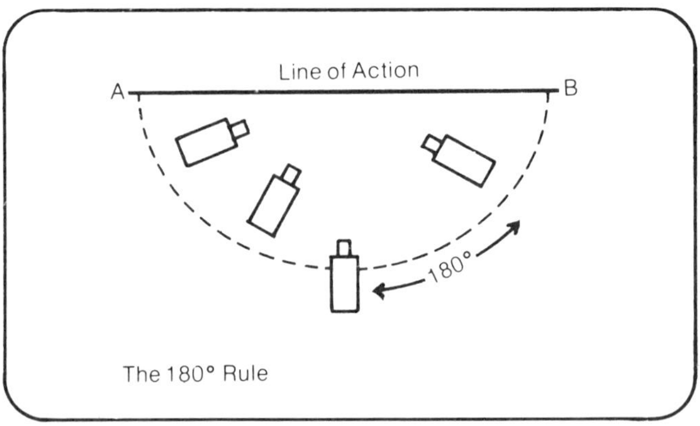

Figure 1: The 180° rule place an imaginary line (A to B) through the action and allows you to film from any position on one side of that line.

imaginary line (A to B) through the action and allows you to film the action from any position on one side of that line. If you make a mistake during filming, you can insert a neutral shot, that is, one made from directly in front of or behind the moving subject. Continuity of screen direction should also be maintained through a series of shots that are supposed to show the subject heading for a specific destination, in order to give the feeling that he is making progress in getting there.

Even if there is no action on the screen, you still must maintain continuity in the direction people look. The medium shot in Figure 2 establishes that the left side of the screen belongs to the woman, and, if she is talking to the man, her eyes must always look to the right. There's no problem if the camera follows the 180° rule and stays on one side of the couple. We moved in for a close-up in the second frame, but stayed on the same side of the woman—her gaze is still to the right, so continuity is okay. But in the next frame we tried to get creative and find a new camera angle. Because the camera crossed the line of action (thus violating the 180° rule), the woman appears to be looking to the left, away from her colleague. The confused audience will wonder if someone new has entered the room.

An interesting problem arises when you have a scene with three people, like the women on a coffee break in Figure 3. The first frame establishes the situation. In the second frame, we move in closer, and

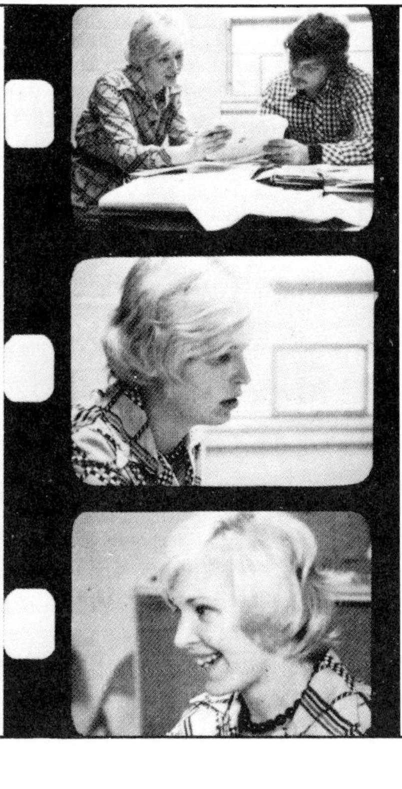

Figure 2: In the first frame, the medium shot establishes that the left side of the shot belongs to the woman. In the second frame, the close up keeps her on the left side, but in the third frame she appears to be looking away from her companion. The camera crossed the line of action.

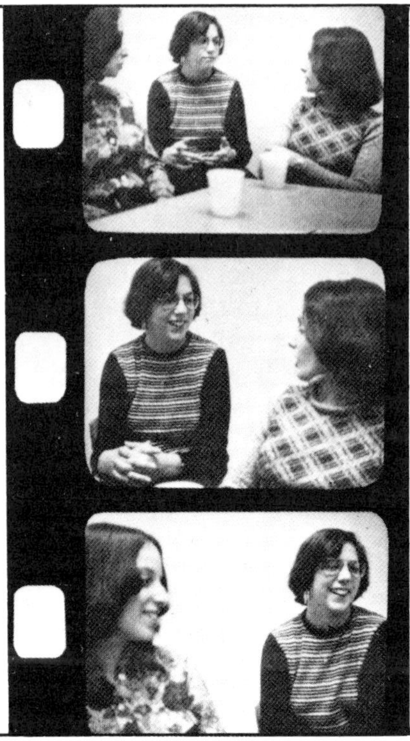

ELINOR STECKER

Figure 3: The first frame establishes the relationship of the subjects. In the subsequent frame, the middle woman bounces from the left to the right of the screen. A close-up of one of the subjects or another shot of all three must appear in the second or third frame to maintain continuity.

in the third frame, we cut to a shot of the middle woman and her friend on the left. As a result, the middle woman keeps bouncing around, from the left of the screen to the right of the screen. If you want to use these two shots, cut-in a close-up of one person, or another shot of all three.

Maintaining continuity takes a little forethought, but it can add immeasureably to the quality of your films.

BASIC LIGHTING TECHNIQUES

Gunther Hoos

The subject of lighting for film can be very complex. Thorough mastery takes many years of practical experience, and knowledge is gained largely through experimentation. However, there are basic principles of lighting that every serious filmmaker can learn.

If you want to make good films, you have to know how to avoid washed-out highlights, shadows without detail, off-color hues, skin tones reminiscent of everything except skin, and cut-to-cut mismatches of overall lighting. Forget about complicated set-ups and dramatic lighting—that's another ball game. Let's deal with very basic, clean and simple illumination of subject and scene.

The introduction of existing light cameras and high speed film has led many filmmakers to believe that they can film virtually without light. But they fail to consider the resulting *quality* of their image. If all that viewers can discern on the screen is the silhouette of someone moving in the aura of an existing light source, they'll quickly lose interest. Fast lenses and films are a liberating influence for the filmmaker, but they are not excuses for bad footage. On the other hand, too much light can also ruin a scene. Even if the scene looks nice and bright in person, on film it may look terrible. Too much light can cause your subjects to look like runaways from a horror film, casting giant shadows on the walls behind them.

It need not be this way! There is *always* something you can do to give your images visibility, solidity and life, even under the most uncontrolled documentary shooting situations. At times it may be as simple as changing your camera angle or your position and exposing manually. At other times the judicious use of a movie light bounced off the wall, or a portable, battery-operated hand light will make a crucial difference. And in films where advanced planning and control are possible, the use of set-ups which include multiple lights, reflectors and directional control devices will result in footage that represents your vision. Control is even possible outdoors. As beautiful as natural light is, there are times when supplemental lights will help to cut contrast, increase dimensionality and improve the richness of color in the film.

But creative lighting does more. Lighting should also influence the color composition of a scene, so that the color rendering in the projected film approaches what our eyes expect to see. Why is this necessary? Because human eyesight, unlike the emulsion of color films, has a self-adjusting mechanism that compensates for the way objects look under different kinds of light. If we see a red apple in the sunlight or in a dimly-lit room, we still know that we are seeing a red apple. This compensation is so much a second nature to us that we are almost unaware of the constant changes in color composition around us. Film emulsions, however, are not capable of compensation. They are merely layers of chemicals which react to light. As such, different emulsions must be produced for compatibility with daylight or artificial light. Therefore the color makeup of the illumination for any particular scene should be balanced so that it matches the ideal color makeup of daylight or tungsten that the emulsion has been prepared to record.

To determine how to balance the color makeup of the illumination, we must be able to measure it in some way. This can be done with sensitive meters. This measurement is expressed in a comparative scale of degrees called Kelvin, and is designated the *color temperature* of a particular light source. The standard color temperature for average daylight illumination is 5400 degrees Kelvin (expressed as K), and the color temperature of artificial light is usually 3200 K or 3400 K. Daylight film and indoor film emulsions are matched to these respective color temperatures, which are the numbers your lighting corrections must ultimately match up to. As long as you know the color temperature that the film you're using is matched to, and the color temperature of the prevailing light source (which is always measureable), you just have to match up the two. Many common light sources have standard color temperatures, a number of which are listed in Table A.

There are various ways to do this matching. It can be a simple procedure, requiring only the addition of a standard #85 filter over the lens, which reduces the 5400 K of daylight to 3400 K. Many Super-8 cameras have this filter built-in. If your lighting is a mixture of both daylight and artificial light—as in a dimly lit room with daylight entering through the windows—you can use relatively inexpensive Rosco conversion gels on the windows or lights. These are pieces of colored plastic or gelatin which can be applied to the windows if you're matching for artificial light, or over the lights themselves if you're matching for daylight. Careful consideration must be given to all sources of light within a shot so that the richness of color on your footage will approximate what the eye expects to see. Often raising or lowering the color temperature in parts of a scene or the subject may be very desirable. Experiment—there is no other way to find the perfect combination of lighting for a scene. It's helpful to have some idea of the color temperature of typical light sources. By knowing what to expect, you'll be better prepared to make decisions regarding the addition, elimination or modification of lights in a scene.

The kinds of equipment we'll concern ourselves with will not be the heavy, non-portable type you associate with Hollywood sets. In fact, if you've shied away from thinking about lighting for films, it's probably because you're not aware of the wide variety of lightweight, versatile equipment available to the "shoot-and-run" school of filmmakers.

Probably most everyone has heard of quartz lights. The lamps are very small and produce a very stable light output. The lamp consists of

Table A

Sources Which Must be Matched to Daylight or Tungsten Film		Approximate Color Temperature Values of Common Light	
Burning		Tungsten-halogen lamps	
candle	2000 K	(quartz-iodine)	3200 K
Sunrise and sunset	2000 K	Photoflood tungsten	3400 K
40-60 watt tungsten household bulb	2800 K	Cool white fluorescent	4300 K
100-200 watt tungsten		Average	
household bulb	2900 K	daylight	6500 K
Ordinary non-studio tungsten		Overcast	
floods (500-1000w)	3000 K	sky	6800 K
Studio tungsten lamps	3200 K	Hazy sky	8000 K
Projector lamps	3200 K	Clear blue sky	10,000-25,000 K

a quartz glass envelope which contains a filament composed of tungsten and halogen. Halogen is a collective name for a group of elements which include iodine; and in fact, iodine is usually what is used in quartz lamps along with the tungsten. Halogen elements have long lives, and using them in the filament prolongs its life, thereby maintaining accurate color temperature and intensity throughout the lamp's lifetime. A quartz lamp is good for about 250 hours of use. Photofloods, on the other hand, rapidly experience a thinning of the filament because they lack halogen; after several hours of use, photofloods will gradually shift toward the red end of the spectrum as their color temperature decreases. However, they don't cost much—about 60 cents a lamp—while quartz lamps start at about $16. Filmmakers who cannot afford to invest in equipment will probably want to go this way.

The numerous portable light kits which are available are designed around the highly efficient quartz lamp. These kits contain just about everything you'll need—accessories included—to light a set or location. In fact, 4000 watts of lighting—and that's a lot—may weigh less than 20 pounds including accessories. If you feel that your shooting will require a range of lighting equipment, consider a portable kit.

I don't suggest using movie lights—with the exception of the Sylvania Sun Gun—unless it's absolutely necessary. Movie lights are camera-mounted and they swivel; in fact, they can usually be taken off the camera and handheld. But they create deep shadows and washed-out highlights in most shooting situations. Because movie lights are very directional, they create areas of intense light which result in an unbalanced effect. You don't have control over your image with them; you can't create a mood or dimensionality. However, they *are* very inexpensive and convenient, and they do, at least, guarantee an image—

which is always better than no image at all. They also are quite durable. If you don't feel that your budget will allow much more, you can experiment with movie lights to at least improve what you get on film.

When lighting a scene, two principles should always be kept in mind. The first is that the lighting should be clean, uncluttered and balanced. This means that objects should cast only single shadows and images should consist of a pleasing combination of highlights, middle tones and shadows. Contrast, unless desired, should be kept very low if you intend to make duplicates of your film. It has a tendency to built up tremendously on Super-8 prints. The second principle to keep in mind is that the illumination of a subject should seem to come from a *logical* direction. If your subject is sitting near a table lamp which is supposed to be illuminating the right side of his face, it would look very silly to have a strong light shining on the left side of his face. Determining the direction of the lights is very important for the believability of a scene. Before any lights are set up, the filmmaker should familiarize himself with the light already present and build on what there is in a logical way.

If the existing light is poor or unusable, the filmmaker must set up a main source of illumination. *The most natural direction for the main light is high above the shooting area and as far as possible from the subject.* We naturally accept the position of the light source coming from above—the sun—as being logical. Other lights are used to sepa-

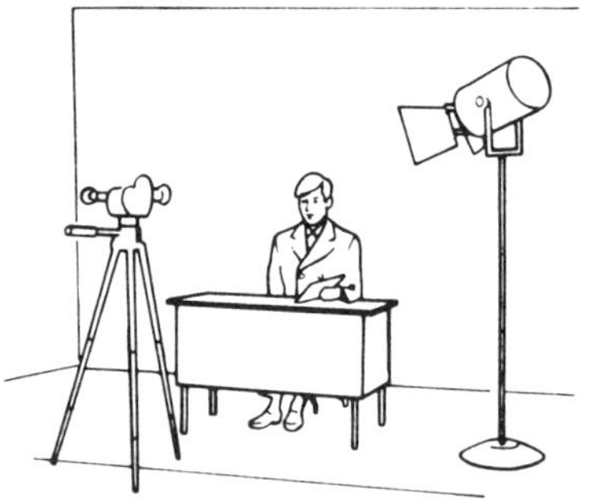

The key light is mounted higher than eye level in order to keep the actors from squinting, create decent nose shadows, and fill out background shadows to make them less apparent.

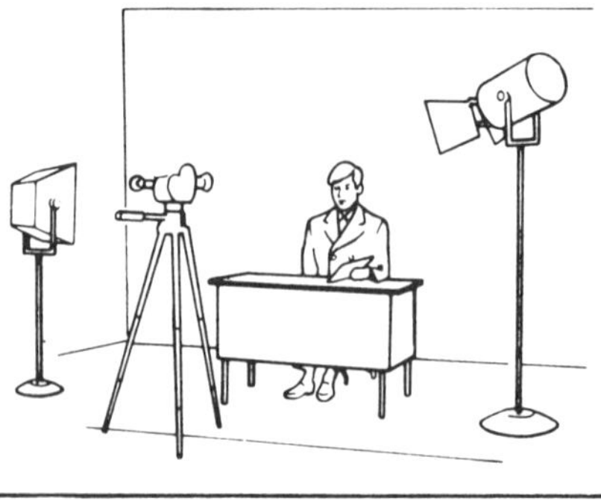

The fill light illuminates the shadow created by the key light—its positioning can be tricky.

rate the subject from the background, highlight the subject's features, add dimension to the subject, and break up the shadows created by the main light.

The classic four-light set-up consists of a *key*, a *fill*, a *back* and a *background light*. The *key light* is the main light source falling on the principal area of action. The key light is mounted higher than eye level in order to keep the actors from squinting, create decent nose shadows, and fill out background shadows to make them less apparent. The *fill light*, generally a softer light than the key light, is often located near the camera. It illuminates the shadow created by the key light. Positioning the fill light can be a little tricky; if it falls too directly on the subject, unattractive double nose shadows can result. The *back light* is located behind and above the subject and may be directly in line with the camera. Its function is to provide highlights on hair and shoulders, thereby giving dimension to the subject. It creates depth and helps to separate the subject from the background. The back light must be carefully controlled so that it doesn't shine into the camera lens and create flare. Usually the back light is of the same intensity as the key light. The *background light*, as the name implies, is thrown onto the background. The light (or lights) may be mounted high, low or on the sides of the scene. The primary purpose of the background light is to kill or subdue shadows from the key and fill lights, and to light up the back-

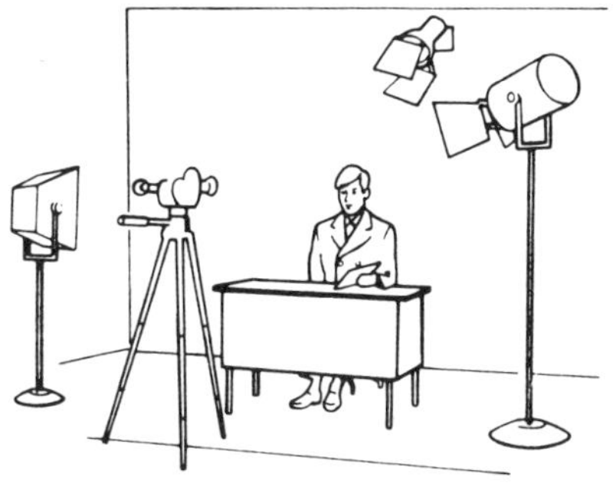

The back light provides highlights on hair and shoulders to give dimension to the subject. It must be carefully controlled.

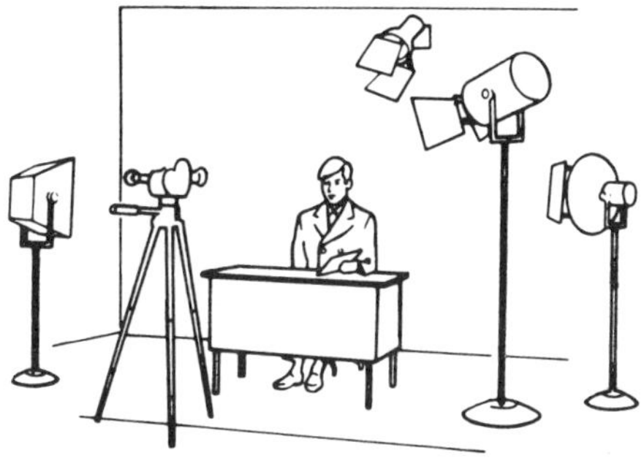

The background light is thrown onto the background and is used to kill or subdue shadows and provide contrast and separation.

ground. By lighting the background to be darker or lighter than the subject, contrast and separation are clearly defined. To keep background shadows to a minimum, try to locate the subject some distance from the background.

Besides the four basic lights which you can direct and angle for specific results, there are other devices you can use to pattern, diffuse or even block out certain portions of light. *Barndoors* are hinged metal flaps used in pairs which are mounted on the exterior rim of lights. Their main purpose is to block light that might otherwise cause lens flare, unwanted reflections, or over-illumination. The *cookie* is an old standby. This is a sheet of opaque material which has a random or symmetrical pattern cut into it. It is placed in front of a light and then illuminated, creating a patterned shadow background. The cookie is useful in situations where it is impossible to light large backgrounds properly or the background is so ugly that lighting it would ruin the shot. The patterned shadow cast by the cookie is usually more acceptable than the original background. If light is too directional, it can be diffused (spread out) in various ways. Cheesecloth may be taped in front of the light source; a piece of wire mesh known as a *scrim* can be mounted directly on the light head via an accessory holder; or a piece of *diffusion material* can be placed in front of the light. Diffusion material such as the eight varieties manufactured by Rosco Labs is a type of cloth made of fiberglass or plastic. It is extremely durable and is sold in rolls. The varying density and texture of the different varieties allow you to alter the diffusion and intensity for each light. Rosco also manufactures reflective media which diffuse and distribute light evenly.

When you are filming people, diffusion of some degree is almost always advantageous. Diffused light is very kind to blemishes, skin pores and wrinkles. Diffusion softens the edge of hard shadows and makes them less apparent. Diffusing makes the transition from dark to light areas very gentle. Also, most lights do not provide a balanced lighting field, and diffusion mediums tend to even out the intense spots.

Very important to quality lighting is the intensity ratio between the key light and the fill light. The ratio can easily be measured with any light meter. Just remember that only the key and fill lights determine the ratio, and all others should be turned off during measurement. For color, a ratio of 1 to 4 is about maximum. For Super-8 it probably should not exceed 1 to 2, because if the ratio climbs, the contrast builds up; and if the contrast builds up, the highlight and shadow details will tend to disappear. To check contrast prior to shooting, look at the scene with a contrast-viewing filter. These are very inexpensive and will save you much grief later on. By looking through one of these, you can determine how much highlight and shadow is in your scene.

Another much-neglected point is the maintenance of lighting consistency from shot to shot. All the tones in a scene, unless a change is called for, should match. The skin tone of a close-up should be the same as in a medium shot; the same goes for the background. Maintaining this consistency requires a developed awareness of light intensities.

Not all lighting must be direct. In fact, most uncontrolled situations that require lighting cannot be lit directly. For situations like these, indirect soft lighting and bounced lighting are usually employed. Rosco diffusion and reflection media are a good choice. These materials, coupled with a bag full of cheap photofloods and an inexpensive reflector, offer a very economical way to achieve balanced lighting without many shadows over relatively large areas. The reflective media do not absorb very much of the light and distribute it very efficiently.

Of course Acme, Colortran, Lowel, Strand-Century and others make shadow-free soft lights for 2,000- to 6,000-watt units. With adjustable-focus quartz lights, umbrella reflectors are used quite often. They provide very soft directional light to small action areas. Both Rosco reflective media and lighting umbrellas can be bought which not only reflect the light, but also change its color temperature, should you wish to do so.

The main difficulties encountered when shooting in daylight are the changeability of the color temperature throughout the day, the tremendous variations in intensity depending on the location of the clouds, the changes in the angle and direction of the light, and the great contrast range. Preparation will help you avoid many pitfalls. Here are some things to consider:

—Never go out without a reflector of some kind, whether it's reflective media or just a sheet of aluminum. If the subject is to be photographed in the shade, the proper subject exposure will grossly overexpose the sunny background. A little reflected light on the subject should help to balance the contrasts. Bring pieces of cardboard, gaffer's tape (2-inch wide cloth adhesive) and reflectors.

—Be aware of reflections from natural surroundings that may cast an unwanted hue on your subject. For example, filming someone in a green field on a sunny day may result in a green tinge on their skin.

—If the sky is completely overcast, a normal film exposure will tend to make the colors look very pale. An underexposure of about 1/3 stop will give the proper color richness.

—Unless you want lens flare—an overall sheet of extra light over your scene—always use a lens shade. Flaring tends to make images appear very flat.

—If you are filming in direct sunlight, make a scrim out of some diffusion material by mounting it in a frame; then have someone hold it between the subject and the sun. The diffusion reduces contrast and improves the important area of the image.

—The best highlighting and dimensionality of subjects comes from backlighting. However, exposure with the sun shining at the camera can be a little tricky.

—If using tungsten-balanced film, be sure the daylight filter is in.

Artificial lights require considerable quantities of power. Before plugging 4,000 watts of light into a socket, check its capacity. Most circuits are fused for only 15 or 20 amps and will quickly blow. To convert amps to watts, figure roughly that each amp allows you about 100 watts of power.

On location, you have to seek out separate circuits if you use a lot of lights, in order to avoid blowing fuses. For long cable runs, use heavy duty cable or else you may experience substantial voltage drops. A 1-volt drop will reduce the light's color temperature by about 10 K, thus changing the color quality of your footage. Consequently, a 10-volt drop will change your light appreciably.

Be thorough and neat when you string cables. Tape them down with gaffer's tape or someone will surely trip and get hit with a 2,000-watt light. Gaffer's tape is indispensable. If all else fails, try to find an electrician. Better yet, find him before you start.

The surface of the complex art called lighting has barely been scratched here. However, you now have a starting point for practical work and more reading, as well as an appreciation of good lighting. Besides, Super-8 filmmakers are notorious for wading in where giants fear to tread.

18 OR 24: THE FPS QUESTION

Dennis Duggan

Eighteen or 24 . . . that is the question. Whether it is better to shoot at the speed set as Super-8's standard in the days of its silent infancy, or to adopt the precedent put forth by filmmakers in the aged formats of 16mm and 35mm.

I am neither an avid supporter of 18 frames per second (fps) as Super-8's "own true speed" nor a fanatic about the "professional" heritage of 24 fps. Each time I begin a new project, I ask myself which standard I should choose. I would be content if everyone settled on either one, but I don't see how a decision can be reached in the atmosphere of misinformation and ignorance that surrounds this question.

Case in Point

A beginning filmmaker recently asked me where he might have a contact print made that would change his 18 fps film to 24 fps. After explaining that only an optical print could perform this feat, at considerable expense to his film and his pocketbook, I tried to ease his pain by questioning him further to see if there might be another solution to his dilemma. As it turned out, he had some footage of a football game and wanted to add narration. That's all. Someone had told him that 24 fps was "the speed of sound." You can imagine how pleased he was to find out that all he had to do was to have his film striped, then add his narration along with "wild" game sounds and music, or anything else, without any fancy optical magic. This may be an extreme example of sound naivete, but it brings up some of the more subtle untruths that stand in the way of a common agreement on this point. Let's separate the facts from the myths one by one.

Picture Fidelity

Some argue that a picture shot and screened at 24 fps is more natural than one shot and viewed at 18 fps. This may have some truth in theory, but 18 fps footage looks perfectly natural, and there is really no such thing as *more* natural.

Sound Fidelity

Anyone who has done much playing with a tape recorder knows that the faster you move the tape, the better the sound quality. Music sounds better at 7½ inches per second (ips) than at 3¾ ips, and serious recordists use only 15 ips for music. The frequency response on the high end of the spectrum is improved as speed increases. The difference between 18 and 24 fps, however, is only the difference between 3 and 4 ips. This difference is usually only audible in a side-by-side comparison, and only to someone with a better ear than mine. If you've listened to a good cassette deck at 1-7/8 ips, you'll realize that speed isn't always that important, although I suppose it might be argued that there is a psychological effect beyond our conscious perception.

Professional Standards

Probably the greatest argument for the faster speed is that it's the frame rate people have been using in other formats for years. And if you plan to blow your film up to 16mm or 35mm, by all means shoot it at 24 fps. You should ask yourself, though, if that is in fact what you're going to do with your film and why. If your films up to now have been technically and artistically less than satisfying, and the word "professional" means high quality to you, don't be fooled. Shooting at a higher speed isn't going to make your films any more professional, in that sense, no matter what it says in an ad. (An amateur is someone who does something for the pleasure of it, not someone who does it badly. A professional makes films to earn money. The pro that enjoys making films is also *entitled* to be called an amateur. Pardon the soapbox.)

Professional Equipment

Some equipment works only at 24 fps, and some performs only certain of its functions at that speed. If the equipment or the functions important to what you want to accomplish as a filmmaker are only available at one speed, then you'll have to weigh the advantages and disadvantages of your choice carefully against the overall merits.

Amateur Equipment

Every Super-8 camera and projector that I can think of works at 18 fps. Many work at 24 fps also. But many do not. Since no one has yet designed a "do-everything" Super-8 camera, we are often forced to use several cameras to incorporate all of the values we might want into a single film. The more sophisticated machines that allow many in-camera effects don't usually permit low-light (XL) filming or the advantages of single-system sound. In the area of this kind of free choice of equipment, in my opinion 18 fps is usually a wiser choice.

Budget Priorities

If the money you spend on film stock for a project is only a small part of your overall budget, then the cost difference related to frame speed won't mean much to you. If most of what your film costs is what you spend on film, processing, fullcoat and printing, however, a choice of 18 fps will mean a savings of 25 percent for each of the above.

Odds and Ends

Sometimes our reasons for making a particular choice are personal and rather esoteric. I chose, after much deliberation, to make a feature-length film at 18 fps, mainly because the most extreme slow motion speed possible with my equipment was 54 fps, the longest dissolve was 100 frames, and the slowest zoom speed on my camera is 10 seconds. I knew all of these effects would look a little more dramatic at 18 fps than they would at 24 fps.

The thing I like best about 24 fps, which its supporters never mention, is that splices are less noticeable at that speed. There may also be a pretty good argument that a student who's only working in Super-8 as an economical way to learn filmmaking before moving into a larger format may develop editing habits that will later have to be changed.

The Question Remains

When I think about my next film, I have this fantasy: I think of how easy it would be to put all my sync sound onto Channel 1 of my Dokorder, while I put a pulse from my Super8 Sound Recorder onto Channel 4. Then, after I have put all the music and sound effects onto Channels 2 and 3, I could use that pulse to pilot the Super8 Sound Recorder for a three-channel mix. Whenever I have this fantasy, I think seriously about settling for 24 fps as my standard speed. But when I think about spending 25 percent more money (or shooting 25 percent less film), and needing 25 percent more light, and having my camera make more noise, then everything gets muddy again. If I do pick 24 fps, then I can use 18 fps to subtly increase the speed in a chase scene. But if I choose 18 fps, I can use 24 fps for the equally subtle effect of kinesthetic slow motion, or to mellow out a pan shot or shots from moving vehicles.

I suppose if it were up to me, I'd make 18 fps the standard speed for Super-8, but I wouldn't try to con other people by claiming they could get a ticket for shooting at faster speeds or some such nonsense. I also know that I'd accept either speed to put an end to the question. In the meantime, we will all have to make our own choices for each new film. All you should ask is that the choice be really *yours* and that it be based on the realities.

DESIGNING AND FILMING TITLES

Elinor Stecker

A film without a title is like an unframed, unsigned painting. They both can be enjoyed, but they seem a little ragged and unfinished. Besides, if a film is very good or very bad, the viewers want to know who the filmmaker is. What does "titles" refer to exactly? Main title, credits, subtitle, end title—they're all called "titles" even though they are different. The *main title* is the actual name of the film; the *credits* list those industrious people who appeared in the film or worked on it in some technical capacity; a *subtitle* gives information or explanation not obvious from the visual action, or it may be the actor's words in a silent film; the *end title* is self-explanatory, although the trend seems not to use it much today. If you don't state "the end" at the close of your film, something should still be added to give a sense of completion. One way is to conclude with your own credit—"a film by. . ." or your own distinctive emblem or signature.

There are a couple of things that can make otherwise great-looking titles appear amateurish. One is the simple matter of alignment. Regardless of what you use for your background—paper, cardboard or clear acetate—those plastic letters with sticky backs, available in every photography store, don't lend themselves to being pushed into a straight line once they've been stuck down. You have to position the letter correctly or lift all of them up and reposition them. The easiest way is to line up the letters against a straightedge.

The most common obvious fault people make in titling is spacing. If you have a short title, don't try to fill the background, also known as a title card, by spreading the letters far apart. Not only does it look peculiar, it also makes the words difficult to read. A good rule of thumb is to place the letters no farther apart than the width of a capital "N." Letters can be placed closer together, even touching, and the words will still be legible. In Figure 1 all the letters are equally spaced. Careful measurement was taken so that the distance between the right side of each letter and the left side of every following letter was exactly the same. Only it doesn't look that way! The reason the spacing looks uneven is because some of the letters are regular and some are curved. The curved letters have more "air" around them than do regular-shaped, straight-sided letters. The eye sees all this air and interprets it as extra space between letters. To compensate for this illusion, curved letters have to be placed closer together than regular-shaped ones. That's what I did in Figure 2, and the effect is improved. If you look closely, you'll see that the letter "A" actually cuts under the "P," and there is less room between the "I" and the "C" (curved) than between the "I" and the "N" (regular).

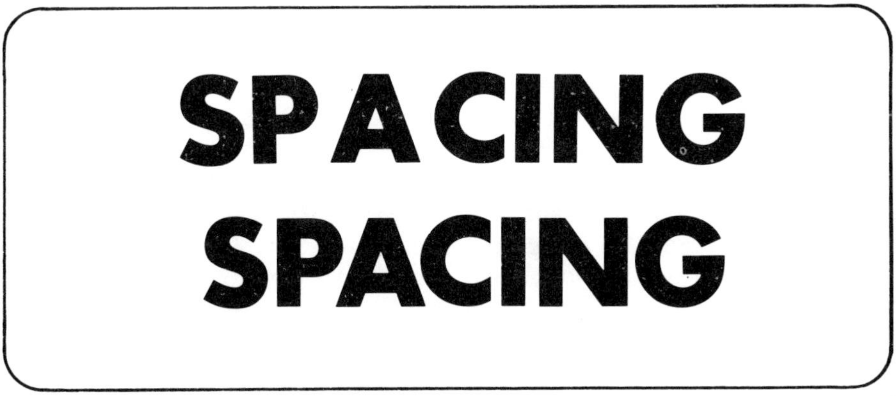

Figure 1: (Top) The letters are equally spaced, though they don't appear to be.

Figure 2: (Bottom) The curved letters have been placed closer together to improve overall look.

Closely related to the mechanics of spacing is the matter of the size of the letters. If the letters are too small they will be difficult for the audience to read. If they are too large, they will look like they're bursting out of the frame. The "large" and "small" size I'm speaking of are relative to the projected frame size. You can use small letters and come so close with your lens when you're filming that they'll overwhelm the screen when the film is projected. A good guideline is to keep the letters no smaller than 1/25 and no larger than 1/5 the height of your background. So that the letters are of consistent size on all of your titles, use the same size letters for all of the titles in a particular film.

Margins are another important consideration. If the letters are large, the title long, or the credits extensive, you might be tempted to push the words almost to the edge of the frame. Not only does this look unattractive, but, even with through-the-lens viewing, what you see is not necessarily what you get. The camera and the projector both may lop off a bit of your titles, and you may find that only part of some of the letters can be seen.

Credits can be arranged either evenly lined up or ragged on one or both sides. In listing your credits, you will help the audience in identifying the people more easily if their names are lettered differently from their jobs or roles. You can use small letters for listing the job and large ones for the person's name; lowercase contrasted with uppercase; or two different but compatible type styles.

One of the best ways to get really professional-looking titles is to use what are known as dry transfer letters. These are sold at art supply stores. These letters come on large opaque sheets of paper and contain many duplicates of each letter. Most manufacturers make them in both black and white, and some companies make them in yellow, blue, red and green as well. You can even get shaded and outlined letters. There are hundreds of different styles of type to choose from, and intriguing new styles are introduced each year. The manufacturers of these letters publish catalogues which are interesting to look through, and best of all, they are free. Your biggest problem in using the dry transfer letters will be in trying to choose the most appropriate type face for your film! The bold, straightforward style that will work well in an industrial film may be completely out of character in a dance film. Whenever you choose, make sure it is simple and legible. Clever and ornate lettering may be attractive, but hard for an audience to read.

The letters are applied by laying the sheet face up over the background. Rub the front of the sheet so that the letter transfers from the sheet back to your background. Use a burnisher or an orange-wood stick (used for nail manicuring) to do this. Once you've applied the letter it can't be reused. Buy more sheets than you think you'll need; you'll make mistakes and have to do some letters over. These letters are easily removed by putting a piece of masking tape over them and pulling the letter off with the tape. Don't try to economize by buying very small letters (the smaller the letters, the more you'll get). The smaller ones are harder to work with, and any small imperfections which result during application really show up when magnified on the screen. If you do run out of letters you can sometimes fake it by substituting other letters. For example, a lower-case "p" upside down is "d." I once needed a lot of "R's," so I rubbed on a "P" and the slanted leg of a "K" and created my own letter.

White is usually the best color choice for letters; it provides the greatest contrast with most backgrounds. It is not a *rule* that you should use white. The rule is that you must have contrast between the lettering and the background or the title won't be legible. For more con-

This title is difficult to read because there is not enough contrast between the lettering and the background.

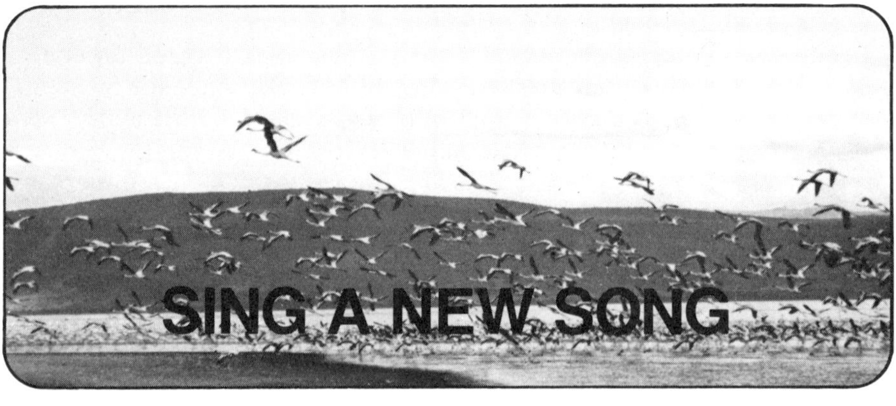

trast you may want to make your own shadow on dry transfer letters. Make the title in white letters on a sheet of clear acetate. Then take another piece of acetate and use exactly the same kind of letters, only this time in black. Superimpose the white letters over the black ones, but throw them slightly out of register to create a shadowed effect.

If you have a deadline for your film and you wait until the last minute to do the titles, you could be sorry. It's just at those rush times that the exposure is wrong, or a finger mysteriously appears in animated titles, or you find that Jeffrey spells his name "Geoffrey." Warning: Make exposure notes, check spellings, and give yourself the time to do the titles over again if you have to. In fact, it will be to your advantage if you practice shooting some titles before you get involved in producing your film. Titles are an art in themselves and the more attempts you make, the better your end results will be. Just don't get carried away—I have a friend who dropped his original project and made an entire movie of just *titles*.

Once you're a pro at designing clean, smart-looking titles, you should start to concern yourself with matching the mood of your titles to the mood of your film. This can be accomplished through the choice of materials you use for both titles and backgrounds, and also through a few special filming techniques.

You should always put thought into having your backgrounds as well as lettering reflect the mood and style of your film by looking around your home or office for all sorts of ideas. Textured placemats, suede clothes, cut-velvet book covers and leather camera cases are all potential backgrounds. Texture adds interest and can be especially important in a black-and-white film. Color-aid papers have a lovely matte surface and come in hundreds of rich colors; they have to be handled carefully since they are easily marked by the oil on your fingertips.

This title has been moved to the half of the frame where there is more contrast so that the title becomes more legible.

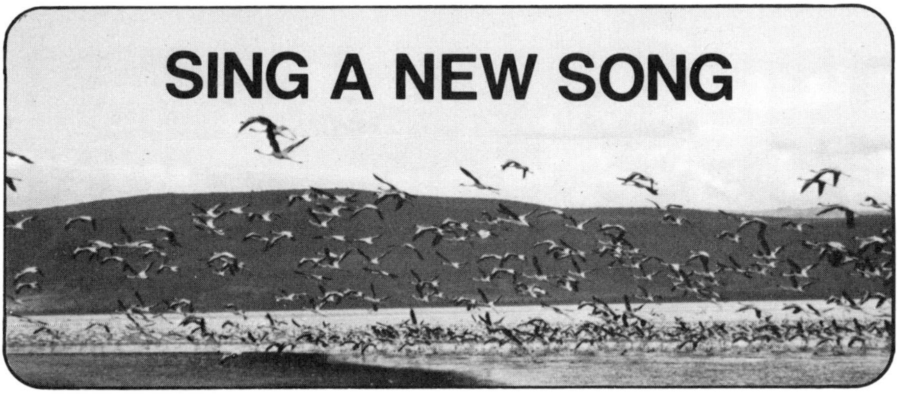

Pantone is another line of hundreds of colored papers; they are less delicate and have a lustrous surface. Both are available at art stores.

Don't use a lot of colors on your title card; the result is apt to be garish and distracting. But you may want to add a second color in the form of a decorative strip or border to provide balance or accent. Beware of a border that goes all around the title. You're likely to run into centering problems, so confine the border to one or two sides. Decorations can be added by using simple drawings or actual objects. Photographs, tissue paper, wallpaper and gift-wrap paper can make good backgrounds if they are not too busy or too bright. A patterned design can be muted in several ways. A piece of wrapping paper in its natural state can be covered with grey acetate, subdued with frosted acetate, or covered with tracing paper.

Some of you must be screaming that you don't want to be bothered with meticulous lettering and clever lighting. Then deliberately make your lettering casual. Informal lettering really has to look that way or the viewers will think you intended to be precise but blew it. So write boldly with chalk, crayons, pastels, felt markers or paint on colored paper. Or stick-on gummed letters or plop down alphabet noodles (uncooked!). Effective casual lettering can be done by writing on an object that appears in the film or is significantly related to it. I've written on autumn leaves and panned the camera from one leaf to the next, and I've done titles on oranges. You can cut letters or whole words out of paper and stick them to an object with double-sided tape, or you can cut nice chunky letters out of photographs and stick them to a background with rubber cement. The letters in the photo below were made as thick as possible so the pictures would show.

You don't have to do any work at all if you use found titles. The most common kind are the monument markers and highway signs that can

Left: The letters for this title were made as thick as possible so the photographs would show. Right: A prism created this unusual title effect.

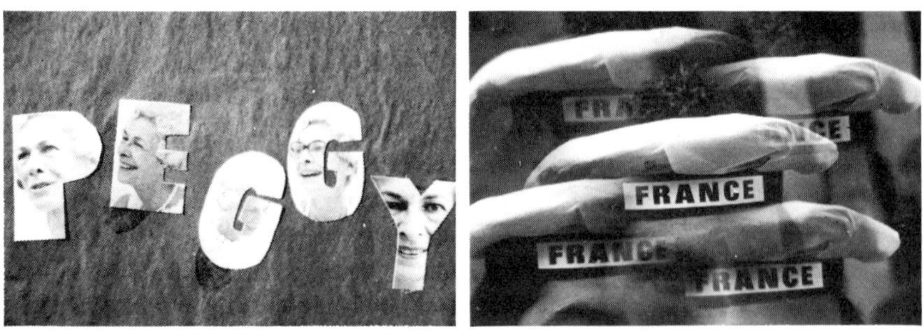

ELINOR STECKER

be nicely incorporated into a travel film. Maps, travel folders, newspapers and restaurant menus are good, too. Embroidered souvenir bags or hats make good titles. Figure 6 was shot through a multifaceted prism placed over the camera lens. This prism can be rotated while you're shooting, and the images on the sides will move while the center one holds steady.

Another effortless way of lettering is to use a plastic label-maker. Or, if you have or know small children, borrow their wooden letters, crepe sponge letters or alphabet blocks. The white letters that fit into grooves on announcement boards are useable if you underexpose so the grooves don't show. You can form lots of things into letters that can be related to the film. My favorite one was spelled out with dry cat food and then was eaten by the star. Pine needles, flower petals, seashells, transistors and other small objects can be arranged into words. I've even seen Band-Aids spelling out the word "Help."

A title that becomes part of the scene can rivet the audience's attention. It can be as simple as a child writing the title in chalk on the sidewalk and then moving away as the camera pans with him. Or it can be plastic letters stuck on the back of a car; film the title and then have the car move down the street. (When I did it the driver put the car into reverse by mistake, causing one very frantic filmmaker to grab the camera and run.) Or zoom out from a title that is part of the opening scene. One other effective technique is to alternate a static title with a bit of action—perhaps the name of a cast member followed by a shot of him coming out of a door. Repeat the sequence for the entire cast.

The great thing about moving picture titles is that they *can* move. This seems to pose a problem to many filmmakers, though. The question I hear most often is how to *superimpose* a title over a moving background. You can place a large piece of glass in a firm support, and the title on a piece of acetate taped to the glass. Focus on the title, making sure that there's good contrast between the title and background, and that there's just a minimum of movement in the background. The background will be in acceptable, but not sharp, focus. The farther back you can get from the title and the more you can stop down the lens, the greater depth of field you will have, thus improving the focus of your background. There are other ways of superimposing—like backwinding, rear projection or letting the lab do it—but the glass shot is frequently the most practical and inexpensive.

Once you start thinking about titles, the ideas never seem to stop. So go ahead—make them—but remember a few important points. The lettering should be simple and legible; there should be contrast in tone between the letters and background; and the titles should be appropriate to the mood and theme of the film. Once you start putting these ideas to use, your films will be more professional and creative than ever—from start to finish.

PROCESSING AND PRINTING

PROCESSING AND PRINTING

GETTING ALONG WITH YOUR FILM LAB

Mark Mikolas

For an independent filmmaker, the selection of a laboratory may be the most important final step in the filmmaking process. It means handing over the results of months, sometimes even years of work, so you'll want to base your selection on solid knowledge of the capability and competence of the lab. And developing a good working relationship with the lab you choose is essential to the ultimate success of your film creation.

The first step in getting good service from a lab is understanding what a lab is and what it can and can't do. By understanding *how* things are done, you can prepare a film properly for the service that you want, and increase your chances for satisfactory results.

Lab Organization

A lab is either a *wet lab* or a *dry lab*. A wet lab processes film (in addition to offering printing and other services). A dry lab may offer some nonprocessing services (such as timing and printing), or it may simply oversee all postproduction steps on a film. In this case, the actual processing work is done by other labs. A wet lab can generally offer lower rates and faster service than a dry lab, since all functions are in-house and the print doesn't have to be sent elsewhere for processing. A wet lab will print on print stocks that they can process in-house. In Super-8 work, Ektachrome print stock is commonly used.

It's important for you to know what is being done to your film, and by whom, when you deal with a lab. Many labs will be honest about what work they do in-house and what they send out, so you can simply

This is an automatic processor capable of processing both Super-8 and 16mm film.

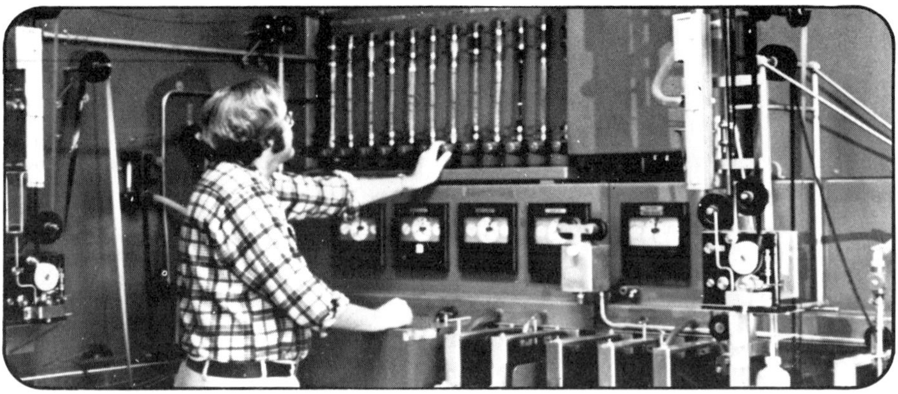

ask them. For instance, Lab X may offer a particular service, such as black-and-white processing. When you give them this particular job, they send it to Lab Y which does the actual work. Because Lab Y will charge Lab X a lower "wholesale" price for this service, Lab X will usually charge you the same that you would pay if you went directly to Lab Y to begin with. However, the service usually takes longer since you will be dealing with a "go-between." And if there are any problems with the job, they are more difficult to straighten out because the lab you turned the work in to (Lab X) did not actually do the work. On the other hand, Lab X, by "farming out" the job, may save you the trouble of going to two places.

A Lab Is a Business

The services a lab can offer depend mainly on the equipment they own. A lab that does not offer timed prints or edge numbers, for instance, is not withholding these services from the filmmaker. They have not invested in the necessary equipment. To do so requires thousands of dollars. Labs offering Super-8 are doing so because they think it's a wise business move. With increased volume, they will be able to afford more sophisticated equipment and to offer additional services.

The Lab/Filmmaker Relationship

Laboratories are growing with the rest of the field. Getting to know a lab and working with them will give you the best opportunity to exercise some control over postproduction services. If a print is terrific, call them and tell them. If you think there is room for improvement, show them and explain. If they are not responsive, or are condescending toward the Super-8 format and blame *it* for their failures, then start shopping again. Discuss good and bad experiences with other filmmakers in your area.

An edge numbering machine prints sequential numbers on the perforated edge of the film.

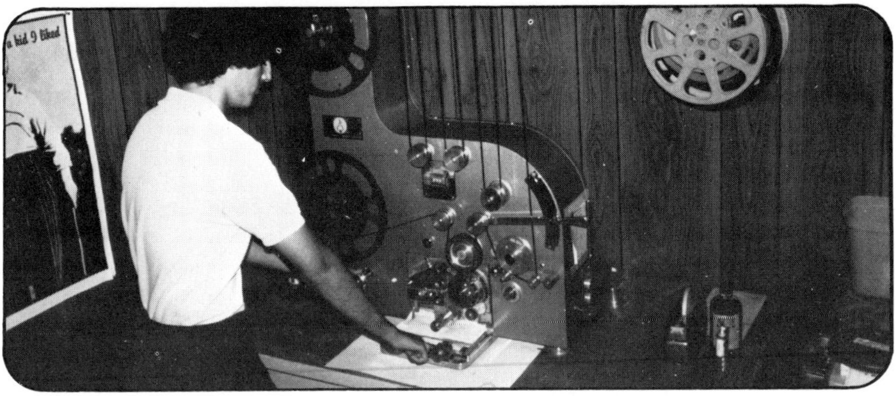

Labs, on their part, can help in several ways to insure a good relationship with filmmakers. Each lab should have available clear instructions about how films and tracks should be prepared for them. For example, if it is important to their timer to know what the original stock is, they should request this information. If the lab has a synchronizer that counts frames, they should specify that A and B roll cue sheets be prepared with frame numbers rather than footage and frames, and so on.

They should also be clear about their billing and credit procedures, and in what form they expect payment. Ideally, a person informed about the lab's Super-8 operation should be available (even listed in the brochure) for filmmakers to check with before work is prepared and sent to the lab, as well as when it is being worked on.

PREPARE FOR BETTER PRINTS

Dennis Duggan and Lenny Lipton

The biggest obstacle facing serious Super-8 filmmakers is the less-than-adequate Super-8 release print. At this stage, we can produce exquisite originals and quality transfers to videotape, but the print from Super-8 falls short of professional standards. Since most of us involved in Super-8 through its formative years have become fairly adept at problem solving, let's take a look at some of the obstacles and see what can be done about them.

To begin with, the nature of the format demands that we squeeze our image reality onto the relatively small Super-8 frame. We know that with top-quality camera and lenses, by limiting our serious efforts to fine-grained film like Kodachrome 40 and taking extra care in the shooting and handling, we can do wonders with that little frame.

Getting professional labs to take our format seriously has been a chore, but we seem to be getting results. It's up to us to get the most out of the labs that are now tooling up for Super-8 work. One way to do this is to have your films printed, even if they're just short early efforts that you don't plan to do much with.

The next problem is the toughest one. Kodachrome 40 camera stock is not terribly compatible with the available print stocks Ektachrome 7389, 7387 or Gevachrome 9.02. The prints from 7387 and 9.02 tend to build up too much contrast. Eastman 7389, on the other hand, has a unity of one—this means the contrast should be about the same in the print as it is in the original. But this very factor tends to give it a very flat or dead look. All three tend to produce, to some extent, a loss in sharpness and an increase in graininess. The degree to which these flaws exist depends on the condition of the original and the proficiency of the lab that makes the print. In other words, a well-made print from a near-perfect original will be acceptable, at least to someone who hasn't seen the original. If we hang in there, the technology in this area will eventually improve.

Don't Blame It on Super-8!

More to the point: Because we are working in a format that is just out of the teething stage, we sometimes blame all our filmmaking problems on the fact that it is Super-8. We see Hollywood films and TV films that may or may not have artistic merit, but are almost always technically together, and we associate this with the fact that they were shot in 35mm or 70mm. We do ourselves and the professionals an injustice with this kind of thinking. Pros don't have it easier than we do, they just make it look easy. They have the advantage of experience that most of us lack—but we usually have the advantage of time. Many

Hollywood pros expend a great deal of energy in keeping contrast low in the original so that the final print will meet their rigid standards. Much of what they accomplish, we can duplicate or approximate, if we're willing to expend similar energy.

Shoot For the Print

For instance, a director may request that the costume department deliver a wardrobe that is entirely in pastel colors. Our version may be to ask our actors and actresses not to wear clothing that is dead black or white. We could go through what clothes they have and pick out low contrast combinations. They can order low contrast sets. With contrast in mind, we can make the best choice of sets from what's available to us. They control the lighting to keep the ratio between the lightest and darkest areas of a scene down to 2 or 3 to 1. They do it by checking each area with an incident light meter. We can do the same thing or at least take reflected readings of all the parts of a set-up with our in-camera meters. For greater accuracy, we could carry a grey card.

A Lowel Soft Light can fill the average room with 1,500 watts of shadowless light—plus, it's lightweight and folds up for easy portability. This unit is the single most useful accessory I have seen for controlling lighting contrast. If the price tag of $168 is way out of your budget, try the 1,000-watt Acme quartz studio light model 710SL (at under $50 with barndoors), or any high-powered light you may already own to construct your softlight. I lined the inside of a large, shallow box with highly reflective mylar and then added a couple of layers of cheesecloth to create my softlight.

For daylight shooting, professional companies use banks of fill light or giant scrims of diffusion material that might be a hassle for a filmmaker with a small crew (usually of one). While these aren't usually possible for our productions, we can try to confine daylight shooting to slightly overcast days, or use reflectors to fill in shadow areas. A 40- by 60-inch piece of white matte board will serve the purpose well. A few holes here and there in the board add a naturalness to the fill and make the board easier to handle in the wind.

Use Contrast Control Filters

Tiffen makes a set of contrast control filters that are graduated from numbers 1 through 5. They are used by professional cinematographers (e.g., Alcott in *Barry Lyndon*) to achieve a diffused effect while retaining most, if not all, of the resolution. I seldom use them for this purpose, but I've found in Super-8 they can produce a slightly softened original that will look normal again in the print. The #1 can be left on the camera all the time. It produces a very subtle contrast drop.

The #2 filter deals nicely with the so-called average lighting situation, and is probably the strongest one you should use if you're not sure you want a print made. Number 3 handles most direct sunlight and direct lighting situations, and would probably be the one to get if you could only afford one. They cost about $20 apiece in series 8. Numbers 4 and 5 will rob about half a stop of light and some resolution, and should only be used in extremely harshly lit situations.

By using the techniques I've outlined, I've been able to get print results that other serious Super-8 filmmakers thought was original footage. One way or another, the biggest drawback in Super-8 is being eliminated. With enough concentrated effort on all our parts, the problem will soon be reduced to no more than another page in the fast-moving history of Super-8.

—Dennis Duggan

Super-8 may be many things to many people, but to most of them it isn't a medium for making prints. The casual chronicler of the life and times of his family probably isn't as demanding as the more dedicated worker, and for the home moviemaker Eastman Kodak, for one, provides what is probably a perfectly adequate printmaking service for both silent and sound movies.

Kodak duplicates the original film on a Kodachrome-type print stock, which is exposed to a low level of illumination before exposure in order to reduce contrast. This step is called flashing, and as far as I know only Kodak offers this contrast-reducing step in conjunction with Kodachrome print stock.

I've had very good experiences with Kodak and their recent printmaking efforts. In particular, Ektasound or other magnetic sound camera original is printed at the cost of about 28 cents per foot, which includes sound duplication onto mag-striped print stock. The major drawback of the Kodak services is the lack of *timing*, or scene-to-scene exposure correction, a routine service at any professional lab.

A Lowel Soft Light can fill the average room with 1,500 watts of shadowless light.

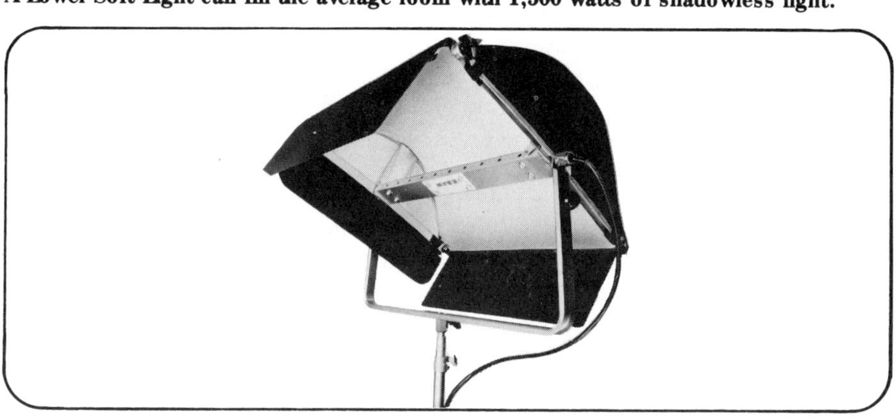

LOWEL LIGHT

It's All in the Timing

Scene-to-scene or shot-to-shot exposure correction, which is accomplished by controlling the intensity of the printer's source of illumination, can mean the difference between a lousy print and a first-rate print, especially if there are uneven exposures.

Despite the fact that the Kodak prints lack timing, that is, are printed from head to tail with one average light, their prints are exceedingly sharp, with good grain, bright highlights and a rich black maximum density (D max). Contrast is acceptable and the colors are quite pleasing. The reproduced sound is extraordinarily fine.

But let me caution you: Before you use Kodak or any other laboratory for the first time, send them a sample roll of film so you can judge the quality of work done by the organization. Better to spend a little money on a 100-foot test roll than a lot more on your 500-foot film.

What I'm telling you now is from personal experience, and the suggestions I am putting forth are, naturally enough, suited to my needs, and not necessarily yours. In the past three years I have completed seven Super-8 films, which have a running time of almost four hours, and in the course of making these films I have shot on practically every stock generally available to the Super-8 filmmaker. I have had prints made by a number of laboratories on several kinds of print stock. There are less than half a dozen organizations in North America that consider themselves to be Super-8 motion picture specialists, and from what I have seen, their prints are more alike in quality than different. I therefore feel qualified to comment on the Super-8 scene with regard to printmaking in general, although much of my experience has been with a local lab, Leo Diner Films, of San Francisco.

Measuring Print Quality

Print quality can be measured in two areas: Image quality and sound quality. Let's discuss image quality first.

One point that's often overlooked is that the Super-8 filmmaker, unlike the 16mm worker, becomes familiar with the look of the original camera film and not with a workprint made from it. Thus the Super-8 filmmaker must compare the *print* of the completed film with a memory of the higher-quality *original* camera film, and not with a *workprint*. Of course, audiences looking at your Super-8 print have never seen the original, so they won't know what they're missing. If you've made a good film, they'll be looking at the film. So the first *secret*, as I see it, of successful Super-8 printmaking is to make a good film.

As I mentioned, the 16mm worker has at his or her disposal camera materials which are part of a printmaking system the manufacturer has established, comprised of both camera film and specially matched print stock. No such system exists for the Super-8 filmmaker. But the saving grace has been the introduction, in the last few years, by both Kodak and Agfa-Gevaert, of low contrast print stocks designed to work nicely

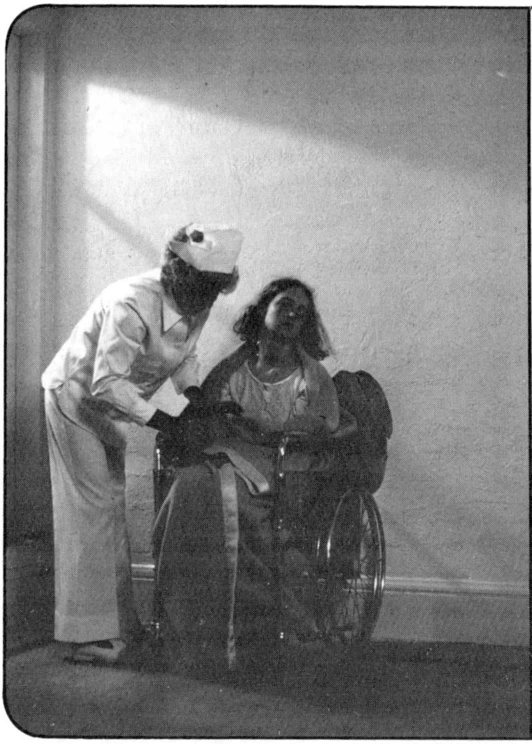

A Lowel Soft Light to fill in the shadows gave the final print of this scene from Duggan's "Afternoon in the Sun," a dramatic effect without excessive contrast.

with higher contrast projectable camera original. So there are two print stocks, Gevachrome 9.02 and Ektachrome 7389, which will work fairly well in conjunction with just about any Super-8 camera original.

However, the real problem becomes knowing which film to select in conjunction with either one of the two print stock choices. After a great many tests, for the time being, I have settled on Gevachrome stock for prints. As they are made by Diner Labs, they have brighter highlights, a deeper D max and better color, especially skin tones, than Ektachrome stock. However, the Ektachrome stock is marginally sharper. Both materials seem to have comparable grain.

Some people advocate the use of Kodachrome as a camera original, since it is so fine grained and sharp. Still other people put down the use of this film because it is often difficult to make good prints from it, due to contrast build-up. Kodachrome 40 can make very good Super-8 prints, when used in conjunction with either Gevachrome or Ektachrome print films. The major hang-up: you can't get predictable, dependable results. (I should say that *I* can't get predictable, dependable results.) The usual advice given is that you should avoid contrasty subjects and employ nice flat lighting when exposing Kodachrome meant for printmaking.

I have found that this maxim simply cannot be counted on. Sometimes Kodachrome shot under low contrast conditions prints well, and other times it doesn't. Very often high contrast subjects shot on Kodachrome (for example, people on the beach who are sidelit) will make perfectly good prints, and other times they won't.

The Ektachromes

Right now I am experimenting with Ektachrome 40, which I find to be a very beautiful camera material, and I hope that its relatively fine grain and good sharpness will eventually produce good prints. The other camera film I have great hopes for is the newly introduced Ektachrome SM 7244, which is the finest grain, softest contrast fast Ektachrome film I have seen. It deserves your serious consideration, but remember, before you select any camera film for your project, shoot tests and have test prints made.

I feel the greatest contribution that could be made to Super-8 print-making would be even better print stocks, with low grain, lower contrast, better color, and most important, better sharpness. Super-8 black-and-white camera film printed on Super-8 black-and-white print stock looks very good. Why can't our Super-8 color efforts look as good, as sharp? The answer is that black-and-white films are simply much sharper than color films of comparable speed. This is true for both camera and print stocks. The high quality of Super-8 black-and-white prints gives me hope for the future of color prints.

Now the subject of sound: After much trial and error, mostly error, I have settled on Kodak to do all of my print sound striping. I know of no other lab that can apply such a good quality stripe to the emulsion side of contact prints. As you probably know, when contact prints are made from Super-8 camera original, the emulsion position changes. While the emulsion of the camera film faces toward the projector lens, contact prints, since they are mirror image, must be oriented with emulsion away from the projector lens. Since this is the case, stripe must be applied to the emulsion side of contact prints, if it is to make contact with the soundhead.

There is no emulsion-striped Super-8 print material, so all prints must be striped *after* processing. A number of labs offer this service, but from my experience the stripe is usually of inferior sound quality and often peels off the print. Therefore my advice: use Kodak for sound-striping prints.

Some labs offer sound-transferring services for the Super-8 worker, and they can take care of getting the print striped for you along with recording or dubbing the track from your sound master. However, these services are not universally available, and I have come to dub my own sound in my studio. This is a simple procedure and one for which you will need no additional equipment, if you're already set up to do double-system projection. I have two such set-ups, a pair of Eumig 807 projectors interlocked by Super8 Sound, and an Elmo ST1200 with a digital switch which is run in sync with a Super8 Sound Recorder.

Both produce tracks that are far better than anything I have ever heard produced by a 16mm optical track.

That's where it is for me regarding Super-8 prints. To sum up: It takes a great deal of care to get prints with an adequate image, but the prints can have superb sound.

—Lenny Lipton

HOME PROCESSING

Robert Price

So you want to process your own! There is certainly no reason why you shouldn't. It's easy, it's cheap, it's fast, and a lot like magic when you see images appearing before your eyes.

For fast processing of your Super-8 film, black-and-white or color, doing your own can't be beat. A roll of black-and-white takes less than an hour. The Ektachromes take about the same time. Unfortunately, Kodachrome's chemical process is still guarded by Kodak, so you won't be able to do that yourself. But with all the other emulsion stocks available there is hardly a need.

Ever need a roll of film processed quick to check your camera operation before that last minute shoot? If an important event is coming up before you can have a roll lab processed, home processing can be invaluable. Another fantastic plus for doing your own processing is in screen tests. In Super-8 you say? Of course!

There are so many companies now producing home processing kits that obtaining one is the easiest part of doing your own. Practically all better photo stores carry them in stock or can order them for you. Mail order firms also can provide everything necessary for home processing. The kit I used cost $25.75, which is neither the least expensive nor most expensive you can obtain, and came from Superior Bulk Film. The black-and-white chemical kit costs about $3 from the same company and will process six rolls if everything goes according to instructions. Kodak also makes a black-and-white reversal kit that works equally well.

The Kodak kit E-4 will process the Ektachrome 160, 40 and 7242 stocks, sound or silent. As yet, there are no emulsions in Super-8 for the new E-6 kit. The breakdown cost per roll figures 50 cents for black-and-white—now that's cheap!

As I said before, as long as everything goes according to instructions, the time and cost savings are fantastic. But buyer beware if this is your first venture in home processing. The instruction sheet with my kit seemed to assume that I already knew something about processing. Since I'd been doing my own processing of still camera films for over 10 years, they were assuming correctly. For the novice, the instructions gave no hint as to correct pouring procedures (tilt the tank) or timing of the solutions. (It takes a long time to pour them out again, so practice with water to get an idea how much time is required for filling and emptying.)

The actual processing steps are very easy. Add the correct solution at the correct time, and pour it back in its container giving yourself enough time before the next step begins. Very simple. The hard part comes in loading your tank.

From Cartridge to Tank

Make sure you have handy a practice roll of the film size you'll be processing, and use it many times to practice loading your tank. Practice until you think you can do it in the dark because that's exactly where you'll be doing it. In fact, you should do some practicing in the dark also. Many things you take for granted by actually being able to see the film loading with the lights on, will become troublesome when the lights go off. I can't stress enough the importance of getting the loading down cold. This is 90 percent of the work, and if not done correctly, you'll net about 10 percent salvageable film when you finish processing.

Next, mix your chemicals. The black-and-white reversal chemicals I used were a delight to mix since all six were in liquid form. Just add water at 70 degrees, and they're ready to use. The kits that contain powders are slightly more difficult, since you'll have to allow more dissolving time whether you stir, shake or mechanically agitate the container. And *do* label your containers after mixing *each* one, not after all are mixed and you forget which concentrate was which.

Assuming all solutions are at the correct temperature and you've practiced loading your tank, you're ready to go. But first, there's one more little problem hardly anyone knows about—opening the car-

Pull film directly from the cartridge and wind it onto supply reel. Wind from supply reel to the larger developing reel in total darkness or with the tank's top in place. The tank will accept solutions much faster if filled in a slightly tilted position. Empty each solution quickly, leaving enough time to start adding the next solution on time. Take the top of the tank off to wash the film—much easier than pouring water through the tiny spout. Here's one way to dry your film. Watch for kinks, twists and emulsion abrasions.

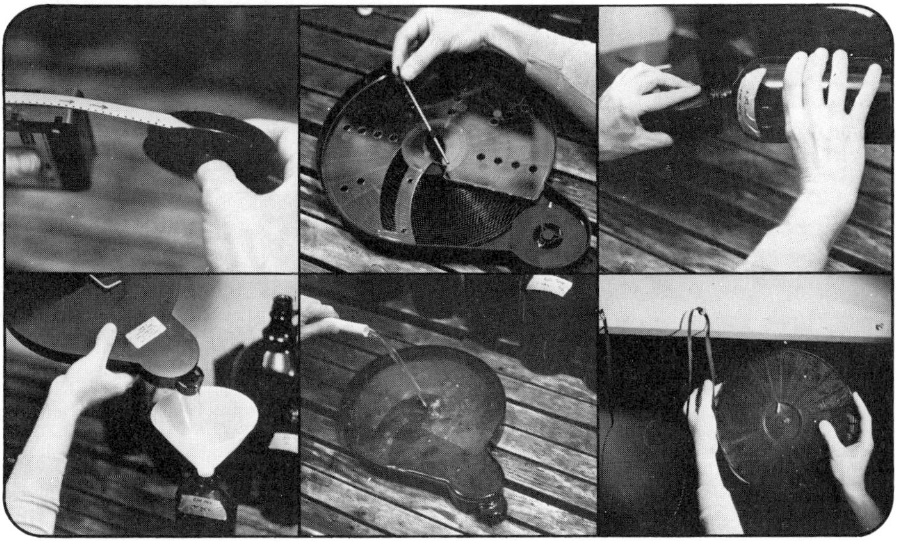

tridge. Under no circumstances should you take a hammer into the darkroom with you and whack away. This will only result in flying plastic splinters that are difficult to remove from your person in the dark, and a lot of bent film.

I found two very easy ways to open the cartridge. One, you can buy a cartridge opener from Kodak which is very expensive or from Superior Bulk Film which is quite a bit less. Two, use my quick and cheap method. I pulled the film straight from the cartridge and attached it to the 50-foot spool included with the processing tank, using my editor rewind to wind it up. The second method was under suspicion of scratching film, but every roll I processed was scratch-free. You can grab the end marked "exposed" and pull—the actual end of the film will come free of the cartridge. Now pull on this end, and you'll feel a slight resistance. Keep pulling until you hear a distinct snap and the film will then pull freely from the cartridge (see photo 1). During the winding process onto the 50-foot spool, protect against bending the film along its travel from the cartridge to the spool; that's how scratches occur. When finished, you'll have a convenient spool of exposed film on your editor rewind, in the dark, of course. The Fujica film cartridges are the easiest to open. Peel off two pieces of tape and the cartridges separate. However, their film stocks cannot be processed at home. Fuji Single-8 users can reload cartridges with Kodak black-and-white or color films to develop at home, but you may have to readjust the Fujica camera's pressure plate to accommodate the thicker film base.

Adding the Solutions

Load the film into your tank, attach the cover and turn the lights on. If you have the spiral reel type tank (such as Superior's "Daylight Tank") which separates each strand of film so chemical action is complete and even over the entire film, filling can be a problem. Try tilting the entire unit so that solutions fill faster (see photo 3). The opening provided for filling is quite small, and you have about 20 ounces of solution. This amounts to a lot of time involved in just filling. That's a lot of time before the film is entirely covered and the solution is working evenly on all the emulsion. Another problem I encountered was that the cover tended to lift under the pressure of filling solutions. Spillage and light leaks occur here. It was much easier to leave the cover off, in the dark of course, and fill first, attach cover, agitate to thoroughly wet the film, then turn the lights on. If you master this approach for the first three steps, you can then leave the cover off for the remaining steps, since they can be done in room light.

During the processing steps make some attempt at keeping solution temperatures constant with wash temperatures. It's the differences between the two that make for image problems.

In the fourth step of the black-and-white process, you'll need to remove the tank cover, if you haven't already, and re-expose the film to light. A 100-watt bulb is fine. This re-exposes the silver remaining in the film that was not developed in the first developer solution. Since there is only a certain amount of silver left, you need not worry about too much re-exposure—the bulb will re-expose only what is remaining. The second developer completes the cycle, and the steps remaining serve only to protect and preserve the image.

Briefly, I was able to work with another processing unit made by Micro Record for $198. Unlike the Superior Daylight Tank, the film is in constant motion within each solution bath in the Micro Record unit. An electric motor winds the film from the supply reel onto the take-up reel and back again while immersed in a covered tank of the proper chemical. At the end of each step, you lift the top motor unit with film attached and seat it into the next chemical tank. All very clean, no muss, no fuss. The drawback is that each step takes longer since the film is completely covered with chemical solution only during the time it is traveling from one reel to the next. Unless the full amount of time is given to each step, the possibility of uneven results and poor density characteristics is great.

Drying the Film

Drying the processed film is an equally painless operation. String a clothesline at least 6 feet long across your darkroom, and loop your film over it, making sure the emulsion side (dull side) faces up where the film crosses the line. Or loop your film over push pins stuck in a wall or bulletin board (see photo 6). Kodak suggests using a large garbage can, clean on the outside. You wrap the film around the outside with the emulsion side out and tape the two ends to prevent unraveling.

Most of the kit companies also make inexpensive drying racks.

Processing Color Film

Up to now, I've covered principally black-and-white processing, but color is also as easy. The total time in processing is practically the same. One limiting factor is cost. The Kodak E-4 for Ektachrome films (2 pint) will process four 50-foot cartridges. The kit costs about $20. Simple deduction brings us to about $5 per roll for home processing. Unless you need instant lab work or specialized effects, send it out. Another factor that is limiting other than cost is obtaining good color results. This involves strict adherence to processing time and temperature figures given in the kit instructions.

Color processing effects are largely a matter of experimentation with developer combinations or changes. This should only be attempted after fully understanding the normal process and what it does to film. Solarization is effected by exposing the film while in the first developer.

What is of primary importance is what home processing can do for you. Without a doubt, it is the best processing you can obtain since you know the lab technician and the lab's quality standards.

EDITING

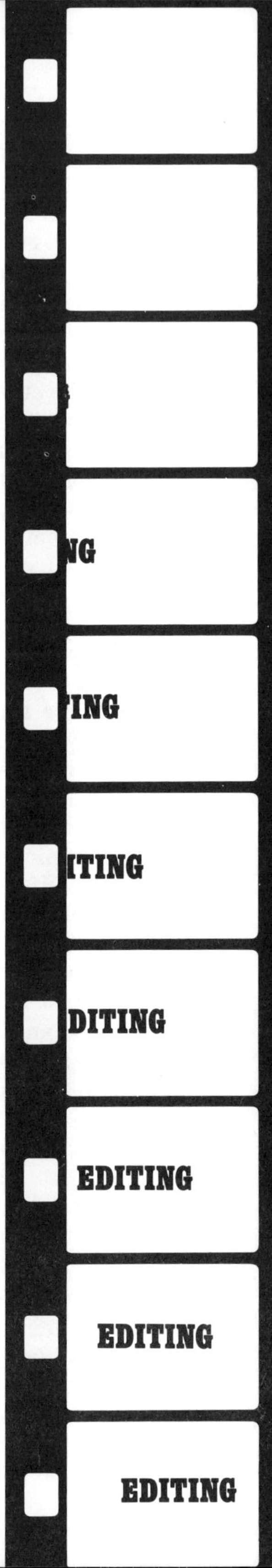
NG
ING
ITING
DITING
EDITING
EDITING
EDITING

HOW TO CHOOSE AN EDITOR-VIEWER

Eileen and Bob Zalisk

Editing is the art of creating a film out of raw footage. The process can be compared to the creation of a mosaic, which is also composed of many tiny pieces. When the pieces are cut properly, the viewer has a sense of the movement and flow of the entire composition, and is not aware of the cuts. The same magic can be produced with film. Through editing, your film can condense time or extend time, and it can convey many different moods. By giving each shot a different screen time, some shorter, others longer, you give the sequence pacing. And through editing, you give a film continuity, so that a scene flows smoothly from one cut to the next.

When you go to buy an editor, we recommend you take a roll of developed film to the store and test several viewers with it, using the guidelines we suggest in this article. Don't be bashful about testing out the unit you're thinking of buying. Because many of the technical features (bulbs, transport systems) of editors made by different manufacturers are the same, it is important for you to know how the unit "feels" to you before you buy it. By testing the unit, you can ferret out defective parts—a shutter that doesn't shut, or a roller that doesn't roll—and it is certainly more convenient to discover this before you take the unit home.

In examining editors, we have applied these criteria, which you might also find helpful: 1) The editor should not damage your film. 2) The image you see on the viewing screen should be clear enough for you to evaluate it. 3) It should be sturdy enough to stand up to repeated use.

Since most filmmakers use their editors a great deal, sturdiness is very important. This means the film reel should attach securely to the rewinds, and the unit should not wobble when the rewinds are turned. Even more important is the weight of the unit and how it is distributed. Ideally, the weight should be distributed low on the unit (it shouldn't be top-heavy), and there should be some provision to keep the editor from slipping around (i.e. good solid rubber feet).

Here's a checklist of features to look for when you shop for an editor. Take it with you when you go to the store.

1) The Reliability of the Film Transport System:

This should be constructed so as to prevent damage to your film. To assess this, look for these three things: a) the sprocket wheel should be aligned so it doesn't tear the film sprocket holes; b) the film rollers should be undercut (sloped) to prevent the film from being scratched; c) the film transport system surface should preferably be stainless steel.

2) The Quality of the Viewing Screen Image:
Don't be sold by size alone. Look for a bright, clear image. Do you want a ground-glass lens (which is sharper, but requires straight-on viewing), or a fresnel lens (which allows a wider angle-of-view).

3) Focusing and Framing Knobs:
These should be accurate and easily reachable.

4) Reel Capacity:
You'll probably want a 400-foot reel capacity if you intend to string together several cartridges.

5) Separate Set of Rewind Guide Rollers:
These allow rapid rewinding of the film, *without* having to subject it to the rigors of the film transport system. A nice plus.

6) Film Marking Device:
Look for one that does minimal damage to your film.

7) Dual-8 Capability:
If you still do a lot of work with Regular-8, this is a feature you might want to look for.

8) Film Cleaner:
Handy for keeping your film free of dust and dirt, but not necessary.

9) Frame Counter:
If you're logging original footage, or need to time cuts, this is a helpful tool.

10) Sound Monitor:
A must if you're cutting a single-system sound film.

11) The Rewind Ratio:
This refers to the gear ratio in the left-hand rewind. In general, the greater the ratio, the less time you spend rewinding.

Once you buy your unit, you can modify it to get the editor you want. One such "operation" we performed on our unit had to do with the rewinds. You've probably noticed that in 16mm editing equipment, the viewing screen and rewinds are always separate units, while in Super-8 they are usually marketed as a single editor unit. There's a reason for this: With the arms separate from the viewer and attached to an editing board, the tension on the film is more evenly distributed as it passes through the transport system. In order to get the same effect with our Super-8 editors, we removed the arms and attached them to an editing board at some distance from the viewing screen itself. It

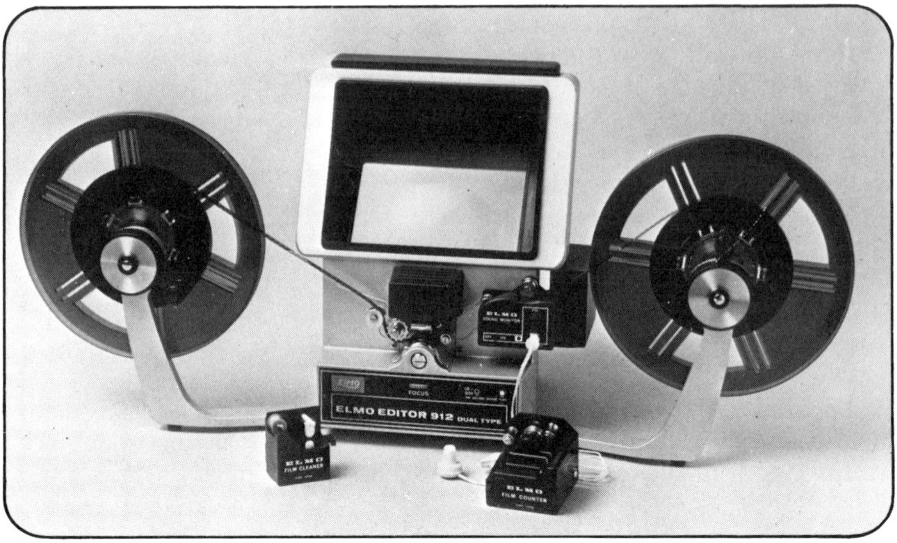

ELMO

There are many editors on the market. The Elmo 912S dual-type for sound and silent film is pictured here.

might be possible to improve editors in the lower price ranges by this kind of minor surgery.

This setup eliminates the wobbliness that often results in ripping the film out of the sprocket wheel and scratching it when winding rapidly. Since the less expensive editors are most prone to this because of their general lack of sturdiness, separating the arms would improve those units. Or you might want to replace the rewinds altogether with a more sophisticated pair (this can get to be an expensive proposition, though).

Other equipment you'll need to get your editing operation in gear include a splicer for splicing your film, grease pencils for marking scenes or cuts, small scissors for making rough cuts where precision isn't required, opaque film leader to mark the head and tail of your film, cotton editing gloves to save wear and tear on your film, and some kind of a filing system to file your film segments as you work. Once you've graduated from these editors, you might be interested in looking at a more sophisticated flatbed editing table.

Editing with an editor is easy and it can make a big difference in the final result of your film. It is the creative part of filmmaking—the art of making a film *more* than just a series of scenes spliced together. Once you edit a film, you will probably never look at another film you shoot or see in quite the same way.

ORGANIZING A BASIC EDITING BENCH

Elinor Stecker

There we were, watching my uncle's movies of Europe, when the screen suddenly went black for 3⅓ minutes. Yes, he had shot a whole roll of film with the lens cap on the camera, and he hadn't bothered to remove the black footage before showing it. I made some clever remarks about his avant-garde filmmaking, and tactfully suggested that he use a scissors.

Understandably, some people dislike cutting out film segments—black or otherwise. After all, film isn't cheap, and maybe you had to hang by your heels to get the shot, or it's a picture of your adorable off-spring. Throwing out film is the hardest thing for the novice filmmaker to do. But you have to be ruthless. Most of your home movies won't require involved editing, but they'll certainly be more enjoyable to watch if you do some corrective surgery. Take out the scenes that are over- or underexposed, out-of-focus, jiggly or much too short. Then remove (but save) all the white leader, except for that on the first reel. This "rough cut," as it's called, will improve your film immediately.

You can leave it at that, but after you've seen the improvement even moderate editing makes, you may want to go on to the creative part of editing, which involves rearranging the order of the scenes and short-ening them to the best length. Here are some basic guidelines to help make your work more efficient and your films more effective.

Rule #1: Keep the cat out of the editing room! Those nice skinny pieces of film are very enticing to felines, and you'll find chewed-up film on the floor and cat fur in your viewer if you let Morris slink around your equipment. Actually, the corner of the room you use for editing should be out of bounds for everyone in the family.

That brings us to Rule #2: cleanliness. Dust particles can damage film by scratching it, so before you start to edit, dust your work area or "editing bench," and wipe it down with a damp cloth. Do your smoking and snacking in a different place—you're entitled to periodic coffee breaks, anyway. Some people also wear cotton editing gloves when they handle film. If you can't get used to them, handle the film only by the edges.

An editor/viewer is really necessary for viewing one frame at a time, although it is possible to do this on some movie projectors. You'll also need a splicer and splicing cement or tapes (some splicers can be used with both cement and tapes); film clippers or small scissors (straight manicure scissors are excellent); 200-foot or 400-foot reels with cans; a film storage shelf; a piece of velvet or lintless cloth; film cleaner; and a can of pressurized air for blowing out dust in the gate of the viewer. You'll work more efficiently if you assemble all the small items and store them together. Finally, good lighting is extremely important.

The first step in editing is to join all those short reels of film together, probably in the order in which they were shot. Then put the film in the viewer and log every scene in your movie. An easy way to do this is on 3 x 5 index cards or lined legal pads. Number each scene consecutively, write a brief description of it, and note whether it was a long shot (LS), medium shot (MS) or close-up (CU). You may also want to note whether the camera was at an unusual angle (high or low), and if there was any camera movement, like panning from left to right or tilting up or down. If the subject crosses from one side to the other, you may want to note the direction of movement. Some people draw sketches on their film logs. You'll want your description to be as short as possible.

With your log in hand, project the film and make notes about the scenes. If a scene was out-of-focus, mark it NG (no good). If there was any camera shake, if it was an especially beautiful shot, or if it was too long, write down these facts. The quality and length of scenes are not always obvious on a small, hand-cranked viewer.

Project your film several times in order to get a good feel for it. Then, in the quiet of your editing room, think about the way you want to reorganize the film. Take the log and a red pencil, and renumber the scenes to show the order in which you want to splice them together. If you're using the index card system, you can spread the cards out and then rearrange them in their new numerical order. Then number each piece of film so it corresponds to the order in which it will be spliced into the film, and file the segments in a systematic way. One way to file them is to simply stick each length of film onto the wall or table edge with a piece of masking tape, and put the number on the tape. You can also make a rack out of narrow strips of wood with a row of headless

Figure 1: Segments of film held with dressmaker's pins pushed through the sprocket holes onto insulation board.

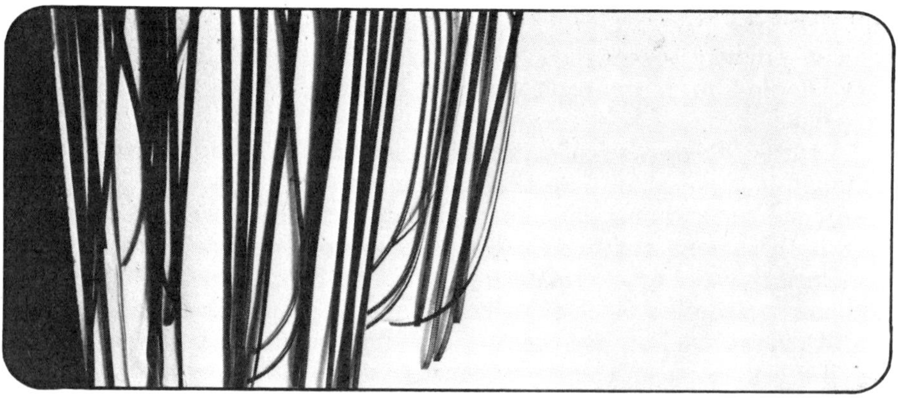

nails hammered into it. Hang the film by the sprocket holes. Editing bins lined with lintless cloth are sold for this purpose, too.

I use an editing board that is made from a 4- x 4½-foot piece of insulation board bought at a lumberyard. I smoothed the rough top edge by covering it with tape and wrote my numbers on it; the pieces of film are hung up with dressmakers' pins (these are long and have nice big heads). In any arrangement where the film is hanging, the longer lengths can be protected by covering the floor with newspaper or an old bedsheet.

Some storage systems require coiling the film—be careful not to pull on the film, or scratches known as "cinch marks" will result. You can store the film in egg cartons, plastic editing trays, or Kodak movie albums. I've taken to eating a lot of cheese since I found one brand that is packaged in round plastic boxes; the 3-inch diameter is the perfect size. Superior Bulk Film Co. sells empty regular 8mm movie cans, and they, too, are ideal. These containers are easily labeled with self-adhesive labels.

Next, take two or three feet of white leader and place it on the take-up reel of your editor. Splice all the scenes together in their new order. Don't forget the titles! Finish with another piece of leader to protect the film. With a piece of white lintless cloth or velvet folded over the film, rewind the film while cleaning it at the same time. This is especially important if you've used cement splices, since the scraped-off emulsion settles all over the film. Project the film and make notes about it—are the scenes too long? Should the order be changed? Should something be omitted?

If you want to time your scenes carefully, you may find it helpful to make a timing ruler. You can put marks on the edge of your editing bench or on a long strip of cardboard. Just mark it off into 3-inch inter-

Figure 2: Film storage systems: 1) ordinary 8mm film cans; 2) plastic cheese box; 3) cylinders cut from bathroom tissue cores; 4) egg cartons; 5) Kodak "Movie Album"; 6) 35mm can.

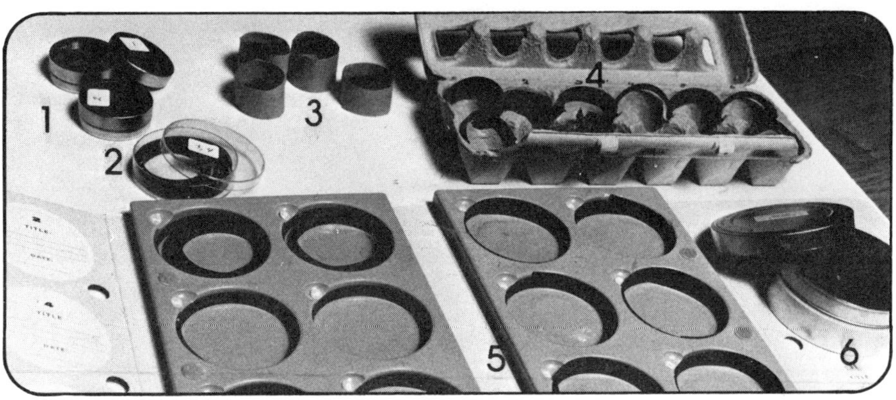

vals—3 inches equals 1 second of time at 18 fps. When you want to cut 1 second from a scene or make sure one scene is shorter than the previous one, just line up the film along the marked edge. A final and crucial step is to clean the film with liquid movie film cleaner before you store the film in a file can.

TIPS FOR BETTER SPLICING

Dennis Duggan

To make an invisible, inaudible and indestructible splice, and to do it every time, is an impossible task for most Super-8 filmmakers. Have the manufacturers let us down in this important area of our work, or is Super-8 simply an unspliceable format?

Traditionally, splicing has been used to join various shots in a work-print and later to conform the original in A and B rolls to that work-print. The end product is a splice-free duplicate from the lab. Many Super-8 workers are true to this tradition and for them, the splice is not usually a problem. Neither is it a particular challenge to the enthusiast who simply weds several 50-foot reels onto one big reel.

Many of us, however, want to produce films with professional values but lack the budget to go the traditional route. We often cut the original, project it, re-edit it, project it some more, and perhaps, if we like the result, have a print made. The splices may be just a few frames apart and are seldom more than a few feet apart. We are asking splicers to do more than they were meant to do, so we often cut our way into trouble. Let's take a look at a few of the tools that might best meet these unreasonable demands.

Tape splicing is easy and clean, and "joins" seldom break. Among tape splicers you'll find the Agfa F-8S, a sophisticated, automated splicer that uses five aligning pins and snap-locks to hold each film end in place. Its four-frame, paper-lined tape is snugged into plastic retainers and a lever-type handle is pulled down. This single motion makes the cut, peels away the paper backing, and neatly lays the tape on the film. As the handle is returned to its upright position, both sides of the film are taped securely, the snap-locks are released, and the spliced film is ejected. Four-frame coverage such as this can be visually and audibly noticeable in projection, but the ease and consistency with which the F-8S works makes it an attractive splicer. Foto 2001 distributes the Quik Splice (plastic) and the Capro (metal) which are simple but efficient splicers that also cover four frames with paper-backed tapes.

A guillotine-type splicer, such as the CIRO, uses economical, unperforated tape that comes in rolls. The splicer perforates the tape as you use it. The design of the unit, which cuts the film on the right-hand side rather than in the center, is unwieldy and not to my taste. This is a personal objection, however, and one that is not shared by many other filmmakers.

I have used the Fujica Single-8 for most of my tape splicing, and feel very much at home working with it. This sturdy metal splicer holds 100-splice rolls of perforated tape. Though a bit less automated than the Agfa, Fuji's unit is easy to handle and offers a few advantages.

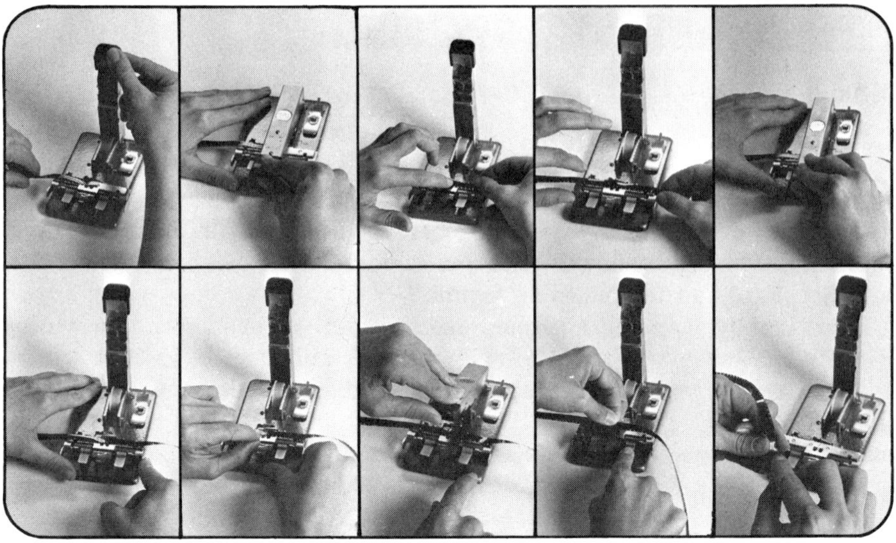

How to Make a Good Tape Splice: 1) With the Fujica Single-8 splicer (for Super-8 too), place film on cutting surface so frames to be cut extend over cutting line. 2) Draw down cutting bar. 3) Place second piece of film (to be spliced to first) on the right side of the cutting surface. 4) The second piece of film can overlap the first piece. 5) Draw down the cutting bar to cut the second piece of film. 6) Two pieces of film are now butted together in position for the splicer. Change the marker from its "film" position to its "tape" position. 7) Draw the tape across the film and press onto two film ends. 8) Cut the tape with cutting bar. 9) Push down the bar to release the film, now covered with tape on one side. Lift film with left hand. 10) Turn film over and press down tape on the other side. Splice is complete.

Because you control placement of the tape on the second side of the film, you have the option of trimming it for use with Super-8 fullcoat (magnetic film) so that the sprocket holes are covered on both sides, but the sound track is not. This splicer's small size and flexibility makes it a handy and quick film repair unit for away-from-home projection mishaps.

There are a few disadvantages in tape splicing. Some projectors will produce a wow at the sound head or lose their loop with a less-than-perfect tape splice. Using a conventional splicer, the tape covers the balance stripe area, interrupting stereophonic sound (if you've got it). However, new splicers such as the Wurker Duoplay and the Braun-Nizo FK-4 are designed for films with stereo sound tracks. These "two-track" splicers apply the tape completely over the emulsion side of the film but only between the sound stripe and the balance stripe on the base side of the film. Thus the sound tracks are left clear and the sound will be undisturbed, even in stereo.

Another problem arises if you use a vertical sound editing bench, with rewinds that were designed for larger formats. Constantly pulling tape-spliced film back and forth through the sync block tends to stretch it in both directions at once, so that a gap forms at the splice. At best, projecting film with stretched splices produces flashes of clear light on the screen. At worst, in rare cases, stretched splices can trick a projector into making its own perforations in your cherished footage. Manufacturers could at least eliminate light flash problems by printing a heavy black line down the center of the splicing tape.

Cement splicing works by first melting and then fusing or welding the frames together as they dry (not by glueing them together). Ideally, a "hot splicer," such as the one Maier-Hancock makes for 16mm and Super-8, should do this best. This sturdily constructed tool certainly does the job, but I would prefer a model specifically designed for Super-8 (with more retaining/aligning pins) and with a price tag (it's now around $300) more in keeping with the economics of our format.

Cement splices can be virtually unnoticeable and are generally recommended by most labs. The most unusual of the cement splicers is the Eumig Chemo Splicer Z01. This unit cuts the film into a zigzag pattern, creating a much greater area of contact than other cement splicers. Eumig's Special Binding Agent (which *must* be used) comes with a ladle for dispensing just the right amount (a single drop) of cement. Splices made with the Eumig system are extremely strong and flat and don't cause a "click" at the projector gate. I personally find this type of splice visually too distracting, but many people swear by it. Bolex, Hahnel and Braun each make cement splicers that scrape the emulsion from a small area of one frame, and scrape the base from the frame that's going to be spliced to it. After applying cement to the two film ends, the film ends must be joined *immediately*. The scraping action of the Bolex is manual, but with practice it can be very precise. The Hahnel and Braun units are almost identical. They both utilize a motor to spin a sapphire wheel which makes a smooth, beveled edge. After much trial and error, I have settled on J&R film cement as the best bonding agent for use with my Braun motorized splicer. It costs about $6 a pint, but it works. It seems the trick with this system is to remove *every* last bit of emulsion from one piece of film without removing *any* of the binder or base. The other piece must be scraped gently to rough up the base without actually removing it. If you don't use quite enough cement, you'll get a little air pocket in the splice and it will eventually *come apart*. If you use too much cement, the film will be weakened and eventually *break*. The cement must be fresh each time you work with it. Craig cement bottles and brushes are available, and they can be filled with just enough J&R for the work at hand. The brush, however, is designed for 16mm use and should be trimmed for Super-8 work.

You should be aware that perfect cement splices *can* be made, and when they are, they're stronger than the film itself. Most important, of course, is the quality of the film. Remember, the unkindest cut of all is not to cut at all.

NO-SCRATCH EDITING

Lenny Lipton

Although my films get screened publicly as well as in my living room, their subject matter makes them resemble home movies. My films dig into daily life and show how my friends and family are passing through this strange world. And I've learned more from home movie techniques than I have from commercial filmmakers.

Until two years ago, I had worked almost exclusively in 16mm, using the traditional approaches inherited from commercial practices. It's not that I hadn't questioned these techniques; it's simply that a large part of the time I wanted to do the same kinds of things the professionals were doing. For example, in 16mm it is usually frowned upon to cut the original camera film directly. One makes a workprint that takes a beating in the course of day-to-day editing. The original rests safely in a can on a shelf until the editing process is complete. Then it is carefully matched to the workprint and is used for printing only.

Two years ago, I asked myself if I could break away from a decade of 16mm experience and work like a home movie maker. The answer to a question like this can always be yes, if one is willing to alter the standard of quality one has gotten used to. Would the continual handling of Super-8 film cause abrasions and scratches, not to mention downright damage and destruction? What would happen to those dangerously narrow Super-8 perforations in the course of editing? How could I add to a shot I had cut too short without showing an obvious splice? I think that over the last two years I have satisfied myself on every point, and I have mastered a direct way to work with original camera film.

In the process of editing a film, I probably screen it at least a hundred times. So the first problem I had to deal with was how to prevent scratches. Where do scratches come from? If there is a burr, or raised edge, where film comes in contact with a stationary part of the projector or editing equipment, the film will get scratched. The best way to check out your equipment for a burr is to run some black leader through it. Black leader has maximum emulsion density, and any scratches will certainly be revealed. (You can make black leader yourself by covering your lens with a lens cap and shooting as much as you need.) Run the leader through the projector with the emulsion toward the lens. That's the way the camera original would be projected.

If you put a sufficiently long length of film through the projector and splice it end-to-end, you'll have a continuous loop which can be run for 5 or 10 minutes. You should be able to run such a loop through your projector for an hour without any marring or scratching. Look at the base and emulsion sides of the film through a low-power magnifying glass, and search out scratches. Suppose you find that your projector *is*

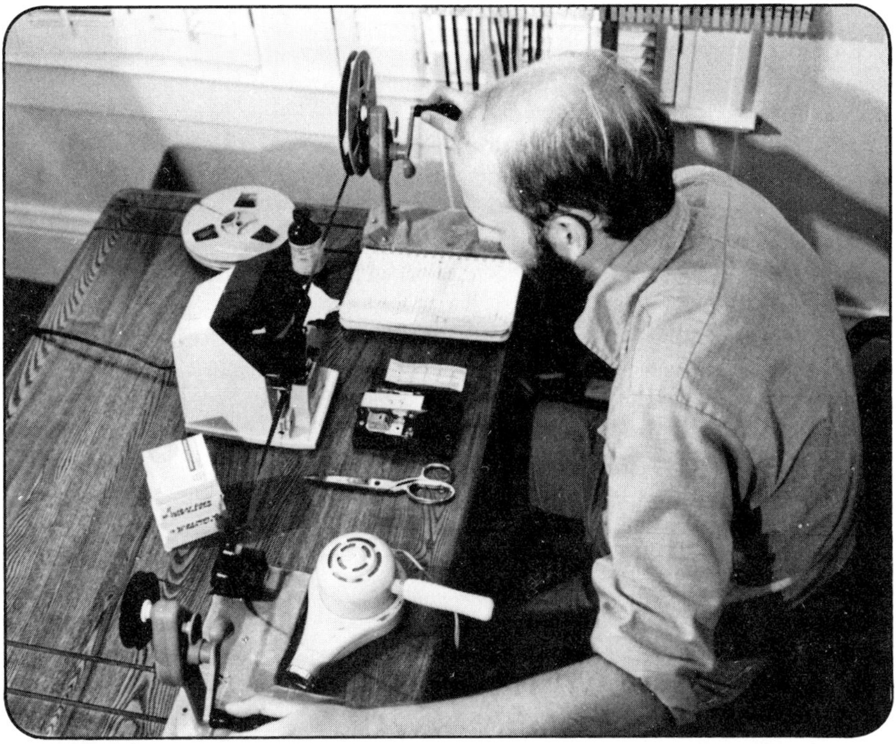

Plan ahead before and during filming so that all your shots run the right length and are in the right order.

scratching your film. It is a relatively simple matter to introduce leader into the projector and isolate the scratch-producing part. Run a few inches in, and run it out. No scratch? Well, run a few more inches in, and out, and then you can see just where the scratch begins. Usually it's in the gate. If you can remove the gate of your projector, you may be able to see the burr causing the damage.

It's curious that the same emulsion so easily damaged can be damaged by itself. If it builds up on a portion of the gate, it can and will gouge out more emulsion in a terrible cycle of emulsion build-up and film destruction. You can check for this by running the film past a clean, white cloth and see if any material comes off. If you are running a striped film, a moderate amount of brownish material from the stripe is all right. So is grey dust. Dust is a part of life and won't ruin your film. But watch out for the orange-colored stuff. That's emulsion dust, and it's killing your film.

Whether the problem is a burr or emulsion build-up, you will probably have to clean your gate. This can be done with denatured alcohol or shellac thinner, both sold at hardware stores. Moisten a cotton swab or flannel cloth with the alcohol and rub away. If the problem is a metal burr, back to the repair shop.

I also advise you to use 3 feet of Protect-A-Print leader at the head of your footage. It will clean the gate and help prevent emulsion build-up. It won't do much about dust, but dust, as I have said, doesn't cause scratches. Run the same kind of checks on your viewer. A viewer can damage film as badly as a projector.

One thing we do have to live with is auto-threading projectors. They can cause a great deal of destruction to film. You have to be very careful with them because there are hardly any other kinds. The Ektasound projectors are channel-loading, a particular kind of manual threading similar to that employed in reel-to-reel tape recorders, and these are kind to film. Whichever machine you choose, pick one with a good loop restorer. Without that, it can be curtains. Sit near your original while it is being projected, and guard your film. Always show your film on your own projector. Don't be conned into believing that somebody has a non-scratching machine, unless you test it out with black leader.

One of the most important steps I took to protect my film was to give up cement splices. They can cause a lot of wear with all the dust and grit produced as they are being made. The coarse emulsion and base particles can grind away at your film like sandpaper. Tape splicing for me has been the answer for one additional reason: Film can be added to restore a cut shot without anyone noticing the splice. Cement splices use up a frame or two when you remake a splice; this can produce an unwanted jump in the image. Not so with tape. I suggest you investigate the Guillotine plastic ($15) or metal body ($40) tape splicers, or the Fuji ($15) tape splicer (prices approximate). The Guillotine and Fuji devices make very similar high-quality tape splices that cover both sides of the film without covering the mag stripe. Only one frame on either side of the frame line is covered, for a maximum visibility, two-frame splice.

After every editing session, or after several projections, wipe your film clean with an anti-static record cloth; you may be impressed with the amount of stuff that comes off.

There are liquid preparations on the market for cleaning and lubricating your film. I personally don't use any, but you might be interested in checking out VSF 299, an anti-static solution which is especially for magnetically striped film. Write to Electro Chemical Product Corp. at 89 Walnut Street, Montclair, N.J. 07042, for information.

I haven't mentioned to you my most controversial proposal for handling film: Give up cotton editing gloves. You see, it is next to impossible to make tape splices and use cotton gloves. I clean my hands every so often with pop-up baby wipes. So help me, it works great. And the proof is in the projection.

I would also like to suggest that you get your film Peerless or Vacuumate treated. A local professional motion picture lab will take care of this for you at a low cost. These processes toughen the film and lubricate it, and work very well. Striped footage can be given the total treatment, but unstriped film that you plan to have striped must *not* be lubricated, since this can prevent binding of the stripe. The lubricating step can be performed after striping, or you can stripe the film first and go all the way with either Vacuumate or Peerless. Eastman claims that the "rail effect," or the holding of emulsion away from the base by the raised balance and record stripe, can prolong the life of the film. Maybe so, but oxide particles can accumulate between the layers, and if you cinch your film—that is, yank on the film to tighten it—it's like sandpapering it. Never do anything like this. If your film has been sloppily wound on your reel, rewind it.

Working with originals would give professionals the willies. Thank God we are not professionals with their built-in prejudices. Editing Super-8 camera film has cut my cost by about a sixth or seventh. It has forced me to make up my mind about each cut. There is a certain cleanness and clearness about working with original camera film with my naked hands that I never had in 16mm.

IN-CAMERA EDITING

Jim Piper

The subject of the one-reeler is pure home movie—two kids at the zoo with their doting grandparents. But the cutting of the film looks very professional: long shot of the kids peering over a rail; another long shot of the monkey island; a close-up of one kid squealing with delight and pointing; a tight shot of a monkey swinging by his tail; a cutaway of grandpa smiling. The shots seem to run just about the right length, and what's more, the splices are absolutely invisible. The A and B rolled print—for that's the only way you can get invisible splices—is superb.

Fooled you. Actually, this film was never strung between the rewinds of a viewer, never violated with scissors. Nor is it a print. It is simply camera stock, projected just the way it came back from the lab. It was edited, all right, but it was edited *in the camera*. That means the person who shot the film—the mother of the children—planned ahead, before filming and during filming, to take all her shots so they ran just the right length, in just the right order.

Effective camera editing saves time and money. It teaches a lot about basic shooting and cutting techniques. It helps filmmakers working with single-system sound cameras to overcome the problem of cutting when sound is displaced 18 frames from the image. But most of all, camera editing is just plain fun, a worthy challenge for filmmakers casting around for something different to do without having to spend extra money.

What Should You Camera Edit?

This doesn't mean *all* films should be camera edited, or that camera editing can always get you the same results as conventional bench editing. If you are after precise timing and calculated montage effects, you have to pay your dues with viewer and splicer. If your film calls for cuts between far-flung locations, you won't be able to shoot in sequence. Or if you're producing a theatrical film requiring careful rehearsals, you'll have to separate the good takes from the bad ones.

At the same time, if, like many filmmakers, you sometimes find bench editing tedious, and long to close the gap between the joy of shooting and the exhilaration of showing your finished film, you might consider camera editing your more casual home movies. Sure, you'll make mistakes at first, but you'll get better at it. One thing you can be certain of, however, is that your home movies will never look better.

In the past two years I've camera edited little one-reel home movies about my wife competing in a horse show, my two boys flying a kite, the demolition of an old building, my older son launching rockets, an air show, a flea market and a birthday party for a friend's daughter.

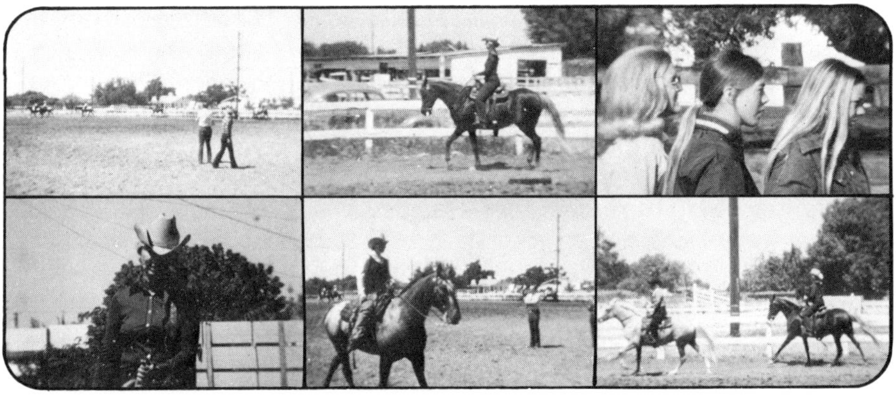

I used wide angle shots followed by tighter shots to establish setting and single out various subjects.

Why did these subjects make good bets for camera editing?

* Each event took place in a relatively contained area, so I didn't have to run around and lose concentration.
* Each event unfolded slowly enough so I could pick subjects and make camera adjustments with care.
* Each event offered opportunities for varied coverage, which is what every editor needs to produce interesting footage.
* I was vaguely familiar with what and where things would happen at each event, so I was able to plan ahead.

Coverage

Your first job is to decide what to shoot and what subjects to include in your movie. Recently, when I shot a one-reeler of my wife competing in a horse show (see sequence pictured), I decided beforehand to get footage of not only my wife (the principal subject) on her horse, but also of the other horses and riders, the judge and ring stewardess, the announcer and the spectators. Secondary subjects like these lend flavor to your movies, and, as we shall see, often rescue you from continuity problems.

About proportion: The equestrian event, I knew, would run some 20 minutes, including the passing out of the ribbons. Before I started shooting, I planned to devote about 40 feet (of my 50-foot Super-8 cartridge) to the action in the arena, and 10 feet to the passing out of the ribbons.

Sequencing

Now comes your first challenge: deciding on the order of shots. To begin, you'll probably want to establish a sense of the overall setting. That's why my first shot was a wide shot—to show the arena, the judge, and the horses and riders (see shot 1 in sequence). Next, you'll want to take tighter shots to reveal more detail and frame your various subjects individually. So if you look at my next four shots (2, 3, 4 and 5), you'll see that they frame my wife, some spectators, my wife again in a tighter shot (to remind viewers that *she* is my principal subject), and the judge looking at another horse and rider. This pattern—an establishing wide shot followed by tighter shots—is commonly used by film editors for orienting viewers in space. But the reverse pattern often creates greater interest: tight shots of gifts, kids smiling, and a cake, followed by an explanatory wide shot of a backyard and a birthday party in progress.

The next three shots of my equestrian movie (6, 7 and 8) go together and require explanation. Note that in shot 6 my wife and horse are traveling right to left. Between takes the judge signaled for the horses to change directions, so shot 8 shows my wife's horse moving left to right. But if these two shots had occurred in sequence, I would have produced a *jump cut*, that is, a sudden, jarring leap of the subject, as if action had been omitted. Sensing this problem, I shot a brief *cutaway* (shot 7) of the announcer before taking shot 8, thereby giving the effect that the announcer was calling for the horses to change directions.

You'll find that it's pretty hard to avoid a jump cut if you shoot the same subject in successive shots from about the same camera position and lens focal length. If you don't have a cutaway readily available, you can avoid a jump cut by panning away from the subject until it leaves the frame at the tail of the first shot, or by changing camera positions or the focal length of the lens (say, from wide angle to telephoto) before taking the second shot.

The alert camera editor looks for ways to sequence his or her shots

I shot a brief cutaway (shot 7) of the announcer.

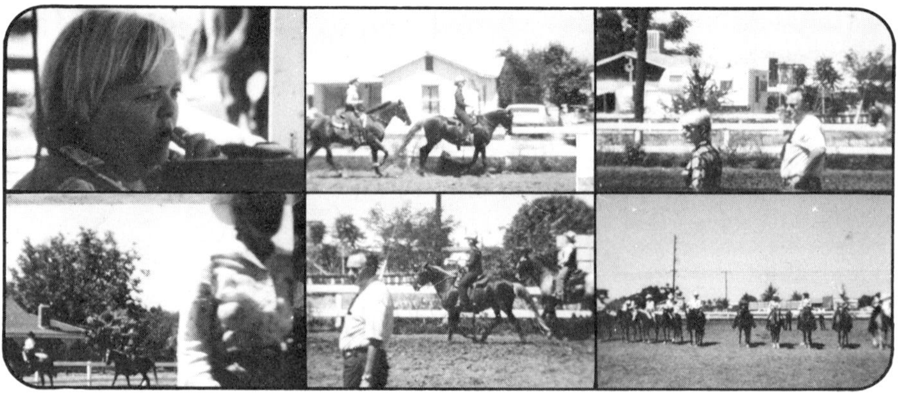

so they tell stories, or at least produce a little drama. I hoped to do this in shots 12 through 17, dealing with the final judging before the passing out of ribbons. The horses are lined up (shot 12) as the judge looks them over one last time (shot 13) before marking his score card. After the first shot of the judge (shot 13), I snuck in a cutaway of my wife (shot 14); after the second shot of the judge (shot 15), I cut away to an interested spectator awaiting the judge's decision. The purpose of these cutaways was to prolong the drama and create more interest. Shot 17 shows the judge walking past the horses to turn in his score card to the announcer.

Managing Time

Now look at the sequence of shots 18-22: The announcer calls out a ribbon winner (18), my wife (19-21) receives her ribbon, and spectators applaud (22). This sequence seems to happen in a continuous flow of time, and all the action seems related. Actually, things moved too fast for me to take the three shots in sequence, so I had to fudge a little. The announcer is really calling out the first place winner; my wife took a third. And the crowd is applauding the fourth place winner. Because I knew the passing out of ribbons would involve repetitive, predictable action, I could plan ahead and take only portions of three cycles of announcing/ribbon receiving/applauding. So what really took several minutes to happen, I condensed to 15 or 20 seconds on the screen.

You can also make time appear to pass more quickly by creating purposeful discontinuities of action. Example: In my kite film, I took a wide shot of my boy running with the kite, trying to get it in the air. I followed that with a close-up of him standing still, smiling and looking at the sky. Cut to the kite, fluttering aloft. The cut from running to standing suggests a passing of time, and the change from wide shot to close-up avoided a possible jump cut.

For the final judging, cross-cutting from judge to wife and spectators prolongs the drama.

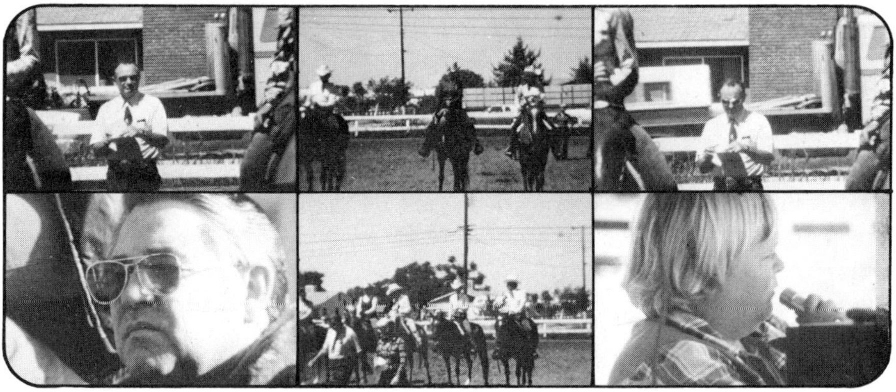

A good time to use your camera's fading or dissolving feature—if so equipped—is at these junctures that suggest leaps in time.

Cutting

It's not easy to sense when to start and stop a shot. Think of the action: Overall, is it flowing, graceful and unhurried, like the equestrian event? Then longer running shots might be in order. Or is the action fast-moving, erratic and shocking, like a football game? If so, a series of brief shots (1-2 seconds) might be appropriate.

Often you can use the completion of a natural action as a guide to cutting. Thus the judge looks up at the announcer and holds up a finger as a signal for the horses to change directions—cut. Or the ball carrier is hauled to the ground and the referee blows his whistle—cut. If the action has no clear-cut conclusion, such as with shoppers in a flea market, then 3 or 4 seconds is usually long enough to let the shot run, unless you're deliberately trying to create a leisurely effect. Cutaways to secondary objects seldom need to run more than 2 or 3 seconds.

If you're shooting single-system sound, you may want to let audio rather than visual events dictate cutting points. For instance, when I shot the air show (in sound), my mic picked up the announcer (off camera) as I shot. I often waited until the announcer had completed a sentence before cutting the shot, even if it meant filming action I didn't especially want. In general, I find when camera editing during single-system shooting, my shots have to run longer to avoid chopping up the sound track.

Using the Zoom Lens

Maybe you've wondered how I managed to take the various close-ups and cutaways of my wife, the spectators and the judge if I couldn't move my camera inside the arena to get close to these subjects.

This sequence seems to happen in a continuous flow—actually I had to fudge a little.

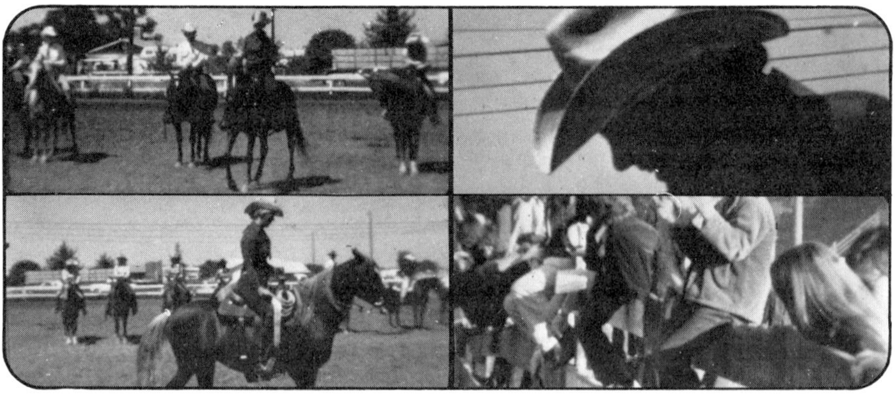

Simple. I took these shots in telephoto, which, as you know, makes distant subjects appear close. That's the great thing about zoom lenses—they allow you to shoot at a variety of focal lengths. The abrupt cuts from wide angle to telephoto, and back, give the impression that you are moving constantly, setting up each shot from a new angle and distance. In fact, you're positioned comfortably and calmly in the same place, alternating between wide-angle shots and telephoto shots. Zooming from one focal length extreme to the other destroys this all-over-the-place illusion, because viewers can see that the zoom starts and finishes from the same camera position.

Technical Matters

Naturally, if you want steady telephoto shots, you'll have to use a tripod. The tripod gives you a place to park your camera, freeing your hands, and maybe your brain, so you can think ahead.

In fact, you'll want to be free from technical hassles so you can concentrate on sequencing and cutting. That's why I always try to set up and shoot with the sun at my back: I have fewer exposure problems that way, and I can let my camera's automatic exposure system take over. I also try to avoid contrasty shooting situations when possible.

I seldom focus because I exploit Super-8's great depth of field in wide angle. Before shooting, I preset the focusing ring at the most workable range for telephoto shots. This may make more sense to you if you consult a depth-of-field chart and note how range of acceptable focus increases as focal length decreases. To make a long story short, this means you can follow-focus on a subject moving toward you by simply zooming out. You never have to touch your camera's focusing ring and risk jiggling your camera.

I realize that not everyone likes to shoot this way, stuck behind a tripod, constantly thinking, suppressing a desire to improvise.

Maybe these filmmakers shouldn't camera edit at all. For many people (including myself often), shooting should be free and spontaneous, like fooling around with a guitar. But in-camera editing requires a different frame of mind—a more cerebral and considered posture toward the craft of filmmaking. The camera editor has to be more like the bench editor than the jazz guitarist. But the great thing about filmmaking is how it calls on the whole range of sensibilities at one time or another. Who can say one approach is better than another?

ANIMATION

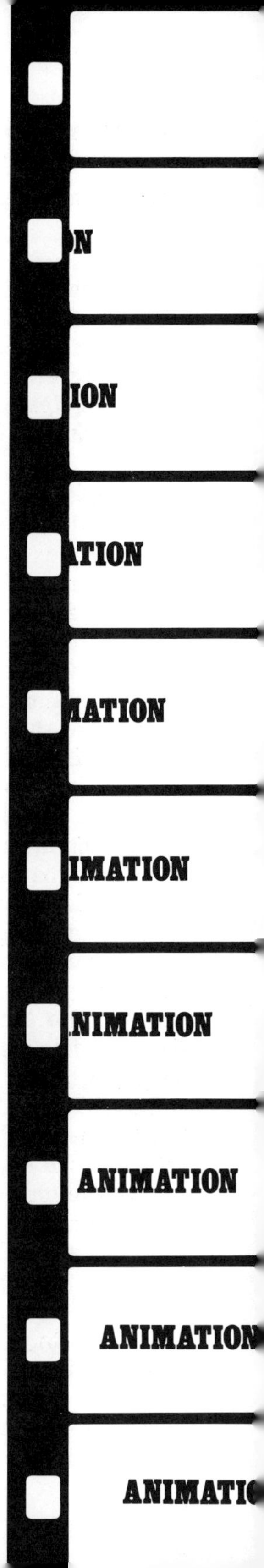
ANIMATION

SETTING UP FOR BASIC ANIMATION

Yvonne Andersen

As a teacher of animation, I receive letters from adults and children which read: "I can draw pretty good and I know how to animate cut-out characters, but I don't know how to operate my camera. Please help me!" In an effort to ward off a lot of near-tragedies, I'll describe the proper equipment and the step-by-step procedure for setting up a Super-8 camera for animation.

Equipment

CAMERA: Your camera should have the ability to take single frames; reflex viewing (what you see through the eyepiece is what you get); the equivalent of reflex focusing through the lens, or split-image focusing; and be capable of fastening to a tripod.

If your camera does not have these features you can still make animated movies, but you will have to spend a lot of time experimenting with focus and the position of the artwork, as well as tapping the trigger to take short bursts of frames.

TRIPOD: Your tripod should be strong and sturdy and able to tilt straight down and in all directions, as well as hold the camera steady. I prefer the Quick Set Husky brand tripod because it can hold Super-8 as well as 16mm cameras. However, there are some others such as Welt/Safe-Lock that serve well for Super-8 cameras.

CABLE RELEASE: Most of the cable releases that come with cameras are fragile and not built for a lot of animation. They are also very uncomfortable to use for a long period of time. You should get a good one, and be sure that it works on your camera. One end of it screws onto the camera, and the other end is handheld between the first two fingers. The end is pressed with the thumb. It should have a large grip.

CLOSE-UP LENSES: A set of diopters should be purchased to fit your camera. These are a set of supplementary close-up lenses which attach to the front of your camera's normal lens in order to increase the size of the image. A diopter set comes in threes, usually +0, +1 and +2. The higher the number, the greater the magnification. Most of the time you will only need one diopter. I use +0 with my Nikon, +2 with my Bolex 280 Macrozoom, and +2 with my Nizo. If you didn't purchase a set with your camera, take it to the store to be fitted if you're unsure of what to buy.

Many Super-8 cameras cannot focus closer than 4 feet from a subject unless a close-up lens is on the camera. Some macrozoom cameras can film very close to the subject but can't cover a wide area of art in the macro position.

Plan to set up the camera so that when the lens is at wide-angle position, it will cover an area of artwork about 11 inches x 14 inches wide. The camera will be about 20 inches away from the artwork.

LIGHT STANDS: Get two light stands and two reflectors. I like the Acme flylight stand and the Acme 10Sl reflector. You could use inexpensive reflectors with clamps and fasten them to chairs, but I think this arrangement is clumsy.

FILMING TABLE: I use a child's small table with a work top of about 18 inches by 20 inches. It should have sturdy legs and be painted flat black, so as not to reflect light.

Setting Up for Animation

1) Fasten the camera to the tripod.

2) Focus the eyepiece to suit your own eyesight. Follow directions in your instruction manual.

3) Screw the close-up diopter onto the front of the camera lens.

4) Load the cartridge in the camera. I use Kodachrome 40 most of the time. This requires BBA #1 light bulbs for the light stands. (These bulbs are 3400 degrees K color temperature, 250 watts.) If we are in a hurry we can get 2-hour processing in Boston of Ektachrome EF film. When we use this we have to use ECA bulbs (3200 degrees K, 250 watts). Kodachrome 40 is preferable because prints are less grainy.

5) Check the camera batteries, as per the instruction manual.

6) Put the filter key in the camera. Super-8 color films are basically designed for use with movie lights indoors. Since most of the cameras are built with an orange filter in place behind the lens, you can use these films outside. However, if you are going to film inside, push the filter key into the slot to remove the filter. Some cameras have a dial instead, with two symbols on it—a sun and a light bulb. Turn the dial to the light bulb for indoor animation with lights.

7) Take a sheet of heavy white paper the same size as your artwork. Draw a black line down each side and across the top and bottom about

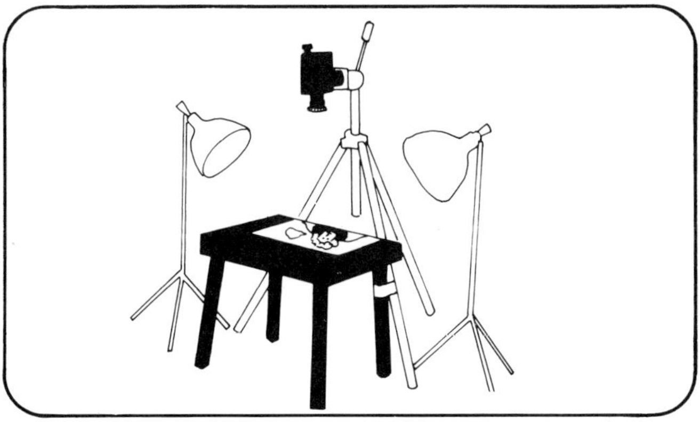

I use a child's small table with a work top 18 X 20 inches, painted non-reflective black.

¾ inch from the outside. Take a pen and make a series of vertical strokes in the middle of the paper. Fasten this paper down to your filming table.

8) Set up your camera facing down at the paper, with the lens set to wide angle. When you look through the eyepiece you want to just barely see the black lines you have drawn on the four sides. Jack the camera up and down on the tripod until it is in the right position. Setting up the camera this way will show you if the camera is exactly vertical, and it is an insurance against the fact that most Super-8 cameras shoot a little more on all four sides than what you see through the viewfinder. If your table is black, and the camera includes a little of the table in the frames, it will not be very noticeable when projected.

In setting up your tripod, you will have to shorten the two front legs a few inches so that they are almost vertically in line with the table legs. They should also be braced against the front of the table.

9) Zoom in toward the center of the paper where you have drawn the lines. When you are all the way in to extreme telephoto, focus on these lines by twisting the focusing barrel of the lens. If you have split-image focusing, your vertical lines will be broken in the middle if you are out of focus.

When you are focusing, zoom back out to your wide-angle position. Sometimes you'll find that the camera sees more than it did before. If this is the case, jack the camera down a few inches and try focusing all over again. You may also find that you are using the wrong diopter for artwork of that particular size. If this is the case, change the diopter; one of them will work. You may have to jack the camera up and down a little to get the right focus. After you have focused in the close-up position, the camera will stay in focus when you zoom back, as long as you have not changed its height.

10) Tape the artwork to the table. Also tape the front legs of the tripod to the table, and tape the back leg to the floor. We use a wide, grey tape for this called carpet tape or gaffer's tape. Be sure the camera is tight on the tripod and that nothing has moved out of position.

11) Fasten the cable release to the camera.

12) Turn off all the lights in the room except for your light stands. Set up one of these on each side of your table, with the reflector at a 45-degree angle, so that the surface of the art is lit evenly.

13) Most Super-8 cameras have an electric eye, which sets itself according to the film in the camera. In this case there is nothing more you have to do before filming. Some cameras, when single framing, require you to take a light reading by looking through the eyepiece at the artwork. You will see numbers and a pointer inside. Manually set the diaphragm according to the number you see indicated by the pointer.

Some cameras enable you to override the electric eye so that you can make a scene lighter or darker. In animation this is important if you have a scene that contains a lot of black. For example, if you have a

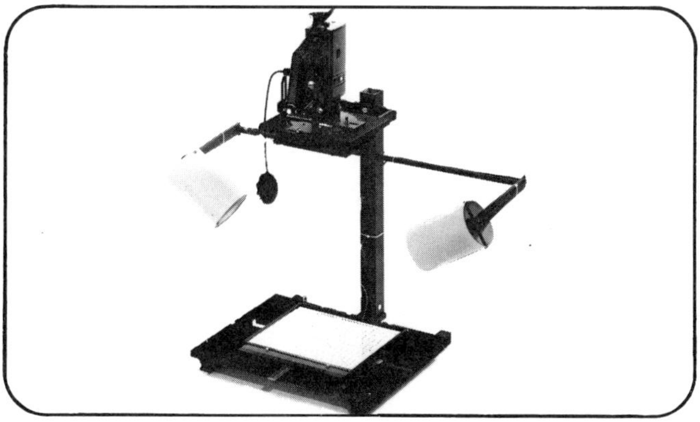

This professional animation stand from Oxberry offers moveable elements for precise and professional animation.

black night sky and a small spaceship moving by, your camera's electric eye will think it's in darkness and strain to open up to see more, which is impossible since you intend to shoot a black object. If you film this scene without setting the exposure manually, the scene would be overexposed after processing.

Place a grey card—a neutral grey test card manufactured by Kodak for determining exposure under artificial light—or anything of a medium color on top of the artwork. In this way you can determine what your "average" exposure should be under your shooting conditions. Look through the eyepiece and note where the pointer is. Perhaps average artwork reads as 5.6, but the black scene reads as 2. In this case, freeze the pointer at the position the medium-colored card reads, 5.6; be sure to follow your instruction manual for doing this. Now you can film the black scene, and it will return from the lab looking very black and rich.

14) If you are filming with a new cartridge, shoot 48 frames before the important animation starts. This is in case the lab happens to mess up the opening length of film in your cartridge.

15) Start filming. In Super-8 we usually shoot 3 frames for every change in facial position. A walking person is moved forward 1/4 inch every 3 frames, and a running person is moved 1/2 inch or more every 3 frames.

Setting up really isn't difficult at all, and it's amazing how much difference a little care will make in your finished film. Now there's no need to yell "Help!" the next time you shoot an animated epic.

INTRODUCTION TO PIXILATION

Yvonne Andersen

Have you ever been watching a film that begins with a medium shot of a man who appears to be driving down a street, and suddenly discover, when the camera pulls back, that there is no car, and the man is driving along on the seat of his pants? That's *pixilation.*

Very simply, pixilation is the single-frame shooting of people, or of people interacting with objects. It creates an unreal, whimsical effect because it unnaturally speeds up normal movement.

In filming the scene we just described, for example, the actor moves forward a few inches at a time, and the camera shoots a few frames of each position. When projected at 18 or 24 frames per second, the movement appears to be continuous.

You can make absurd things happen in pixilation, because you have almost as much control over events as you do in animation. What you are actually doing is turning a live actor into an animated character.

In the film *Fat Feet*, directed by Red Grooms, and filmed by myself, there is a street scene with cardboard cars, live pedestrians, drivers and a painted city backdrop. The cars, flat cut-outs about three-quarters actual size, are painted on heavy cardboard.

The driver sits behind the cut-out car so that we can see his head through the window, and the camera shoots four frames. The actor then moves the car forward a few inches. An assistant runs into the scene to turn the hubcaps of the car slightly, then runs out of the scene. The camera takes four frames, etc.

In the scene pictured here, Arthur DeTore drives a cardboard car through the city streets. Dominic Falcone, the policeman, stretches out his hand to stop traffic. Because of the stop-action nature of the filming, we were able to gradually lengthen the arm of the policeman until it was about 6 feet long.

We made the hand by stuffing a glove, wiring it onto a stick and covering it with a sleeve. The whole contraption was hidden up Dominic's coat sleeve. He held onto it, and during the filming, an assistant pulled the fake arm out a little bit at a time.

With pixilation you can also film interaction between large puppets and live actors. In the film, *Plague*, by Amy Swartz, 14, we see a cranky old lady talking to some children. She begins to harangue them in a crackly voice: "You're always trying to change things! Why don't you leave everything the way it was!" Then, with a flash of lightning, she changes them into old people who sit in chairs behind her.

The old lady was made of chicken wire covered with papier-mache, which was then painted. She wears a real sweater and has fake hair from an old Halloween wig. Amy shaped the eyes and lips out of colored plasticine so she could change their shape every few frames to give the effect of the old lady speaking. The actors who were in scenes with her had to hold their positions between shots so that Amy could run into the scene and change the shapes of the mouth and eyes.

You can also make pixilated films using real scenery, either indoors or outdoors. Most of our pixilated films use painted backgrounds, costumes and props. Our backgrounds are painted on heavy white background paper which can be purchased by the roll from theatrical supply houses.

When we are working with children, we frequently make the costumes out of white butcher paper. We just staple the pieces together and paint the paper. We use makeup on the faces, or make masks from paper bags or papier-mache. The props are cut out of heavy cardboard.

If the scene you're doing doesn't require interaction with an inanimate object (as in Amy's film), and you simply want to change the pace of the scene from normal speed to a more magical tempo, you can have the actors walk very slowly through the scene, with the cameraman single-framing them.

The faster the single-framing, the more closely the action will resemble normal speed when it is projected; the slower the single-framing, the faster and more frantic the action will be. When the thumbs of the camera people get tired, they can yell FREEZE! The actors should hold their positions until the camera people are ready to start again.

Coffin Child, by Mark Weiner, 16, is a good example of this kind of filming. The setting is a room with a window, and a coffin in the middle of the floor. As an animated sun sets in the window, Count Dracula slowly rises from his coffin (extending his claws over the side, of course). Once he has risen to his full stature, he hops over the side, stopping to change the sign on his coffin from "The Count Is In" to "Out For a Bite," and dances off. Pixilating this scene gives it an unreal, eerie look.

We usually have two cameras covering big scenes. The first camera catches the long shot or overall action, the second gets the crucial

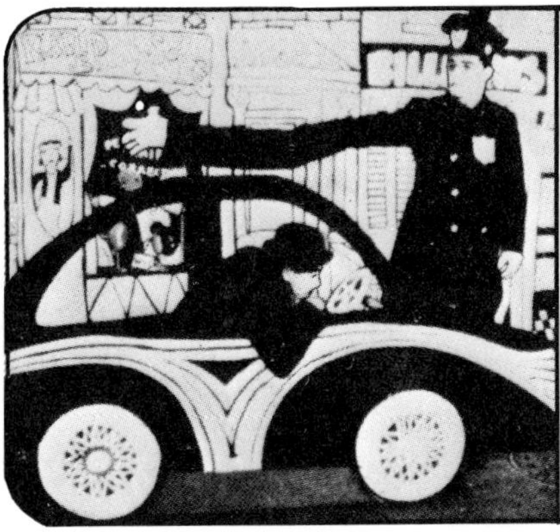

With stop-action filming, the "long arm of the law" was gradually lengthened.

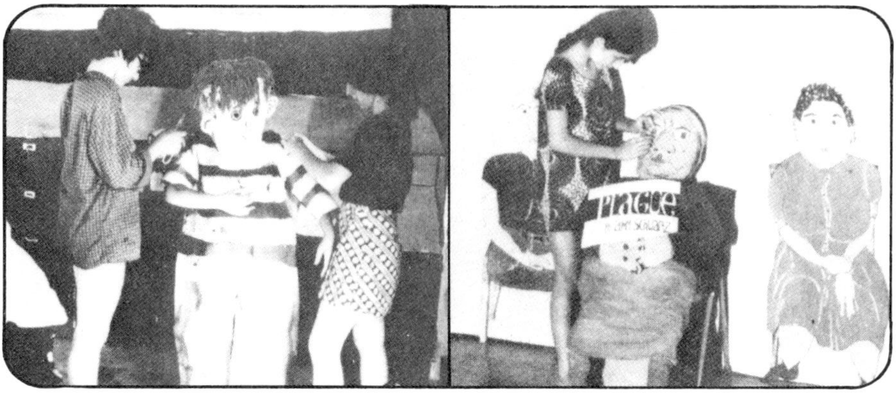

Between frames the plasticine eyes and lips of the crabby old lady are reshaped to give the effect of her speaking. Make costumes out of white butcher paper—just staple the pieces together and paint with poster paint.

close-ups and medium shots. In *Coffin Child*, the camera moves close up when Dracula's hand turns over his sign to say "Out For a Bite."

We usually have a rehearsal before shooting, with the camera operators watching the action through the lens. Then the actors walk through the scene very slowly, and we do a take. Of course, all this is silent filming. The music, effects and voices are put on afterwards.

We enjoy making pixilated films because it's fun to make big sets, and it gives our animators a chance to be actors.

CLAY ANIMATION

Yvonne Andersen

A clay bus rolls over a clay hill and screeches to a stop. The bus door opens and a horde of screaming children pours out. The bus driver, much relieved to be rid of the little devils, wipes his brow and melts into the ground. Screaming with exuberance, the clay children run through an archway. Above the archway we read the words, *KRAZY TIMES ZOO.*

Clay is a fascinating medium to work with. It is sensual to handle and look at, and it has the ability to shrink, grow and flex. We found that in close-ups even the press marks and fingerprints look good.

Though I have been using the term *clay animation*, the medium we actually use is Plastilina, a soft, grey-green, nonhardening substance. We get ours at Newton Potters, 96 Rumford Ave., Box 96, West Newton, Mass. 02165. It's called Plastilina #2, and comes in 2-pound wrappings at about $2 each. The order number is 20111. There are cheaper grades of Plastilina, but this grade is softer, easier to manipulate and holds up longer.

Our ground surfaces are sheets of ¼-inch plywood, 24 by 32 inches square, covered with a Plastilina landscape. The backgrounds are either solid black velvet paper or a second sheet of plywood covered with Plastilina.

Three-dimensional animation is a lot of fun, but it takes more time than flat animation and requires more storage space for your characters and sets. The time factor is related to lighting and focusing. Since the characters cast shadows, they have to be rehearsed a bit to determine how to set the lighting. We generally use four or six lights instead

In close-ups of clay characters even the press marks and fingerprints look good.

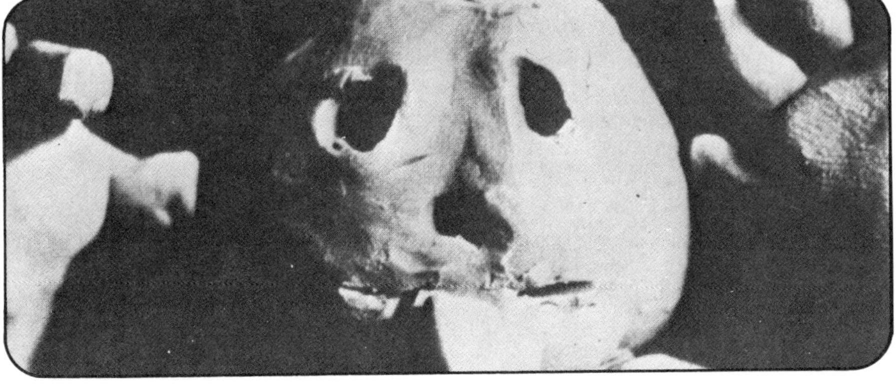

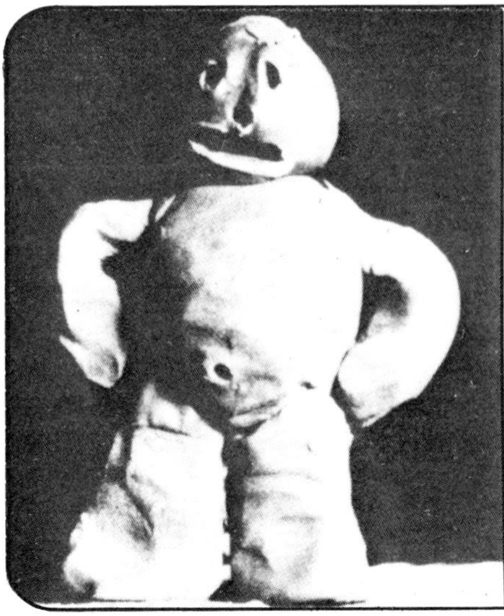

Clay figures can be made to shrink, grow and flex.

of the two normally needed for flat animation. Also, the characters do not remain a fixed distance from the camera, but move toward and away from it. You must determine where you want the focus to be sharp and how much depth of field you want (*i.e.*, which parts of the scene should be in focus and which should appear blurred). Depth of field varies according to the light available, the lens opening you use, the focal length of your lens and the camera-to-subject distance. I like to include some shots in which a character's face is seen sharply in close-up and the background is blurred.

We have also animated with colored Plastilina. This gives pleasing results, but you have to be more careful when manipulating the characters, since the colors tend to spread into each other.

When shooting clay animation, we take four frames for every ¼-inch movement, as this seems to give us the best results for the least work. Also, we find that a lot of movement is not so necessary if your characters look interesting enough. Sometimes just enough movement to keep the characters alive is enough.

After you have made your film, you can scrape the Plastilina off the boards, ball up the animals and people and put the entire setup into a covered container. Next year, when you're ready to make another clay animation, you can open the container and form a whole new cast and landscape.

SAVING MONEY ON CEL ANIMATION

Carl Lamm

Nothing in this world is sadder than the face of a would-be cel animator in a film supply store. That 3-minute cartoon he so lovingly storyboarded will require roughly 2,000 cels. At $30 to $50 for a box of 200, he is faced with a bill as high as $500 for cels alone. Frequently, he gives up in despair and goes back to cut-outs, puppets, pixilation or other animation techniques. Don't despair. You don't have to knock off your rich uncle to afford cel animation. With a little ingenuity, you can create professional-quality animation at a fraction of the cost professionals pay.

Start saving money by cutting that mammoth cel bill by over 80 percent. The cel, a clear sheet of acetate plastic, is the heart of the drawn film. Since the oil embargo of 1973, the price of these prepunched animation cels—a by-product of the petrochemical industry—has skyrocketed. But you can beat the system by going straight to a stationery store for a box of "Sheet Protectors," clear folders designed to cover student reports. Made of acetate plastic, Sheet Protectors come in the same gauge as animation cels, .005, are punched with three holes and measure twice the standard size of 8½ by 11 inches. And the cost? Depending on where you live, you will pay $7 to $8 for a box of 100 covers, which can be cut in half to make 200 8½- by 11-inch cels. Now the cels for that 3-minute film will cost less than $80, an appreciable savings.

Of course, professional cels do provide better quality than the ones you improvise. If you hold a Sheet Protector at an angle to a bright light, you will notice thin lines running across the sheet. These linear imperfections will not affect the image you paint on the acetate, but they will necessitate careful positioning of lights to avoid picking up the pattern in filming.

Another drawback to Sheet Protectors is the loss of an inch or more around each side of the acetate, which cuts down the size of your camera field. This will be no problem if you purchase an animator's field guide, which lets you calibrate the exact field your camera will be able to film. You can copy a guide from an animation book or go to a film supply house such as Heath Productions, which sells unpunched guides for $6. A guide is absolutely necessary if you plan close-ups and pan shots. But if you don't want to bother, you could avoid the whole problem by buying Sheet Protectors in the 9- by 12-inch or the 11- by 14-inch size. The larger sizes are a bit more expensive, however.

Even cheaper than Sheet Protectors are unpunched "Report Covers," which come in the same sizes but in a thinner gauge. These are a bit more difficult to work with, because of the thinness, and require you to buy a three-hole punch for roughly $10 at any office supply or stationery store.

Once you have bought the acetate covers of your choice, you will have to cut them in half along the fold. Scissors or an X-acto knife will do the job easily, if not quickly. Be careful to protect the sheets once you have cut them, since acetate scratches and picks up dirt easily. It's a good idea to slip a piece of paper between each cel to prevent scratching when they're stacked together.

Now you'll have to make your own peg bars to fit the holes in your improvised cels. Using one of your cels, mark the holes on an 8-inch length of balsa wood and cut shallow holes in the balsa with a knife. Sand wooden dowels to fit the registration holes in your cels, making sure they don't end up too small (cels will jiggle) or too large (cels will tear). Wedge the finished dowels in the holes you made in the balsa wood, fix with heavy duty wood glue and shellac the entire peg bar. The thickness of your peg bar will depend on your animation board, but I find that ½-inch balsa wood works well and will not warp. Since most homemade animation boards are made from ¾-inch plywood, you can probably cut ½-inch grooves in the plywood to make the peg bar flush with the board. If necessary, use a thinner bar and shallower grooves, but beware of warping.

Now that you have cels, a peg bar and some sort of board, the next menace to your budget is animation paint. Most pre-mixed professional animation paints cost over $1 an ounce and come in 2-ounce squeeze bottles. A wide selection of colors is available.

If your cartoon requires a lot of colors, as most do, you can save a bundle by purchasing your paint in the hardware department of a large discount store. Look for acrylic latex paint, which adheres to acetate plastic just like the real thing. The smallest amount available is usually ½ pint, which holds 4 fluid ounces and costs $1.50 to $2. When the thick acrylic latex is diluted, you end up with about 6 ounces of paint,

Figure 1: Fit dowels in balsa to make a custom peg bar.

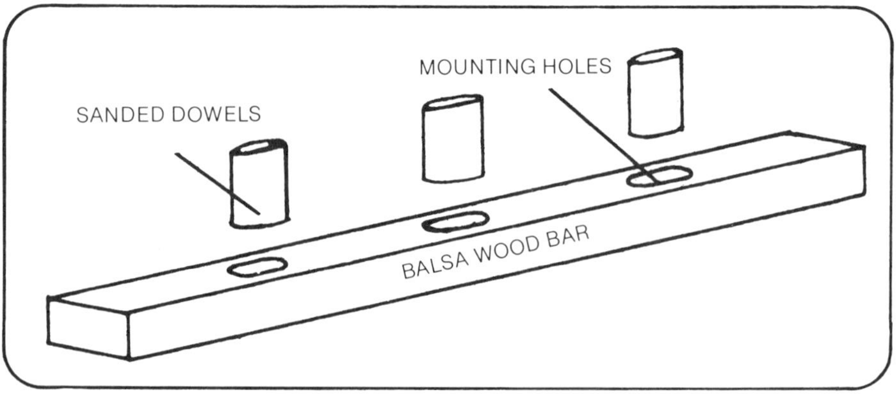

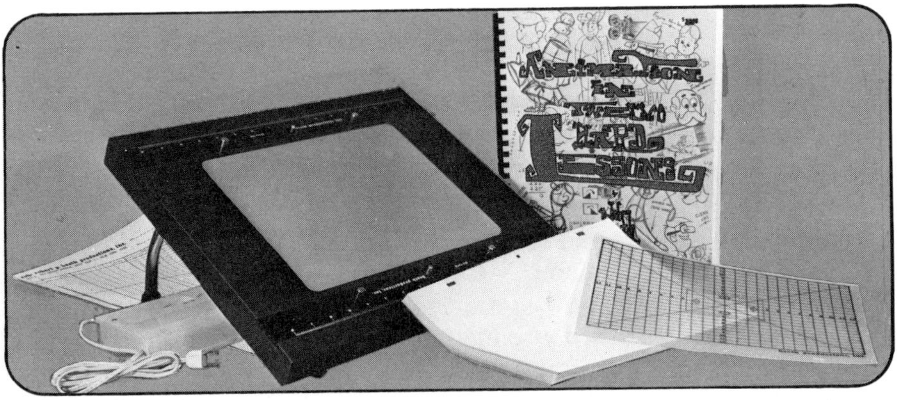

This "correspondence course" in cel animation by Heath Productions will develop your professional techniques.

costing less than one-third the price of professional animation paint.

However, you have to do a little work to earn your savings. Diluting paint requires care. If you overdo it, the paint will become transparent when dry. Leave it too thick and the image will be distorted.

Hardware store paint comes in a limited number of shades, so you'll also need to mix your own colors. Experiment with different mixing ratios and write down the formula when you find a good mix, so you can use that color again. Your drugstore or dime store will stock cheap, plastic squeeze bottles for storing mixed paints. Label the bottles with the mix ratio. Over time you will build your own palette of colors.

Another problem with cheap solution is "flicker," the bane of most amateur animation. A flicker effect is caused by electrical appliances changing power needs, which in turn cause small changes in the amount of voltage getting to your movie lights. The camera can pick up changes in light too small for the eye to see.

Professional animators spend over $1,000 for motors which, among other things, keep the amount of voltage coming through the line at precisely the same level. You can buy a similar device for under $10. The "Electric Outlet Control Panel," manufactured by Rogers Co. of New York, can be found in most hardware and discount stores. The rectangular device contains a fuse box and four to six electrical outlets. Plug your photo lights into the panel and warn your family not to turn appliances on or off while you're filming. Voltage control is not perfect, but the device will minimize flicker, making it virtually unnoticeable. You could also build your own voltage control device, if you have a knack for that sort of thing.

You don't need professional equipment to produce professional quality animation. A little thing like poverty shouldn't stop you. Cel animation is cheaper than you think.

CREATING STICK PUPPET ANIMATION

J. K. Takahashi

Stick puppet animation and Super-8 filmmaking are a natural team. They offer the director the opportunity to have a multi-character cast, to exercise absolute control of every movement, and to capitalize on the savings of Super-8 filmmaking. All that's needed is a camera capable of single-frame shooting, a few lights and the building materials for puppets and sets. Because the production will involve miniature sets and characters, the cost of materials will be substantially less than it would be in a "life-size" production. You can expect the major expense to be the filmmaker's time.

I was a student at Kalamazoo College in Kalamazoo, Michigan, when I did my first film based on stick puppet animation. My friends at school had expressed great interest when I told them some of the old Japanese folk tales passed down to me by my grandfather. At the same time, a friend of mine, David Webber, saw a film by Jeri Trinka, the Czechoslovakian filmmaker who makes feature-length films with elaborate sets and extensive casts of fully-articulated puppet characters. (That means the puppets have torsos capable of twisting, along with movable arms and legs, and flexible joints and fingers.) After some discussion, we decided to put together a short version of a *Chambara*, the classic Japanese period sword-fight flick.

The plot was simple. An unemployed samurai, or *Ronin*, wanders through 18th century Japan making his living as a mercenary. He takes up with a courtesan, kills her lord, and after a dazzling demonstration of his lightning sword technique, flees with her. The lord's son vows to avenge his father's death and family dishonor.

Designing the Fully-articulated Puppets

The actions and movements of the characters demanded fully-articulated puppets. Luckily, both David and I had some experience in woodcarving. We chose balsa and pine as the medium for our puppets. After hanging around a lumber shop and gleaning the scrap box for materials, we began the job of designing the puppet bodies for the production.

The torso for our prototype was a 2½-inch piece of a 1½-inch cylindrical dowel. To form the shoulder span, we loosely screwed a 2½-inch piece of 1-inch by ¼-inch pine into the top of the dowel. A shorter piece of the same proportions served as the hip span. The movement of the shoulders and hips created the illusion of a torso twisting. The arms and legs were ½-inch dowels. They were screwed into the shoulders and hips, and hinged to allow full lateral and rotational movements. Knee and elbow joints consisted of a system of wires wrapped around the dowels, joining the two pieces of each limb. To simulate hands, we

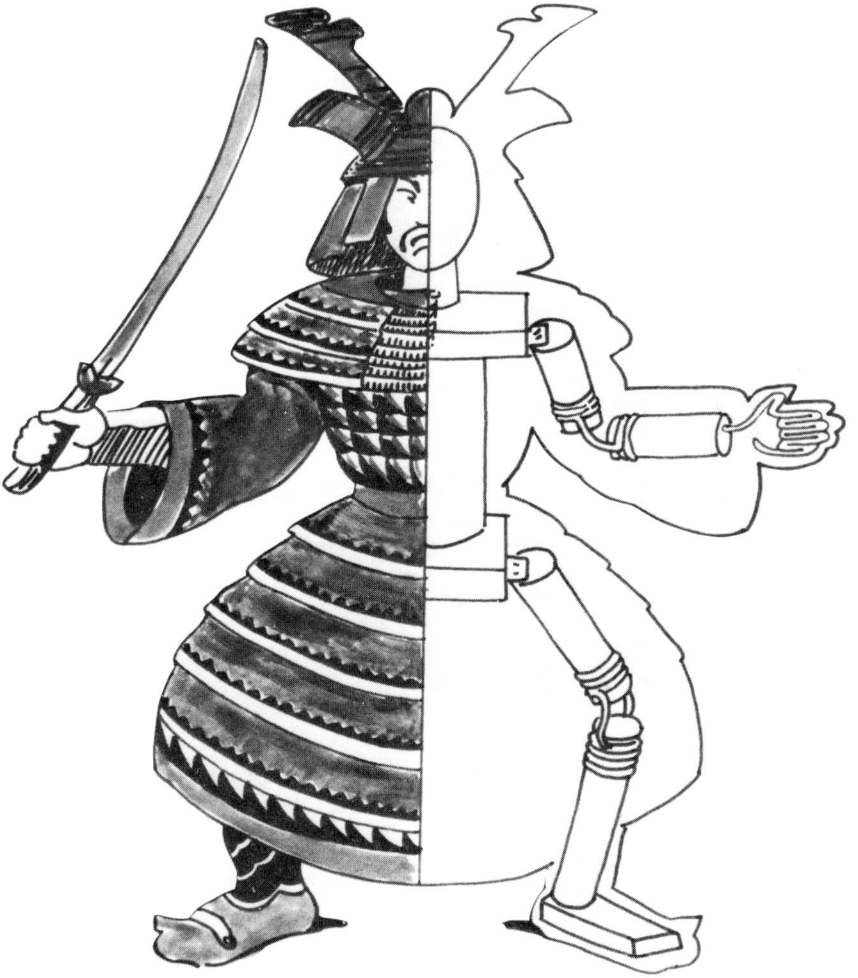

The actions and movements of the characters demanded fully-articulated puppets. The torso for the prototype was a 2½-inch piece of a 1½-inch cylindrical dowel. To form the shoulder span, we loosely screwed a 2½-inch piece of 1-inch by ¼-inch pine into the top of the dowel. A shorter piece of the same proportions served as the hip span. The movement of the shoulders and hips created the illusion of a torso twisting. The arms and legs were ½-inch dowels. Knee and elbow joints consisted of a system of wires wrapped around the dowels, joining the two pieces of each limb.

used pipe cleaners, twisting short lengths of cleaner to look like fingers and palms. The feet were simple blocks of pine which were painted like clogged feet (we could have hinged these, but chose to fake it and hide them under the kimono robes). When fully assembled with balsa head in place, the prototype stood 7 inches tall. (We used this arbitrary figure as the basis for scaling down all facets of the production.) Remarkably, the figure was capable of most human movements. We could even produce a reasonable facsimile of someone bending over and doing push-ups.

We decided that the faces would be immovable, masklike caricatures, slightly reminiscent of those used in Kabuki, Noh and Bunraku drama (classical Japanese drama). We modified the severity of the faces with specific, Western-stylized features, since our audience would be American and probably not knowledgeable about Japanese theater. The hinged jaws and moving eyes of Czech filmmaker Trinka's puppets were beyond our means, so we relied on strong individual face styles and lighting changes to establish emotions, moods and intentions.

We built only four basic bodies to use interchangeably among the

Additional frames were added: 1a, the hand resting on the handle, 2a, the blade a quarter of the way out.

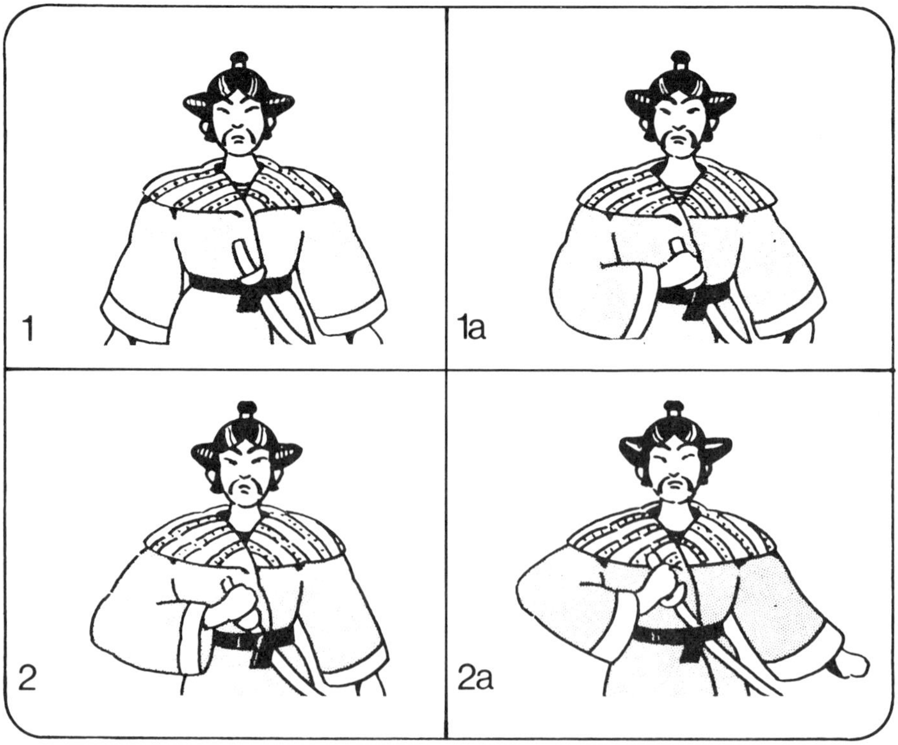

seven characters, since no scene had been planned for more than four actors at one time. (Throughout the filming, as the need for different characters arose, we would make slight alterations in the bodies and even change the faces to give the illusion of "a cast of dozens.") Another friend, Eebie Ryder, took the puppets and designed miniature kimonos for each of the characters, complete with individual *mon* (family crests), accessories and hardware. We were now ready to begin test shooting with our Bauer C3.

Test Shooting: Estimating the Duration of Movements

We test shot in Plus-X and Tri-X to see which film delivered the desired latitude and gradation, and to see how our ideas on animating puppets worked. Could we manipulate puppets and get a realistic effect? About the only thing we knew about animation was a need to move everything in a 24 fps time frame.

Using intuitive judgments of the speed of things, sometimes trying the movements and actions with a stopwatch in hand, we would work out "how far a given point would move in X seconds," taking into account the forces of acceleration, deceleration and intention. For example, the simple act of drawing a sword in combat contains three basic actions: the position of the hand on the handle in preparation for the draw, the unsheathing of the blade, and the position of the blade for battle. Estimating the action at slightly more than one-quarter of a second, we made an allotment of seven frames (24/4)+1, for that action. Because the tip of the sword moves faster, and through a greater arch than the rest of the sword when it is moved into position, we would estimate relative speeds of the parts and their acceleration.

All of this meant that in seven frames we would have to begin slowly and end with a blinding flash of the sword tip. In the test shooting we created three basic frames, one for each basic action. Frame one was the hand at rest, frame two the hand on the handle, and frame three the positioned sword. To get different rates of the act of drawing the sword we would add more frames to each action. For the combat draw we had seven frames to fill, so we added a few frames between each of the original frames. (The additional four frames were added as 1a, the hand resting on the handle, the blade a quarter of the way out, 2b, the glimmer of the totally unsheathed blade, 2c, the sword two-thirds of the way to ready position.) To get the sword back into the scabbard, we would shoot the same basic frames *in reverse*, and create different speeds by adding on in the same manner. You might think about puppet animation planning in terms of stroboscopic treatment of movement. The test reels were used to try out different movements and different rates of movement for each action: walking, hand motions, fighting stances, and the final test, the movement of multiple objects in time and space relationships. A movement chart is helpful in these circumstances. Our big fight scene involved the manipulation of four charac-

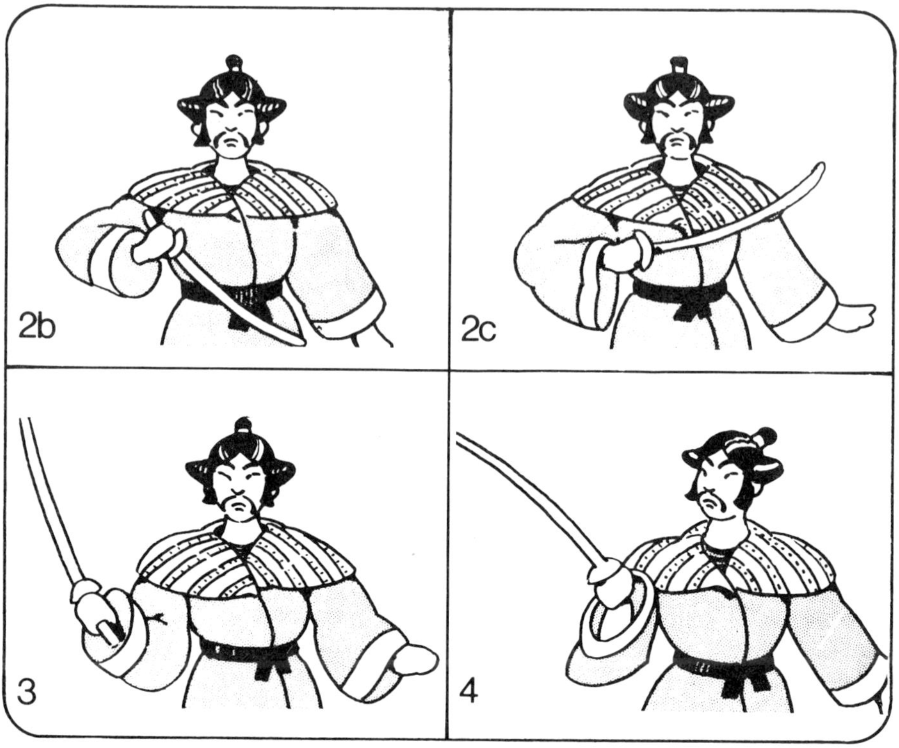

Frame 2b shows the glimmer of the totally unsheathed blade and in 2c the sword is two-thirds of the way to ready position.

ters simultaneously, each actor moving in reaction to and causing reactions in the others. If you want cutaways and different angles of a scene, you need a chart listing each frame and the relationships of the characters in each frame. Our tests proved we had exercised good judgment in our manipulations, and that the Tri-X gave us what we wanted. Now we had to create the sets.

Constructing the Sets

Using plaster of paris, cardboard and tempera paint, we built three basic sets: a nondescript road, the interior of the lord's house and the interior of a tunnel. The road set was a simple table top covered with a tempera-plaster mixture. To create different points along the road (a mountain pass, a seacoast, a farm village, a forest and a rock plain), we positioned a rear-projection screen behind the table and projected "Japanese scenery" on it. In combination with lighting changes, props and natural materials such as branches, pine needles and stones, the projections effectively changed the scenes. To get different angles we would simply pivot the table and switch the projections.

For the interior of the lord's house, we used a plain cardboard box. The three walls were latticed and covered with rice paper to look like the houses of the period. To create another room, a latticed sliding doorway was inserted just before the far wall. The roof, which was a fake set of beams and tiles, was built solid since the lighting could be done from the "fourth wall" and through the paper. By switching the lighting and the props we could create the illusion of a mansion.

By far, the most difficult set to produce was the tunnel. The Ronin digs through a mountain to provide a safe passageway for pilgrims, a task he has undertaken in penance for his amoral life. The climax of the film takes place in the tunnel, when the agent of vengeance confronts the "hero." The script called for three stages of work on the tunnel. We ended up with one 2-inch by 2-inch by 1-inch plaster rectangle with a rough cylinder (the tunnel) through the middle. The side of the rectangle served as the virgin mountainside into which the Ronin chisels at his moment of repentance. We filled one of the ends of the cylinder with stone and plaster.

To shoot the tunnel scenes we carved a hole in the left wall about 6 inches from the filled-in end. From that point we could capture action close-ups and manipulate the puppets. The rest of the tunnel shots were taken from the open end, shooting down the left wall to conceal the hole.

We had pieced the materials together at our leisure, and by the eighth week we were ready to shoot. David and I locked ourselves in the studio for 48 hours straight. (We were snowed-in anyway.) The major fight scene, which has a screen life of just under 1 minute, took us 3 hours of positioning the four figures and squeezing the single-frame release. Once we had edited the shots we disposed of about 50 feet (mostly the results of the last manic hours of reshoots and puppet structural failures). Our final product is about 10 minutes long.

The film is a very funny "Kurosawa" flick, a strange combination of realism in the sets and costumes, and the stark contrasts of the puppet faces and the projected background. We had created a samurai limbo for a total expenditure of $57.93 and more than 672 person-hours.

SPECIAL EFFECTS

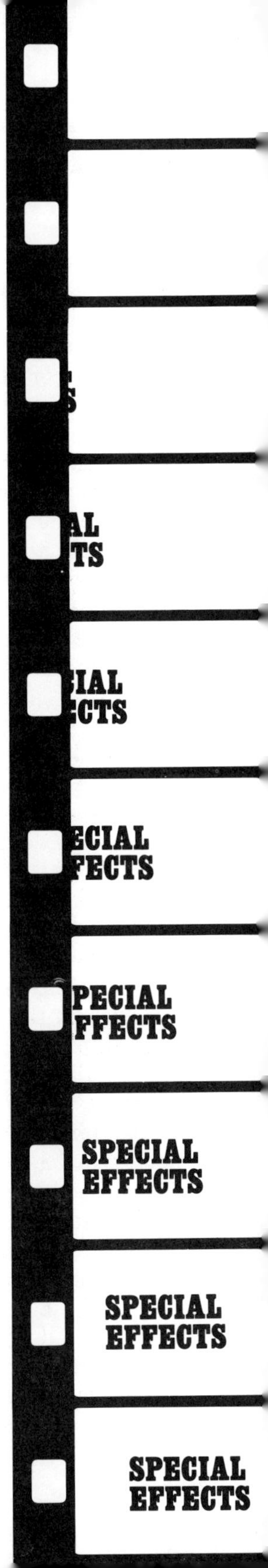
SPECIAL
EFFECTS
SPECIAL
EFFECTS
SPECIAL
EFFECTS

DOUBLE EXPOSURE: IT'S ALL DONE WITH MIRRORS

Rod Eaton

There's more than one way to superimpose images, and for those of you who have had it with backwound double exposures, there's always the *mirror shot*.

With mirror shots you can superimpose a "ghost" figure over a live-action scene, superimpose titles over background images and add other semitransparent images to create dramatic effects in your film. And because the mirror shot is an "in-camera" effect, you'll get the best quality image possible on your original film. This technique also allows you to see the finished composite *as* it is being shot, and it doesn't take a lot of time to execute.

In theory, a double exposure should be simple enough to produce. You expose the film once, wind it back into the camera, then expose it again. But when your film comes in small black, tamper-proof cartridges, winding it back requires an accessory backwinder. Although many Double Super-8 and Single-8 cameras allow backwinding, only a few Super-8 cameras have that capability. Even then, they can only be made to double expose short sections of film (usually less than 100 frames). And even if you can live with that limitation, there are other problems to consider.

If you don't expose each pass through the camera properly, you'll end up with a shot that is 1) too dark, 2) too light or 3) all of the above. When making a double exposure in the conventional way, it's usually necessary to underexpose each shot about one stop. It's also difficult to position the two images exactly as you would like them to appear in the final composite image. In some cases, the positioning of the two images isn't critical. But if you want to place a title *exactly* in a certain area of the first picture, forget it. Since you can't see the composite picture until the film is developed, alignment during shooting is an approximation at best.

With mirror shots, you can easily produce the double exposure effects you need, *without* the problems associated with backwinding. All you need is a thin, 6-inch square piece of high-quality glass known as a *beamsplitter*. When you position the glass in front of the camera at a 45-degree angle to the optical axis of the lens, the camera will photograph through the glass as if it weren't there. The highly polished surface of the glass will act as a mirror, reflecting whatever it "sees." This reflected image will be photographed at the same time as the subject in front of the camera. The result is a composite of the two images —a double exposure.

Suppose you're shooting an old-fashioned ghost story, and you want a specter to appear in front of your heroine. Set up the camera, lights, glass and actors as shown in the illustration. With the set lit and the ghost's light off, the camera sees only the set and heroine. When it's time for the ghost to make his appearance, his light is brought up with a dimmer control and the ghost makes an eerie entrance. When his light fades out, he makes a ghostly disappearance. In doing this, you must light the ghost carefully, so that only the ghost, and not the background, will be reflected in the glass.

The image of the ghost that you see in the viewfinder (and eventually, on the screen) will appear to be transparent—you'll be able to see the set (that is, the set behind the heroine) through him. While that's appropriate for a ghost, it may not work as well in other situations and may seem like a limitation to this technique. But you would have a similar transparent look with a conventional double exposure.

But there are advantages to this technique. Because you can see the entire composite image—set, heroine and ghost—in the viewfinder, it's possible to place the ghost exactly where you want him in the scene. You can determine the overall look and effectiveness of the composite *before* you film it, as well as balance the lighting to achieve the best image quality. There's no fooling with *f*/stops: the camera's automatic exposure system will give you the right exposure for the composite. And, since the entire scene is filmed at the same time, the ghost and heroine can react to each other—even speak to each other naturally (or supernaturally)—and you can record the scene in sync.

To keep the principals in focus, the ghost should be the same distance from the camera as the heroine. If that isn't possible, shoot with a wide angle lens and use bright lighting (to give you a small lens aperture). That will help keep both subjects in focus by increasing the depth of field.

You'll need something to hold the beamsplitter glass in place while shooting. You could fasten the glass to a tripod or light stand to hold it in front of the camera, but you're better off building a frame that will

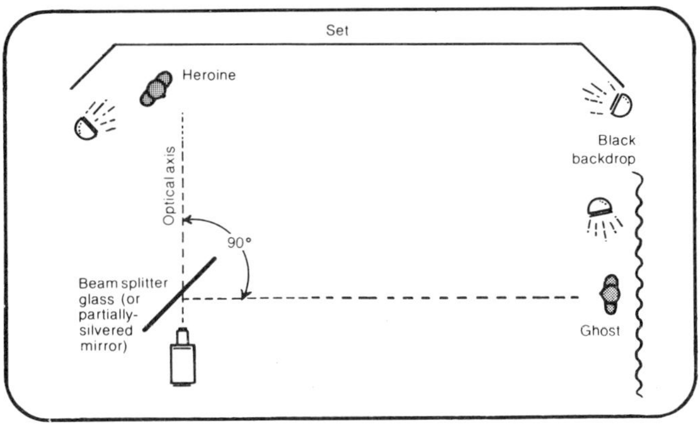

With mirror shots you can superimpose a "ghost" figure over live action scenes, or superimpose titles over background images and create other dramatic effects.

fasten directly on the tripod and camera. This will make it easier to work with the set-up, and will help protect the glass from fingerprints, scratches and breakage.

In place of the beamsplitter glass, you may wish to use a partially silvered mirror (sometimes called a two-way mirror). The partially silvered mirror should transmit 50 percent of the light that strikes it and reflect the other half. The advantage of using a mirror is that it will produce a cleaner image—glass may produce second images caused by light reflecting off the back surface as well as the front. (Both beamsplitters and partially silvered mirrors are available from the Edmund Scientific Company, Barrington, N.J. 08007.)

Both of these devices can be used to superimpose titles over a live-action background. To do that, you'll need to prepare titles that can be backlit. Make them by cutting letters out of sheets of black paper (stencil-fashion) or by painting black paint onto clear acetate sheets, leaving the letter areas clear. Another possibility is to make high-contrast photo negatives that have clear letters on a dense black background. (If you don't have access to a photo darkroom, you can have these titles made for you by a graphic arts company.)

Place your title—backwards—on the front of a light box. It must be backwards because the glass will reverse it "in the translation." Position the light box so the title is reflected into the glass and can be filmed over the background. Since the title will probably have to be placed fairly close to the camera, you may have difficulty trying to keep both title and background in focus. Try to find a compromise by focus-

Scrooge was a wonderful 'mirror ghost' in MGM's 1938 "A Christmas Carol."

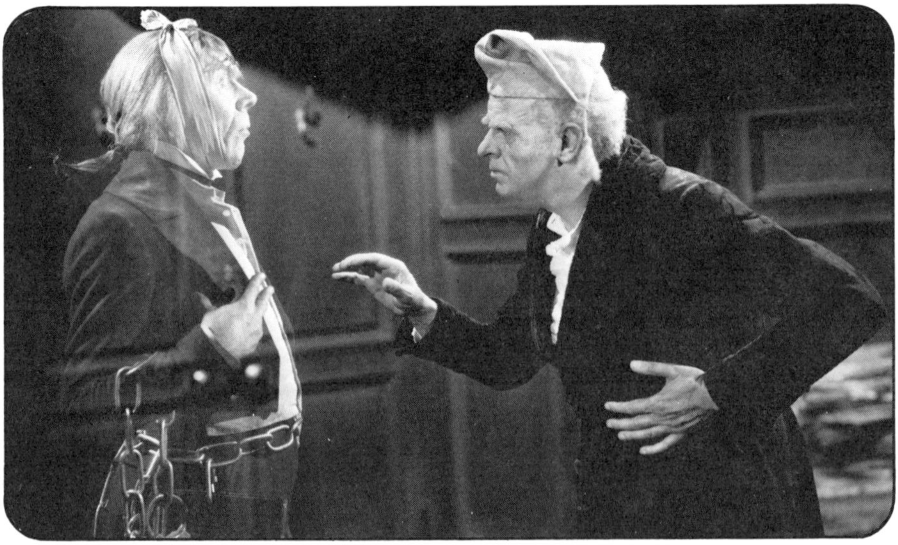

MGM

ing at a point between the two distances. Or, begin the shot by focusing on the background, then fade in the title (by bringing up the lamp in the light box with a dimmer control); as the title fades in, shift the focus to the title, throwing the background out of focus.

You can use the same light box set-up to add interesting and unusual visual effects to a scene. For a shot inside a church, for example, you might like to have an ethereal ray of light streaming in through a window. It's easy to make a "sunbeam" mask from black paper, place it on the light box and position it to produce the envisioned effect.

Masks can also be used to give someone a shining halo or to make an "enchanted" tree glow mystically. You might even adapt the technique for use with table-top animation to produce laser rays for a science fiction film or bombs bursting in air for a war movie.

This method of producing double exposures has limitations, of course. Both components of the shot have to be in close range and aligned at 90 degrees to the camera. You won't be able to make a double exposure of a heavyweight prizefighter sparring with the Washington Monument—unless you can find a way of bringing the Monument to Muhammad. And while the technique is ideally suited to studio production, it becomes cumbersome to use outdoors. However, with some ingenuity and a combination glass-holder/light-box arrangement built along the lines of a giant matte box, who knows what you might come up with?

SHOOTING DAY-FOR-NIGHT

Rod Eaton

Shooting day-for-night means just that—shooting during the day but making the film look as if it was shot at night. That might seem like a lot of extra effort when it's just as easy, with an XL camera and fast Ektachrome, to film in almost no light—a dimly-lit street corner, for example—and still get an acceptable image.

Well, the fact is, more and more, filmmakers *are* shooting at night instead of faking the effect with a day-for-night shot. Faster films and lenses, smaller, more portable lighting equipment, and a trend toward realism have all contributed to making day-for-night shots a rare occurrence in commercial filmmaking.

But the technique has by no means disappeared altogether. The movie *Jaws* contains a day-for-night sequence, as does Truffaut's homage to filmmaking, *Day for Night*. Day-for-night will remain in the filmmaker's vocabulary, because there are some scenes, such as a large expanse of water or a vast area of land, that are impossible or *very* difficult to light. You can't film without light, so in these situations, shooting day-for-night is the only alternative.

Day-for-night shots are a true cinematic convention. Like the fade and the dissolve, repeated usage has made the illusion acceptable to audiences. Day-for-night really doesn't *look* like night, but filmmakers and audiences have agreed that it *means* night.

Let's consider the way night really looks. At night the primary light source is the moon; during the day it is the sun. The moon reflects the light from the sun, and it does a good job of it. If you were to make a time exposure by moonlight, you'd find that the resulting photograph would look as though it had been made during the day. Colors would look "right" and there would be shadows and highlights. There would be some differences, however. The sky at night is black or very dark blue, and because moonlight is highly diffused, shadows would have a soft edge.

Our eyes, however, don't see things the way color film does. Because our eyes have little color sensitivity in dim light, we perceive only greys. This gives night an almost black-and-white look, with the only color coming from areas that are lit artificially or by bright moonlight.

In the theater, it has been the practice to place blue gels over the lights for "moonlit" night scenes. Moviemakers apparently borrowed this custom for day-for-night shots. A good day-for-night shot is typically underexposed one and a half to two stops and has an overall blue coloration. In addition, everything should have a low-key, shadowed effect; the sky should be dark, and you should be able to see practical (real) lights and their effect.

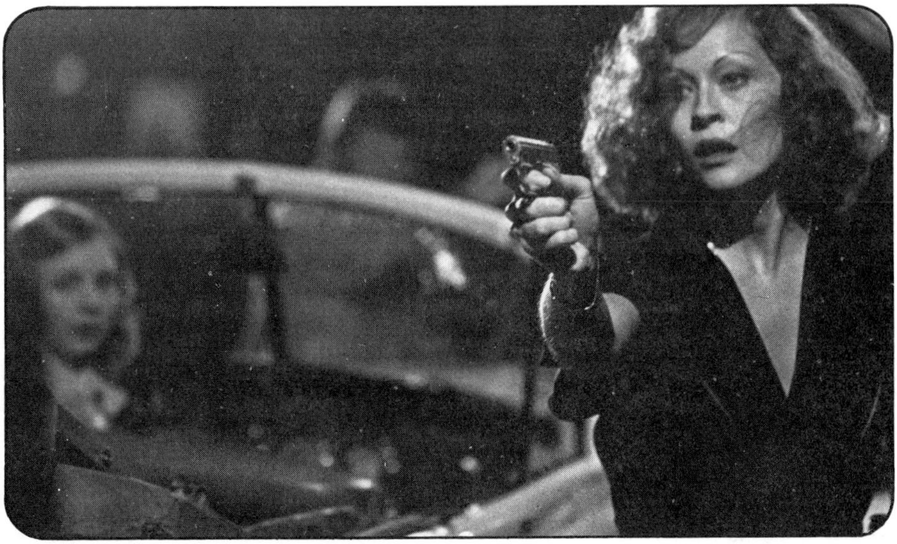
PARAMOUNT

A good day-for-night shot is underexposed and has an overall blue coloration, as in this scene from Polanski's "Chinatown."

In order to underexpose the film for day-for-night shots, you need a camera that will allow you to manually set the aperture, or override the automatic exposure system in some way. It's a good idea to start out with an underexposure of one and a half to two stops and shoot some test footage. Exactly how much you will need to underexpose will be determined by personal preference and by the demands of the story. How dark *should* it be? How much do you want the viewer to see?

The simplest way to get even blue coloration in the shot is to film with the camera's built-in filter set for artificial light. Super-8 color film is balanced to render colors accurately under artificial (movie) light. The reason for doing that is very simple: When you film in daylight, you place a filter in front of the film to filter out the excess blue of the sun. (In many Super-8 cameras, the daylight filter is always in place. You push it out of the way when you attach a movie light or insert a "filter key.") Shooting in daylight *without* the filter will give the film a blue cast that looks very much like a typical day-for-night shot if the film is underexposed.

Another method for coloring the film blue is to shoot through a deep blue filter. Spiratone sells one they call "Contrast Blue" that will produce a nice moonlight effect. You can also try filming through blue theatrical gels, which are available in many shades of blue, including one called "Moonlight." These gels aren't optically perfect, however, and may distort the picture a bit. In either case, if you're shooting with a filter, have the camera set for daylight. The electric eye will compensate for the light the filter "steals," so you will still need to underexpose manually.

Surprisingly enough, the best light for shooting day-for-night is bright, or slightly hazy, sunlight. This will allow you to work with shadows, which are necessary for a convincing night look. The sun should light actors from the back, side or three-quarter side—never from the front. What you're looking for is a heavy shadow effect. With sun coming from behind the actors, you'll get a rim light or halo effect around the edge of their bodies which will help separate the characters from the background.

Photographing the sky so it appears dark can present some problems. One possibility is to try to eliminate the sky from the picture whenever you can. You can also use a polarizing filter (Hoya makes one) to darken the sky. Polarizing filters come in mounts that allow you to turn the filter. After you place the filter on the camera lens, you can look through the viewfinder and rotate the filter until you get the effect of a darker sky. The effect of the filter depends largely on the angle of the sun to the camera. The sun should be at a right angle to the direction of your shot. Since this angle gives you good side light, you can darken the sky and still maintain shadows on actors' faces.

Another way of getting dark skies is to use a graduated neutral density (ND) filter. Half of the surface of this filter is dark, while the other half is clear. The line between the dark half and the clear half is soft. You place the filter over the lens with the dark half on top, and move the camera so the sky is juxtaposed on the dark half of the filter. An ND filter doesn't affect colors, but it does reduce light intensity. The amount of light reduction depends on the strength of the ND filter. Graduated ND filters are available from Tiffen.

For a day-for-night shot to be really convincing, you should be able to see ordinary night lights, such as car headlights, street lights and building lights. If you're filming under bright sunlight, these lights may not be visible at all, and even if they are, they won't appear as they do at night. Sometimes you can fake the effect. For example, if one of your characters is carrying a flashlight with which he discovers a body, you could build a modified flashlight with a very bright lamp. You might consider "converting" a high-intensity desk lamp, which uses a 12-volt lamp powered by a 110- to 120-volt transformer. It's really very simple: Take the desk lamp apart and assemble the components inside a flashlight tube. Run the power cord along the actor's arm and down a pants leg, and plug it in.

You can also use a bright movie light, held outside of the picture, to cheat the effect of car headlights. Placed inside a window, one or two movie lights will look like normal room interior lighting from the outside.

But perhaps the best alternative is to shoot your day-for-night shots during the "magic hour"—the time right after sunset. At this time of day, if you're using high speed film, there is still enough light by which to film. Night lights begin to turn on and the sky begins to darken—you've got your scene! You might still need to underexpose a bit, but probably not more than one stop. And you can still set the filter for artificial light (or shoot through a blue filter). The magic hour won't last long—after a few minutes you won't have enough light to shoot by. Plan your shooting carefully and be ready to start as soon as the sun sets and the light is right.

Somehow, there's something glamorous about day-for-night. It seems to be a part of Hollywood's Golden Era—part of the past. The technique exemplifies all that is magical about making movies—being able to create realities and bring your visions to the screen.

TIME-LAPSE TECHNIQUES

William C. Wind

Do you remember a scene in one of Walt Disney's first nature films—the scene in which dozens of flowers burst into bloom on the screen? Do you remember a recent aspirin commercial in which an entire day passed by in less than 30 seconds? Or another commercial in which rolls were baked to a golden brown in 10 seconds? Perhaps you've never thought about it, but all of these sequences, and many more you've probably seen, were filmed in time-lapse.

Time-lapse is an extension of the technique of fast-motion or undercranking. By single framing at extremely long intervals, it is possible for the camera to observe certain types of movement in a way that the human eye cannot. The growth of a plant, the creation of a cloud, the crystallization of a chemical—all occur on a time scale beyond human perception. Time-lapse expands your perception and allows you to study such movements for scientific gain, or for the pure aesthetic pleasure they can provide. Many filmmakers either ignore time-lapse completely, or they are put off by stories of expensive equipment and hard-to-learn techniques. As a result, they overlook an area with enormous creative potential—one which actually requires no special equipment at all. As far as the techniques are concerned, they *should* be a part of every filmmaker's repertoire, and it is the purpose of this article to show that they are easy to learn.

Basic Time-lapse Equipment

Any Super-8 camera can be used to film time-lapse sequences. A single frame release on the camera will make the job easier, but it is not an absolute necessity. With a little careful practice, it is possible to click off single frames with the continuous-run release. However, if your camera *has* a cable release socket for remote control, use it by all means—it will reduce the possibility of unwanted camera movement since you won't have to push the trigger. Many Super-8 cameras have been designed so that single framing can be done only through a cable release socket.

A tripod *is* an absolute necessity for time-lapse work. It should be cross-braced for maximum stability. Time-lapse filming is similar to animation in that any camera unsteadiness will ruin a time-lapse sequence. You will also need an interval timer or an intervalometer. These come in two varieties—human and mechanical. For your beginning work in time-lapse, forget about mechanical timers. Almost any time-lapse sequence can be filmed with finger-power and a watch, or you can simply count, "one, one thousand, two, one thousand. . ." Later on, if you decide that you need a mechanical timer, you will find units available with a wide range of prices and capabilities. The simplest units fall in the $50 to $150 price range and do little more than release single frames at pre-selected intervals. Other units can cost thousands of dollars and do everything but wash the dishes; for example, the Hervic/Multilapse Intervalometer (over $2,000) can control your camera as well as your flood lamps and electronic flash, at intervals from 4 frames per second to one frame every 45 minutes. In addition, it has a built-in hold circuit, a slow timer, a fast timer, a frame counter and a release thrust control.

The timer I use is the Pulsar, from American General Products, Inc. It's a small, yet versatile unit that costs about $225 (including complete unit with 4 NiCad batteries, charger and tripod bracket). The Pulsar allows Super-8 cameras which have a cable release to take single exposures at an infinitely variable time sequence from 2 frames per second to 1 frame every 10 minutes. It also has a "4 fps" setting which can be used for "Keystone Kop" or pixilation effects. The Pulsar is powered by self-contained NiCad batteries for outdoor work, or by an AC converter/recharger when line power is available. The basic unit is about the size of a small Super-8 camera and weighs less than 2 pounds.

Other timers you can use include: Timefram (about $300); Pacer III (about $175); and the Samenco Movie Control Model MC-6AS (about $250). The Timefram unit allows time-lapse exposures at infinitely variable rates from 2 frames per second to 1 frame every 50 minutes. The Pacer III's time-lapse interval is infinitely variable from 5 seconds to 10 minutes. And the Samenco MC-6AS lets you use intervals from 1 second to 10 hours. In addition, some Super-8 cameras have built-in or add-on timers.

General Time-lapse Techniques

Research is the single most important step in the production of good time-lapse movies. Whenever possible, observe your subject beforehand and time the movement you plan to film. This information will let you determine the proper frame interval for any desired amount of screen time. Then use the formula given below to determine the frame interval setting:

$$\frac{\text{Movement Time in Seconds}}{\text{Screen Time in Seconds} \times \text{Projection Rate (fps)}} = \text{Frame Interval in Seconds}$$

If long division isn't your bag, there is an excellent little time-lapse computer bound into a Kodak pamphlet called *The Seventh Here's How* (AE-90, $.95). It will do the division for you.

Once you've figured out the frame interval you want, your next consideration should be location problems. If you are working outdoors, scout your location carefully. Look for details that could detract from the main subject. Some common disturbing details are shadows moving across foreground objects; airplanes and other vehicles zipping by in the background; insects and birds popping in and out; and flare from the sun as it unexpectedly moves into the picture. If you are working indoors, close all drapes and check the background for clocks.

Exposure can be a big problem in time-lapse work. Many Super-8 cameras do not operate at full speed when taking single frames and, therefore, may require exposure compensation. Normally, the owner's manual will tell you what to do. If you are in doubt, check an old roll of film taken with the camera you intend to use. If each scene begins with a light frame, you will need to close down your aperture by a half stop or a full stop when you shoot single frames. If your camera has an automatic exposure system (and most Super-8's do) you should run a test roll, shooting single frames under a variety of lighting conditions. Keep a record of your exposure settings and results so that you will be able to determine any necessary compensations. If your camera has a manual override for the exposure control, you may have to use it for all time-lapse filming. When working indoors, use only artificial light and make sure your lamps are fresh. Photofloods tend to dim gradually with age, and even with automatic exposure compensation, the change in their brightness will be noticeable over a period of hours. For best results, use the new quartz/halogen lamps.

Any Super-8 camera can be used for time-lapse sequences. You'll need an interval timer (intervalometer)—either human or mechanical. Filming blooming flowers is easy, but it really should be done indoors.

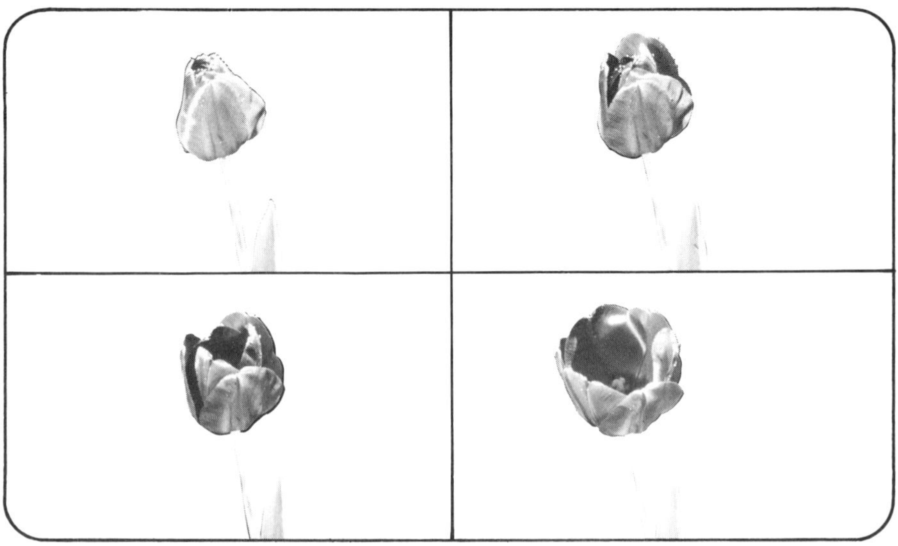

Once you begin filming, there are several basic rules to observe. First, as you begin each sequence, rapidly click off 20 or 30 frames. These frames should not contain any movement, and will serve to "establish" the setting for the audience. They can always be cut out during editing if they are not wanted. Second, make sure your frame intervals are consistent so that you will get smooth movement on the screen. If you find that reading your watch becomes a drag, try using a metronome to keep you on the beat. Third, if your subject starts to move out of the frame, *don't* attempt to follow it. It is impossible for you to move the camera smoothly during a time-lapse sequence (take my word for it). Let the subject move out of the frame and then reposition the camera. If you are fast, you will lose only a frame or two of the action while you move the camera. The screen effect will be the same as a cut, which is far less jarring to the audience than a jerky pan.

Normally, you will not be looking through the eyepiece while filming time-lapse, and light rays entering a reflex viewing system through the eyepiece can bounce around until they fog the film. So the fourth and final rule is to cover the eyepiece when your eye is not against it. Some cameras have a built-in light trap for this purpose.

Special Techniques: Flowers

Every time-lapse situation is different but it is possible to mention a few of the more typical ones, along with suggestions on how to get started in each of them. First, let's consider blooming flowers. Filming them in time-lapse is quite easy, but most people are surprised to learn that it really should be done indoors. Outdoors, the wind will move the flowers around, even on the calmest days, resulting in a kind of "pansy palsy" (forgive me, but it really looks as horrible as it sounds).

For your first experiment with flowers, go to your local florist and ask him for two cut flowers which are just on the verge of blooming. When you get home, put one flower in the refrigerator. Take the other flower, clip about a half-inch off the end of the stem, and put it into a vase or bottle half-filled with warm water. Now, set up your camera and lights. Remember, you are trying to create an outdoor effect, so use just one direct light placed at a 45-degree angle above the flower. To fill in the shadows, use light reflected off a white card or wall. Your background should be neutral but natural looking. A piece of blue or grey poster board will do the job.

When you are all set up, turn on the lights, but do not begin filming. Instead get out your watch and time the flower as it opens. Not only will this give you your frame interval, as described earlier, but it will enable you to observe any movements the flower might make as it opens—many flowers turn toward the brightest light. After you have observed and timed the first flower, get the second flower out of the refrigerator and film it. (For further work with flowers, you might want to try potted plants.)

Special Techniques: Food

If you have an oven with a window, filming pastries can be great fun. Some pastries bake faster than others, and the baking times given in the package directions are seldom accurate, so it would be wise to bake a test batch before the actual filming. Use about the same amount of pastries as you plan to film, and use a preheated oven for both batches. When filming a pie, use a fast frame interval. Hot air trapped under the crust may cause it to expand and collapse rapidly as the pie bakes. When setting up your lights, place them at a 45-degree angle to the window and wipe the window clean of smudges (inside and out). Turn the oven light off during filming if color balance is critical.

Special Techniques: Scenery

Time-lapse sequences of clouds will add interest to any travel or nature film. While it is possible just to point your camera at the sky and start shooting, your pictures will be much more impressive if you include part of the terrain in the frame—and that takes planning. Canyons and mountains are generally the most interesting terrain, but some very dramatic time-lapse sequences can also be shot on the prairie. For mountain scenes, try to catch the afternoon clouds forming behind the peaks. For canyon or prairie shots, pick out a large cumulus cloud or a thunderstorm cloud and film it as it approaches or passes in the distance. When composing your shot, be sure to keep the foreground clear. Framing your shot to include nearby trees and rocks may be the traditional approach to scenic pictures, but when you see the finished footage with gyrating leaves and creeping shadows, you'll wish you'd left them out.

Sunrises and sunsets are nature's fade-ins and fade-outs. By shooting them in time-lapse, you can use them to punctuate your films. However, sunrises and sunsets are extremely tricky to shoot since the light levels vary considerably. I am sorry to say that automatic exposure control is not the answer to the problem. Electric eyes tend to underexpose when the sun is up, and overexpose when it is down. The best I can do is give you some general hints that have helped me.

Start out by using one exposure setting for the whole sequence. Use a setting that is one *f*/stop slower than your normal daylight setting for the film you are using. Try this method to film a variety of different sunrises and sunsets, then analyze the results. Did you lose the vivid colors of the afterglow? Were the edges of the picture too dark? For each sequence, decide on the corrections to be made (and if you decide to change exposure during filming, do it *very gradually*). Then, record your corrections in a notebook and go back out to shoot some more sunrises and sunsets. After you have shot a few dozen, you will begin to have a pretty fair handle on the exposure problems.

When in doubt about exposure, choose a smaller lens opening—overexposed pictures are always a wash-out. And unless you really know what you are doing, don't film a sunrise or a sunset on a perfectly clear day. The unobstructed rays of the sun can do horrible things inside your camera. Besides, a sunset on a clear day is really very dull. If there is a heavy haze on the horizon, though, and if you have a long telephoto lens, you can recreate some great sunsets.

Finally, although shadows are usually unwanted distractions, they can also make some of the very best time-lapse subjects. Shadows of man-made objects such as buildings, fences and towers, have great visual impact—especially as they pass across other man-made objects (such as brick walls, wooden planks and flagstones). Here is a never-ending source of abstract patterns for experimental effects. Shadows of natural objects, however, are my personal favorites. Picture the following sequence. First there is a black screen. Gradually, the upper half of the screen lightens to a dark blue. Suddenly, little points of orange light dot the lower half of the screen. Slowly, the orange spots grow larger, snaking out in different directions. The upper half is now a rich blue and we know it is the sky. Below, the orange shapes continue to displace the black shapes and we discover that we are at the edge of a canyon. The orange shapes reach deeper into the canyon like molten metal flowing into a mold. The black forms slip off the sides of the canyon like sinister amoebas. Then, instant recognition. Sunrise over the Grand Canyon.

The night before I shot this sequence, I camped out on the North Rim of the Grand Canyon. Before I went to sleep, I set my portable alarm clock for an hour before sunrise and put it in the sleeping bag with me. When it went off (about 5 a.m.), I dragged myself to my feet, gathered up my tripod, my camera, my watch, a cable release and a flashlight, and walked to a viewpoint I had scouted the previous day.

As I set up, the first hint of light was appearing on the eastern horizon. I aimed my camera to the southwest, and with the aid of the flashlight, set the manual exposure control to the normal daylight *f*/stop. Then I opened it up one stop. Positioning myself so my shadow would fall across the camera, I began clicking off frames at five second intervals. Ninety minutes later, I had clicked the shutter 1,080 times (I didn't own a mechanical timer then) and my fingers were sore, but I had managed to film 45 seconds worth of pure gold!

Granted, not everyone has access to the Grand Canyon, but I have shot similar sequences in Texas, North Carolina, Montana and Illinois. It really doesn't matter where you are. As long as you plan carefully and stick with it, you'll get your "dream scene."

DO-IT-YOURSELF MATTE SHOTS

Rod Eaton

You can use a partially silvered mirror—called a *beamsplitter*—placed at a 45-degree angle to the camera lens to produce superimposed images. The Schufftan process takes this idea a step further by enabling you to replace selected portions of the picture with other detail—placing live action into a miniature set, for example. This is a technique generally associated with optically printed matte shots.

The Schufftan process—or Schufftan shot—was a popular device among filmmakers of the '30s. Since then, it has been made virtually obsolete by optical printing techniques. But for Super-8 filmmaking, with its paucity of available optical effects, the Schufftan process allows you to make shots that would otherwise be "impossible." In fact, the Schufftan process can give you better results than optical printing because the composite image is filmed on one piece of film on one pass through the camera. Optical printing requires several generations and numerous passes through the printer, resulting in loss of sharpness, increased graininess and contrast and the possibility of misalignment and image jiggle.

To begin, you'll need to build a "Schufftan Box," named in honor of the German film technician, Eugen Schufftan, who is credited with the development of this technique. The box, which is mounted on a tripod, holds the camera and beamsplitter in the proper 45-degree relationship. In addition, the box contains two pieces of thin, optical quality (undistorted) plate glass: one piece is in front of the lens and perpendicular to the optical axis, the other on the side, parallel to the optical axis. The box should be enclosed to prevent extraneous light from entering and painted flat black to reduce internal reflection.

Figure 1 shows the general construction of a Schufftan box. We can't give precise dimensions, since they will differ depending on your camera. Actually, the bigger you can build the Schufftan box, the sharper the matte lines will be, since the glass pieces on the front and right side that position the mattes will be closer to the point of focus of the lens.

Let's assume that the beamsplitter everyone uses is the one sold by Photo Control (4¾ by 6¼ inches) in Minneapolis. For most Super-8 cameras, the beamsplitter would be about 6 inches from the front of the lens (measuring to the middle of the beamsplitter, on a line perpendicular to the optical axis). The rest of the box dimensions would be about 9 inches high (depending on the height of the camera handgrip), 9½ inches long and 4½ inches wide. As a rule, the glass pieces should be as far from the lens as is practical (more about that later). Make sure you can't see the edge of the beamsplitter or the glass with the lens at wide angle.

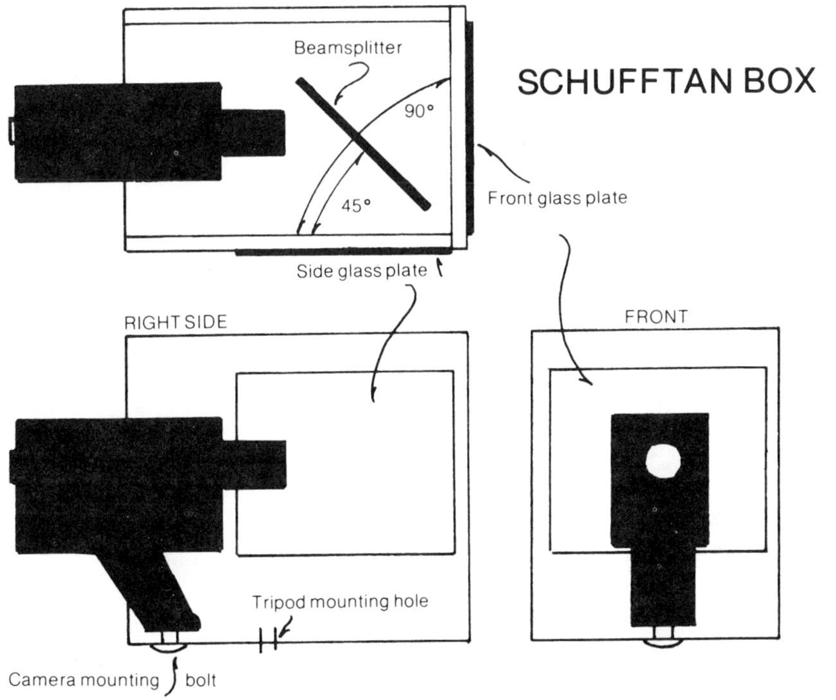

Figure 1: The Schufftan process uses a partially silvered mirror called a beamsplitter to produce superimposed images.

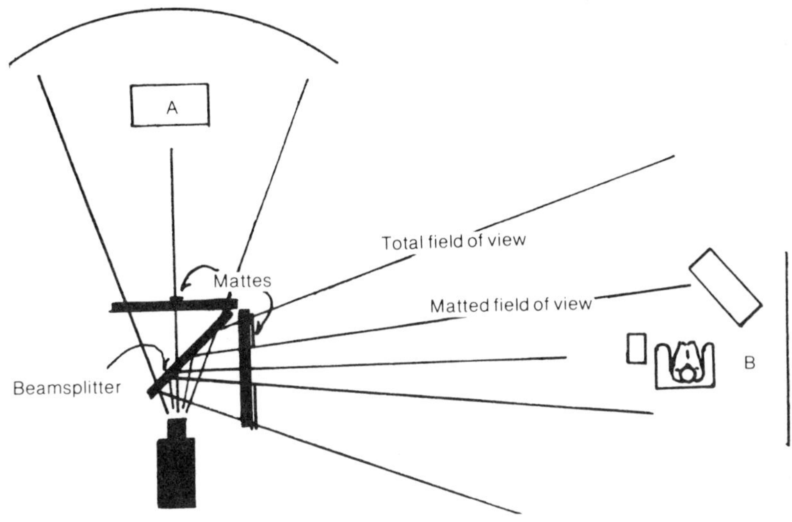

Figure 2: Assume that set A is a miniature house with a window in front.

As with mirror shots, the beamsplitter reflects an image of whatever is at a right angle to the camera. This image, along with the image seen through the beamsplitter, is photographed on the film. The two glass pieces, however, will enable you to position complementary masks—or mattes—in the path of each image to control the composite (Figure 2).

Assume that set A in Figure 2 is a miniature house with a window in front. You are going to "matte in" an actor "sitting in the window," by using the Schufftan process. The actor is actually seated in set B, a full-size interior of the "inside" of the miniature.

The first step in producing the composite is to look through the reflex viewfinder and, with only set A lit, outline the miniature window opening on the front glass with a grease pencil. Next, cut a piece of black paper to fit the area outlined and attach it to the glass with a dab of glue. A certain amount of trial and error may be involved in getting the paper to fit exactly, but when you're through, the paper should matte out the window exactly.

Next, make a matte for the right-side glass. This matte will be the exact reverse (that is, the complement) of the first, since you want to matte out everything except the portion of the scene that is to appear in the window of the miniature. With both sets lit, you'll see the composite through the viewfinder, and you can position four strips of black paper (top, bottom, right, left) on the glass until the reflected image of the actor is properly matted into the miniature set. As I mentioned earlier, the farther away from the lens the mattes are placed, the sharper the matte line will appear.

Schufftan shots take a lot of preparation and time, but they bring your vision successfully to the screen.

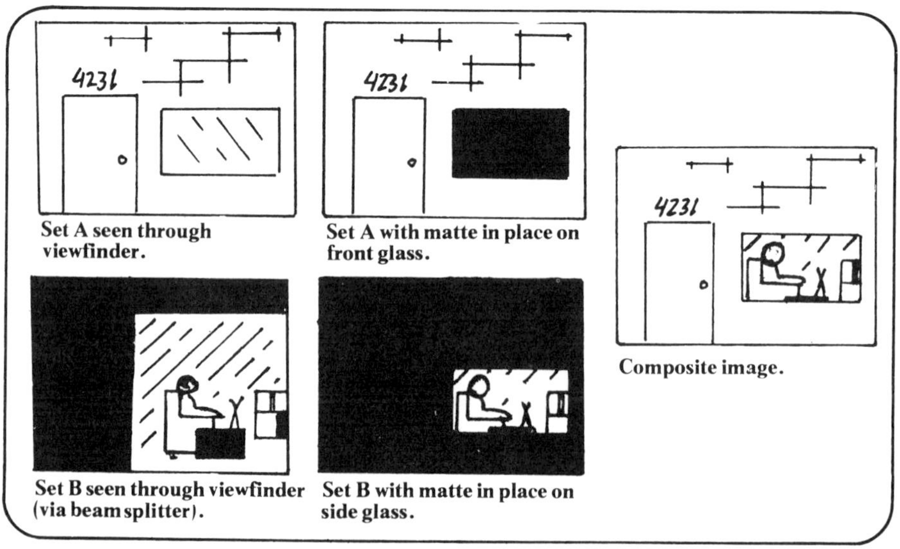

Set A seen through viewfinder.

Set A with matte in place on front glass.

Set B seen through viewfinder (via beam splitter).

Set B with matte in place on side glass.

Composite image.

The Schufftan process offers virtually unlimited possibilities for producing interesting and unusual shots. Naturally, it does have some limitations. There is the obvious problem of keeping both parts of the composite in focus. This can be solved, to some degree, by using a wide-angle lens and plenty of light to give you greater depth of field. The set-up requires a rather large area—a problem if you don't have access to a shooting studio. The technique can be used outside, but lighting may prove a problem. Since the sun is a fixed light source, it will light the two components from different angles. This difference may spoil the effect. And, because of the complexity of the set-up, it's difficult to pan and impossible to zoom.

Schufftan shots take a lot of preparation and time. But, like all good special effects, the time and planning are worth every minute if the effect lets you bring your visions successfully to the screen.

HAUNTING HORROR EFFECTS

Rod Eaton

Establishing shot: *A gloomy Transylvanian castle perched forebodingly on a rocky cliff, silhouetted against the night sky. Cut to castle interior: A dank, dark crypt. Fog billowing close to the floor almost obscures the coffin in repose in the center of the room. A door creaks open slowly and Professor Van Helsing enters warily. He carries a wooden stake, a huge mallet, and a shining gold crucifix. As the prof pushes aside the thick cobwebs, a started bat screams and flies towards the camera, its eyes gleaming malevolently.*

Van Helsing walks to the coffin. He brushes ages-old dust from the lid to reveal a name—Count Dracula. The prof cautiously begins to raise the coffin lid. Suddenly, a brilliant flash of lightning illuminates the crypt, and to Van Helsing's terror he realizes that...

From Murnau's *Nosferatu* (Germany, 1921), to Warhol's *Blood For Dracula* (America, 1975), the monster movie has been a cinematic staple. The ghoulish special effects we take for granted, and admire, in horror films *are* within the realm of possibility for most Super-8 filmmakers—even those with limited budgets. For example, to locate your next film at Count Dracula's Transylvanian castle, all it takes is an establishing shot of a miniature castle-on-a-mountain set. Or you can simplify the process even further by cutting a castle silhouette out of black paper. Place the cut-out a foot or so in front of a dark blue paper sky; locate a photo lamp so the light falls only on the backdrop, not on the cut-out; and create a moon by punching a small hole in a piece of construction paper and fastening the paper in a slide mount. With a slide projector, you can then shine a moon anywhere in your sky.

No Dracula film would be complete without fog. If you decide to do it first-class, you can buy your own fog-making machine for about $250, or rent one from a theatrical or motion picture supply house. Expect to pay around $50 per week, plus transportation costs *and* time in transit. A fog maker vaporizes a chemical fog juice (about $15 per gallon) into a white fog, mist or haze. If a low-hanging fog is desired, the vapor should be sprayed through a cage containing dry ice. Much less expensive than renting a fog maker is buying a few chunks of dry ice, which you then submerge in water to produce a dense, white ground fog. Wetting down the floor of the set before making the fog will help keep the fog near the ground. (Wet floors can also pose serious electrical hazards, so be careful not to let power cables get wet.)

Once you're inside Dracula's castle, you'll need plenty of cobwebs and some sort of cobweb spinner to make them. Most of these machines consist of a small electric fan with a cuplike container for cobweb cement attached to the front. When the fan is turned on, the cobweb cement is forced out of the cup in a thin stream. The fan blades blow this cobweb filament into place. Theatre House, Inc. sells a small machine for about $35. The price includes a pint of cobweb cement and a pint of solvent used to thin the cement and clean the machine. Their cobweb spinner attaches to an electric drill, which you supply. If you want cobwebs, but don't need strand-by-strand effects, you can use pieces of fine gauze material. Hang the material from the ceiling, attach it to points on the walls, to furniture, skeletons or corpses. Tear holes in it, shred sections of it, and you'll end up with massive cobwebs that look like they were made years ago.

For the most realistic cobweb effects, you should light the web from behind or from the side. The cobwebs also should be dusted lightly with cobweb dust (sometimes called fuller's earth). And the dust can be applied liberally to all areas of the set to give an authentic ancient patina. Although finely sifted flour can also be used to simulate dust, it will look *very* white, and will only be appropriate in some horror films.

Besides fog and dust, a respectable horror film requires bats. The rubber variety can be found in novelty shops or a local toy store. By attaching a fine black thread or nylon fishing line to the backs of these toys, you can suspend them from the ends of some long poles and make them "fly." Keep the pole well above the camera's view and bounce the bats up and down a bit so that their wings will flap.

Getting a bat's eyes to glow is a cinch if you have some of the reflectorized tape (red, green or white) used on bicycle and car bumpers. Cut small "eyes" from the tape and stick them onto the bat. The tape will reflect the light from a photo lamp placed near the camera.

Another lighting effect you may need is lightning. In commercial films this is often simulated by igniting finely powdered aluminum, or by using powerful arc lamps. For the average Super-8 filmmaker, both

A fog maker vaporizes a chemical fog juice into white fog, mist or haze, as in "Brides of Dracula" (1960).

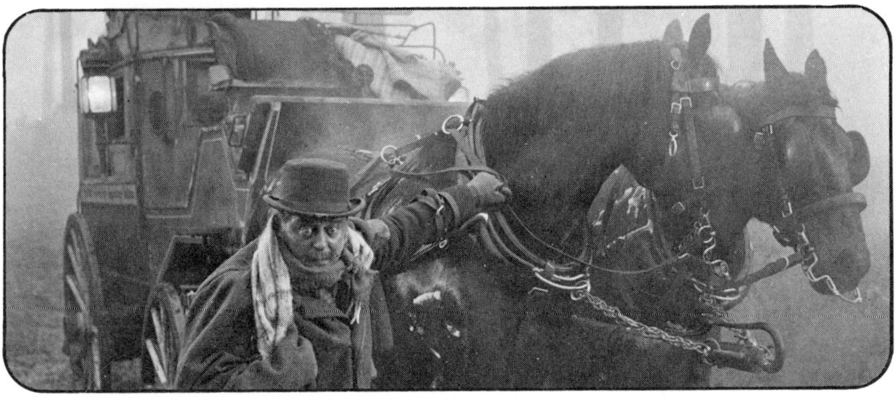

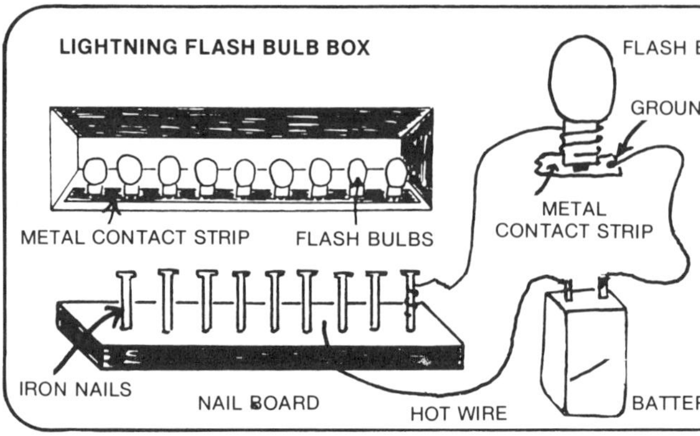

A wiring diagram: The bell wire loops around the base of each flash bulb.

of these methods are impractical. Few of us use or have access to arc lamps, and the pyro-aluminum technique requires costly equipment and is extremely dangerous. Two inexpensive alternatives are using a flash bulb box, or blinking a photo light. The photo light method is the easiest. By hooking the light up to a push-button switch or a dimmer control you can control the flash. Remember that no two lightning flashes are the same, so vary the intensity and duration of the flash. A cold blue light is best for a realistic effect, so use a blue-colored photo lamp (5500 degrees K), or place a blue gelatin filter over the light.

A box with flash bulbs in it can also produce lightning effects. The box can be constructed from cardboard—it's cheaper and easier to work with than wood.

Paint the inside of the box white to reflect the light. The flash bulbs should be wired as the diagram shows. Looping a section of the bell wire around the base of each flash bulb provides good electrical contact, and helps hold the bulb in place. The flash bulbs will go off when you strike the hot lead from the battery against the nails on the nail board. It's a good idea to have a clear plastic cover on the front of the box to prevent injury in case the flash bulbs break. Depending on how fast you pull the hot wire along the nails, you will produce a flash of lightning composed of several individual short flashes. Again, you may wish to use blue flash bulbs, and if you want to make the flashes brighter, connect two bulbs to each nail to double the light output.

All the special effects mentioned here are already familiar to most audiences. But remember, new forms of terror are constantly being created. In *The Exorcist*, audiences were shocked when Regan MacNeil spewed forth green bile. Did it matter that it was only a mouthful of pea soup?

HOW TO MAKE BLOOD PELLETS

Kenneth Gullakson

The portrayal of violence is sometimes essential to the filmmaker's statement. Until now, the creation of realistic-looking gunshot impacts on the human body has been limited to Hollywood, where a professional "hit man" charges $100 a day for the effect. We didn't have that kind of budget for *The Theta Factor*, so I set out to duplicate the effect at home. The results were no less than spectacular, and I only spent $2. Here's how you do it.

First, you'll need to buy some number 00 empty gelatin capsules, which I got at a pharmacy for $1.69 for a box of 100, and one pound of paraffin wax, available at large supermarkets for less than 50 cents. The other supplies are things you already own or can improvise. Assemble an eyedropper, a needle, thread, tweezers, scissors, an X-acto knife or razor blade, a glass of cold water, a small saucepan and an aluminum cup. You'll also need a 2-foot long blow tube with roughly a 3/8-inch inside diameter. I used a section of telescoping curtain rod for this. Finally, whip up a batch of your favorite fake blood. How much you need depends on how gory you want your movie to be.

Place chunks of the paraffin into the aluminum cup and put the cup into a saucepan of water. Keep the water level low to prevent the cup

Figure 1: Capillary action will hold water in the capsule.
Figure 2: Use tweezers to pull the softened gelatin out of the wax shell.

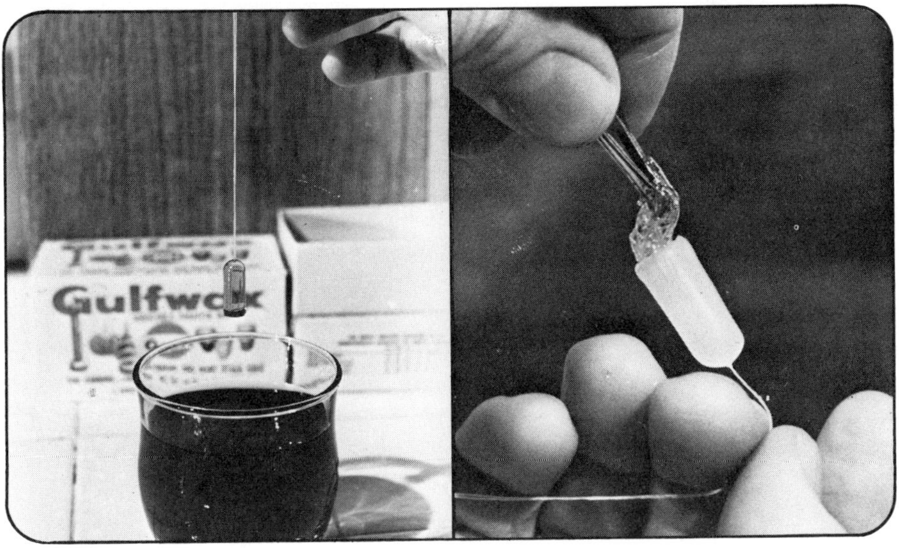

from floating. Heat over a low flame to melt the wax, and keep it in a molten state throughout the entire procedure. Now thread the needle, pulling the ends of the thread even and tying them with a knot. Trim off the tail of the knot. Pull apart a gelatin capsule and discard the shorter half, keeping the longer, narrower half. Insert the needle into this part of the gelatin capsule and push it through the closed end, pulling the thread until the knot stops against the inside surface. Holding the thread with one hand and the capsule with the other, place the capsule in the glass of water, with the open end up so it will fill completely with water. Lift the full capsule out by the thread. Capillary action will hold the water in the capsule. (See Figure 1. I have colored the water to make it more visible.) Dangling the full capsule at the end of the thread, quickly dunk it in and out of the cup of molten paraffin. Allow the paraffin to harden for 4 or 5 seconds, then give it another dunking. This should insure that the wax case is thick enough to hold up under gentle handling, yet thin enough to crush easily upon impact.

Immediately place the capsule in the glass of water to cool and harden for 2 or 3 minutes. Remove the hardened capsule from the water and use the X-acto knife or similar tool to cut off the little cap of wax which has formed on what was formerly the open end of the capsule. Be careful not to crush or crack the wax coating. By this time, the water will have softened the gelatin shell of the original capsule. Using the tweezers, carefully grasp the edge of the gelatin capsule. Pull the soft gelatin from inside the wax shell (Figure 2) and throw it away. Be careful not to grasp the wax shell during this step, as it is easy to crush. Hold only the thread.

Fill the wax shell with the blood surrogate of your choice, using the eyedropper. Now dangle the wax shell full of "blood" by the thread (capillary action again!), and dip the open end into the molten wax a few times to seal it off. Remember to dip only the end, not the whole capsule, since too much wax build-up will prevent the capsule from collapsing properly on impact. Place the capsule in the cold water once again to harden. Wait a few minutes before removing it and clipping off the thread from the end of the blood pellet. It is now ready for use.

Carefully place the wax capsule in your tube, aim and blow. When the pellet hits your target, the impact will crush the wax, splattering blood in a very impressive way.

MONSTER MAKEUP

Don Dohler

Having trouble casting a monster, ghoul or a weird beastie for your Super-8 horror film or sci-fi fantasy? You have at your disposal all the materials needed to produce grotesque effects on the head and face of any willing subject. This type of makeup creation isn't the province of the masters of macabre in big-time Hollywood studios. It's mostly a matter of knowing what you want to do, and applying your artistic abilities to the job at hand.

Like other creative mediums, makeup presents a range of possibilities, from the very involved and costly mold and foam-rubber appliances (like those used in *The Planet of the Apes*) to simple putty and grease stick. However, there is a technique midway between the complex and the simple that is suitable for just about anyone with a little creative drive. Basically, it's a "buildup" technique involving the use of liquid latex and sheets of raw cotton.

Ed Litzinger, a Baltimore makeup artist who has done work for many local films and plays, has been using this buildup technique for more than ten years. Ed is an expert at creating weird makeup. Over the years Ed has created werewolves, corpses, aliens and creatures too wild to describe on paper, so he was the natural choice when I sought an artist to aid me in the writing of this article.

For a subject—that is, the person to be made up—Ed and I decided on George Stover, a local actor who has been through this sort of thing before. Since the entire process was to be photographed, we needed someone who could withstand an extra hour or so during the process while camera angles were set up and lights positioned.

Before you begin a makeup creation, you should have a basic design or idea of what you want the final product to look like. Naturally you'll have a picture of the "creature" in your mind, but sketching the front and side views on paper might help you while you're doing the makeup. If your drawing abilities are nonexistent, don't worry—you can improvise as you go along. And even if you do the drawings, you'll probably want to make changes along the way. In any event, Ed and George and I decided to do a metallic alien makeup; something far removed from the typical monster and exaggerated enough to show the potential of the technique.

Assuming that you have some idea of the type of creature you're going to design, you must be certain to have at your disposal all of the necessary materials. Most of these will be available at local hobby or arts and crafts stores; but if they are not, you can order them by mail. Here are the required materials and where you're likely to find them:

1) *Liquid latex:* Found at arts and crafts stores.

2) *Sterile raw cotton:* This comes in sheets and can be found at your drugstore.

3) *Liquid theatrical makeup:* Look for this at theatrical supply stores.

4) *A rubber head cap:* Also called a "bald cap"—this can be found at your theatrical supply store and in variety stores before Halloween.

5) *A few medium and fine width paint brushes.*

6) *A roll of inch or inch-and-a-half width masking tape.*

7) *A pair of scissors.*

8) *Talcum powder.*

A few words about the materials: Liquid latex usually comes in quart ($3.50) or gallon ($10) cans. It's not a dangerous substance, but I wouldn't recommend drinking it. When you apply the liquid latex, it has the consistency of thick paint. When it dries, it becomes a flexible rubber solid.

The sterile raw cotton is essential. Do *not* purchase synthetic cotton —its properties are different from what you need, and it is difficult to mold and shape. The same holds true for cotton balls, because they are *spun* cotton and too "springy" to be shaped when used with latex.

If you can't find a rubber cap, you should improvise some sort of covering for the hair. A fairly thick plastic bag, taped around the subject's head down to the hairline, might do the trick. But whatever you use, be certain that it will keep the makeup materials out of the subject's hair. Liquid latex, when dry, is almost impossible to remove from a scalp full of hair (although latex is easily removed from smooth surfaces and skin).

With your materials at hand, find a place to work. I'd recommend a basement or garage—any place where a bit of mess won't matter. Wherever you work, I'd suggest putting newspapers or a painter's drop cloth on the floor. Also, protect the clothing of your subject, since it's almost certain things will be spilled. Now, you are ready to begin.

First, put the rubber cap or protective covering on the subject's head. Next, use strips of the masking tape to seal off the area between the rubber cap and the skin. The tape and rubber cap give you a clean, unencumbered area on which to work. In some cases, you may want to use a couple of strips of masking tape across the subject's eyebrows to protect them—but usually this is unnecessary unless the subject has extremely bushy eyebrows.

When the face and head areas of the subject are fully prepared, dip a clean paint brush into the talcum powder and apply a light dusting all over the areas to be made up. This serves two purposes: it puts a protective coating on the subject's skin, and it aids in the removal of the completed makeup.

Now, using another clean paint brush, apply a *thin* coating of latex on the areas to be made up (face, masking tape and rubber cap). This coating acts as the basis for the cotton, which will stick to the latex.

Begin the process of building your makeup by peeling off strips of the

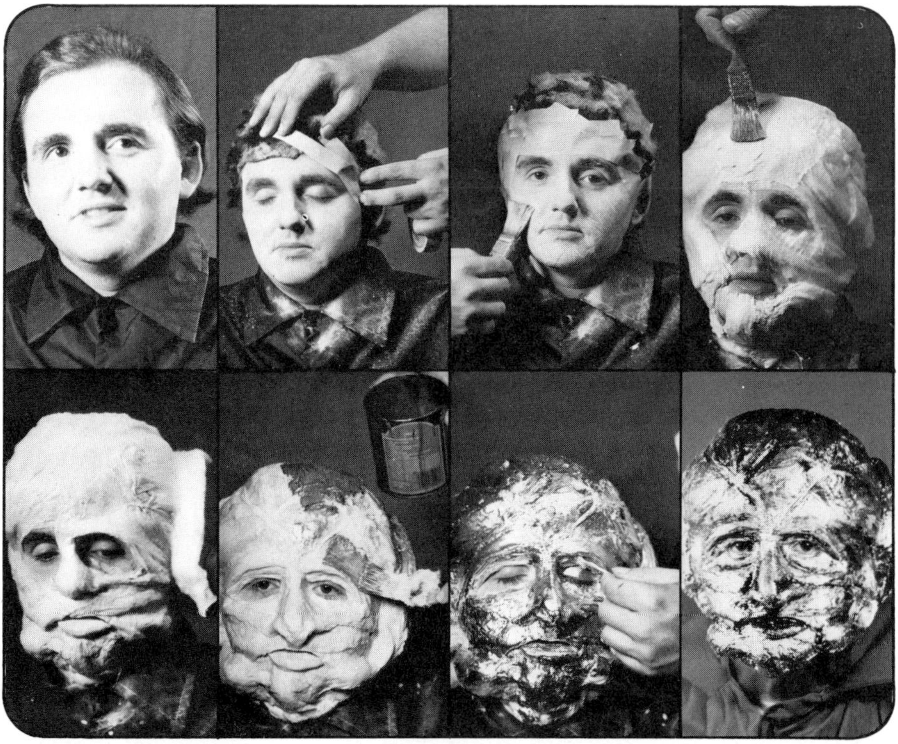

1) The handsome subject before he is transformed. 2) A thin coating of latex serves as a basis for the makeup to come. 3) Some basic shaping is completed with the cotton conforming to the muscle structure of the face. 4) A coating of liquid latex is applied to the cotton basecoat, which will help the second coat of cotton adhere to the first. 5) The lip formation is completed. 6) The makeup artist forms an "alien" ear with a narrow strip of cotton. 7) A second ear is formed. 8) The cotton/latex creation is given some color. 9) The monster is complete.

cotton; start placing them first at the top of the head and working your way down. Keep in mind the normal direction of the head and face anatomy—at least for this first coating of cotton. This is just the base coating for what will eventually become an exaggerated "creature." As you apply the cotton strips, brush them down and into place with thin coats of latex. After you have applied one layer of cotton to the entire head and face (making sure to leave the area around the eyes open, of course), add another thin coat of latex.

Now you are ready for the real creativity of the process: the building and shaping of extreme and grotesque features. There are really no rules here, except that you should try to keep certain muscle structures in mind and build up your layers evenly. Don't build up too much on one particular side at a time—keep your design uniform.

For a large lip, Ed cut out small strips of cotton, applied latex to them and preshaped them into what he wanted before applying the lip to George's face. If you want your design to have lines, wrinkles or—as in Ed's creation—popped-out veins, this preshaping method works better than trying to shape small deformed features directly into the existing cotton/latex buildup.

When working around the eyes, be sure to taper the makeup and feather it out toward the skin. You should not build up thick layers of cotton and latex too close to the eyes, unless you want them to be extremely deep-set eyes (which might pose a problem with lighting and shadows when you are filming). When you color your creation later, you will color the exposed skin regions around the eyes to blend with the rest, giving your makeup a uniform, natural appearance.

In the final stages, Ed Litzinger molded extreme jowls and long, somewhat pointy alien ears which extended down and almost met the jowls. He also drooped the eyes and enlarged the nose considerably.

Once you have completed your design to your satisfaction, let the latex dry a while (about 15 minutes or so) and then begin coloring it. Liquid makeup is your best bet for coloring the skin that remains exposed. Stay away from certain grease stick makeups that are clearly labeled "not for use around the eyes." Let me emphasize that a big part of the credibility of the total look of this makeup is the blending of the skin around the eyes with the actual cotton/latex mask, so the liquid makeup (which can be used around the eyes) is essential. Color is entirely a matter of personal choice, unless you're setting out to create a particular creature (*e.g.*, a werewolf would be brown). Makeup colors come in a wide assortment, and they can also be mixed together for interesting results. For the metallic alien, Ed used both silver metallic and gold metallic colors. Liquid makeup costs about $1.50 per bottle, but it goes a long way. For creating highlighting or accenting certain facial structures, you can use black grease pencil, which comes in a tube. Or you could highlight a particular color—say, green—with a darker shade of green grease pencil to get contrast.

After your makeup is colored and blended into a natural, uniform look, sprinkle talcum powder on it (or theatrical face powder—sometimes referred to as "neutral" powder). This helps to cut down on the shine of the makeup and the inherent stickiness of the latex. If you use metallic colors, as we did, you must use black talcum powder, which is especially suited to a metallic look.

You should now have a completed makeup creation, ready for action in your latest horror film or sci-fi epic. And if you want to put hair on top of the head, I'd recommend a fairly good quality nylon wig. These are available in most theatrical stores and cost from four to eight dollars, depending on the length of the hair. I would *not* recommend the more readily available crepe hair wigs. They don't look real—especially when photographed—and tend to give themselves away as imitation hair. Crepe hair is only useful for facial hair, where small pieces are cut and applied (with either spirit gum or the liquid latex) to form eyebrows, mustaches or small beards. But here again, it's better to use small pieces and strands of the better quality nylon wigs. In general, stay away from crepe hair if you really want a natural look.

The alien makeup Ed Litzinger created for this project was a full-head mask, meaning that the cotton/latex buildup extended down the back of the head to the neck. For your first try at this technique, you could stick to a simpler facial creation and use a wig to hide the rubber cap and masking tape. A facial design will slip off the subject easily with a little tugging and pulling. The whole-head mask, however, might have to be slit or cut at the back of the head before being removed. If you need to use the mask again (yes, it *can* be used again later), the subject can slip the mask on; you then cover the slit with small amounts of latex, cotton and the makeup color you used originally.

Like any project involving the use of specific materials and creativity, this cotton and latex makeup process will demand some experimentation. There are absolutely no rules for the type of features you design—it's all a matter of adding latex and cotton, and refining your final look. Don't be afraid to use your hands; after all, that's where most of the creativity comes from. If you're willing to invest the time and effort, you'll discover that this simple process can yield results as good as any of the masterpieces you've seen in professional films. Good luck!

HOW TO SHOOT A . . .

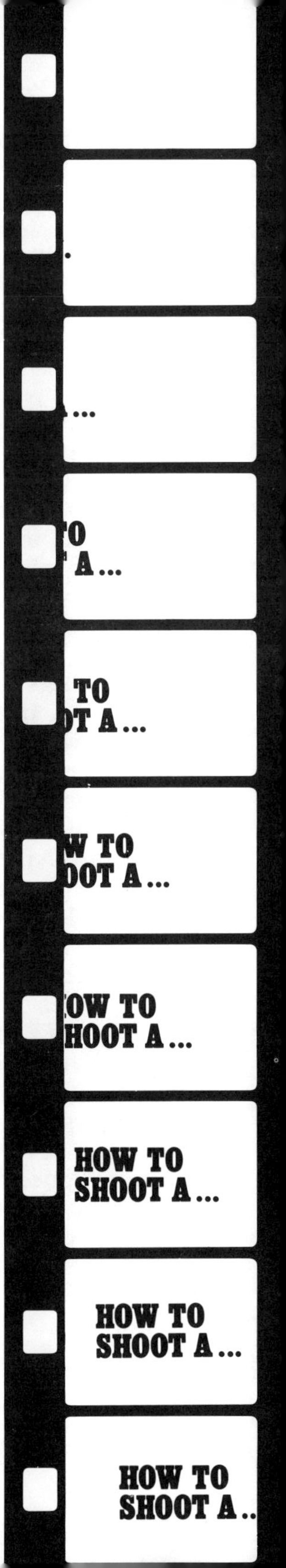
HOW TO
SHOOT A...

CHASE SCENE

Rod Eaton

Remember *The Great Train Robbery?* That was the 1903 Edwin Porter film about a gang that robbed a train, only to be hunted down and killed by a posse. The story was simple, but that 8-minute film established a new style of editing, camera placement and storytelling. Frequently overlooked by film historians, however, is the fact that *The Great Train Robbery* also gave the American cinema the Western and the chase scene.

In the 72 years since Porter's film, Hollywood has ground out scores of Westerns. One unconfirmed estimate places the number at three million. And each of these horse operas has at least one chase scene. Good guys chasing bad guys, bad guys chasing good guys, Indians chasing cowboys, the cavalry chasing Indians and bad guys, and John Wayne chasing everybody.

But the Western movie doesn't have a franchise on chases. Comedies, mysteries, thrillers, action/adventure films, all may include a chase scene. In the last few years, directors seem to have been competing to create the best chase scene in one of three categories—fastest, most hair-raising or most improbable. As a result, we have been given an incredible car chase through San Francisco in *Bullitt*, and a car/elevated train chase in *The French Connection*. We have also seen chases involving airplanes, bicycles, canoes, dirigibles, equestrians, Ferraris, giraffes, hang gliders, infantrymen, jet sleds, kangaroos, llamas, Mounties, narcs, ostriches, Peugeots, queens, rickshaws, steamrollers, tanks, unicorns, VWs, WACs and X (*The Creature from Outer Space*), to name just a few.

Regardless of who chases what, the shooting formula remains basically the same—only the embellishments change. The experience of shooting and editing a chase scene offers you a comprehensive mini-course in filmmaking. Practically every element of camera usage, film language and sequence building is present—pans, tilts, zooms, follow-focus, use of various focal length lenses, continuity of screen direction and action, pacing and parallel editing. If you're a beginning filmmaker, a chase scene can teach you a lot. If you're an old pro, a chase may provide a good refresher course. So, before we begin planning an exciting chase scene you can shoot, let's review some of the basics.

Continuity of Screen Direction

The most important aspect of shooting a chase scene is continuity of screen direction. If the hero is chasing the villain from screen left to right in shot #1, this direction must be maintained in all subsequent shots. If, in shot #9, the action suddenly moves in the opposite direc-

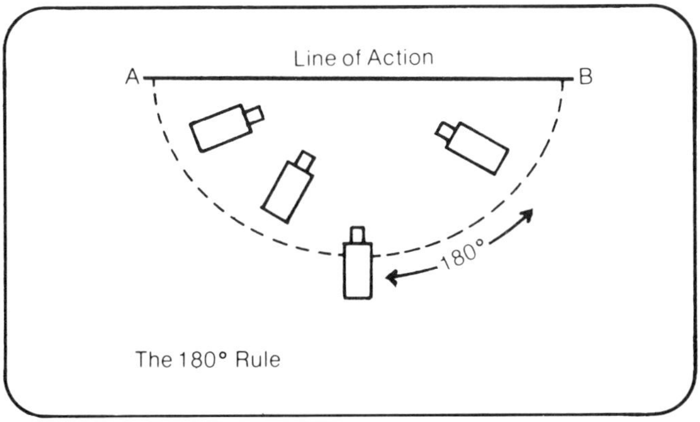

Figure 1: To insure continuity of screen direction, follow the 180-degree rule.

tion—from right to left—the viewer becomes confused. He will wonder, justifiably, why they have turned around.

In order to insure continuity of screen direction, follow the 180-degree rule. The 180-degree rule places an imaginary line through the action and allows you to film the action from any position on *one* side of that line (Figure 1). If you inadvertently cross over the line to shoot, the screen direction will be reversed.

For example, imagine you are shooting a parade. The street is the line of action. You can film the parade from anywhere on one side of the street, and the parade will continue to move in one direction, that is, from screen left to screen right. If you cross the street and shoot, however, it will appear that the parade has changed its mind and is going back home, because you will see the action moving from screen right to screen left. For the same reason, football games are always televised according to the 180-degree rule, with cameras stationed on one side of the line of action. If there were cameras on both sides of the field, you would have difficulty understanding the game. You'd become disoriented and couldn't tell for sure who just scored or which team had the ball.

If you want your chase to change direction, you have to show it change. A shot showing the hero turning around and running the other way can be followed by shots which move in the new direction. Sometimes you can use a shot taken head-on, or from directly behind the line of action (points A and B in Figure 1). These shots are ambiguous in terms of direction and can be used to change screen directions. If your chase scene is lengthy and complex, it's a good idea to shoot a few change of direction shots—just in case. It's easier than you think to wind up at the editing table with left and right pieces of film that cannot be cut together. If you think ahead and get a change of direction shot to insert, you could save yourself some embarrassment.

And don't consider selling your camera just because you made a mistake in screen direction. Console yourself with the fact that it happens to the best of us. When the pros do it, they send the backwards section of film to the lab and have it optically reprinted to flip it around. Then they cross their fingers and hope no one notices that the license plate is reversed and the driver is sitting on the right (or wrong) side.

As with every rule, there are exceptions to the 180-degree rule. If there is some obvious visual reference point in a shot, it may be acceptable to shoot from both sides of the line. For instance, if the hero chases the villain past a gazebo, you could shoot from both sides of the line of action. The audience will understand that the camera has changed position, since the gazebo provides a landmark to keep them oriented. Or suppose a shot shows the chase going from left to right, and in the background we see a man on a hill watching the chase. The next shot is taken from the point of view of the man on the hill. As he sees it, the chase is moving from right to left, so the action would be shown moving that way. Again, the 180-degree rule is being violated, but since the reason is clear, no one becomes disoriented.

Building Excitement in Your Chase Scene

To keep a chase scene exciting, there must be a time and space relationship between the pursuer and the pursued. The audience wants to know how far the hero is behind the villain so they can anticipate the moment he will catch him. This relationship can be established in a number of ways. You can place both protagonists in one shot, clearly showing the space between them. Or you can show the villain race past the camera, and without cutting, have the hero pass a few seconds later. This gives the viewer some idea of the time distance between the two characters.

Another way to establish a time/space relationship is to show each character passing a certain point. For example, one shot shows the villain jumping a fence and running out of the frame. A few seconds, and a few shots later, we see the hero hurdling the same fence. The distance between the two has been defined in terms of screen time. Although the hero is several seconds behind the villain, we know that he is still hot on his trail.

The focal length of the lens (or the position of the zoom lens) you choose for each shot can also be used to advantage in filming a chase. Don't think of a zoom lens as simply a convenient device to frame and compose each shot. Different focal lengths have different characteristics, and these differences can be exploited.

A short focal length lens (wide angle) gives you a greater depth of field—objects near the camera, as well as those far away, will appear in focus. Wide-angle lenses also tend to exaggerate size and movement toward and away from the camera.

A long focal length lens (a telephoto), on the other hand, has a shallow depth of field and minimizes movement toward the camera. Telephoto lenses also make objects appear foreshortened, that is, flat and two-dimensional, giving them a squeezed-together look.

If you understand these lens characteristics, you can choose a zoom position that will help you realize the shot as you visualize it. It may mean walking closer to your subject instead of simply pushing a button and zooming in with your big 10:1, but the extra effort is worth getting the picture quality you want. The extreme wide-angle position, for example, will make it seem as though the hero runs from a distance to the camera in a very short time (because of the exaggeration of movement), and he will remain in focus throughout the shot. Shooting the villain from a distance with the lens at full telephoto, on the other hand, gives the effect of his running for all he's worth, but appearing to get nowhere.

Editing Your Chase Sequence

The time to think about editing your chase sequence is *before* you begin to shoot, not when filming is completed. A good editor makes the best cameraperson, realizing the importance of having a variety of angles, shots (long shots, medium shots, close-ups) and cutaways to choose from when editing. "You can't edit what you haven't got." That's a rule you should keep in mind when you're shooting.

When editing a chase sequence, the important thing is to keep the action moving. You can do this by varying the type of shot and the length of each shot. This will help establish a pace that will heighten the excitement of the chase. Shot length is frequently dictated by the action. A long shot may show the villain coming from around a corner in the distance, running down the block toward the camera, knocking an innocent bystander into the street, leaping over a baby buggy, then leaving the frame in close-up. The hero, close on the villain's heels, chases after him—stopping long enough to help the bystander to his feet and kiss the baby. This shot may be 20 seconds long, but it's packed with action. It could be used in the film intact, without cuts. Following this lengthy shot you could use several short close-ups—the villain glancing over his shoulder as he runs, the hero's feet flying over the pavement, the villain's hand reaching for his gun. As the chase nears its climax, you can cut each shot progressively shorter to increase the tension of the situation.

Another way to add to the excitement is to use the technique of cross-cutting—cutting back and forth from the hero to the villain. There are other filmic elements that can also be added to the chase to provide parallel action. For example, after several shots of the hero and the villain have established the chase, we cut to a drawbridge over a river, then to a close-up of the warning lights flashing. The audience immediately realizes that there is a connection between the chase and the bridge. Then there are more shots of the chase; another shot of the bridge as it begins to lift; a close-up of the warning lights flashing; the villain running on the bridge; a long shot of the bridge rising; the hero on the bridge, in hot pursuit; the villain leaping the widening gap, stumbling; a close-up of the hero's feet—will he make it?

Although there are many rules governing film editing, each filmmaker ultimately develops his own style of cutting. In order to decide if a particular cut works effectively, you might project the film several times, and change the cut single frame by single frame, until you're satisfied with the way it plays.

Planning the Great Chase Scene: The Story

Now that we've covered the basics, let's start planning The Great Chase. Even if it's going to take up 90% of the film, a chase needs a reason for being—something has to happen to precipitate it. A chase isn't a plot, it's only a device. Something has to motivate your characters to chase after one another. Here's a hypothetical plot that may give you some ideas.

Our hero, Simon Goodfellow, is a cub reporter for the *Bingville Bugle*. While covering a Cat Fanciers' meeting, he stumbles onto a nefarious scheme to overthrow the country by electing Iman Idiot to the presidency through a massive write-in ballot. Goodfellow manages to steal into the movement's headquarters and photograph a list of the subversives. He converts the information into a micro-dot, which he conceals in an upper first incisor root canal. He then heads for Washington to alert the CIA.

Meanwhile, the bad guys discover Goodfellow's plan. To stop him, they disguise themselves as Avon ladies and kidnap Simon's fiance, Chastity. As luck would have it, Goodfellow arrives at Chastity's farmhouse just in time to see the gang drive off with her. A harrowing car chase follows—the cars speed along narrow country roads, barely avoiding colliding with trees, bridge abutments, tractors and swords that have been beaten into plowshares. Finally, the bad guys' car misses a turn, careens off the road, crashes through a fence and comes to rest in front of a haystack. Simon leaps out, rounds up the gang, rescues Chastity, and they live happily ever after. Fade out.

A car chase offers unlimited possibilities for an exciting chase. It also poses a few problems. Most Hollywood car chases include multiple fender-bending smash-ups, and almost always end up with at least one car totally destroyed. There's no reason why you can't make a film like that, except it may deplete your filmmaking budget through 1997. Imagine your film budget: four rolls of film & processing, $24; two photo lamps, $2; one Cadillac Eldorado, $10,000. You also have to take into consideration speed laws, other motorists who may have no desire to become part of a high-speed movie chase, and safety.

The Storyboard

The first step, after you have a story, is to plan the chase scene shot by shot. The traditional storyboard is a good way to proceed. By sketching each shot in storyboard sequence, you will get an overview of the progression of the action. You can plan screen direction and change of direction, and decide on camera angles and lenses for each shot. The storyboard will be useful during filming, too. It will help eliminate errors if you use it to check the direction and continuity of each shot, especially when you are shooting them out of sequence.

Once you've outlined your sequence on a storyboard, you have to find a suitable location for your chase scene. To a certain degree, this and step one evolve together, since locations will suggest certain action and camera set-ups. In our story, the car chase takes place in the country—a wise choice, since shooting in the downtown area would present insurmountable problems. For this chase we would look for little-used back roads, or private roads that you could seek permission to use. Depending on how you feel about it, you may want to talk to the local police department. They should know about your plans, and if they're convinced that you're serious about your filmmaking, they may be willing to help.

Whose cars are you going to use for the chase? Who will drive? In most shots you won't be able to see the driver clearly, so anyone can drive. It makes sense to have the best driver you can get, especially if any of the driving is difficult. If you use a stunt driver in place of the actor, have the replacement wear the actor's costume, and, if need be, a wig and make-up. Before you film each shot, block it out with the drivers. Let them drive through the shot slowly a few times so they're familiar with the car, the road and the moves they must make. While they're practicing, you can check your camera coverage and rehearse any moves the camera will make, such as panning, zooming or follow-focusing.

If you'd like to speed up the image on the screen, you can undercrank the camera, that is, run it at a slower than normal speed. If you normally film at 24 fps, you could undercrank at 18 fps during parts of the chase. When projected at 24 fps the cars will appear to go faster

Many shots were used to create the famous chase scene in "Bullitt."

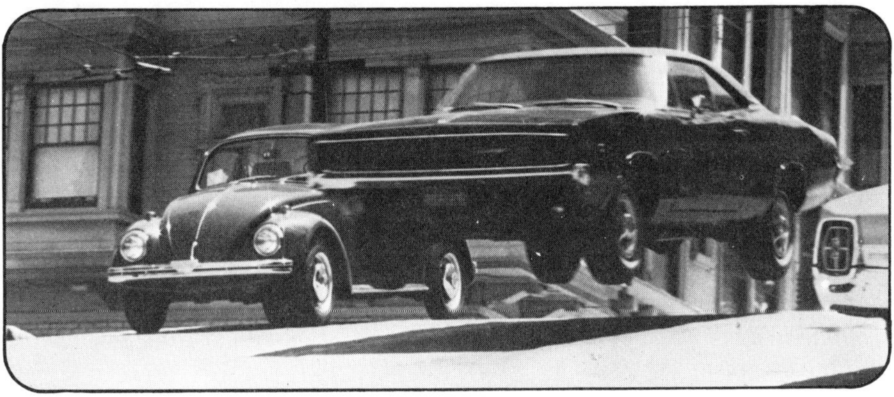

WARNER BROS.

than they really went. Keep in mind that you can only stretch this technique so far. Shooting at 12 fps will usually look faked—dust will settle too fast and the movement of the cars will be jerky. But with a combination of slight undercranking, wide-angle shots to exaggerate movement and clever, fast-paced editing, you can create a feeling of real speed, even though the cars were driven slowly and sensibly. *Above all, don't take risks.* The only good accident is the one you plan.

During the filming of the car chase, station crew people on the road to warn of approaching traffic. You'll need to work out some kind of communications systems between these traffic spotters, the director and the drivers. If a shot is to begin with the cars coming into view around a curve, you could waste a lot of film waiting for the drivers to decide if you're ready for their entrance. Walkie-talkies or citizens' band radios would be ideal, but a system of car horn honks may suffice. Or you can station people with flags just out of camera view but in sight of the director and drivers to signal "action."

It's always a good idea to shoot action sequences with more than one camera. You can cover two or more angles at the same time, giving you ample film to edit without having to restage the action. You could also film the action at various speeds and choose the best looking shot during editing. Before you use two or more cameras, though, check some film taken with each to see if the frame lines all match. There is some difference between certain cameras.

If you're daring, a camera can be mounted on the outside of a car—say just behind the rear wheel—and operated from inside the car by remote control. Universal mounting brackets can be clamped onto a bumper or fender for mounting the camera, or you can rent a heavy-duty suction mount from a motion picture supply house. These units, designed to support heavy 16 and 35mm cameras, will adhere to the smooth side or top of a car. Make sure your camera insurance policy is paid up, just in case. You may discover, too late, that your film gear isn't covered under your household policy.

Remember to shoot lots of cutaways such as close-ups of the speedometer (can be filmed on the freeway with the car going 55 mph), foot on the brake pedal, hands gripping the steering wheel, or the other car in the rear-view mirror. Cutaways will add extra excitement to the chase and they can also get you through some rough spots in the footage.

At the climax of Goodfellow's car chase, the script calls for the bad guys to drive off the road, smash through a fence and end up in front of a haystack. Finding a haystack is easy enough, if you make arrangements with a farmer to borrow one. Driving off the road doesn't have to be difficult either, as long as you pick a spot that doesn't have a deep ditch or other hazards surrounding it. (NB: We recommend that inexperienced drivers limit their chase scenes to action *on* the road.) But crashing through the fence requires a little preparation.

First you'll need to build a fence. It can be constructed out of any old lumber, and the lighter the better. It only has to look real and solid for a moment. Most important, it has to be constructed so it will come apart without offering much resistance to the car. Here's how you do it: Make cuts most of the way through all the main pieces of wood, on the side facing away from the camera. Don't nail anything together—parts of the fence can lay in notches and grooves. The only parts of the fence that should be fairly solid are the posts. These can be pre-cut to snap off at the ground, or you can instruct the driver to go between them.

If the car you are using is a veteran of our streets and highways, you may not mind a few more dents and scratches in the front. Otherwise you can pad the nose of the car with a mattress or several thicknesses of cardboard and rugs. Shoot the crash-through-the-fence from behind the car. By breaking the action into several short shots, you need only pad the car for the actual crash—the shots leading up to it and after it can then be shot from any angle. The entire action will be assembled in editing. (To avoid injury, I suggest driving slowly and undercranking the camera.)

An important element in making this car chase come to life on the screen is sound. Racing motors, squealing tires, the crash when the car hits the fence, the sound as it comes to a stop before the haystack—these sounds will add realism and help sustain excitement. Unfortunately, all of these sounds will have to be added in postproduction, since for the most part, they will have to be faked. Your fake fence won't produce a convincing crash and cars being driven at 30 mph don't sound like cars being driven 50 mph. But the sounds you need can be found on sound effects records and post-dubbed onto your film. This will be a time-consuming process, but it's worth the effort.

There's our chase. Filming a foot chase, a horse chase, a ski chase or any other chase is just as easy. The points to remember are careful planning, rehearsals and safety. Now what has four legs, sixteen hooves, eight tires, runs, gallops and roars, goes like mad and is only eight millimeters wide?

SCIENCE FICTION MOVIE

Rod Eaton

What if? What if time travel was possible? What if the world was overrun by gigantic insects? Or a nuclear holocaust left only a few survivors on the earth? These possibilities are pure speculation, of course—but they *could* happen. That's what makes them science fiction. That's also what makes them ideal candidates for film.

In fact, science fiction and film seem to be made for each other. Film, with its capacity to visually portray fantasies, is an ideal medium for fantastic ideas. Film can take a viewer to other worlds—within the mind and without. It can create a different universe, a new dimension. Film can leap through time and space, as was demonstrated by Kubrick's brilliant cut from a bone thrown by an ape to a satellite orbiting the earth in *2001*.

Creating an SF Film

What kind of science fiction film are you interested in making? In making your decision, you'll find that stories tend to fall into one of these broad categories: one of the most popular is stories that take place in the future. *Metropolis, Planet of the Apes, Clockwork Orange, THX 1138, Soylent Green* and *A Boy and His Dog* all are set in the future. Since anything could conceivably happen tomorrow, the future is an ideal setting for science fiction.

Second in popularity are stories involving aliens—usually hostile aliens. *The Thing, War of the Worlds, Invasion of the Body Snatchers, Village of the Damned, The Day the Earth Stood Still* and *The Man Who Fell to Earth*, as well as a host of lesser efforts in the Earth vs ______________ mold, fall into this category.

Space travel has always fascinated sf fans, and the fascination isn't lessened by reality. *Destination Moon, Forbidden Planet, This Island Earth* and *2001: A Space Odyssey* all involve space travel. To the sf filmmaker, this class offers special appeal in the scope of the special effects possible.

Creature films have given us *The Beast From Twenty Thousand Fathoms, Them, The Fly* and a horde of others easily forgotten. Creatures include prehistoric beasts, man-made monsters and giant mutations—Nature gone wild.

A final category of themes is one I call *Grande Disasters*. These are the films that pit civilization against an insurmountable threat—the end of the world is generally at hand. *When Worlds Collide, The Andromeda Strain* and *On the Beach* are fine examples. *Crack In the Earth* and *The Day the Earth Caught Fire* are on a lesser level, but typical.

These five categories, of course, don't include everything. Many films don't fit neatly into any one category. For example, *2001* deals with alien contact and space travel and is set in the future. There's ample room in each category for creating good science fiction films.

When deciding what type of sf film you want to make, try to keep your ideas within the limits of your abilities and finances. It's easy to visualize a galactic war—hundreds of incredible spaceships marauding through the universe, destroying planets, stars and each other. But it's another thing entirely to put the concept on film. If you have the time, money, facilities and expertise to tackle such a movie, by all means do so. But know your limits.

Although the fanciful, the amazing and the incredible may be what draws you to sf filmmaking, good sf may include these elements in very small amounts. It's easy to get involved in an elaborate production and assume the effects will carry a weak or non-existent story. Such is never the case. Special effects may be required by a film like *Forbidden Planet* or *War of the Worlds*. In fact, it would be difficult to imagine these films without effects—certainly *2001* would have been a different film without its incredible special effects. But it's a mistake to assume effects are mandatory for an sf film—they are not. *On the Beach* has no effects that come to mind. We are told there has been an atomic war, but we never actually see it.

Writing the Story

With a firm grip on the realities of your production capabilities, you've decided what type of sf film you will make. The next step is to formulate a premise on which to build your story. A science fiction premise should be based on scientific facts, but since sf is speculative, the science and technology can be speculative. Let's create a hypothetical sf film premise.

Few people doubt the influence television has on our lives, even though there's little consensus on the nature of that influence. Imagine a future form of television: instead of merely watching a picture, people

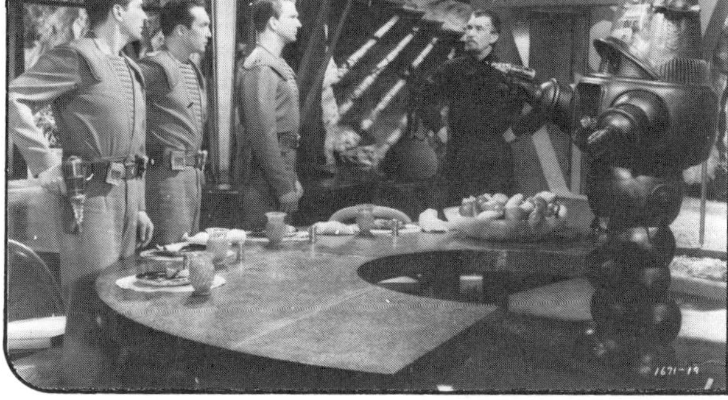

Superlative special effects helped make "The Forbidden Planet" one of the all time best science fiction films.

"plug into" a receiver. They don't watch and listen—they experience. Sights, smells, sounds, sensations—all are real. So real, in fact, that it's impossible to distinguish between the experience and reality.

There's our premise. Is it possible? Experimenters know it's possible to stimulate the brain electrically to produce sensations of color, smell, fear and pleasure. Our device—we'll call it sensavision—is only slightly more sophisticated. It's certainly possible in the near future.

What would we be like if a majority of people spent most of their time plugged into sensavision? Unable to distinguish between real experiences and programmed ones, would we lose our individuality? Since memories help make us each unique, what happens if all of us share exactly the same memories? Not similar memories (we each have personal memories of Kennedy's assassination), but identical, very real, very personal memories?

Given this premise, what are the possibilities? How would people react to sensavision? Would they prefer fabricated programmed lives to real ones? Which would be their "real" life? What story possibilities does the premise suggest?

When writing your story, remember that sf isn't in a special category that exempts it from the rules of good fiction. Many sf films seem to overlook this fact and give us stories that would be laughed at in any other genre. The producers of *Star Trek* faced this problem at the beginning of their television run. They found that many television writers had little understanding of sf. *The Making of Star Trek* (Steven E. Whitfield and Gene Roddenberry, Ballantine Books, 1968) explains how one common writing problem was dealt with. When in doubt about dialogue or character's actions, writers were advised to mentally transfer the scene to a contemporary setting. Thus Kirk would become the captain of a battleship instead of a starship. In this more familiar setting, believability could be better gauged.

This mind game—shifting action to a familiar setting—should eliminate the most offensive sf dialogue devices, the "explanation." Imagine how you'd react if a man sitting to you on a bus turned and said, "This is a cigarette lighter. When I rotate this wheel rapidly the serrated edge turns against this piece of flint. Friction causes a spark, thus igniting this wick which is soaked in a low-temperature ignition fluid. From the resultant flame I light my cigarette."

No one, however, seems surprised to hear a character in a science fiction movie say, "This is an ion-ionizer. When I depress this stud, sub-miniature electronic circuitry based on an oscillating quartz chip emits a positively charged hyperbolic field. Ions, drawn from the air through this chamber, are passed through the field, thereby over-ionizing them. The unstable ions move past this wick which is soaked in a low-temperature ignition fluid. From the resultant flame I light my cigarette."

There may be some things in an sf film that need explaining, but you

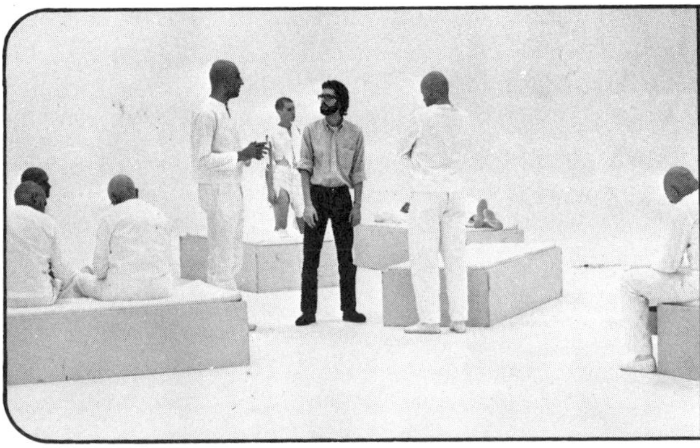

WARNER BROS.

Stunning futuristic effects were simply achieved in "THX 1138" by shaving the actors' heads and dressing them in white overalls.

can find a more subtle way of doing so than simply having a character tell us. After all, movies are, first and foremost, visual. In most cases seeing something is better than being told what is happening. *2001* never bothered to explain much to the viewer, but the film didn't suffer from a lack of information.

Let's go back to our sensavision premise and expand it a bit more. How far into the future we are can be left unspecified. What is the future like? Worldwide shortages of food, energy and resources have placed great strains on an overcrowded planet. Life has become bleak, drab and monotonous. Government is unable to do much—it has its hands full dealing with civil unrest. Cities are decaying, jobs are scarce, the air is foul, food is synthetic and unappealing, there is no recreation. There is little left but to exist.

Into this world comes sensavision. Given the option of existing in the real world or plugging into programmed lives of adventure, romance and excitement, which would you choose? Recognizing the advantages of an anesthetized populace, the government makes sensavision available to everyone who wants it. Nearly everyone wants it.

There are any number of story possibilities inherent in this premise. Because I think science fiction films tend to lean too far toward the Grande Disaster concept, I would opt for a story involving one couple's lives in this bleak future world. The man decides he can't cope with reality any longer and asks the appropriate government agency to install a sensavision receiver in his room. The woman believes living—even a bleak life—is better than the sensavision non-life. After repeated attempts to convince the man he should experience life rather than drop out and accept a programmed existence, the woman realizes she can't hope to compete with the sensavision programs. Ultimately, she, too, plugs in.

Producing the Film

How would a film like this be produced? Because the concept and story have been developed with limited production requirements in mind, the film could be made easily with a minimum of special effects, sets and so forth. Our city of the future could be filmed around any locations that are suitably rundown—old sections of town, condemned buildings, decrepit apartments. How will our future citizens dress? In glittery suits of silver and plastic? That wouldn't fit our premise. Simple clothing of drab, dark colors would reinforce the mood and feeling we want to create. Small, subtle touches like Velcro fasteners instead of zippers and buttons will convey the feeling of a future time. Color-coded ID patches on sleeves would also suggest the anonymity and regimentation of our future world.

Since we've established that our future isn't based on sophisticated technology, it would be inappropriate to have sets dressed with elaborate gadgets. Instead, contemporary furniture and props, carefully aged, become the future's "antiques." As usual, furniture stores, theatrical companies, theater groups, display firms, even friends and neighbors may be good sources for locating and borrowing props and furniture for your sets.

The sensavision unit will have to be built. How would such a device look? A big, black box covered with rows of flashing lights, a myriad of instruments and hundreds of switches? Probably not. Think of its function in terms of the premise. It is a mass-produced device, like our TVs, designed to go into homes and be used by the average person. Considering the miniaturization already accomplished in electronics, the sensavision unit would probably be small. It's certain to be easy to operate and, since it comes from tomorrow's equivalent of GE, it would look good—not a crude prototype.

How would a person plug in? Would he wear electrodes on his scalp like an EEG machine? Or would there be some sort of cap? If the story requires that we be able to see what the user is seeing, how will this be handled? Will there have to be some type of monitor screen on the unit? For the sensavision unit to be believable, each of these questions must be answered in keeping with the premise.

Using the same premise and the same story, it would be possible to

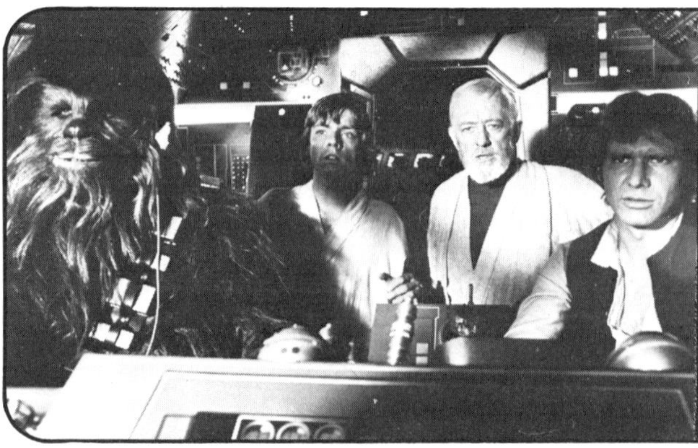

The special effects in "Star Wars" carried the art to new levels of sophistication.

make a full-scale Hollywood-type production with giant sets, elaborate costumes and a cast of thousands. Instead of shooting the film around existing locations, a miniature city could be built. Schufftan mattes could be used to combine live actors with the miniature and to create images on the sensavision's monitor screen.

Of course, if it's special effects that you're interested in, you might prefer to design a film around effects work. Stories set in the future offer lots of possibilities—but so do stories of alien invaders, trips to outer planets, awakened pre-historic monsters or the world being threatened with a take-over by the Coca-Cola Company. Any of these concepts may provide the basis for a good sf story and a good sf film. But make it a *good* science fiction film—the world's already crawling with bad ones. (Perhaps there's an sf premise there: the Earth is dead and millions of years from now an alien creature finds the only remains of our civilization—a print of *The Green Slime*.) Make characters, action and dialogue believable. Think out costumes, props, locations and sets, special effects and budgets in terms of your story and premise. Create the uncreatable, the unimaginable, the incredible. After all, film is an ideal medium for fantastic ideas.

SPORTS FILM

Francis A. Breen, Jr.

If you really want your movies to *move*, there's nothing like a fast-paced sports film. And for me, there's no sport like basketball—women's basketball.

Four years ago, coach Cathy Rush and the "Mighty Macs" of Immaculata College, Immaculata, Pennsylvania, were driving their opposition into oblivion, and I decided to grab some of the action with my new Super-8 camera. Combining footage from several games with titles and shots of newspaper headlines, I assembled a 20-minute film. With the help of my wife, who was to become my assistant camera operator, I talked my way into a victory barbecue and showed my film. Presto, the Macs had their own cinematographer. Since then, I've followed *my* team all over the country, recording their victories (many) and their defeats (few), as well as sharpening my filmmaking skills. My game plan for a winning film applies to both men's and women's basketball, and to many other indoor sports events.

Equipment

Don't believe all the gloomy words you hear about dark-as-the-pit gymnasia. A good XL camera (with a maximum *f*/1.2 lens) and Ektachrome 160 will provide a decent exposure almost anywhere the players can see the ball. A 5:1 zoom ratio is adequate for any size gym; I use a Bauer C5 XL. You'll also need a tripod with a good *pan* or *fluid* head to follow action smoothly up and down the court for two hours.

Ektachrome 160 is the "Old Faithful" of indoor sports filming, but you can often get away with Kodachrome 40 in the brighter gyms. Slip a roll in your camera and check the lightmeter to see if it gives the okay. Kodachrome will give you more brilliant (saturated) colors and finer grain.

How many rolls of film should you take? That depends on the scope of your ambition. To capture your benchwarming offspring's fleeting moments of glory, two or three cartridges may do the job, but come prepared to catch an All-Star performance. If you're shooting a "training" film to help players analyze how well they're doing, figure five rolls for each 20-minute half. For important games, I used two cameras, one at a high vantage point and the other at floor level, and shot up to 40 rolls. Of course, that includes a lot of crowd reaction shots, close-ups and similar gingerbread, and ultimately requires a firm hand at the editing table.

My pre-game checklist includes: camera with fresh batteries, second camera as a backup or for an assistant, tripod, extra set of batteries, 20 rolls of Ektachrome and Kodachrome (better to have film left over than to run out), crayon for numbering rolls of film and a trash bag for film wrappers. Pack up your gear in a gadget bag, make sure you have separate compartments for fresh and exposed film and start your drive to the hoop.

Setting Up

Obtain permission to film the game ahead of time from the athletic director. This will avoid legal problems and last-minute hassles. Arrive early enough to find a "50-yard line" seat high above court side, preferably a comfortable spot with ample room to set up your tripod. Don't obstruct the view of the paying customer. Well-attended games may force you into unusual locations. In Cleveland, Mississippi, I filmed one of the Macs' games from a swaying catwalk suspended from the ceiling of a very high gymnasium. At the University of Villanova Field House in Philadelphia, I alternately sat, stood and knelt on a window sill. At Glassboro State College in New Jersey, I filmed from a scaffolding on wheels which some energetic fans started rolling courtside during the game. Most of the larger gyms have areas designated for filming, eliminating these problems. At times I have filmed from the press box, and during a championship game at Madison College, Virginia, I shared a huge platform with an ABC television crew.

Lighting

Once you have a place to hang your hat, check out the lighting conditions. Most Super-8 cameras have a built-in #85 daylight filter that must be removed when shooting indoors under tungsten light. *Beware of gyms with fluorescent lighting.* As far as your camera is concerned, fluorescent light is sunlight. Leave the filter in place. If you remove it, Type A Kodachrome and Ektachrome will come out an overexposed sickly green. Ektachrome G, however, requires no filtration whatever the light source.

Is the gym lit up for TV coverage? Bright spots on the highly reflec-

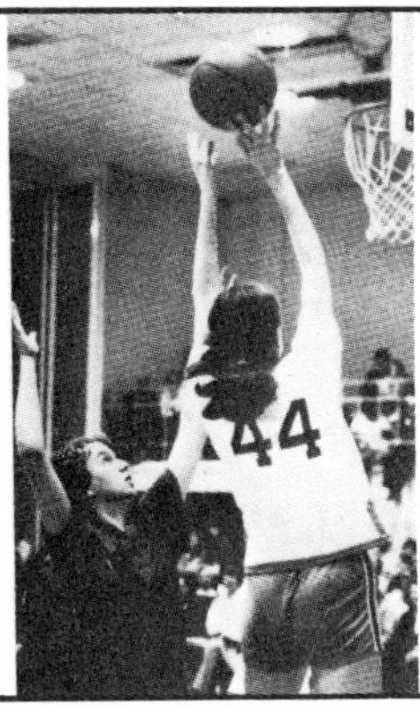

Once you've established the overall action, concentrate on your star.

tive hardwood can fool your lightmeter, closing your lens and underexposing everything but the glare. My film of an important game the Macs played with Maryland was all but ruined by a pulsating shutter as my camera swept up and down the court. I should have taken an average light reading off the court surface and set my *f*/stop manually. This can be done by using the built-in meter in your camera to find the *f*/stop of an evenly lit section of the floor and then shooting the entire game with this setting. If you can't set your *f*/stop manually, avoid shooting down on the court from a high perch. Instead, shoot across court from floor level. Fans on the opposite bleachers will provide a consistent background and your lightmeter will read true.

The One Big Game

You've never shot a basketball game before and probably never will again, but this is the big one, so you want to get it right. Arrive at the gym at least an hour before the game to acquaint yourself with the size, layout and lighting.

From a high central location, shoot some player introductions before the tap off. Follow the opening action for a few minutes, keeping most of the players in your field of vision. Once you've established the overall action, concentrate on your star for a while. From the same vantage point, zoom in (don't lose that sharp focus) and follow her (or him) with or without the ball for a few minutes. If she's hot, stay with her. If not, pull back and follow the ball. At time-outs and dead ball situations, shoot brief bursts of the scoreboard. Now move to courtside and shoot some floor level action, always maintaining a balance between team play and your star player. Try different areas along the sideline and behind the basket. High or low, remember to stay on the same side of the court throughout the game or you will violate the 180-degree rule and reverse the flow of action. Be sure to catch the final seconds of the game with the fans streaming onto the court. If somebody cuts down the net, be ready to shoot it. Finish up with a shot of

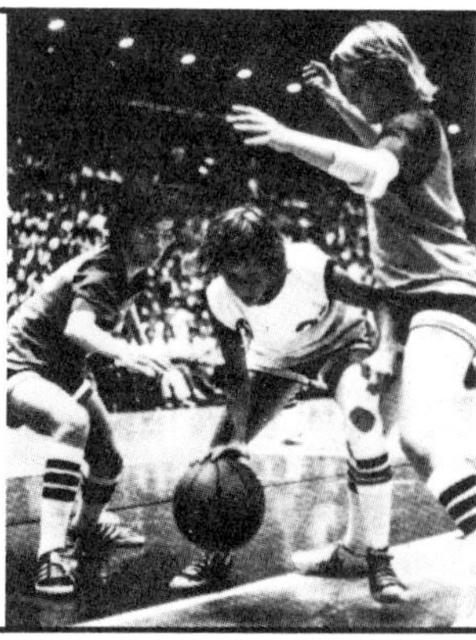

Your sports film should be filled with action and emotion.

the program showing the teams, the date and the site of the contest. This can be spliced to the beginning of your film as an introduction. Your entire production can be tucked neatly into a half dozen rolls of film. We'll discuss editing a little further along.

Training Films

You can help your team to victory by providing the coach with game films designed to show strategies and skills in action. You may even get the athletic department to pick up the bill for your filmmaking. The coach will tell you if he wants to emphasize offense, defense or perhaps a particular player.

Pick a high central location and set up your tripod. Remove ten rolls of film, number them consecutively and stack them nearby for quick snatching. Zoom in on the mid-court logo to focus. Pull back to include 50 to 75 percent of one half court in your field of view. Shoot the opening tap-off and follow play until the first break in the action. When panning from right to left, always keep the ballhandler in the right quarter of the frame. You want the player to be moving *into* the frame, not running out of it. Foul shots are dull and waste film; pick up the action at half court after a score unless you wish to focus on the defensive press. Once again, use breaks in the action to shoot 2-second bursts of the scoreboard. Know the sound and feel of your camera and try to end your roll of film at a break in the action, even if this means wasting a few feet of film. You will miss less and make combining rolls easier.

Highlight Films

The backbone of your "highlights of the season" film will be condensations of five or six key games throughout the year. When these were first shot as training films, editing consisted simply of splicing together the ten or so rolls in chronological order. Now you need to chop them down to show your team at its exciting best.

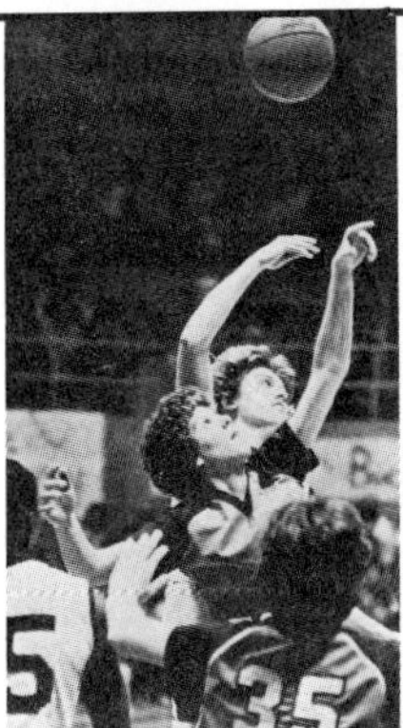

Use slow motion to capture the grace of the players in action.

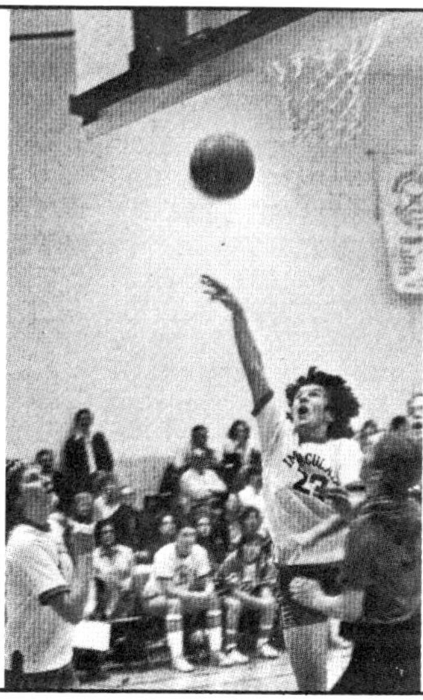

IMMACULATA COLLEGE

Try shooting at floor level to avoid light bouncing off hardwood.

View each game several times, selecting ten or twelve good sequences: a fast break, a stolen ball, a long set shot, *etc.* Vary the length of shots to avoid monotony and splice in cutaways of a huge cheering crowd, a single pom pom waving, a close-up of the team mascot, the scoreboard and so forth. A finished sequence could be: tap off in slow motion (15 seconds), close-up of an intent cheerleader's face (4 seconds), long jump shot soaring 30 feet into the net (10 seconds), crowd cheers (2 seconds), medium shot of your team slowly working the ball around to an open player who scores (25 seconds), the scoreboard (2 seconds), and a series of four driving lay ups, each lasting 4 to 6 seconds and coming in rapid sequence, ending with the crowd cheering (8 seconds). Well, you get the idea.

If this game was shot mostly from a high vantage point, follow it with a game shot mostly at floor level. During the season, film one big game with two cameras, one high at mid-court, one roaming at floor level. Find identical sequences shot by both cameras and intercut. For example, show your team on a fast break with the top camera, then cut to the low level camera's close-up footage of a player scoring. This can be a real show stopper!

I began one year's highlight film with an interview of the coach talking about the coming season, which I shot with a single-system sound camera. Then I swung abruptly to the titles, *Drive to the Hoop*. . .*with Cathy Rush*. . .*and the Mighty Macs*, and shifted into the first edited game, which was accompanied by a swinging Dixieland jazz number on the sound track. For the second game, I used a voice-over narration by one of the players, identifying her by a close-up at the start of the game. Before the next game, I inserted some footage of the team clowning around at practice. Then I threw in some tears, a loss for humility, and finished with a graduating senior giving her summary of the season.

Your team may not win three consecutive national championships, nor go to the finals five years in a row as the Macs did, but even if you're filming the local high school team, you're getting involved in a dynamic way with the fastest sport on legs. Good shooting!

WEDDING MOVIE: FOR LOVE OR MONEY

Chris Jones

The first wedding I filmed was a very unusual event. It took place in St. Louis, at the Climatron, a huge botanical garden housed in a glass, geodesic dome designed by Buckminster Fuller. The ceremony involved a good deal of moving around—different parts of the ceremony took place in different areas of the dome which were connected by narrow paths and staircases. Besides doing a lot of legwork, I gained some insight into the problems of shooting wedding movies.

Basically, the three most serious problems I faced were: planning my movements, setting the accurate exposure, and planning which shots to take. I had never filmed an event with such constant motion. I overused my zoom, and several important moments came out much too grainy and indistinct. To make matters worse, the weather was very bad the day of the wedding, and it was very dark at the bottom of the garden. Consequently, the entire film looked slightly underexposed, even though I was using Ektachrome 160. I also had trouble keeping the faces of the wedding party turned towards the camera, a problem which could have been solved by more careful planning of my shots. But let's consider each problem separately. With the benefit of hindsight, I can give some practical advice to those of you who would like to try filming your own wedding movies.

Planning Your Movements

Once you know you will be shooting a wedding, you should try to attend the rehearsal. At the rehearsal, determine where you can stand and at what points you will be able to change positions during the ceremony. An important thing to remember about filming a wedding is that the action doesn't wait for the filmmaker, nor can a scene be redone if you aren't ready the first time. So in order to insure adequate results, you must know in advance not only where you are going to stand, but what you are going to shoot, and from what camera angle you can best shoot it. Here are some examples of possible camera positions that offer flexibility for your camera work, particularly if there is a lot of subject movement during the wedding. First, there are the positions from which you can shoot the actual, physical location or setting for the wedding—the church, backyard, living room, etc. If you arrive early, you can take establishing shots of the actual location and be in a good position to capture the arrival of guests and the wedding party. Second, there is the aisle position near the altar, for shooting the procession (the bride comes down the aisle towards you). You may find that this position is too obtrusive, unless the wedding ceremony is itself quite casual. During any wedding ceremony, the key word is dis-

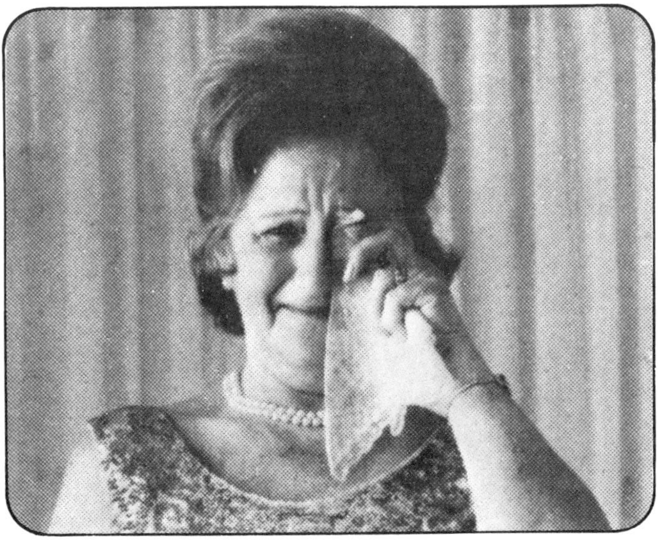

Use quick close ups of the parents of the bride and groom.

cretion. The less the people at the wedding see or hear you, the better they will like you. You should remember that the actual event is as important to the participants as your film of it. So stay out of the way as much as possible by using your zoom for close-ups. Plan to remain on the fringes of the crowd. Finally, after the ceremony, you should place yourself at the top of the aisle to follow the action as the wedding party leaves the altar to form the reception line.

Equipment and Exposure

For an indoor wedding I always have used Kodak Ektachrome 160 film; for outdoor weddings, I use Kodachrome 40.

Since most Super-8 cameras have automatic exposure control, if you keep the sun behind you outdoors, you should get good results. Indoors, existing light cameras (XL models) with fast lenses and increased shutter angles, are useful. Testing the available light can be very critical, however, depending on the camera you use. I usually use a separate lightmeter, and if there is time, I shoot a test cartridge at the rehearsal.

One problem that can occur with an indoor wedding at night is that the predominant available light may be fluorescent. Fluorescent light with daylight coming in through windows creates very few problems. But fluorescent light at night, or a combination of fluorescent and incandescent light, is a problem. Where the dominating light is fluorescent, a color temperature meter is of no value as fluorescent light cannot be measured on the Kelvin scale (Kelvin readings measure the color temperature of the prevailing light. Color film can be adjusted by means of filters to the color temperature of the prevailing light in order to give natural color rendition.) Under these circumstances, an experimental shoot is very valuable, if you have the time to wait for the processing. Also, try shooting with or without the standard built-in filter (No. 85A), and at both the indoor (tungsten) and outdoor (daylight) ASA ratings recommended on your film package. There are a variety of fluorescent tubes on the market, ranging from daylight tubes, which come fairly close to daylight colors, to cool white tubes, which can render things blue and green and make flesh tones look very sickly. For a list of filters you can use to accurately expose your film under fluorescent lighting, you can write the manufacturer of the film you use, or consult filmmaking books with filter charts, such as *Independent Filmmaking*, by Lenny Lipton (Straight Arrow Books, $7.95, paperback edition).

Another exposure problem might occur if you plan to shoot indoors—inside a dimly lit church, for example—and then move outdoors without changing film. If you turn your filter key, or flip the lever on your Super-8 camera to adjust for the indoor/outdoor lighting sources, the slight color difference created by the filtered light might be noticeable in your projected film. However, you can use a neutral density filter to cut down the daylight reaching the film as you move outdoors, and you can stop shooting *before* the daylight is prevalent. Then change your camera angle and your position (to avoid a jump cut), and start to shoot again outdoors, in full daylight.

Planning Your Shots

There are certain moments during the ceremony which must be captured on your film: the procession, with an individual close-up of every person in it; the giving away of the bride; the exchange of rings; the blessing; the kissing of the bride; the exit; and the bride and groom's departure for their honeymoon. If there is a reception, it's also a good idea to show the cutting of the cake and toasting. Once the action for each of these moments is on film, you will have an easily understood narrative in which everyone who was in the ceremony, as well as many of the guests, plays a part. Beyond this narrative account, there is one important point to remember: take as many close-ups of the bride and groom and as many cutaways of others as you can. A good technique is to use quick close-ups of the parents of the bride and groom, capturing their expressions during the ceremony.

You should not attempt to shoot a film which depicts the entire ceremony, from beginning to end, unless of course you want to make a full record of the event. It is enough to capture important action sequences which lend themselves to a dramatic re-creation of the event.

Memorable Movies

The results of my first attempt at a wedding movie pleased the couple so much that before long, other people started contacting me to do their weddings and I have received a lot of requests from people

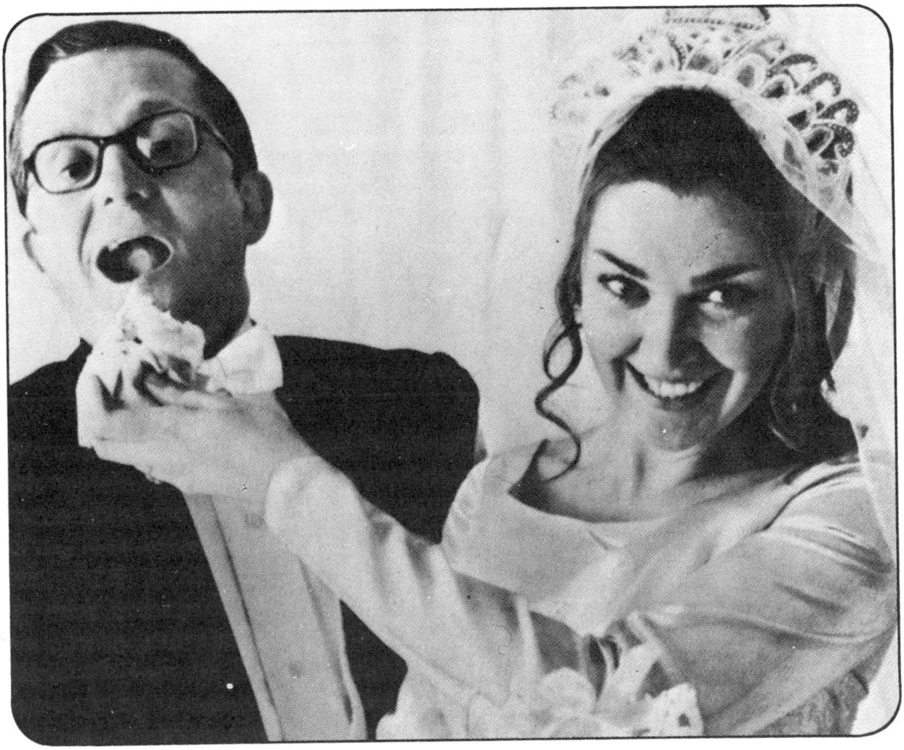

Show the cutting of the cake and the toasting.

who have heard of my work by word of mouth. This was enough to convince me that I could go into business filming weddings. But filming a wedding in Super-8 makes sense for a number of reasons and the business angle is only one of them.

Super-8 cameras and projectors are now common household items, and therefore, a logical medium for recording and seeing family events. A family need not rent special equipment to see the film. In addition, Super-8 movies of weddings have an advantage over still photographs since the entire atmosphere of the event, including sounds, can be recorded and shaped into a memorable film. Viewing a Super-8 film can be done with almost as little effort as paging through a photo album. And most important of all, the Super-8 medium allows you to be very inconspicuous at the wedding itself. You require no special lights and no assistants. The camera is relatively quiet and some compact models will fit into your pocket. This gives you freedom to move around during the ceremony, without interrupting the ritual itself with glaring lights or noisy and cumbersome equipment.

UNDERWATER FILM

Joe Thompson

Super-8 is really the perfect medium for anyone who wants to explore the fascinating world under our seas. Filming underwater is not difficult and can be mastered by any filmmaker willing to first learn the rules of safe diving. You'll be introduced to a world whose colorful creatures are natural subjects for film.

Ten years ago, while I was employed as a research submarine pilot, I purchased my first Super-8 camera to record a typical at-sea operation to show my family and friends. I was surprised at the results—the saturated colors and contrast of the film were quite astounding. Although I was an underwater cameraperson geared for professional results with larger format equipment, I could not control the urge to have a Plexiglas housing built for my newly acquired Super-8 camera.

The First Step

If you have the urge to try this greatest of all filming experiences, you should learn to dive properly. This involves becoming a qualified scuba (self-contained underwater breathing apparatus) diver. The first step you should take is to contact the local skin diving equipment shop in your area. Practically all dive shops today offer courses in scuba diving. Other organizations that certify divers are the NAUI (National Association of Underwater Instructors), PADI (Professional Association of Diving Instructors), NASDS (National Association of Skin Diving Schools) and the YM/YWCA. Contact one of these organizations and take a qualifying course.

After certification the next step is complete self-indulgence in the good old written word. Read everything you can get your hands on about diving and filming. *Skin Diver* magazine, sold at most dive shops, will give you an excellent rundown of the diving world and frequently has articles on underwater filming and photography. There are books by the dozens, and the best thing you can do is to visit your local library, camera store or diving shops and inquire about books on underwater photography.

Equipment You'll Need

Snorkeling: A great way to introduce yourself to diving and filming underwater is snorkeling. Equipment is quite inexpensive—all you need for snorkeling is a face mask, snorkel and a pair of fins for your feet. Floating face down in shallow water, breathing through the snorkel tube, you can spend hours viewing varieties of fish, shellfish, sponges and plant life. You can also hold your breath and take a dive under for a closer look at marine life. It's important to wear protective clothing so your back doesn't get severely sunburned as you float.

To film while snorkeling or diving, you'll need a watertight housing (usually made of Plexiglas) for your Super-8 camera that lets you get at camera controls. There are housings available for almost every popular Super-8 camera. Many of the manufacturers that make these housings will also custom-make a case for your Super-8. One company in particular, Ikelite Underwater Systems, offers a variety of inexpensive Plexiglas housing for Super-8 cameras as well as underwater lights and other equipment. Generally, the price of these cases depends on the number of controls they have for operating the camera.

What kind of camera should you use? With the proper housing, many of the Super-8 cameras on the market will work for underwater filming. However, it's best to use an XL camera because you'll be filming in low light and will need the extra light gathering advantages of these cameras. You should also choose a lens with a good wide-angle setting. A zoom lens with a telephoto setting is almost useless underwater because images seen by the camera will appear closer than they actually are, stretching the normal focal length of your lens by about one-third. Light rays passing through the water, the housing and camera lens are refracted or bent, causing images to appear closer. Thus, a wide-angle setting will give you a normal image. I use a Beaulieu 5008S mainly because of its fast *f*/1.2 lens and 6mm (wide angle) focal length.

Diving: At this stage of the game, you're probably wondering about scuba gear. I can honestly say that practically all of the nationally

Filming underwater is not difficult and can be mastered by any filmmaker willing to first learn the rules of safe diving.

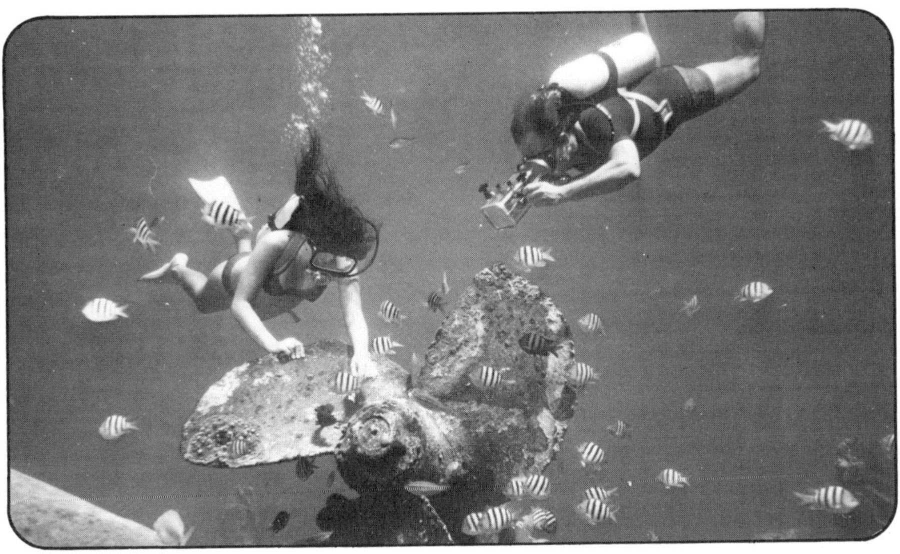

advertised diving equipment is good and reliable. It has to be. No reputable dealer wants to gamble on a lawsuit from a diver who got into trouble because of poor equipment. An excellent way to find out about the best equipment to purchase or rent is to join a local skin diving club. Most of these people dive because they love to and want the best equipment available. They'll be glad to tell you the advantages of the equipment they personally use. Another good advantage of joining a local club is that you'll nearly always find an underwater photographer or film buff. The instructor of your diving course should also be able to recommend up-to-date equipment. Today equipment for the properly outfitted diver can range in cost from $450 to over $1,000. If you only plan to dive a few times a year, on vacation for example, you can save by renting equipment from a diving equipment shop. Diving equipment is a personal thing—you should choose equipment that suits your particular needs and feels right to you.

Taking the Plunge

Once you have your diver certification, equipment and your favorite Super-8 in waterproof housing, head with a diving buddy to a spot where you'll find subject matter to film. Again, local dive shops or skin diving clubs can direct you to the right spots. It's a good idea to pick a subject to film ahead of time. It might be a rare type of fish or marine life or simply a document of the preparation for the dive, boat trip and dive itself. Get together a good outline that does nothing more than tell a story. That's the most important thing in any type of filmmaking. An old-timer in the film business taught me years ago the magical "W" formula: who, what, why, where and when (and how). Consider these when you make your film outline. I usually go on location with my outline, and from that I work up separate little sequences or stories to film. Never be afraid to deviate from your outline—that's the beauty of documentary filmmaking.

Going underwater with your equipment the first few dives will seem awkward, but don't let that bother you. Check your camera housing for leaks and proper balance. It should hang suspended in the water (called "neutral buoyancy") and handle quite easily. When you and your partner or diving guide are in the water, it will be difficult to communicate. It's a good idea to agree ahead of time on some hand signals to help coordinate your filming.

Shooting Techniques

It's extremely important to approach fish slowly with a minimum amount of motion. This may take a bit of practice, but it's worth the effort. Sudden movement or jerking the camera around in a fast pan will frighten fish away. Concentrate on one subject at a time trying to get long, medium and close-up shots. Due to the light refraction mentioned earlier, fish and other subjects will appear in your viewfinder

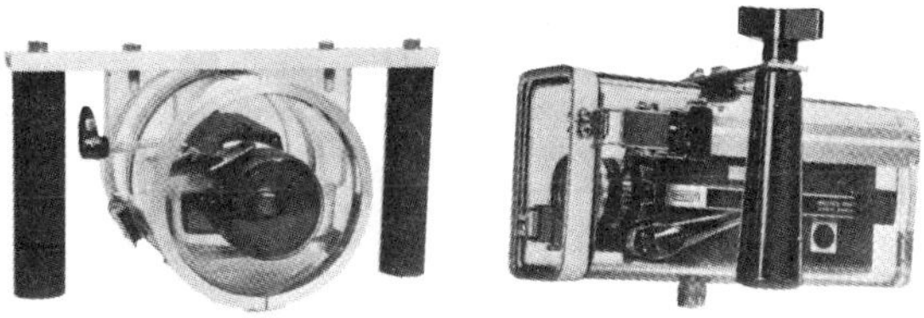

A watertight Plexiglass housing for your Super-8 camera, such as those made by Ikelite Underwater Systems, will allow you to film while snorkeling or diving.

closer than they actually are. *Set the focus by what your camera sees and not by actual distance.* If your camera doesn't focus through the lens, set the focus about one-third closer than the actual distance. For example, if a subject is 6 feet from your camera, set the focus scale at 4 feet.

Underwater, your camera can move freely and easily in any direction, and it's a great temptation to begin panning and tilting. You should immediately get in the habit of holding the camera level and steady. Stop and position yourself for each shot. Keeping a steady orientation will make the film much more enjoyable to watch. One technique that does work well is holding the camera in front of you and very slowly moving with it, propelling yourself with your fins. The effect is like that of a dolly shot.

Film Stocks

The two film stocks I've used with success underwater are Kodachrome 40 (K40) and Ektachrome 160 (E160). K40 generally gives you warmer tones to soften the blue-green tint underwater. If you're planning to dive in dark areas (bottom of a reef, canyon wall, *etc.*), it's a good idea to load up with E160. For filming at night with underwater lights, again E160 is your best bet unless you plan to shoot extreme close-ups under lights. In that case, you might switch back to K40.

Lighting and Exposure Tricks

Getting the proper lighting and exposure can be tricky underwater. The best time to film is between 10 AM and 4 PM during the summer months. Remember that once underwater, the light fades drastically the deeper you go. Only a portion of the light that strikes the water's surface actually enters the water—much of the light is reflected away. Since many fascinating creatures hide in the shadows of shelves and caves underwater, you'll have exposure problems trying to capture these subjects. Your camera's automatic exposure will set itself for light in the surrounding area, so you'll have to override this manually and open up the lens one-half to one full f/stop.

There's another problem with filming underwater—color rendition. Water absorbs color, especially reds and oranges, and the deeper you go, the less you'll be able to pick up warm tones on your film. Everything will appear to have a blue-green tint. There are color corrective filters, lens adapters and color corrected dome ports (on camera housings), but these will do little good if the colors simply aren't there to begin with. I personally don't believe in supplementary filters or lenses.

To lessen the blue-green tint, it helps to take medium and close-up shots. Keep your lens set at wide-angle and slowly move in on your subject. Avoid using the zoom for close-ups. Keeping as little water as possible between you and the subject will help you get the best color possible and minimize haziness from dust-like particles that are often suspended in the water.

Dangers of the Deep

Dangerous marine life shouldn't present you with any problems if you know what to look for. Creatures like the spiny sea urchin, for example, can stick you with one of its spines. It's an uncomfortable experience but not fatal (you shouldn't try to pull the spine out—let your body dissolve it). Since each diving area has its own idiosyncrasies regarding dangerous marine animals and plants, it's best to dive with local divers or guides who can point out trouble spots. Be sure to keep your gear in tip-top shape and remember the rules you learned during diving instruction.

The one creature that seems to inspire awe and respect is the shark. I've had numerous encounters with these magnificent creatures, and I regard them as less of a problem than unsafe diving practices. The poor shark has been maligned for centuries. If a shark makes you the least bit nervous, simply get out of the water.

Adding a Sound Track

Let's assume now that you've shot your film, edited the footage and are ready to put on a sound track. You can add narration and select appropriate background music, but your film won't capture the feeling of the dive without sound effects. Adding some regulator and bubble sound effects is really quite easy. Simply place your air tank and regulator in your bathtub filled with water, turn on the air and record the bubbling sound. Next, add some exhalation sounds to simulate breathing with scuba gear, and your underwater scenes come to life again. Keep the sound effects subtle (low volume) so they don't dominate the music or make the narration difficult to hear.

Getting involved in the world of undersea Super-8 is an experience that I'll guarantee you won't soon forget. Take that diving course, put your Super-8 in a housing and venture into a world unlike any you've ever seen before. Good filming.

INTERVIEW

Carole Kahn

So you've lined up an exclusive interview with would-be tennis pro Renee Richards, and you think you've got it made. Well, maybe. Getting a good subject to interview is only half the battle. Knowing how to get the most out of that person, and then being able to capture that living, breathing personality on film, is the other—and often more difficult—job. The filmed interview can be an intimate, emotional insight into another human being, or it can be a boring, disconnected "talking head." Which you end up with depends as much on you the filmmaker as it does on your subject.

How do you find out what makes another person tick? How do you get underneath that person's skin, and then share that knowledge with the rest of the world? Let's start at the beginning, with the preliminary work that must be done before a camera even comes into the picture. First, there is the background research. Is your subject part of a larger story that might be told through the interview? What can you find out about the person's activities or style, even before you meet? All of this research will pay off later when you're deciding on film possibilities.

The First Encounter

When you first contact your subject to set up an appointment, you have a good chance to get a "feel" for his or her personality. Try to figure out whether you can get more out of this person by using a sympathetic approach or a more abrasive, challenging role—or a little of both. You can, and should, figure out in advance most of the questions you will want to ask—but *how* you ask them can be decided at the moment, depending on how the interview is going. For example, after several minutes of a generally sympathetic interview with Russian dissident Vladimir Bukovsky on a recent segment of TV's *60 Minutes*, CBS correspondent Mike Wallace asks the Russian, who has been in and out of Soviet mental asylums: "Well, then, let me ask you—I'm serious—is it possible that you *are* a little mad?" Bukovsky stutters, "Is it possible that I. . .? Well. . ." Wallace interrupts: "Just a moment. Well, here is a fellow, a young fellow, you've spent one-third of your life in prison, or in the hospital, in the asylum, in prison camps, and every time you came out you tweeked the nose of the system once again. It's almost as though you wanted to go back." (©1977, CBS Inc. All Rights Reserved.)

Wallace's sudden challenge prompts a fascinating response from Bukovsky. He relates how he once caught three ants and put them inside an aluminum mug: "Of course, they tried to get out of it, and every time I shaked them down. They made some hundreds of

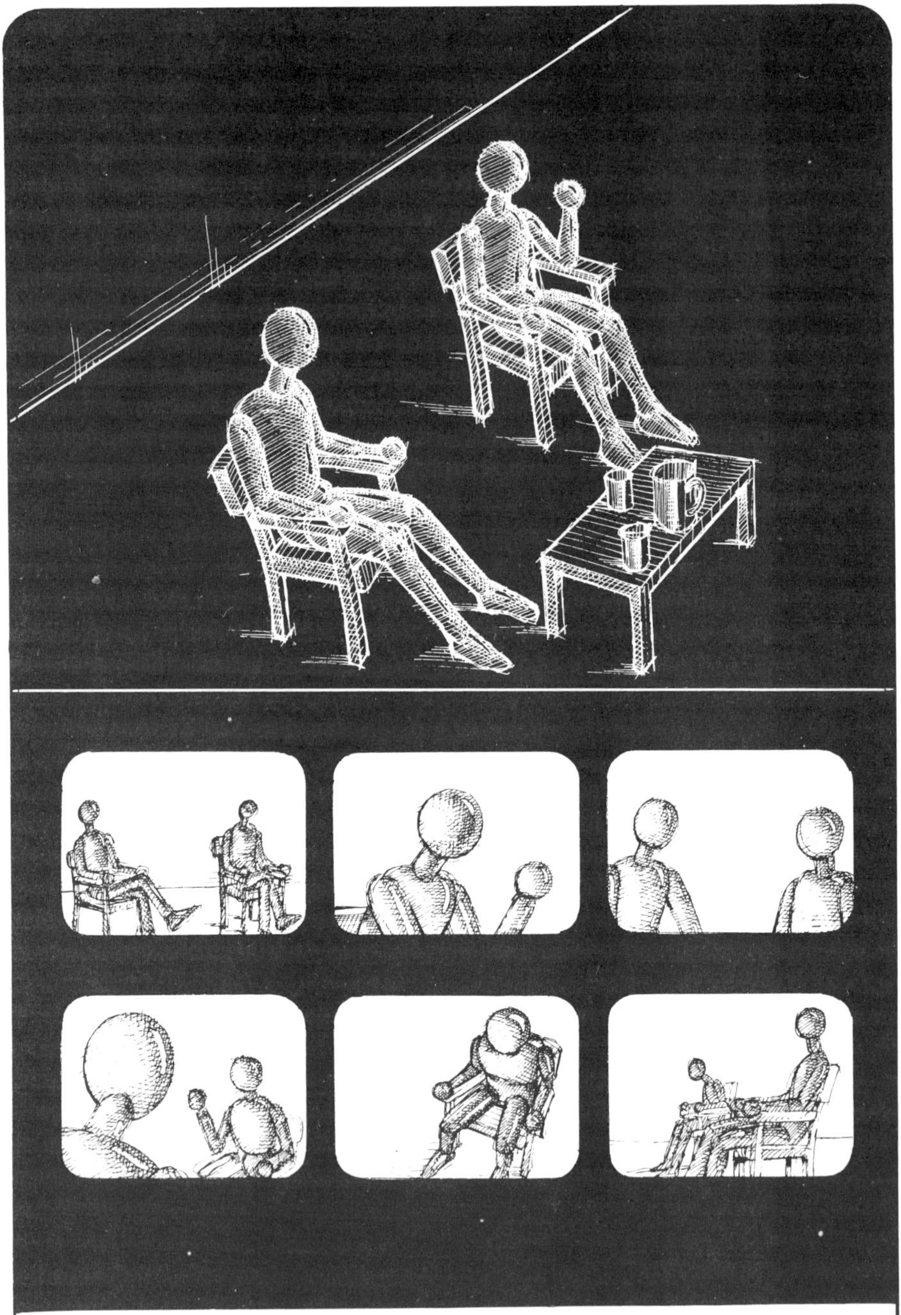

The filmed interview should be an intimate, emotional insight into another human being. How do you find out what makes a person tick and then share that knowledge with the rest of the world? Varying the frame size or focal length of your shots is vital to making the interview hang well together.

attempts to go out. But after that, they stopped completely. They never tried to go out again. I left them on the grass, and the day ended and night go and the next day go, and they never tried to go out. That's the way our people in the Soviet Union are." And when later on, at the end of the interview, Wallace persists and asks, "Why you? Why Vladimir Bukovsky?" Bukovsky answers, "If not me, then who?"

Sometimes when you're dealing with a very shy or very uptight subject, it's a good idea to do a preliminary interview with the person on audiotape only. The absence of the camera makes the interview seem less official, less threatening. And the material you get on the tape may turn out to be the most usable, most natural conversation you're going to get.

In any event, use the opportunity of this pre-interview to observe your subject in action. Does he or she have any characteristic gestures to which you might want to alert your cameraperson. What sort of clothing is the person wearing? You might want to suggest that similar clothing be worn for the "actual" on-camera interview. Are the surroundings appropriate for the on-camera interview? Do they reflect the person's lifestyle or vocation? Does the person have any suggestions for another setting where he or she might feel more comfortable?

Plan Your Camera Moves

Once you've done your homework, know the sort of person you're dealing with and the kinds of questions you intend to ask on-camera, it's time to coordinate the interview with the person who's going to be doing the actual shooting. Don't attempt to be both interviewer and cameraperson at the same time. It rarely works. Explain to the cameraperson what you're trying to get out of the interview. A good cameraperson should listen carefully while filming. If previously sensitized by you to the subject and the subject matter, the person doing the filming will have a "feel" for when to zoom in for that telling close-up.

Some reporters work out a signal system with whomever is doing the actual filming. I prefer to simply say out loud something like, "Well, that last shot was a medium shot, let's do these next questions in close-up." Of course, if the meaty part of the interview unexpectedly comes in the middle of a long shot, you've got to rely on your cameraperson to zoom in for the close-up at the right time. You can try to get the subject to repeat the answer later on, after alerting the camera to stay in close, but it takes deft questioning to recapture a spontaneous moment.

Shooting Techniques

Varying the frame size (or focal length) of your shots is vital if you want your interview to cut together well. It's a good idea to change the frame size with each major new question. If you like part of an answer and think you can get the subject to tighten up the part you don't like on a second go-round, do another take, making sure the frame size or the camera angle is different from the first response. For example, if you used a medium shot the first time, use a close-up the second time, or vice versa.

Shots showing the interviewer and the subject in head and shoulder close-ups, as well as extreme close-ups, are basic for filmed interviews. The wider shot is particularly useful if you want to relate the subject to something in the background, and the extreme close-up can be priceless to show emotion. A zoom-in can be editorially useful—underlining a critical moment in the interview, a key point in the response. Like all zooms, it should be used sparingly, or it will lose the very emphasis you are trying to create.

Camera angle is also important. In most cases, you will want the audience to know that the subject is speaking to an interviewer rather than directly to the camera. So the best position is the three-quarter profile where the subject looks slightly off-camera at the interviewer. But you will need more than frontal shots and frame size changes to get the piece to cut together well. Suppose, in the final edit, you want to cut the first part of an answer with the last part, cutting out the middle. To avoid an awkward "jump cut," you will need a "cutaway" or insert shot of something other than your main subject. A reverse camera angle is one of the simplest and most frequently used cutaways. This can be an over-the-shoulder shot, looking from your subject to the interviewer, or a shot of the interviewer alone, in close-up, listening. You can shoot these at a later time and, in both cases, avoid the need for lip-sync. You can simply use the dialogue from the section of original track you cut out as voice-over sound for your cutaway shot.

It's also a good idea to do some listening or reaction shots of the subject, particularly if you, as the interviewer, do some of your questions lip-sync. Such shots not only provide insurance in case you have to edit your question, but also provide for an interesting change of pace, making the viewer feel more involved in the interview. The audience gets to see both interviewer and subject talking and reacting, as if each viewer were on the scene. All of these shots—including your lip-sync questions—are normally done after the interview is completed. Listening and over-the-shoulder shots are filmed without sound, so you may later add the voice-over. One way to get such shots to look natural is simply to continue the conversation—without recording it—after the interview is completed.

Alternatively, you might wait to film your own "listening" shots until the interview subject has gone. The cameraperson may advise you to change position to take advantage of better lighting possibilities. This is fine so long as your head faces in the same direction as in the interview. Try not to look too smiley, or too serious. The best "listening" shot is one in which you are attentive, nodding your head a bit as if reacting to something the other person said, or looking thoughtful and inquisitive.

You can add variety to the "people" shots with other cutaway possibilities. Be aware of chances for cutaways in the room in which you're filming. Is there anything on a desk that would add to the interview? In the background? If the person being interviewed has been fiddling with papers during the interview, and that was visible in a wide shot, have the subject repeat it for a close-up of the action.

Also be alert to visual possibilities in what the subject says during the interview. For example, if the subject talks to you about a tennis game, plan to film a few shots of a tennis game later on. If the person mentions a particular painting as meaningful in his or her life, you might film a pan of that painting. If the person's family is mentioned, you might show a family photograph of a shot of the subject going through the family album. All of these shots can be interwoven into the fabric of the interview to make it more interesting, and more revealing of your subject's personality. Unlike a cutaway to the interviewer, which is mainly useful for editing purposes, this kind of shot adds content to the interview. For example, shots of *Penthouse* publisher Bob Guccione photographing models and dealing with his secretary and other magazine staffers did as much to tell us about the real Guccione as did the things he actually said to Morley Safer in a recent *60 Minutes* interview. Guccione talked like a pretty straight businessman, but his shirt open to the navel and his chest draped with silver jewelry added a touch of the "swinger" to the staid business image. Similarly, in another Safer interview with basketball star Bill Bradley, it was scenes of Bradley in a game, on the road and in the locker room which gave the audience a real feel for the man and the kind of life he leads.

Other Creative Possibilities

By no means does an interview have to be a mere question and answer session. There are many ways to make an interview come alive. You can talk to other people who know the person—people who might reveal things your subject might not. You can record and film interactions between your subject and other people. Consider this exchange on a recent CBS *Who's Who* program between a surgeon, Dr. Irving Cooper, and a young child whose mother wanted the doctor to operate so the child could walk again:

Dr. Cooper: "You think we ought to go ahead with the next operation, or do you...do you?"

Girl: "You know what? There's three good things about the operation and there's three bad things."

Dr. Cooper: "What are the three good things and what are the three bad things?"

Girl: "You kind of get sick with the oxygen. When you put it on your nose, it kind of makes you like real drowsy and you feel funny."

Dr. Cooper: "Okay. That's one bad thing."

Girl: "And the clamp's kind of uncomfortable."

Dr. Cooper: "That's a real bad thing. I...I agree with that. What else?"

Girl: "And they stick needles in your head."

Dr. Cooper: "That's right."

Girl: "It hurts just a little bit."

Dr. Cooper: "Now tell me about the good things."

Girl: "I can ride a bicycle."

Dr. Cooper: "You can ride a bicycle now?"

Girl: "No, I will be."

Dr. Cooper: "Oh, you will. I hope so."

Girl: "Yes. I can...I'll be able to walk to my friend's house."

Dr. Cooper: "I hope so."

Girl: "And I can run, skip and jump."

Dr. Cooper: "Well, those would all be good things, sweetheart. I hope...I hope I see you do that. We'll try like the dickens."

More than anything the doctor could himself have said, more than Dan Rather, the interviewer, could have said, this brief interaction with the child gave the audience a feel for the gentleness of the man and his honesty in dealing with even the littlest of patients.

In deciding on related scenes that might enhance your interview, consider scenes that might reflect memories as well as current events. The subject may be in these scenes or may not. A traveling shot from a car, for example, may provide a picture of the subject's neighborhood, as we hear the person talk about what it was like to grow up in that community. You, as interviewer, could also use such a scene as a background for your own voice-over narration. Or you can put yourself in the scene, and do a stand-up lip-sync piece to tell the audience more about the person you're interviewing.

Narration can be a valuable tool in tying the different pieces of your portrait together, particularly when you're trying to relate the individual to a larger story. Scenes shot for narration should be complete in themselves. That is, they should have a variety of wide, medium and close shots, and cutaways if necessary, so that the edited scene tells a story by itself.

Pay Attention to Details

In all filming, but particularly in the interview format, it's important to pay attention to details of lighting, background, appearance and clothing. You may not intend it, but dull lighting or hair that is mussed will have a definite editorial effect on your interview. For example, I once filmed interviews for a news story of two men who had opposing viewpoints. One, a Congressman, came to the interview wearing a light blue shirt, medium blue suit and a colorful tie. He was filmed in his brightly lit, cheerfully decorated office. His opponent, an officer of a nonprofit association, came to the interview in a drab olive suit, matching tie and white shirt. His office was equally drab and dark. When the piece appeared on television, the association officer demanded a public apology, claiming we had deliberately made him look bad. The moral: if you want your subject to come out at his or her best, don't be shy about suggesting appropriate clothing to wear for the interview, and be sure to check out the location in advance—at the very least you'll know to bring more lights.

Whether you're out to film that interview with Renee Richards or your elderly grandmother, avoid the tyranny of the "talking head." Plan to vary your film with some of the techniques we've discussed. You'll not only hold your audience's interest, you may also get a deeper insight into your subject, a closer look at who that person really is.

THE DOCU-
MENTARY

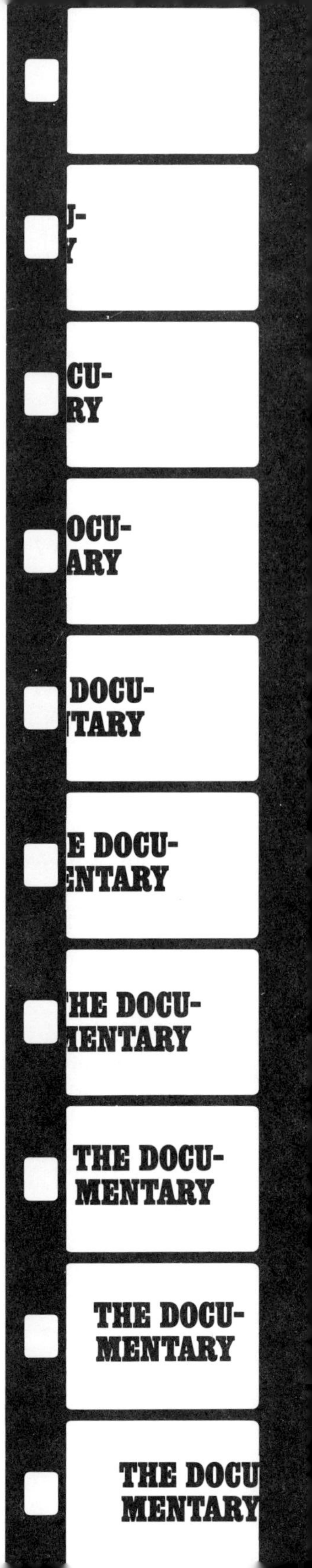
THE DOCU-
MENTARY
THE DOCU-
MENTARY

INTRODUCTION TO DOCUMENTARY FILMING

Rod Eaton

The history of documentary filmmaking is as long as the history of the motion picture itself. The very first motion pictures made and exhibited to an astonished public were, in a sense, documentaries. *Arrival of a Train at Ciotat Station*, made in 1895 by the pioneer filmmakers, the Lumiere brothers, was less than 1 minute long. But the new medium was so powerful that audiences pulled back in fear as the train seemed to rush out of the screen toward them.

At about the same time in America, another film pioneer, Edison, was producing similar records of real events and people. *President McKinley's Inauguration* (1898) was typical of his work. For these early filmmakers, anything that moved provided interesting subject matter; they were as fascinated with the actions of a baby eating or workers leaving a factory as they were with the antics of presidents and kings.

But the novelty of moving pictures soon paled, and the public demanded more than just movement. Through the work of Melies, Porter and others, the "story" film was born. Although dramas and comedies were the hits of the day in the early 1900s, some filmmakers continued to focus their cameras on the drama of the real world. The Russian filmmaker Dziga Vertov edited documentary footage into *newsreels* which were used to inform the Russian people about the Bolshevik Revolution. Vertov called his films *Kino-Pravda*, which means *camera-truth*. In *Man With a Movie Camera* (1928), Vertov created a vivid picture of Russian life and, along the way, thoroughly documented the filmmaking process as it existed in the 1920s.

Two Americans who shared Vertov's interest in the drama of the real world, as opposed to the "reel world" of the theatrical motion picture, were Robert Flaherty and Merian C. Cooper. Flaherty made the classic documentary *Nanook of the North*, a study of Eskimo life in Northern Canada, in 1922. Cooper, who later moved into Hollywood film producing (he made *King Kong*), made *Grass* (1925), which follows the nomadic wanderings of the Bakhtiari tribes of Southern Persia, and *Chang* (1927), the story of a Laotian village besieged by tigers.

During World War II, military and governmental needs for motion pictures created something of a technological revolution. Sixteen millimeter equipment, previously considered strictly an amateur "home-movie" format, proved ideal for low-cost film production. Filmmakers found that the small, lightweight 16mm cameras were more suitable for journalistic use than the large, cumbersome 35mm professional cameras. After the war, the 16mm medium was not only acceptable, it was omnipresent: thousands of 16mm projectors left over from the war effort insured that films shot on the smaller gauge could be shown anywhere, and they were.

Documentary filmmakers were quick to realize the advantages of the smaller gear, and the lower production costs of 16mm. In addition, the advent of sound had allowed documentarians to add another dimension to their work. But it wasn't until the introduction of lightweight, portable sync sound recording equipment (around 1960) that filmmakers were able to explore all the possibilities of the documentary form.

Today, we're in the midst of yet another technological revolution. Again, an "amateur, home movie format" is being accepted in the documentary field as a smaller, lighter alternative to 16mm equipment. Super-8 cameras, with their built-in sophistication and sync sound capabilities, seem ideally suited for the demands of the documentary filmmaker.

But what exactly is a documentary film? We have used the term "documentary" to describe a number of seemingly different types of films. What do these films have in common? First of all, they all deal in facts. The newsreel gives us facts, pure and simple. General interest films, such as travelogues, give us facts but seek merely to offer us lighthearted entertainment. Scientific documentaries seek to educate us. The sponsored documentary, such as a public relations film, usually seeks to publicize a product. Instructional films communicate facts (usually technical) in an effort to teach something.

Then we have what we might call the *committed documentary*. Dealing with matters of social concern, it seeks to inform people, to influence them, to move them to action. This is documentary as defined by the famous British documentary filmmaker John Grierson, and practiced by journalists like Edward R. Murrow and Fred Friendly at CBS in the '50s. It has been said that this form of documentary exists in the grey area between journalism and art. As such, it puts certain demands on the filmmaker. Here's how screenwriter Wolf Rilla sees

With coaching, Jacques Cousteau caught "The Smile of the Walrus" for his 1972 film.

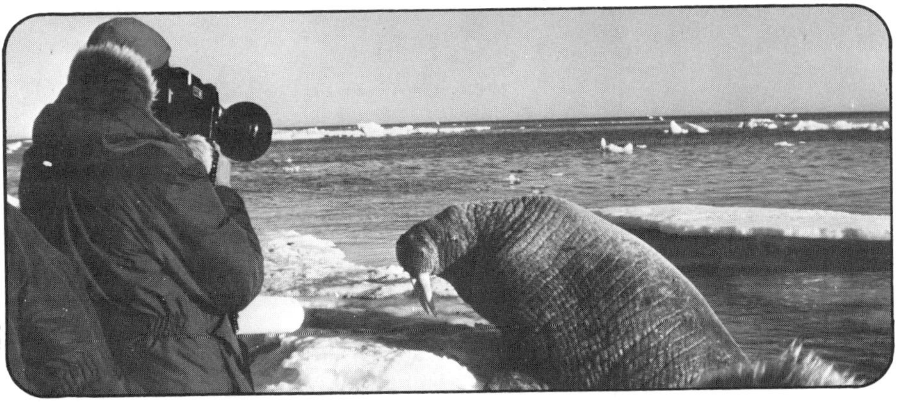

ABC

those demands: "Above all, the writer must remain faithful to the facts without prejudging them. . . he lets (what he has seen) speak for itself. He asks questions, but leaves it to his audience to look for the answers. The moment he supplies prefabricated answers, the committed documentary becomes straight propaganda. The distinction is a fine one and the dividing line cannot always be seen. . . Propaganda could be described as commitment imprisoned by dogma."

The most recent development in the documentary form is known as *cinema verite* (while verite means truth, a more accurate "translation" of the term is "direct cinema"). This through-the-keyhole approach requires subjects who are (supposedly) oblivious to the camera, a patient filmmaker and an unlimited supply of film. Because truth can be easily manipulated during both filming and editing, the film may ultimately communicate the subjective vision of the filmmaker, rather than the "truth" it promises. Since a definition of truth is beyond the scope of this article, let's move on to the actual production of a documentary.

Making a documentary film differs considerably from other types of filmmaking. With few exceptions, you have little or no control over where, when, how, or even if an event takes place. You can't direct the action. You'll find yourself filming in awkward, uncomfortable, inconvenient locations. Light may be bad or nonexistent. Sound recording problems turn into nightmares. And if you run out of film at a crucial moment, you can't holler CUT and ask for a retake. Fortunately, these problems can be dealt with, if not eliminated completely, by careful preparation, meticulous preplanning and anticipation.

Preproduction

First, what is the subject of your film? Let's assume that the students at a nearby college are staging a demonstration, and you decide to make a documentary film about it. Will your film be *about* the demonstration as a single, isolated event? Or is your subject the reasons behind the demonstration? Or is your subject really something else entirely? Student unrest. Police brutality. Public apathy. It's essential to have a clear understanding of what your subject is before you begin to film—although it's likely your original concepts will undergo some changes once you begin.

It's also important to keep your intended audience in mind. Who are they and how much do they know about your subject? What prejudices do they have about it? Are you going to attempt to change their views? Enlighten them? Motivate them?

Regardless of your subject, it's important to learn as much as you can about it. The filmmaker can take a lesson from the journalist and employ the Five Ws: who, what, where, when and why (and sometimes how). Research, ask questions, find answers. While you're collecting data and interviewing people, look for human interest stories that are both dramatic and representative of a general situation.

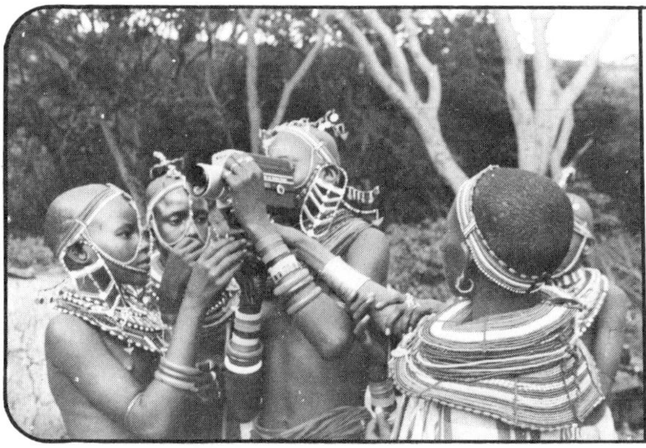

In a documentary, everyone gets into the act. Here young Masai women turn the camera on the filmmakers.

Then add the Three Ls: locations, logistics and legalities. When you know where and when the events you will be filming will take place, scout the locations. Determine what kinds of lighting problems you'll have to deal with; locate the electrical outlets and determine if there is adequate power for your lighting and other equipment. You can begin getting ideas for camera placement to cover anticipated action. Logistics covers equipment, supplies, crew, transportation, meals and accommodations. You'll want to make detailed lists of the equipment and supplies you'll need on location.

At this point you can pull all this information together into a production budget. How much will this documentary cost to make? Your estimate should be as accurate as possible. If you're not sure if you'll be on location for three days or four, figure four days into the budget. Add 10 to 20 percent of your total budget on top of the budget to cover unexpected contingencies—renting additional lights, repairing a broken camera, bailing your key grip out of jail.

Perhaps the most important aspect of calculating the film's budget is the shooting ratio—how many feet of film will you have to shoot to get one good foot in the final film? If you shoot three 50-foot cartridges and wind up with a finished film 50 feet long, your shooting ratio is 3:1. In most filmmaking, shooting ratios of 4:1 and 5:1 are common. In documentary work, however, since you have so little control over the subject, the ratio almost invariably goes up.

Legalities are a frequently overlooked aspect of documentary filmmaking, and failure to secure model releases, obtain filming permissions or investigate performance rights could result in a lot of trouble, embarrassment, delays and lawsuits. A model release is a short contract negotiated between you and each person who is recognizable in the finished film. Releases aren't needed if you're filming someone in a public place being themself, especially if the film isn't intended to sell anything.

If there's any doubt about your right to film in a given location, investigate and, if necessary, obtain permission to film in writing—

especially if it's private property.

If you're planning to film a performance such as a concert, play, sports event or even a rehearsal for a performance, you will definitely need permission to film and may be required to pay the performers some sort of performance fee. You may be able to convince the performers to waive their rights, but these negotiations will take time since unions—sometimes more than one—are involved.

Production: Lighting

Because documentary work often takes you indoors to film meetings, performances and people at work and at home, light may be a problem. Many Super-8 cameras are of the XL variety and can record an image on fast film even in very dim light. But even an XL camera will produce a better picture if you can augment the light level with photolamps. Non-XL cameras depend on higher light levels.

The question is, do you light a location to get a better photographic image at the risk of making your subjects doubly aware of your presence?

If there's not enough light and you choose not to supplement it with photolamps, there's another alternative: have the lab force-process your film. Force processing—also called pushing—involves developing the film for a longer period of time than it is usually developed. This results in the film having a higher sensitivity to light—or if you prefer, a higher ASA rating.

If you decide to light a location, you have several different lighting systems to choose from. Quartz light is the choice of most professional filmmakers. It's lightweight, highly portable, and for its size, puts out a lot of light. However, quartz lighting units are very expensive, so you may have to rent units rather than buying them. If you do rent, the Lowel "Tota-Light" system is a good choice.

One of my favorite ways to light is to use inexpensive photolamps—both the 500- and 250-watt sizes. Photolamps cost less than a dollar apiece and come in both 3200 K (for tungsten balanced film) and

PYRAMID FILMS

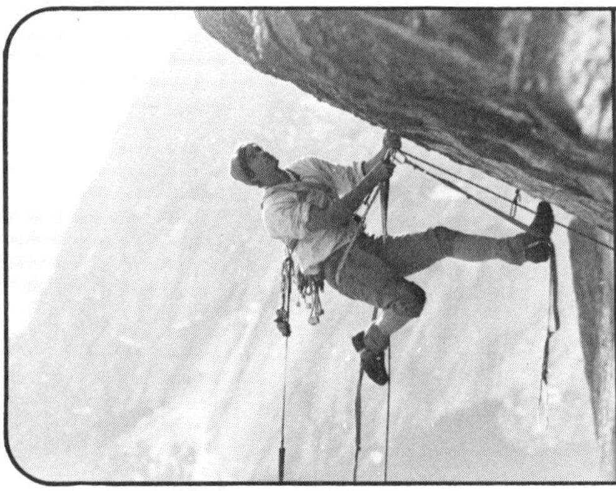

Documentary filming can be high adventure —imagine this!

5500 K (for daylight). Their only disadvantage is a relatively short life—about 4 hours. Since photolamps fit a standard light socket, you can try replacing regular lightbulbs with photolamps for more natural-looking lighting. Make sure the socket and surrounding area—shades, fixtures, *etc.*—can take the increased heat.

Lighting an interior, especially a large one, is complicated by the fact that you have no control over where people will be in the room. Unless you're fairly certain they will stay in one area—around a table, perhaps—you have no choice but to light the entire room. If the room's ceiling is white and not too high, you can point its lights toward the ceiling and bounce light back into the room. This results in softer light overall and tends to eliminate harsh shadows.

The worst thing that ever happened to color filmmaking was the invention of the fluorescent light. Because fluorescent lights are deficient in the red area of the spectrum, they photograph with an unsightly blue-green tint. The color is particularly unbecoming on skin tones. There are several ways to deal with fluorescent lights, other than turning them off and relighting the room with photo-balanced lighting. Kodak Type G Ektachrome 160 has a color balance that is partially corrected for use under fluorescents, and may give acceptable results, especially in situations where the light is mixed (*i.e.*, fluorescents overhead and sunlight entering through a window).

Another approach is to shoot daylight balanced film (set your camera's filter for daylight) and use a filter on the lens to correct the color. Daylight balance is closer to the color of fluorescent lamps than is tungsten. A "CC" (color coring) filter like a 20 magenta will add the missing red.

Tripod or Handheld Camera

Most documentary filmmakers prefer to handhold their cameras rather than mounting them on a tripod, favoring the complete flexibility and mobility handholding allows. Fortunately, Super-8 cameras are light (compared to their 16mm and 35mm counterparts), so they're easy to handhold through long periods of filming. To gain additional support without giving up much freedom of movement, the camera can be supported on a body brace, a lightweight metal frame that hangs on your shoulder(s), allowing your entire body to act as a camera support.

Anticipation and Patience

There are two words you should keep in mind when shooting documentary footage: anticipation and patience. Anticipate the action and the shots you want, and have the patience to wait for them to happen. From your research and your initial concept of the film, you'll have an idea of the kinds of shots you can expect to get.

Always shoot to edit. Cover the action from different angles and shoot plenty of cutaways.

Although television news reporting has made the handheld "look" acceptable, with its shifting focus, frequent zooms and sometimes shaky camera work, you should still strive to make your shooting as smooth as possible. *Documentary* is not synonymous with *sloppy*.

Sound Recording

Recording sound for documentary films is complicated by the same factors that make filming difficult: lack of control over the subject, bad locations and the need to be able to move and film quickly. It's a good idea to have an assortment of microphones on hand to better cope with the sound recording problems that come up. For example, if you can't get in close to the speaker, a good shotgun mic might be the answer. A shotgun is the microphone equivalent of a telephoto lens.

A member of your crew should have the responsibility for keeping records. Number each film cartridge and roll of recording tape as it's used and record, on a separate log sheet, the date and location, content, speakers, pertinent technical data (lighting, filters used, force-process or normal, sync or wild) and any other information which might prove helpful.

Postproduction

The shooting's done—now the real work begins. Somehow you've got to put miles of seemingly unrelated pictures and sound together into a meaningful film. The only way to begin is to look at everything several times—begin to get a feeling for the footage. You'll start seeing things you probably missed when you shot them, and you'll see how different shots will go together.

One of the things that may become apparent during these initial viewings, if it wasn't apparent during filming, is that the film you shot may bear little resemblance to the film you *thought* you would make. Very often, your concepts undergo some interesting changes during the production of a documentary film.

As you begin to edit, you're faced with the problem of bias. Whether or not it's possible for a documentarian, or a journalist, to be free from bias can be debated endlessly. The specific documentary approach you have decided to take will help determine how you shape the film.

Making documentary films can be many things. It can be frustrating and difficult. It can present problems never encountered in other types of filmmaking. But it can also be rewarding. It can be a demanding challenge—both to your ability as a filmmaker and as an individual.

Super-8 technology is equal to the challenge. Sophisticated new cameras with their lightweight, low-light filming capability, sync sound, long zoom ratios and small, unobtrusive bodies seem specifically designed for demanding documentary assignments. Fast film stocks allow shooting under low light and adverse light conditions. Labs offer force-processing, workprints and duplicates. Sound recording equipment and sync sound technology have caught up with 16mm filmmaking, as has the availability of professional editing equipment. And Kodak's video transfer system has opened new doors for distribution of Super-8 film on color videotape and commercial television broadcast.

Making documentaries also gives the filmmaker the opportunity to become involved, politically and sociologically, in issues and events that interest and concern him. It gives filmmakers the opportunity to add insight to information, to move people to action. John Grierson said it best: "Documentary film promises us the power of making drama from our daily lives and poetry from our problems."

SHOOTING AN ADVENTURE DOCUMENTARY

Gerald Vinarcik

There are several techniques you can use to improve film continuity when shooting action documentaries such as films on mountain climbing, probing the ocean depths, or hunting and fishing.

The first step is to shoot lots of scenes which will lay the groundwork for the "unexpected." This requires planning. For example, there are many cut-in scenes you can shoot in advance—things like looking over maps and brochures, tracing the expected route, and making the final decision as to destination. If you include shots of these activities in your film, they will set the stage for what follows.

The packing of special equipment (rods, reels, guns, ammunition, climbing boots, parachutes, etc.) is another activity to film. Use plenty of close-ups. The audience may be unfamiliar with these items, but if you show the equipment in detail early in your film, its function will be better understood when it appears later on, in the midst of the action. You should also include a few shots of traveling to the "jumping off" point. This could mean shots of a plane, a car or a mule. But no matter what they include, they will make good film transitions to your scenes of the actual adventure.

Once you arrive at your destination, you can build audience anticipation by showing the equipment as it is unloaded; the boat being launched, or a few of the hazards of the trip (steep cliffs, dangerous animals, *etc.*). Also, when you have arrived, take advantage of the lulls in the action. Lunchtime activities, the cleaning or repairing of equipment, sunset and daybreak, can be used to carry the story along. When you have finished with these details, find some shots that will wrap up the entire adventure. Look for something different. Air bubbles rising, coiling a rope, slipping a gun back into its case, all of these things can be used as effective endings. Don't drag the audience back home unless you have a definite purpose in mind.

Once you have shot all the "plannable" footage, your next step is to film the actual adventure. Capturing the unexpected requires special techniques. Always have the camera loaded. Set it at a predetermined exposure so you can shoot immediately. Depending on your subject and environment, you will usually become aware of an "unexpected" happening at a predictable distance and exposure. For example, when shooting underwater, that unique fish usually appears at 6 feet and your lighting conditions are generally *f*/8; when shooting the rapids, a whirlpool or double hydraulic would begin to appear 25 feet ahead. When the initial shock of the event has subsided, take a more calculated shot. More often than not, that first take will include some once-in-a-lifetime shots.

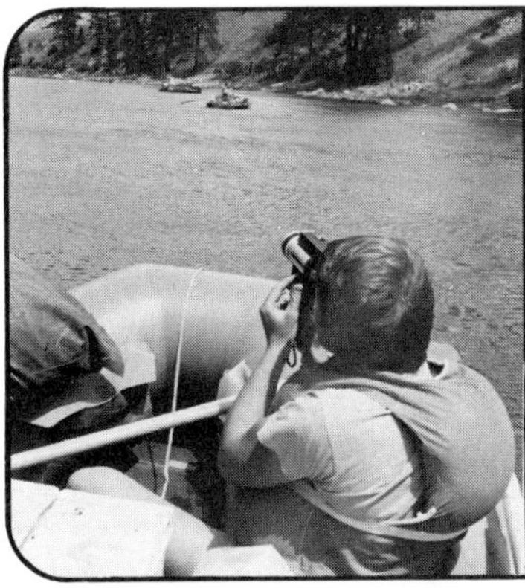

Your Super-8 camera is a good traveler, try it on a river.

The greatest single asset to adventure filming is a second camera. It is never out of film at the same time as your regular camera, and it is cheap insurance. It can be inexpensive and, in the hands of a second cameraman, it can provide a completely different perspective of the same action. It also can be used to take production shots while you film the documentary itself. If you have a second cameraman with you, all the movements for the second camera can be pre-planned. However, even if you are on your own, you can ask an inexperienced person to operate the second camera. A guide or any willing bystander will generally do a good job if you set the shot up for them. Meanwhile, keep track of your adventure shots. During lulls, arrange them on paper to tell the story. See what's missing. The time to fill in the gaps is while you are still on location. This is also the place for setting up re-enactments which will round out your story. Say someone falls, but you miss it? Set this episode up again by having a rock slipping underfoot. There are a multitude of scenes that can be acted out; only your imagination limits you.

Interesting cutaways for an adventure story are easy to come by. Flowers, animals, scenery and the other people in the adventure help to make the story more interesting to watch. They can also be used to smooth out the continuity of the action. If your shots show mountain climbers on the side of the mountain and then on top of it, you might want to make the sequence more believable by cutting in a few shots of the mountainside itself. These shots will "explain" the gap in the action to your audience.

Finally, most adventure trips take one or two weeks and there are many dead spots. If you collapse the time to a couple of days in your story, the action will be as exciting to watch on the film as it was to experience.

ROOTS: FILMING A FAMILY HISTORY

Betty McAfee

Too many people think of "home movies" as a lesser, amateur film form, but two recent experiences I've had suggest just the opposite—that such films can be profoundly significant.

A few months ago, a Super-8 filmmaker friend asked me to collect sound for her as she documented a quilt show in San Francisco. The quilts I saw there fascinated me, especially those on which a family's life story had been lovingly embroidered, square by square. On these quilts, quiltmakers recorded births, deaths, houses, animals, portraits and family events. Each square told a story, with the whole quilt becoming a documentary tale. It struck me that the quiltmaker's long winter evenings in front of the fire, with an embroidery needle and thread are like my long winter evenings in front of my editor with film and cement. Both of us are trying to document the essence of our family's life.

Shortly after the Quilt Show came *Roots*, that remarkable television experience that recounted one family's moving history. Alex Haley's search for his family story is everyone's search. Once more, I realized that Super-8 home movie making is an attempt on our part to preserve the stories, events and characters that comprise our family's moment in time. Inspired by quilts and *Roots*, I'd like to recommend some possible ways to make new kinds of "family film quilts" which, when taken out of the closet in the years ahead, will help later generations know their family roots better.

Not long ago, a Super-8 filmmaker invited me to his home for an evening of film viewing. One of his films stays etched in my mind. This young husband and father had collected numerous black-and-white photographs of his wife, himself and their children. With his macro-zoom Bolex camera on a tripod, a couple of photoflood lights and a great deal of patience, he filmed the pictures, one after the other. Sometimes he zoomed in on a detail or lingered on a particular picture. Having arranged the pictures in chronological order, the effect on the screen was of him and his wife growing up from infancy to adulthood, meeting, getting married and beginning their family life with the birth of their first child. The effect was stunning. David's gift to his family will, I am sure, be treasured by them in the years to come. His technique could be applied to a more extensive family film project that might include grandparents and even great-grandparents. For such a film, you might add a sound track of an elderly person in the family recounting the family's history. Putting together a photographic film about "Our Family's Roots" could be a fine family summer project.

Last winter, a friend asked me if I would take some footage of her father as he took a favorite walk beside the ocean. He was in his late seventies, and she wanted some imagery of him in this later time of his life. He and I happily cooperated with her wish.

I let him start his walk while I stayed on a high dune, beginning the film with a wide-angle shot that showed him crossing the sand toward the ocean. Then I joined him on his walk, filming both intimately, with close-up shots, and more objectively, with wide-angle shots that showed him with the rocks and ocean behind him. I filmed his boots as the waves came up around them, his stride as he walked, his footprints in the sand, his stopping to look at things washed up on the shore, his brief chat with a neighbor also walking on the beach and a final shot of him heading back across the sand.

My friend persuaded her father to sit down and chat with her with a tape recorder running. She used a lavalier mic pinned to his collar so he would not be self-conscious as he talked. They talked about his visit with her, things they had done and the things he loves about the ocean. When this tape is played with the film, the effect is powerful.

Birthdays are times when we all feel compelled to film our children. I'd like to advocate the taking of 50 to 100 feet of film on or around the birthday of each child, but *not* of the birthday party. The task would be to capture the essence of your child in that year of his/her life. You could start the film with the child holding a poster that gives his/her name and age as a title shot. You might follow this with a lingering portrait of the child's face in close-up, moving over the hair, into the eyes, then holding on the whole face. The next shot might include the whole body of the child, perhaps in slow motion, running in a field or down a street, climbing a tree, or getting in the car and driving off, depending on the age of the child.

In this portrait you could include brief shots of your child with his/her special friends, not standing in front of the camera giggling, but involved in a favorite activity—playing a game, riding bikes, going to the movies, goofing off. Also important are shots of the child with the family, doing something that is part of everyday family life, and shots of the child alone, reading a favorite book, catching butterflies, taking care of a pet, fishing, sewing. Your film could end with a shot of the front page of the newspaper on the child's actual birthday, setting the child's life in the context of the larger world.

Your child should script the film, deciding each year what to include. Making such a film can help you know your child better, and preserve a glimpse into the child's world at a particular age. When strung together, years later, the total footage will be a highly personal documentation of personal growth.

I have a daughter who has become a professional French horn player, and over the years, I've filmed many of her experiences as a developing musician. My best and favorite film of her was made one afternoon, very much on the spur of the moment, when the evening sun was golden in the sky. I asked her to come outside with me, my camera and her horn. I filmed her and her horn every way I could in that beautiful orange-gold sunlight. She held the shiny bell of the horn at various angles so that I could film on its surface reflections of flowers, brown grasses, fences, her face and the sun itself. To catch the reflections, I zoomed in on them, set my focus and zoomed back out for various framings. Sometimes I shot the brilliant, slightly distorted reflections on the bell, sometimes the whole horn and sometimes the whole of my daughter and the horn, standing or sitting with various backgrounds.

I had trouble keeping myself and my camera out of the reflections, but found angles of shooting that eliminated me. I also let my reflection be part of the image a couple of times, which turned out to work well in the film. I did an in-camera fade on one shot so I could have a good ending shot.

The editing was simple since I only shot a couple of rolls of film. I striped the original footage and transferred a recording of my daughter playing a Haydn horn concerto onto the stripe. With the sound-on-sound capability of my Elmo 1200 projector, I added a voice-over narra-

I filmed my daughter in the evening sunlight, catching reflections of flowers, grasses, fences, her face in the shiny bell of the horn.

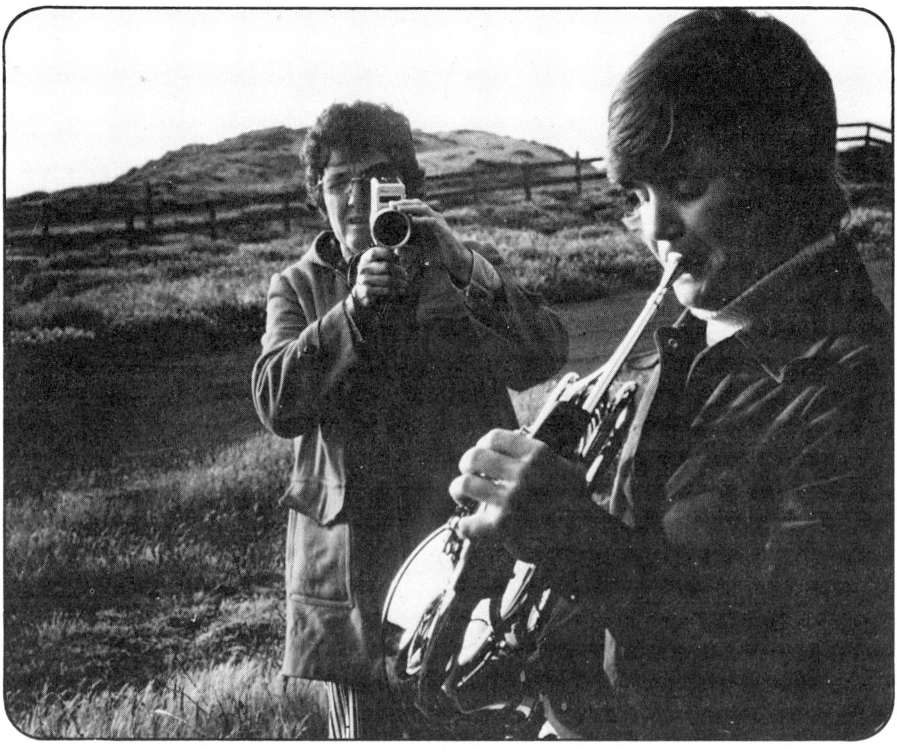

BETTY McAFEE

tion taken from a taped interview I'd done earlier with my daughter talking about music and what it means to her.

The film is a very special film, particularly within the family. But it also turned out to be a film other people enjoy, simply as an art piece. To me, this is home movie making at its best.

Perhaps a hundred years from now, if the world still exists, someone will take our Super-8 home films off a shelf and carry them to a film show somewhere, where everyone will marvel at our telling of life in these strange times we call today.

MONEY AND MOVIES

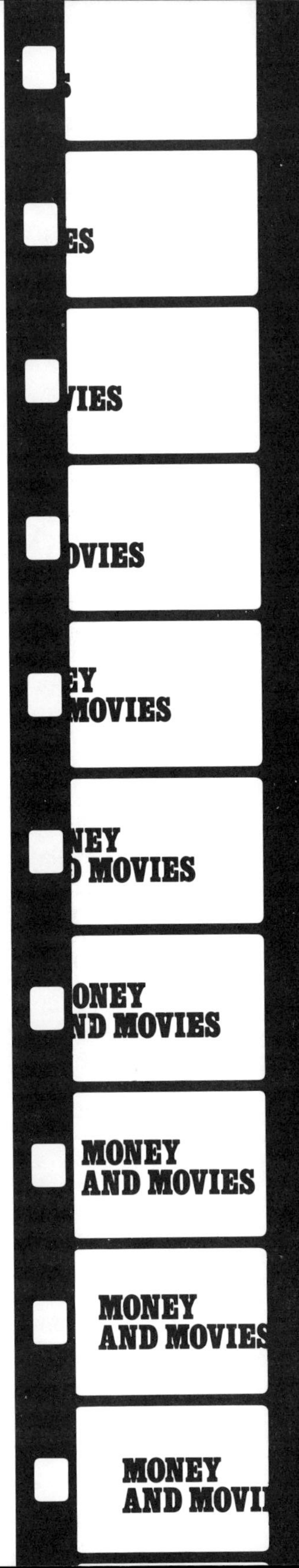
MONEY
AND MOVIES

START YOUR OWN FILM BUSINESS

Raul da Silva

Okay, you've been sitting around wondering how that guy with the deep-pile carpet, suede suit, and Porsche 911S got that way. He talks like you, walks like you—heck, he's not even as good-looking as you. What's he got, man?

Hunger, and the notion that if someone else can win, so can he. Stop wondering. How do *you* get off the ground? First, tell yourself you're going to make it. Don't sit there with your Super-8 gear, hoping. Convince yourself. Make the commitment. Then tear out this article, my friend, because *this is how.*

Think market. Let's pick one that's fairly obvious, like the big equipment dealer. Let's make him target number one. Why would he need a film? He not only needs *a* film, but he needs a film every *month or two.* Why? Because he's got a huge list of varied customers. All he has now, if anything, are a lot of poorly photographed brochures. He *needs* some motion picture footage. He may not know that, but that's where you come in. Your job is to show him not only how film can save him lots of time and fuel, but also how it will go a long way to sealing that potential deal out on Route 104.

We picked out target number one. Let's see how we canvass the lucky guy. If you're thinking of walking in and saying, "Hey Mister, wanna buy a film?"—forget it. I'll tell you right now that his answer will be, emphatically, "No!"

Gather 'round, gather 'round. Call one dealer. Tell him that you want to use his company as an example on your *sample reel.* What for? Why, to help other companies and business operators in your county have the chance to look into a time-proven method of demonstrating products and services. You merely want to film his operation to show your prospective "clients" how effective a demonstration film can be, and how it can save them dollars. They can spool it into a projector and show their customers each piece of equipment in operation without ever leaving the office.

So, your subject agrees and you're ready to embark on your adventure. Now you've got to invest some dough. What kind of camera? There are several rules to follow: First, it is true that the most expensive cameras are *usually* the best, but beware. Don't purchase a camera simply because it's loaded with features. If you're not going to use an intervalometer, for example, why buy one?

The best approach to take when buying a camera is to check on service and parts availability. If you can locate other pros in your community, get personal recommendations. You want to make an investment, not buy a toy. A good rule for finding a dealer to purchase your equipment from is that the larger the dealer, the more negotiating power you have by virtue of their volume.

The easiest way to produce such a film is to go single-system. Buy mag-striped stock, shoot it silent, edit it, then transfer a mixed sound track on ¼-inch tape to it. The reason for this is simple: ¼-inch tape is sound standard. Any sound studio (even hole-in-the-wall) can mix to ¼-inch. You can go to someone like Tommy Valentino in New York City (151 West 46th St., N.Y.C. 10036) and buy a music and sound-effects library for less than you would imagine. The libraries come on records and transfer quite easily from catalogued, easily identifiable bands.

Mixing rigs can also be fairly inexpensive. For Super-8 one-shot films, like the filmed monthly equipment bulletin we're talking about, forget the overly expensive tape decks. There's absolutely no way you can justify that kind of expense in terms of qualitative comparison. A good Sony TC 800B (the one Super8 Sound converts for sync sound) is not only a fine location recorder with the right mic, but you can actually buy several and put them in tandem or side-by-side for mixing (with a small Sony quality mixer like the MX-14). The Uher 1000 is also an excellent choice.

Where to put the production money is in voice. Don't go to a talent agent, but if you know of a good college actor, or voices you like on local radio or TV, you might try approaching these people to do your film voice-over on speculation or for a low fee.

Don't get into using commercial disc music available in record stores. The sound-record copyright law passed in 1972 can get you into trouble. Music libraries contain either original material or music in the public domain—that is, their copyrights have expired. It is, therefore, safe to copy from them; they are sold for this purpose. But you cannot, by law, copy a commercial sound recording. Some will argue, but you still want to remain ethical, even if you could get away with it. For a complete copy of the law, you can write to the Copyright Office, Library of Congress.

After you shoot your film and edit it to contain all the elements in

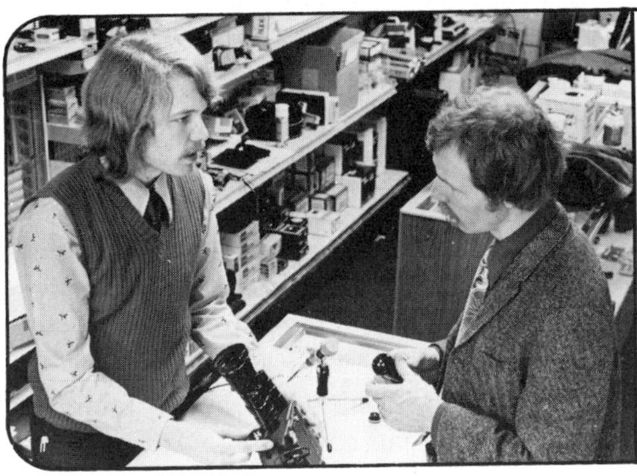

Filmmaker Andrew Olenick examines a Beaulieu Super-8 system and discusses service and parts availability at Hahn Photographic.

your shot-list, start drafting out a tight script containing only factual information. If you have a facility with words, it won't hurt to romance your subject material a bit, but try to use restraint.

Have the voice professionally recorded. There's no reason to pay more than $35 an hour to a sound studio. Sometimes, they'll throw in a quick mix for you if you have all the elements tucked under your arm when you take your talent into the studio for the session. *Do not*, I repeat, do not try to save money on voice. The impact of a professional voice (and sound track) will go a long way in showing your stuff to prospective clients. If you have done professional recording for others, it's obvious you can do your own, but I know very few producers that pay as much attention to sound as they do to the visual. Voices start at about $15 per hour. I've paid that and up to $2,000 an hour.

Your script is the backbone of your production. Keep in mind that it will be your salesman each time you use it. If you need help drafting a script, find it. The true mark of a professional is that he knows his limitations. The most successful producers select specialized talent for specialized jobs. Help for writing in smaller cities can be solicited from college English departments or the local newspaper. An ad in the classified column of your newspaper may also help.

Since you're going to keep your costs low, you want to record short sequences of narrative casually with plenty of space between complete thoughts. This will enable you to bring background music up during the moderate pauses. Then transfer your mixed track directly onto the Super-8 mag stripe by connecting your tape recorder to your sound projector. There will be plenty of margin for alignment and you won't have to worry about sync. Here's an example of a script opening.

SCENE 1
Establishing shot, exterior of Agway equipment dealer's showroom
ZOOM SLOWLY FROM FRONT DOOR AND PAN TO ROW OF FARM IMPLEMENTS
Central Agway has operated out of 2000 Elm Street since the days of Franklin Delano Roosevelt. In all this time their reputation for service has become known throughout the county. (2 second pause)

SCENE 2
SLOW PAN ACROSS LOT FROM HIGH POINT OF VIEW
Farm equipment is just one division of the large Elm Street Agway dealer. Let's look at some of the products and services that can benefit *you*—from Agway. (1 second pause)

Don't overload your script. Remember this is your *sample* script. Three or four products or services will be adequate to show your prospective clients how they can use Super-8 to help their business grow.

Placing a good, easy-to-operate projector in your client's office will assure you repeat sales. You'll want to show him brochures from the various manufacturers of self-contained projectors. These are encased,

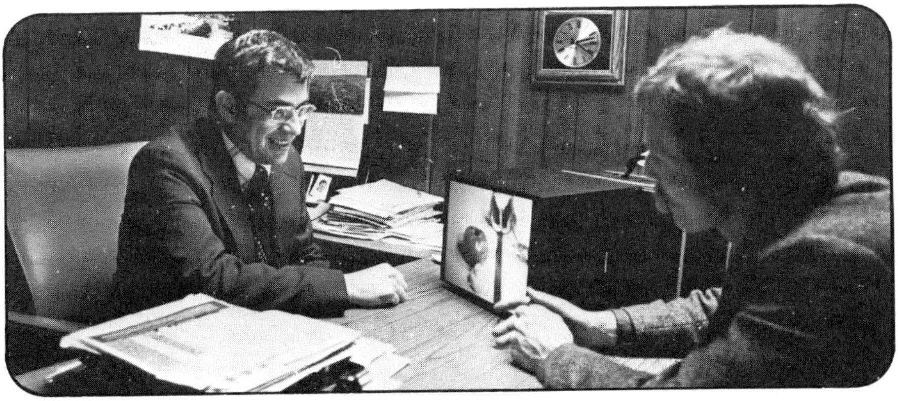

Introduce a good, easy-to-operate rear projection screen to your client.

desk-top units which are comprised of the projection unit and a small pop-up, flip-out, or rear-projection screen (average price about $450). Give him an idea of the wide choice he has. One possibility is the Kodak Supermatic cartridge-type projector. Other self-contained projectors include Bohn-Benton, Fairchild, MPO, Target, and Technicolor. Some of these projectors are continuous-loop, which means that they need no rewinding after each showing of the film. A continuous loop-projector is quiet, impressive, and most important, *very* easy for most people to operate. Many times it's just a matter of pushing a button. This is a selling point, so don't forget to mention it. Another possibility is the Beseler "Cue/See," which utilizes a silent film cartridge and a separate sound cassette. If your client wants to go full hog, you can suggest a free-standing exhibition cabinet which can be equipped with a self-contained projector. Rappaport Exhibits, for example, manufactures an entire line of futuristic cabinetry which can be used in conjunction with MPO Videotronic or Technicolor projectors. If there's an audiovisual dealer or lab in your vicinity, they will be glad to load your client's film for you on continuous-loop. If not, you can contact a large service like Audio Graphic Films in Hollywood who, besides distributing continuous-loop projectors, is also one of the largest cartridge loading services in the country. Making your client's film is only half the job—being sure that he can display it properly and under the most exacting conditions is the other half. If you can write an annual contract out of his annual sales budget, you will want to include the projector.

Take note: I do *not* suggest that you use a continuous-loop projector for showing your *sample film* for two reasons. Open-reel projection is quicker to handle in the event the film breaks during your presentation. It will also make things simpler for you should you want to delete or add a sequence to the film.

What is your time worth? What should the budget be? Some producers take the most that they can. I've not seen people with this type of philosophy stay in business too long. You are, first of all, a businessman, and secondly, a filmmaker. Your profits can come out of a 15-percent commission on everything you buy and handle during the project (like the projector), and the balance from a set hourly rate. You can also negotiate a package deal based on your estimated cost of operation and overhead. Do not try to make your entire living from one client unless the account can afford it in terms of volume. Average hourly rates vary all over the scale depending on where you are geographically. Naturally, you cannot charge New York prices if you do business in Lansing, Michigan.

Organize your budget. Below is a sample budget log. Since you will be the best judge of price in your area, you'll have to estimate the cost of each item. The price of your time depends on several variables: a) what your competition is doing in your area, and how much goods and services cost; and b) how professional you rate yourself. Are you just starting off and learning on the job? Or, will you be doing a fast, slick job, knowing how to cut corners and save money for your client? If it's the latter, you should be earning somewhat more money than the neophyte. Your time should be sold at anywhere from $10 to $35 per hour. Rate yourself honestly and you cannot lose.

BUDGET

Out-of-pocket money

1. *Film stock:* cartridge or spool, striped with magnetic oxide. Allow for at least 5:1 shooting ratio for yourself. That means if your film is is planned for 5-minute running time, purchase 25 minutes of film. (Cost:) $__________.

2. *Processing:* For best results have the stock manufacturer process the film if at all possible. (Cost:) $__________.

3. *Sound Effects:* Can cost from $16 and up for a needle-drop (one segment) unless you have a library or can make a deal with a sound studio that is recording your narrator. (Cost:) $__________.

4. *Music:* Again, from $16 a needle-drop and up. The sky's the limit here. You obviously cannot afford to go to a top music source. Try dealing with a local radio station, audiovisual dealer, the media or film department of a television station that may have resources. Library music is inexpensive if you take your time to look around. Your best bet is to invest in your own library. (Cost:) $__________.

5. *Voice Talent:* Negotiate, negotiate. (Cost:) $__________.

6. *Mixing:* If you don't do this yourself, you will naturally have to shell out the money for it. Make a deal with the sound studio if you don't have your own mixing rig. Studio time usually starts at $25 an hour. (Cost:) $__________.

7. *Cartridging:* As mentioned before, an audiovisual dealer, your friendly Super-8 lab, or the fellow who sold you the continuous-loop

projector can cartridge your production reel for you. If you do it yourself, it is naturally not out-of-pocket money. (Cost:) $__________.

Time (What you will charge for your time on an hourly basis)

1. *Scouting:* Meter reading at location site, taking notes prior to making up shooting script. (Time x Rate=) $__________.
2. *Meetings:* Don't forget that meetings take up time. Try to make these short and efficient, otherwise don't charge for them. (T x R=) $__________.
3. *Shooting:* Plan for efficient shooting at minimal time by writing a well-designed shooting script. Think in terms of efficiency as opposed to continuity here. For example, plan all your exterior shots at one location for one time segment, interior in another. You will edit the film to continuity according to your script later. (T x R=) $__________.
4. *Scripting:* Chances are you should be able to write a clean, terse script after your client meeting. If you absolutely feel you cannot, then this item should be in the out-of-pocket money section of your budget. (T x R=) $__________.
5. *Sound Studio Directing:* Some of the producers reading this have their own sound studios. If you do not, this item goes in under your time *and* out-of-pocket money. Plan your time here. Ask the studio to let you hear some voices they may have on tape. When recording, don't let anyone nibble at your time with idle conversation. If you want to talk shop, ask everyone out for a Dutch-treat lunch. (T x R=) $__________.
6. *Transfer:* If you don't have at least one good reel-to-reel deck, you should not be in the Super-8 production business, but in case you have to transfer, just ask a friend who has a deck. (T x R=) $__________.
7. *General Production Management:* (T x R=) $__________.

Some of you may feel that a film costing about $850 and a projector

Olenick demonstrates a continuous-loop projector which is impressively quiet and very easy to operate.

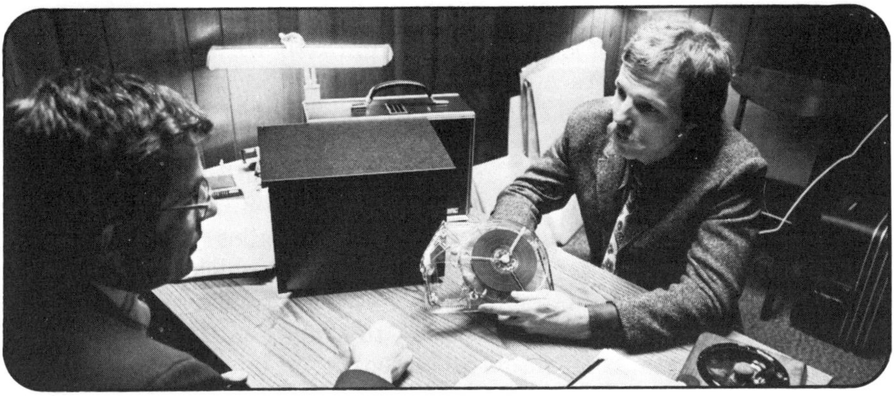

costing $450 may be too much. Think about this: An Agway dealer has $15,000 worth of agricultural spray to be utilized by an aerial applicator. His customers range all over the county. He wants to show them techniques in different field locations. He needs a film. It is worth not only his $15,000 supply on hand, but future sales exceeding $100,000. Or consider this: An International Harvester dealer has new farm equipment coming in. He has one unit to be used as a demonstration model. It would cost him to take it out to his customers to show *one* application each time. You could make a film showing *five* applications in five different locales for him. The only cost to him would be the gas in his car, the film and projector. With the film, he can show the five applications to all his present and future customers. His savings continue for as long as he carries the piece of equipment.

Here's a checklist on production steps to take in getting your sample reel(s) together:

1. Find a good equipment dealer—get permission to shoot.
2. Draft a shooting script based on logical continuity.
3. Film sequences using best possible light.
4. Edit your film so that it makes visual sense.
5. Draft final script for studio recording.
6. Obtain rough timing to match to tape and edit script if necessary. Record narration.
7. Have a good selection of light background music and sound effects (to fill for ambience) prepared from commercial library source.
8. Obtain studio sound mix, being careful not to disrupt the rough scene-to-scene synchronization as per your original script.
9. Patch your tape recorder into your Super-8 sound projector for transfer to mag stripe. Give it as many passes as it takes. If the tape was planned well, only one pass will be needed.
10. Obtain circulars from self-contained projector manufacturers.
11. Make up presentation kit of your open-reel sound projector, sample reel and packet on office projectors. *Do not* give away circulars; just use them in a three-ring binder as presentation material. You want your client to purchase his projector through you.
12. Start visualizing the deep-pile carpet.

What are some other areas you can approach with the sample reel presentation? My fingers always do the walking through the Yellow Pages. There you'll find all types of potential business contacts for one-shot films. Don't rule out larger markets such as auto dealers, but even though many of them display an auto in action in Super-8, the films were made in 16mm first and printed on Super-8. They are usually large-budget productions with all the budget goodies you'd expect. A local dealer, however, may be selling a specialty vehicle, or truck that has applications out in the field, or he may want to show his prospects the service department without having to take them through and disrupt work. Use your imagination when looking at business prospects. A cabinetmaker may want to keep film samples of work he's sold. A plumber may want to keep a document of a particularly rough, complex installation. A custom motorcycle maker may want to record models he has sold. A baker who makes specialty wedding cakes may want to show his wares. (Right now he's got either stale cakes or plastic models, none of which are ample or adequate.) It goes on and on like that. If the budget is absolutely tiny, you have the equipment which allows him to record right on the mag stripe through your sound-on-film projector. Introduce him to film. One contact leads to another. Don't be ashamed to take your films to a Rotary meeting, or the local advertising club.

The most common objection you'll be faced with when starting will be cost. Try to start with low-cost offerings. After your prospects realize the utility, impact and immediacy of film, they'll know it's worth putting an investment into on an annual, if not monthly, basis. You may not get rich, but a good living is there waiting for you. Just reach out and grab it. No time for daydreaming now!

HOW TO MAKE MONEY WITH WEDDING MOVIES

Lucien Aigner

The Super-8 wedding can be a terrific money-maker for ambitious photographers and filmmakers eager to turn pro.

How do you get started? Certainly not by going out and buying a lot of expensive hardware which will end up gathering dust on your shelf. Instead, get hold of a Super-8 camera and take a few hundred feet of film at the next wedding you attend. My advice is that you just start shooting. Even if it's a wedding where you are the still photographer, you should have plenty of time to shoot movies between your other shots, when you are just waiting. Your first masterpiece will not win a Golden Eagle, but it will be a beginning. It will open your eyes—it might even sell. Mine did.

What camera? My advice is to use the simplest of the Super-8 models, such as one of the XL cameras. This type of camera has the great charm of nearly full automation and a shutter that will take complete advantage of available light when used with Kodak's high speed Ektachrome 160 film. You can put a movie light on top of your camera, though for your first venture I don't recommend such an arrangement. Using a light will make you more conspicuous, and the light's cord can be awkward, although for dimly lit churches, your lighting will be better. In any case, an available light camera model is nearly a must.

What do you shoot and how? We all have seen still photographs of weddings in which the photographer seeks to capture only the climax of an action—that fraction of a second when the bouquet is in the air and the girls are reaching for it. The arm of the bride is lifted high and in one single shot all that went before and is about to come is revealed. But when you are shooting movies, this is not so. You not only can, but must, catch the whole sequence. You must lead up to the climax, otherwise your film will look choppy. And capturing the whole sequence requires a special type of anticipation since you will have to start shooting a few seconds before the climax occurs. In addition, the movie camera gives you a chance to film scenes that are hard to get with a still camera, for example, the bridal party coming down the aisle, or the congratulations and handshaking in the reception line. It is very hard to get scenes like these with a still camera. You must wait patiently until both the bride and groom appear through an opening in the line of guests who are passing by to shake hands and kiss. And then, when you click the shutter, the line moves and somebody blocks your view, so all you get is the back of some happy guest. With movies, this does not matter. Interruptions add to the drama of your scene.

But shooting these scenes is not all you must do. There is sound as

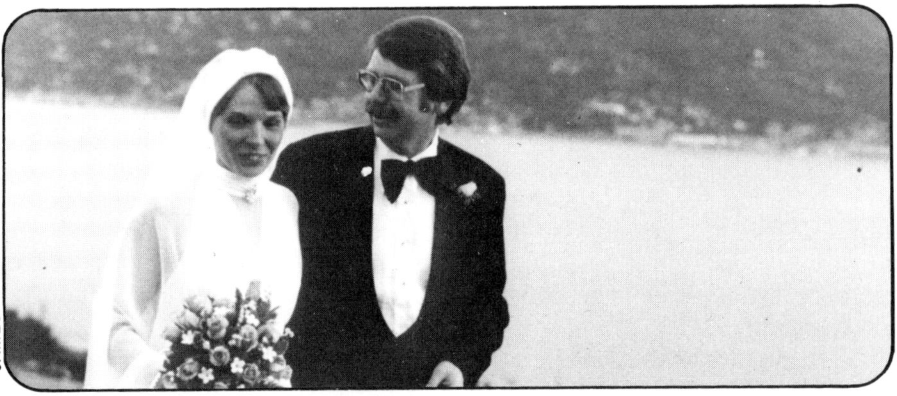

JAMES KASSON

You can use a neutral density filter to cut down the daylight reaching the film as you move outdoors.

well. I suggest that you use a portable tape recorder—a cassette model will do. You don't need much sound, just enough to give authenticity to your movies. You will need a few bars of the music that was played at the reception or in the church, since it cannot be substituted by post-recorded music effects. Also, you should get a few minutes worth of background sound at the reception, including sounds of laughter and small talk. A minute or two of sound taken while you are standing near the bridal couple in the reception line can also come in handy. You can add the rest, and the most important part as far as my experience has shown, when you show your product to the bride and groom. As they watch a silent version, you record their spontaneous remarks. Or you ask them, after they see the movie, to describe the story of their wedding as if they were talking to a friend who couldn't be at the wedding. In effect, they will be making a voice-over, or narration of the film.

Once you have all the sound elements, you are ready to edit. Perhaps you will want to seek advice from an "expert"—a radio announcer, a high school or college electronics teacher, or a neighbor who is a sound buff. What is involved is both the editing of the picture and the editing and mixing of sound. If no help is available, you can take your edited film to a sound recording studio and they will help you out, especially if they are local and you promise them your wedding business. You can arrange editing and mixing of the sound for a flat fee.

What is most important in this entire process is the fact that when your movie is delivered, it can be enjoyed using whatever projector the family has. If they don't have a sound projector, your tapes can be played on their cassette recorder. Furthermore, you don't really need sync sound with lip sync dialogue, since you don't want all the sound that accompanied the wedding—it's too confusing. It gets into your way and will make the addition of narration very difficult. The narration, meanwhile, is the very thing that will make your film more personalized and therefore superior to an amateur's product.

As a professional you will, of course, want to know how this new product will affect your sale of other films or of still photographs. Some still photographers feel that it is foolish to bother with movies since your total sale may not be much higher than it would be without them, and since movies will cut down on the sale of candids for wedding albums. This is a possibility, but need not be so. An easy solution is to work out a package, including both movies and an album with fewer pictures. Another solution is for filmmakers to work with local wedding photographers.

As to the finances of wedding movies, I have found the results rather favorable. The ratio between cost and sales is good. Your investment for a 12-minute wedding movie with sound might include the following: 4 or 5 cartridges of color film, about $20 to $25; processing of same, about $10 to $15; cost of a workprint, about $15 (you shouldn't fool around with your original footage during the editing stage because you might scratch it and deliver it in that sorry condition to your customer); tape recorder rental, about $5; tape, about $3 to $6; assistance in editing and mixing sound, about $25; two extra prints of the final film, about $30 (these are important because you can sell three prints instead of one, and the $450 which you can charge the customer ($150 each) will appear more justifiable).

All this adds up to an investment of about $110, against a sale of $450. Your finished product will be an edited print and an edited cassette tape which are roughly in sync. You make a sync mark on both the film and the tape to indicate exactly where they should be cued up for showing, and you are in business. It might be necessary to make final adjustments to fit the projector and tape recorder of your customer. These instruments are not always compatible with the ones you have used. Also, customers with sound projectors may want their prints sound striped. But once these final details are set up, your film will have an enormous charm for the bride and groom, their families, and their friends. It will recall the total atmosphere of the wedding with authentic sound and personalized narration.

I should also mention titles. These may be shot at the studio and added to your original. And there are many other nice details and shooting techniques which you can use to further enhance your product. (See the main portions of this article.) What I have outlined here is only for starters. Good luck and good shooting.

SHOOTING PUBLICITY MOVIES

James Percelay

Tired of paying for your films out of your own pocket? If your films are of professional quality, you might consider getting someone else to pay for them—public relations departments of universities, hospitals and other institutions are good bets. If you offer your time, labor and expertise in return for a full expense account, you'll be surprised how many institutions will be willing to have you (instead of a costly professional agency) make a public relations (PR) film for them.

I speak from experience. During my sophomore year at Drew University in Madison, N.J., I produced a PR film for Drew's admissions office, and I think both the school and I benefited from the production. I was fortunate enough to have the University's complete cooperation—after all, the more they helped me, the better their film would turn out. In addition, I was able to get academic credit for the project, and can present the completed film to potential employers as a sample of my work once I graduate. Finally, I was able to do all this for free (beyond my tuition and room and board, that is). The University also benefited: they received a high-quality public relations film at a fraction of the cost of a professionally produced version.

Getting the funds to produce a PR film for your school is simple—all you have to do is prove to them that they need one. I did this by calling the PR departments of comparable schools and gathering specific data on how many of them had such films. Then I drew up a report on the possible applications of the film (it could be shown at high schools, trustee meetings, national college conventions, *etc.*). As a clincher to my sales talk, I pointed out that a professional agency would charge $1,000 per completed minute for this film (the average price quoted by three New York agencies), compared to the $50 per completed minute a student-made, Super-8 film would cost. Next, I drew up a detailed budget which accounted for every possible cost that might be incurred.

Finally, to prove that I had some film experience, I compiled a resume of past awards, including a "Special Award" in the Kodak Teenage Movie Contest and 2nd place in the R.I. State Film Contest. My resume also included previous experience (various internships at local TV stations), as well as teaching jobs (at local YMCAs and state-funded art programs). It took me almost three weeks to arrange my complete proposal (budget, resume and film experience), but it paid off, and I was granted my $1,000 budget.

Preproduction

Grant in hand, I set out to find crew, actors and a scriptwriter. When I posted billboards in the student union advertising these positions the response was quite good, perhaps because of the novelty of a film production on campus. Because the University's media center only owned silent cameras (Rollei SL 84s and Canon 518s), we decided to shoot the film in a documentary style with voice-overs, instead of synched dialogue (we would dub in sound effects or incidental dialogue later).

The film would focus on a day in the life of six representative Drew students, revealing the University through the eyes of these students as they went to their respective classes and participated in sports and other activities. We wanted to keep away from the cliched narrative tour-of-the-campus format common to college PR films, and felt this style would be more palatable to the film's target audience, which would be composed primarily of high school students.

The film begins with an opening montage (of archival photos) portraying Drew's 100-year history, over which the titles are superimposed. The last photograph in the montage dissolves to a lone student (one of the six the film focuses on) walking across the campus and reflecting on his expectations and college experiences. He walks to the campus radio station where he begins his weekly radio show. After he puts on a record we cut to his dormitory where his roommates are listening to his show while studying. Somewhat bored with academia, they soon depart for some refreshment at the campus pub. The next morning begins with the whole campus waking up and walking to class to the energy of the Brandenburg Concerto. As the music fades out, the film proceeds to cover four of the students in their respective classes. With the dubbed-in classroom dialogue in the background, we hear voice-overs of their thoughts about their particular course of study. The voice-over technique is used again when the film focuses on the school's physical education program. The film closes with a student, after watching his friend at baseball practice, riding his bike into the University forest preserve. The credits are superimposed on this final scene. The complete film runs 20 minutes.

Formulating the Script

Before you begin your script, it's important to make an outline of the ideas you hope to communicate in your film. For example, my scriptwriter (a graduate English student) and I thought back to our senior year in high school when we were looking at colleges, and recalled some major points that we felt were insufficiently stressed in Drew's PR program at that time. They were: (a) Drew's attractive campus, (b) the small student/teacher ratio, (c) the value of a small liberal arts school and (d) the school's proximity to New York City. We stressed all these points in the film.

When writing your script, be careful not to date your film by focusing on colloquial jargon (such as "right-on"), short-term hairstyles, fashions, fads and public figures or popular singing groups appearing on campus.

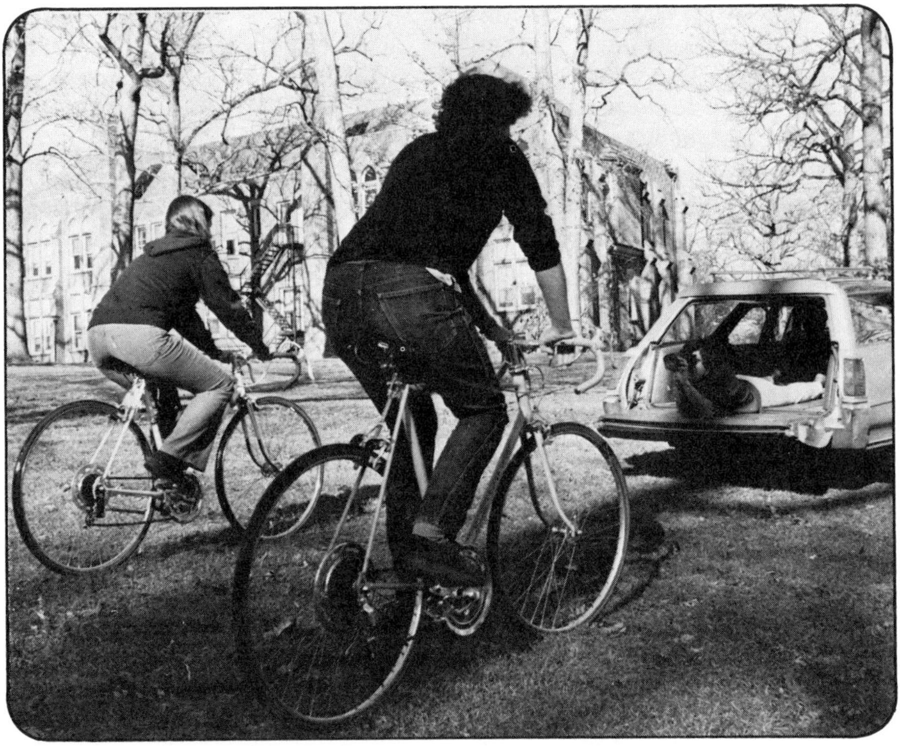

A heavy car with semi-deflated tires makes a smooth tracking shot on uneven terrain.

Although you've sold this as a student-made film, it should not *look* as if it was made by a student. There are several things you can do to get a polished, professional look. First of all, always use a tripod, use the same film stock throughout the entire film and shoot at 24 fps. These measures will help you avoid jerky zooms and pans, as well as enabling you to use the better projection equipment available. Go for little extras such as superimposed titles. Assuming that you're going to A & B roll your film, professional superimposed titles are quite simple.

Production Problems

Shooting on a college campus posed many problems, one of which was scheduling. Because of classes, exams, lectures and various extra-curricular activities, just about everyone's schedule conflicted with everyone else's, and we were forced to shoot on weekends and at night.

The fluorescent lighting in Drew's classrooms presented another production problem. These lights emit a significant amount of ultraviolet (UV) which adversely affects indoor shooting (light coming in from windows has a similar effect). Since I didn't want the students to appear as if they were ill in class, I had two alternatives: to use Ektachrome 160

Type G or to overpower the green influence of the fluorescent lights with quartz movie lights. I chose the latter, for two reasons: I didn't want to change film stocks in midfilm, and I knew that Ektachrome 160 had poor resolution when printed. Shooting with Ektachrome 40 (K40), I needed six 1,000-watt Berkey Colortran lights to light the indoor scenes evenly. The lights created a new problem, however. The heat and glare from the lights disrupted the relaxed atmosphere in the classrooms and as a result, it took numerous shootings to get the spontaneous footage I was after.

By using lots of lights, we often overloaded the wiring in some of the University's older buildings. In order to rectify this problem, I placed rheostats on each of the fill lights and then replaced the popping fuses with Mini-Breakers. These screw-in circuit breakers allowed me to reset the circuit in a trial and error fashion, as I gradually lowered the rheostat until the circuit stopped overloading. I might add that this voltage reduction could only have been applied to the fill lights, as the resulting change in color temperature would have been quite obvious if applied to the key lights.

With the aid of the Public Works Dept., the author uses a cherry picker to film a high shot over the college building.

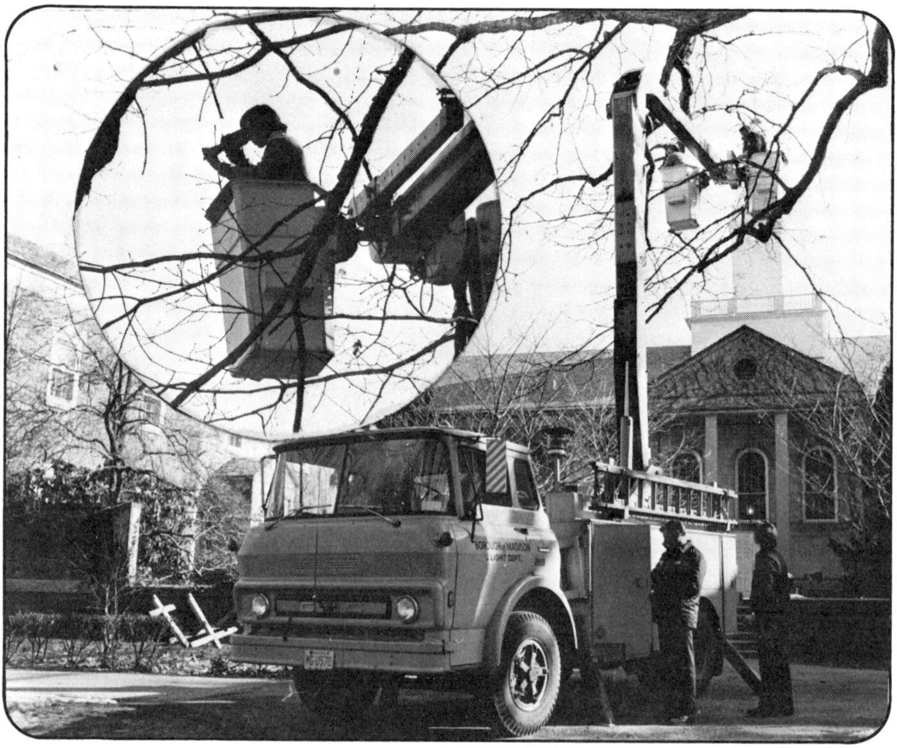

Upon examining my final footage, I found, to my dismay, that the film looked perfect! So what's the problem, you ask? Well, K40, like all present Super-8 stocks, is designed for projection, not printing. Therefore, when using a stock like K40, it's necessary to shoot indoor scenes very softly lit and outdoor scenes slightly overcast or cloudy (this will compensate for the significant increase in contrast once the stock is printed).

Postproduction/Editing

Before you even run your original through a viewer, I highly recommend that you have it "Vacuumated." Vacuumating is a film treatment which removes the moisture in newly processed film and replaces it with emulsion hardeners and preservatives. The process is offered by Vacuumate Corporation (207 West 25th St., New York, N.Y. 10001).

After I rough-cut the Vacuumated original on a Vernon viewer (making temporary splices with Kodak Presstapes), I had a workprint made. After editing the workprint I took it, along with the original, to the Super-8 editing facilities of Team Lance Super-8 in Brooklyn, New York. There I conformed the original to the workprint on Team Lance's ten-plate flatbed editing table (manufactured by Super-8 Research Associates). While I didn't have the films edge numbered, I did slate before each shot, and this made conforming quite simple. (I had been warned that the edge numbering techniques used by many Super-8 labs often result in ink splashes on the image area of your film.) In addition, I was able to view the workprint in sync with the original, since the flatbed has two separate viewing systems in interlock. In setting up the film in an A and B roll fashion (which I had never done before), I used Team Lance Super-8's Precision 4-gang synchronizer and a Maier-Hancock Hot Splicer. If you plan to have your film printed, I strongly recommend using cement splices (Maier-Hancock, Bolex and Hahnel are about the best in my opinion). Tape splices tend to stretch under the tension of a printer, often resulting in white flashes at each splice.

After shopping through *Super-8 Filmaker*'s report on lab services, I decided to send my film to Newsfilm in California (Newsfilm Laboratory, Inc., 516 No. Larchmont Blvd., Hollywood, Calif. 90004). I chose Newsfilm for a variety of reasons. To begin with, Newsfilm is one of the only labs capable of printing dissolves down to the length of 12 frames (of which I had many). Second, Newsfilm offers an inexpensive low-contrast master which saves wear and tear on your original, as well as printing time. Third, this lab was quite courteous and allowed me to stay in telephone contact with the technician working on my film.

The Sound

While the film was shot silent, I achieved "lip-sync" with some careful planning. To pull this off, I shot the speaking parts from a considerable distance away from the speaker, or at a sharp angle from the mouth (both methods made exact lip movement undiscernible). Next, I timed each speaking part and recorded the appropriate length of dialogue onto fullcoat. This was then edited into the master track.

The final sound transfer onto the film was performed at Super8 Sound in Cambridge, Mass. My three edited fullcoat tracks (one voice, the other music, the third sound effects) were placed on their Super8 Sound recorders (modified Sony TC800Bs) in sync with an Elmo ST 1200. While viewing the film as the recording was being made, I was able to adjust the levels at crucial points in the film (using a Sony MX-14 mixer).

Packaging the Film

One of the major selling points of a Super-8 public relations film is its portability—the ease with which it can be taken to (in this case) high schools, meetings, *etc.* Of the projectors available, continuous loop cartridge projectors fulfill the requirements best. These units are small, maintenance-free (they require no threading), and do not need to be rewound (a must, if the film is to be used at a convention or as part of a display). There are three companies that dominate the market: Fairchild, MPO Videotronic and Technicolor. Two other projectors you might also want to consider are the LaBelle (lower cost but shorter run), and the Beseler Cue/See, which has stop-action capability that lets it double as a filmstrip projector.

Before you have your film printed, investigate the machine in which you plan to have it projected. For obvious enterprising reasons, the projector industry has not standardized the Super-8 continuous-loop cartridge. You may find that your film has to be printed onto the thin "Estar" based stock (Estar is Kodak's trademark for their brand of polyester film) in order to fit into the particular machine you choose. If so, you must have an internegative made of your film. The reason for this is that the only Estar print stock commonly available is color positive stock and must therefore be exposed to a negative image in order to produce a positive print. Of those labs which offer a Super-8 internegative, Geo. W. Colburn Laboratory of Chicago is one of the most reputable. While making an internegative is quite expensive (about 65 cents/foot), it gives you a quick way to make inexpensive, durable copies. (Estar based films are far more resistant to wear than those with acetate bases.)

When you're looking for a cartridge machine, keep in mind that any cartridge mechanism subjects your film to a lot more friction than an open reel projector would. Features such as rotating film guides, as opposed to stationary ones, will save a tremendous amount of wear on your film (the MPO cartridge has such a feature).

Producing a Super-8 public relations film for your high school or college (or any other institution for that matter) gives you a chance to produce a semi-professional film and also opens the door to many other possibilities. You can use your film as a solid sample of your work when you go looking for a job, or you can enter it in film contests. And if you don't think that's possible, take a look at the PR film produced for Princeton University—it won an Academy Award! In any case, I found the project a good way to get some production experience while producing a professional product—one both my client and I can be proud of.

EDUCATION

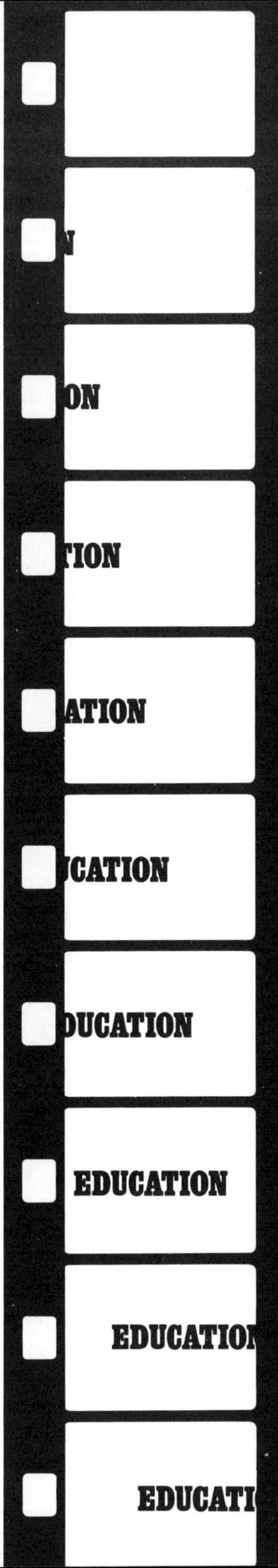
N
ON
TION
ATION
UCATION
DUCATION
EDUCATION
EDUCATIO
EDUCATI

FILMMAKING FOR CHILDREN

John Lidstone

Children seem to be born filmmakers who treat the camera as a perceiving, inquiring and expressive extension of themselves. Children can work with film just as they work with any other medium—clay, wire, paint, paper—discovering, experimenting, and exploring its potential. More often than not, what they capture visually is a delight both to themselves and to their audiences.

When encouraged to work freely, children tend to find their own creative level quickly. This means that film teachers will need to accept a ten-year-old's film at *his* level with none of the sophistication of an adult film. Often the child has a better understanding of what is most natural for him than the adult does. This does not mean, however, that the teacher, parent, group leader or camp counselor working with children in film does not have a well-defined role as an instructor.

The trick is for the film instructor not to overplay his hand. If he doesn't, the child's filmmaking can be truly creative rather than merely imitative. For example, most Super-8 cameras are designed for any amateur to operate, but children still need help with the technical aspects of the camera and with other equipment needed to produce even the simplest film. Film instructors can play a major role in this area of technical assistance, and they can do so without thwarting the child's individual style. To do this they must keep pace with *his* needs rather than their own.

One way to meet the child's need for technical instruction is to have each beginning filmmaker participate in four basic training sessions which introduce him to the fundamentals of simple film production. Each session should be set up so that film shot during one session can be processed in time for viewing at the next session. The student should have an overview of the complete filmmaking process at the conclusion of the four sessions, but actually they are only the beginning. There will be a constant demand for technical help even with the simplest procedures as each child works his way through his own first film.

First Session: Children can learn basic camera operation in a series of dry runs. These should involve him in loading the film, focusing, reading the automatic exposure meter, using the zoom lens, panning, setting up the camera on a tripod, and handholding the camera.

The class can be divided into two parts. Some simple animation can be done by one group indoors: for example, each child might spell out his own name using cut-out paper letters of his own invention. This will introduce the child to the feel of a "live" camera as it is actually running, and it will let him learn how to set up and arrange lights. While part of the class is animating, the rest can try some outdoor shooting which could involve simple acting. If any of the children have their own cameras, they should be helped to interpret the instruction manuals. At the end of the first session, each child should be familiar with all the basic camera operations, and each should have shot both indoor and outdoor footage.

Second Session: By this time, film shot during the first session will have been returned from the processor and can be shown to the students. A group discussion following the screening should pinpoint why some footage was more successful than other footage. At this point, it might be helpful to review procedures with which the class seemed uneasy, repeating some of the dry runs of the first session.

This is also a good time to acquaint the group with the operation of the projector and to set up some simple rules for the care of equipment.

Once again, there should be an opportunity to shoot actual footage, but this time the students should shoot things which *they* select and which relate to a common theme. For example, they could work around topics such as "Smiles" or "Opposites" or "Windows"—but whatever they choose should be simple so that it can be used in the next session for editing. A title for the anticipated sequence of shots could be filmed using animation techniques that were learned in the first session.

Third Session: Film from the second session should be projected and the reasons for any technical problems explored. Some technical problems which usually occur are: blurred or jumpy footage; sequences which are out of focus; zooms which are too fast or too slow; and film which is underexposed or overexposed.

After discussing these problems, the idea of editing can be introduced. Children should be able to see the difference between editing in the camera and editing on a table using splicers and reels to hold the film. The physical process of editing can be explained by actually cutting up footage previously shot by the group. Because children are inveterate TV watchers, they will already know about transitions from scene to scene and they will be able to see the many choices open to the filmmaker as he organizes the shots of his film in the editing stage. If there are enough editors (reels and viewing machines) and splicers, the class should have an opportunity to practice with both types of equipment, using discarded film to make actual splices.

Fourth Session: Using footage shot around a common theme, the group can now go through the steps needed to produce a finished film. A particular sequence of shots can be chosen by the group and then spliced together; a title can be added at the beginning of the sequence; and blank film (leader) can be placed at the very beginning and end of the reel so that the projector can be threaded up more easily. With a tape recorder as basic equipment, a sound track can be made. It need not be synchronized with the picture. At this stage, making a sound track should be simple enough to demonstrate the principle involved without overburdening the child's capabilities. As technical skills are

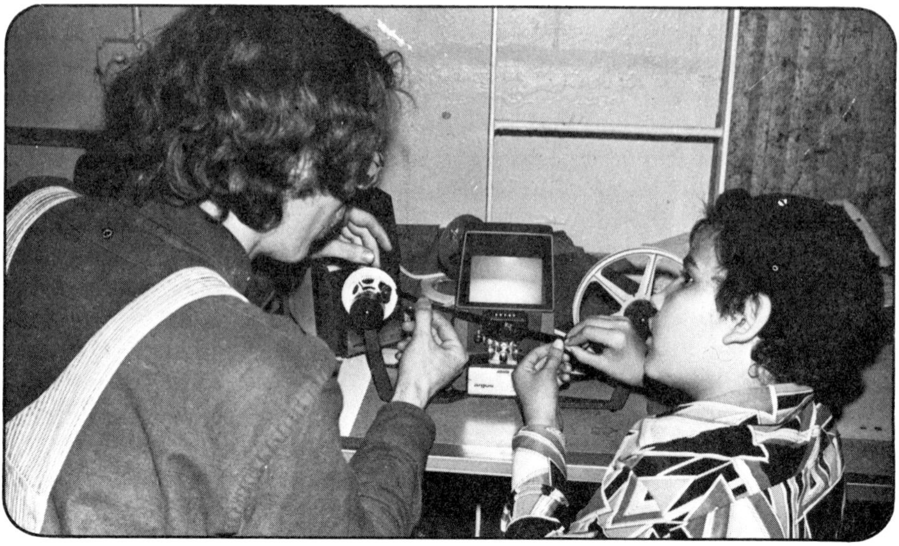

There will be constant demand for technical help as each child works his way through his own first film.

mastered, the child will be able to do more complicated sound tracks.

These four sessions cover a lot of ground, and it is likely that each session will have to be broken up—especially if time periods are strictly adhered to during the school day. In a camp situation or in after-school programs, it is best to run each session continuously. If it is possible, an assistant to the teacher should be present. Depending on the size of the group, one assistant can be assigned for every six or seven filmmakers. Things will go much more smoothly in this part of the filmmaking program if there are assistants, but it is possible to work alone. One instructor can handle up to 15 youngsters effectively. If a school is short on editing equipment, films can be edited in the camera with good results, and this is an excellent introductory exercise for any filmmaker.

A good filmmaking program is designed so that each filmmaker is on his own as soon as possible. The logic of the four sessions outlined here is to make each student technically independent of the instructor as soon as his knowledge and abilities permit. While it is fun to work on class projects, the child can only express his individual ideas if he knows how to work on his own as well as within the group. When the child is working on his own, the role of the film instructor is that of Mr. Fix-it, motivator, organizer, and expediter. When the group works on a class project, the instructor's role *can* become more traditional.

But traditional teacher roles do not seem to work well for most film programs after the initial period of organized instruction. The best results occur when teachers work on a one-to-one basis with students. This is only effective up to a point, however, as most young filmmakers seem to need their own goal if they are to finalize their film ideas. Planning a film festival or special event at which student films would be exhibited is a good way of giving youngsters a definite goal.

Exciting films made by children come out of situations where the film teacher is sensitive enough to the needs of his students to know when he should be the central figure and when he will be more effective in a supporting role. This is creative teaching, and this is what generates creative filmmaking for children.

MAKE THE GRADE AS A FILM TEACHER

Jim Piper

Personal filmmaking. Each student producing an entire film from start to finish. Scripting, shooting, editing, preparing the sound track. The whole thing.

As an alternative to team-produced, vocationally oriented filmmaking, this one-student, one-film approach is catching on all over the country, especially in liberal arts programs in high schools and colleges.

But a lot can go wrong on that perilous road from script to screen. Anyone who teaches such a course should never lose sight of the many problems—in delayed feedback, in the twin tasks of conceptual and technical mastery, in self-esteem—that face every beginning filmmaking student. In my 4 years of teaching a Super-8 personal filmmaking course in a California junior college (see Figure 1 for course profile), I've learned a few things that might be of interest to other filmmaking teachers.

Getting Film Ideas

Students often tell me that one of the hardest parts of the course is finding an idea for a film. To give students some idea of what's possible when working with relatively simple Super-8 equipment, I start the course by showing the class prints of films made by former students. These screenings are followed by short lectures and discussions about premises, plots, characters and overall themes. (If you haven't accumulated any prints yet, try renting films or borrowing from some other film teacher.) I've also developed a number of sure-fire "film starters," as I call them, for students who just can't decide on film ideas:

1) *The film based on a recorded song, published poetry or prose excerpts:* The song *is* the film idea, as well as the film's sound track. The student's job is to shoot and cut the film to enhance the song, poem or story.

2) *The simple documentary:* A how-to film based on an activity the student knows well, such as skiing, playing tennis or hang gliding.

3) *The film based on a "given premise":* I compile a list of brief starting points for films, then invite students to let their imaginations take over. Examples: A student, late for class, can't find a place to park; in a nightmare, a homeowner is confronted by appliances that come alive and turn against him.

4) *The "commissioned" film:* A short film produced for the benefit of someone else, as if it were commissioned. The "client" must be contacted and interviewed to find out what kind of film he can use, and the film has to be aimed at a real audience.

5) *Rap sessions:* Students bring in their discarded film ideas and rap

about them. An idea that one student couldn't get off the ground may soar in the mind of another student.

I break the term down into three units of about equal length, and I check students' work twice during each unit. The *preproduction unit*, about six weeks long, stresses scripting and planning. During this unit I require a written treatment and later a detailed screenplay or shooting script. The *production unit*, running five weeks, stresses shooting and the preparation of the rough cut. Early on in this unit I ask for one earnest reel, uncut. And as the unit closes, I want to see the rough cut. The five-week *postproduction unit* deals with reshooting, fine cutting and preparing the track. During this time I look at fine cuts without tracks and, later, with tracks. Lectures, individual student film productions and the class film run concurrently.

Learning Basics by Writing

For the treatment, I ask for a two- or three-page summary of the approach the students plan to take and what sound system they plan to use. If the film is going to be a documentary, the treatment should clearly state the purpose and mood of the film. If a story film, the treatment should sketch out the plot and indicate who the characters are. For sound, students have a choice between simple cassette tracks wild-synched to visuals with a variable-speed silent projector, and magnetic sound-on-film with dialogue and other sounds post-dubbed.

When the scripts come in, I read them to see if the sequences of shots students are planning will achieve the ends proposed in their treatments. For example, imagine a treatment that says, "I want to communicate how lonely hitchhikers can be." Then imagine that the corresponding sequence of shots in the script reads like this:

1) LS: Hitchhiker on a city street.

Figure 1: Break the term down to three units: Preproduction (scripting and planning); Production (shooting and rough cut); Postproduction (fine cutting and sound track).

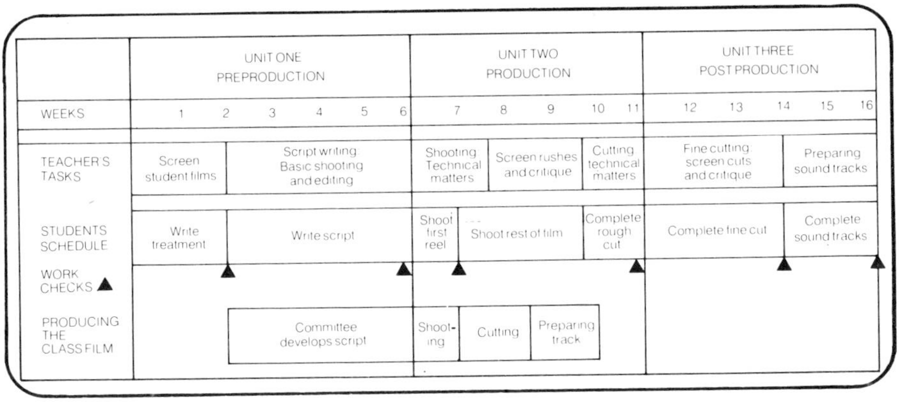

2) LS: Car approaches hitchhiker.
3) CU: Car speeds by hitchhiker.
4) MS: Hitchhiker sees another car and raises his thumb.
5) LS: Second car speeds by hitchhiker.
6) LS: Hitchhiker walks along street.

I'm not sure that the six shots add up to "loneliness." Frustration, perhaps, but not loneliness. So I might suggest that the student set the scene on a deserted (*i.e.*, lonely) country road, instead of a city.

But I'm getting ahead of myself here, because before students can write that first shot of their scripts they have to know something about what I call the basic options of shooting and editing. Shot options include those decisions about whether to shoot a long shot, medium shot or close-up; whether to move the camera or leave it stationary; whether to shoot a complete action in one take or break it up into several takes. Cutting options include decisions regarding the pace of cutting, the treatment of time, the visual emphasis of various shots.

I cover much of this early material in lectures, emphasizing points by rescreening a few of the student films I showed earlier. During screenings I invite comments about the shooting and cutting, and pass out dittoes of scripts written by former students to generate still more discussion. I also set aside some class time to go over pertinent sections of the course text, *Personal Filmmaking*, which I wrote myself.

Practical production procedures also figure in these lectures and discussions about scriptwriting. I have devised a system based on letters and numbers for helping students see the connection between shooting and cutting. Sample sequence:

A-1 LS: Car approaches in distance on country road.
B-2 MS: Hitchhiker turns and sees car.
A-3 LS: Car coming closer.
B-4 MS: Hitchhiker thumbs a ride.
A-5 LS: Car speeds by hitchhiker.
C-6 CU: Hitchhiker disappointed.

The letters refer to shooting; the numbers to cutting. Thus shots A, B and C from the rushes are to be cut up and spliced together to produce the sequence 1-6 in the finished film. The brackets around A-5 and C-6 serve as a continuity reminder: The actor must look and move in the same screen direction in both takes in order for the shots to be match cut.

About Sound

In planning the final ingredient, the sound, I urge students to simplify their sound requirements. In their scripts, students write brief descriptions of the sounds they plan in a column opposite their shot descriptions. For instance, opposite the shots 1 through 6, above, the student might enter: "Sad guitar music mixed with the sound of a car speeding by."

Teaching Technical Matters

My next job is to give students enough technical information about cameras and shooting so they can move into actual production with confidence. With Super-8, I've found I can explain many technical matters of filming as special cases of the basic aim-and-shoot home movie style. Yes, I tell students, you can handhold most of your shots, except in extreme telephoto. Yes, focusing is easy, unless you have to shoot very close or the light is poor or you plan a long zoom. Yes, your camera's automatic exposure system will work just fine, if you don't shoot toward the sun and avoid contrasty situations.

I usually spend a class period letting students handle cameras, explaining which buttons do what. I have also produced a few simple demonstration films of no-no's, to show what happens, for instance, when you shoot Type A film unfiltered in sunlight, or when you forget to focus before zooming in.

All this technical information leads to the first reel, which is due about the sixth week. I screen these first reels privately with students, and I note three things: Is the camera working properly? Is the footage free of elementary technical errors? Has the student adopted a shooting style appropriate to the purpose and mood of the scene? If there are problems, we can work them out before the student shoots more footage.

On to Cutting

About halfway through the course, I introduce the class to the film room—an 8- x 16-foot storage room with work surfaces where students can come to work any time. After I've demonstrated the use of the equipment (a silent and a sound projector, several viewers and splicers), I give an equipment test. Each student must know how to operate both projectors, as well as how to clean the film gates and change lamps. Each student must also make three neat wet splices capable of passing my severe twist test.

This session helps prepare students for the completion of their rough cuts, which are due about two-thirds of the way through the course. As the production unit closes, I make appointments to screen each student's rough cut privately. At this screening, I can make suggestions for reshooting on the one hand, and for further cutting on the other. Often a single roll of film will go a long way toward patching up a weak film. As for further cutting, my suggestions center on how the student might recut to remove unnecessary head and tail footage, improve tempo and pacing, improve continuity, or simply delete some ineffective shots altogether. The fine cut comes in about three weeks before the term ends.

Finally, Sound Tracks

At this point, I show students who have planned cassette tracks how

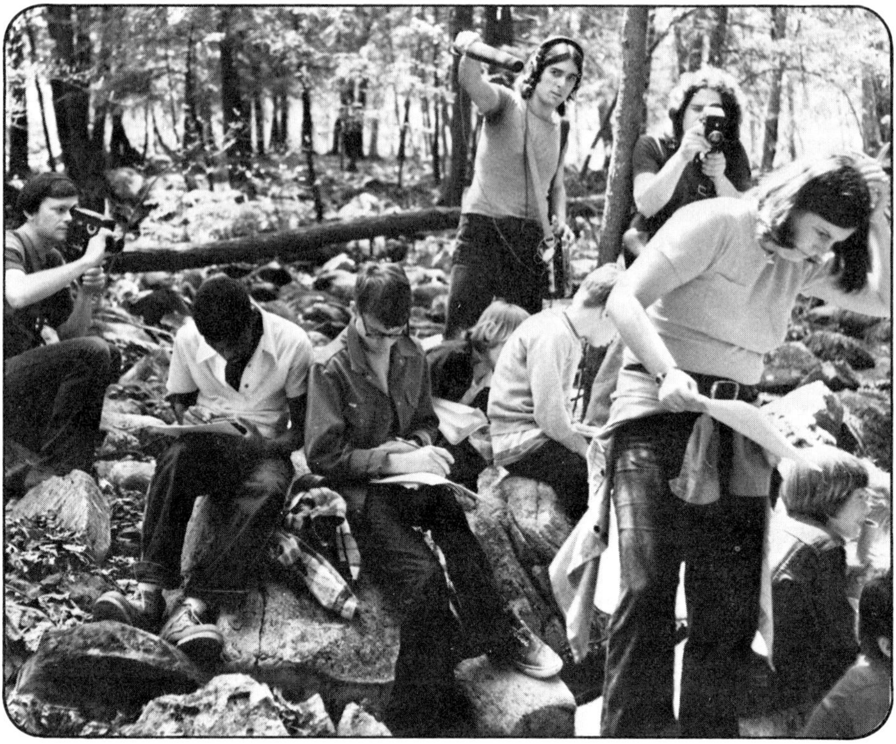

Tell students to handhold most shots, except extreme telephoto.

to time sequences in their films and create cassette tracks by pause-editing with a stopwatch. Then I show students working with the mag projector how to record on their striped film first with a microphone, then from a tape recorder or record turntable. If anyone wants to mix, I demonstrate the use of the four-track recorder for creating a two-channel mix, and the operation of the sound projector's sound-on-sound device.

Producing a Class Film

Nothing quite transforms classroom activities into practical understandable experience as much as producing a class film. Our class film, *S*M*A*S*H*, came to life early one term when a student with a twinkle in his eye had an idea to do a class film about an unsanitary, fly-by-night vasectomy clinic and one of their fearful patients.

A script committee worked out the story, and listed all the shots we'd need. The case included a drunken doctor, a man-hating receptionist, a grubby nurse, the patient, his willful wife, and some extras. Two students rounded up props, and we shot the film in one long day, in a delightfully ratty student apartment. Three students shared filming chores as I stood by, assisting. Three more students volunteered to cut the film, and later on, four other students dubbed the speaking parts, which were short and simple. Finally, I used our sound projector's sound-on-sound device to mix in a little offbeat music. All 23 students were present during shooting, during the screening of the rushes and several cuts of the film, and during the dubbing and mix-in sessions.

Exceptions, Exceptions

But to tell you the truth, my course doesn't run quite as smoothly as these remarks might suggest. Too often students miss the due dates for the assignments and fall behind. Some students seem incapable of writing any kind of script at all. I never feel I have enough time to teach the basics properly, and the last third of the course, riddled with individual problems, sometimes threatens to turn into a nightmare as the festival date bears down on us. So I end up making a lot of exceptions. It's not that I'm such a soft touch. It's just the kind of course it is. For teaching personal filmmaking means giving personal attention. Bending the rules. Taking risks. Fitting the course to the student, instead of the other way around. The course takes a lot of my time, and my colleagues think me mad to want to teach it. Ah, but their courses seldom end with anything quite so cozy and educational as our festivals—which make it all worth it.

BUILD YOUR OWN

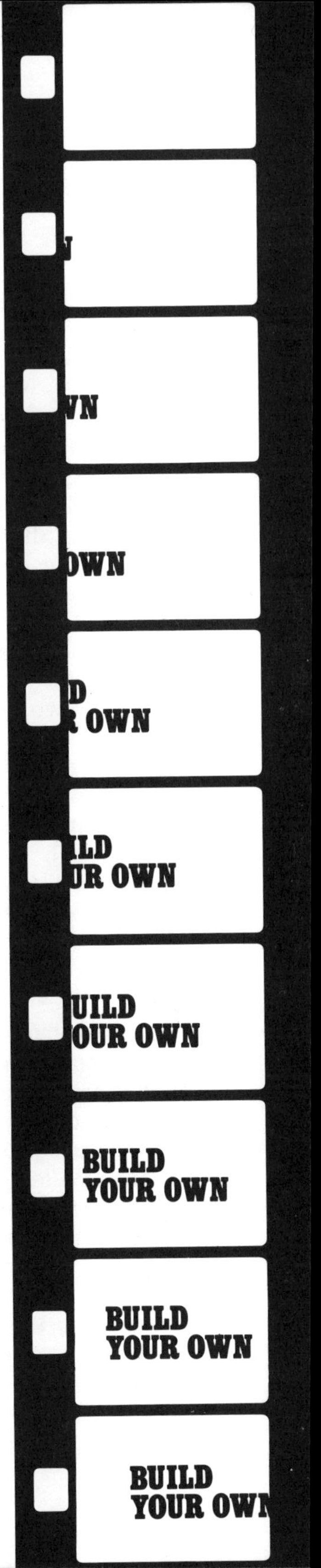
BUILD
YOUR OWN
BUILD
YOUR OWN

SOUND MIXER

Roger Simister

Violins sob as Herbert and Hermione stroll along the moonlit beach.

"I'm afraid...it's all over between us," she whispers.

"No!" he shouts. "You can't mean that!"

Surf crashes on the shore.

An artfully mixed sound track can leave your audience weeping...or trembling...or giggling. Combining dialogue, music and sound effects isn't difficult if you have a sound mixer, and you can build your own for less than $13. The mixer I built has one input for a microphone and two high level inputs for tape recorders. You can feed the output (your mixed sound track) directly into the mic input of your sound projector or tape recorder. For best results, use the mixer with a dynamic microphone. Condenser or crystal microphones may not have the necessary volume or impedance to produce a quality sound track.

Radio Shack and similar electronics stores will carry the parts you need to build your own sound mixer. Buy a chassis, two 5K pots, two 10K pots, two one-megohm resistors, a phone jack, four phono jacks and four ¾-inch knobs. Tools you'll need are: a soldering iron, solder, long-nose pliers, wire strippers, a 3/8-inch hand drill, a hacksaw and a vise. Of course, you can also buy very inexpensive mixers from electronics outlets such as Radio Shack and Lafayette, but beware of mixers which can only accept input from microphones. As a filmmaker, you'll probably want to use tape-recorded sound. Adapting a mic mixer for tape recorder input may be too difficult for an amateur; it's easier to build your own sound mixer to suit your purposes.

Building Your Own

First, prepare the chassis by drilling holes for the controls and input/output connectors. The pots (potentiometers), which will control the level of sound, should be mounted on the front panel of the chassis in 3/8-inch holes (see Figure 1 for spacing of mounting holes for pots R1-R4). The mic jack (J1) on the rear panel also mounts in a 3/8-inch hole, but the smaller phono connectors (J2, J3, J4) only need a ¼-inch hole (see Figure 1 for spacing of input/output jacks J1-J4).

Before mounting the four control pots you'll have to cut their shafts down to a 3/8-inch length. Hold the shaft in a vise and cut it with a hacksaw. You may also have to sand off the primer coating inside the chassis near the microphone and phono connectors. This will insure a good electrical connection to the chassis.

Next, mount the four control pots (R1-R4) on the front panel of the chassis as shown in Figure 2. Note that R1 and R4 are marked for 5K resistance, while R2 and R3 are marked 10K. This will help you place the pots in the positions marked on the diagram. If you mix up the resistance levels, the level of sound will be reduced. You can now mount the microphone jack (J1) and phono jacks (J2-J4) on the rear panel opposite their respective controls (Figure 2). Place the two one-megohm resistors (R5, R6) on wires leading from the 10K pots (R2 and R3) as shown in the diagram. Use number 22 or 24 insulated hook-up wires to link the connectors, resistors and pots, keeping all wires as short as possible.

You're now ready to solder the components. But before you begin, here are a few tips. Always "tin" your soldering iron before starting by applying some solder to the tip of the iron. The solder should melt and adhere to the tip, leaving a shiny surface. If it doesn't, the tip is dirty and should be cleaned. Strip both ends of the wire to be soldered and loop or bend the end of the wire onto the connection with pliers.

Touch the tip of the iron to the connection and wait a few seconds until the connection is hot enough to melt the solder. Then apply just enough solder to cover the connection.

The last thing to do after you mount the control knobs is to stick some of those plastic labels on the mixer, so you can tell at a glance which knob controls what.

Sound Mixing Tips

Once you've built your sound mixer, bought, borrowed or stolen the necessary tape recorders and edited your sound tracks on separate reels of magnetic tape, you're ready for the big mix. If you've never mixed sound before, be forewarned: it may well take more than one sitting to create the sound track your film deserves.

When you're ready to start worrying about the proper recording level, the mixer's output pot will help you evade your projector's auto-

Figure 1: Top view of mixer showing input/output connectors.

Figure 2: How to wire-up the components of your sound mixer.

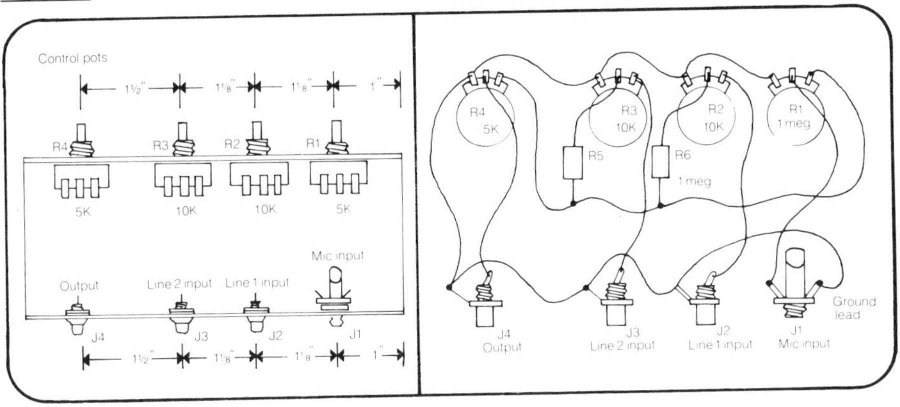

matic gain control. If you're familiar with automatic gain circuits, you know that no matter how loud or soft you record sound onto film, the automatic gain plays it back at a consistent level. This device is a boon in one respect—no matter how much voltage you feed into your projector, you won't "over record," producing distortion. But filmmakers curse the automatic gain when it makes a babbling brook sound like a waterfall or records the chirping of crickets at the same level as the roar of a passing train. By using the output level control on the mixer, you can mix in a level of sound so low that it won't activate the automatic gain circuitry inside the projector. With the automatic gain circuit inoperative, you can record sounds as loud or soft as you want them to be in your finished film.

To find the best setting, feed a steady sound source such as music through the mixer and into the projector, which should be in the record mode. Turn up the mixer's output control until the projector's automatic gain just begins to affect the sound, and you have found the setting you want. If you turn the output control past this point, you will be able to hear the automatic gain bring all your sounds up to one level.

When you're all finished, you can transfer your newly mixed sound track to your film's magnetic stripe or just play it on a tape recorder as you show your film. You'll be amazed at how much a sophisticated sound track can do for your film.

ELECTRONIC CLAPBOARD

Joel Kauffman

The ability to be a one-man film crew is one of the things I've always liked about Super-8. Now that I've developed an easy way to establish sync, lone-wolf filming is even more practical.

Of course, everyone knows you can sync a film by having your subject clap his hands to start the scene. This works fairly well in controlled situations if your subject claps loud enough, keeps his hands within the area being filmed and returns his hands to a normal position before beginning to talk. In many scenes, however, this just isn't possible. I used to set the camera on a tripod, start it rolling, dash in front of the camera with a clapstick, give the cue and dash back to the camera, wasting film all the while.

So I set out to build myself a sync unit that could be activated from behind the camera. I envisioned a handheld device that would emit a beam of light and a sound simultaneously, sort of an electronic clapboard. After some scrounging and searching, I was able to assemble all the parts I needed at a local radio/electronics store. The key to my sync system is the Mallory "Sonalert," a device which produces a shrill noise when activated by current. Since the Sonalert runs on 9 volts, I bought a 9-volt battery and battery cap, but I couldn't find any 9-volt

Figure 1: Components arranged in a chassis.

Figure 2: Completed sync device with sound and light emitting from same direction.

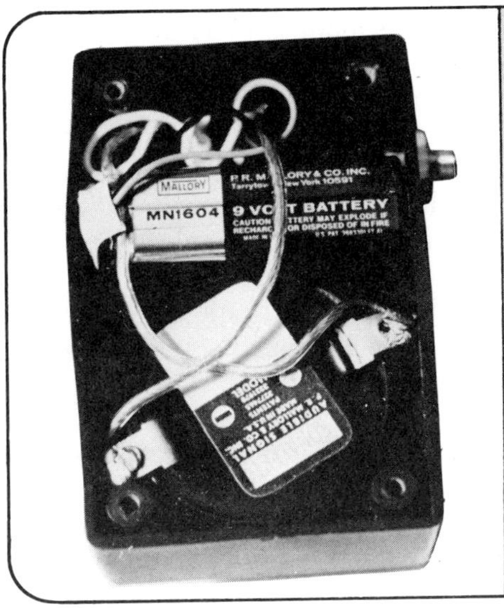

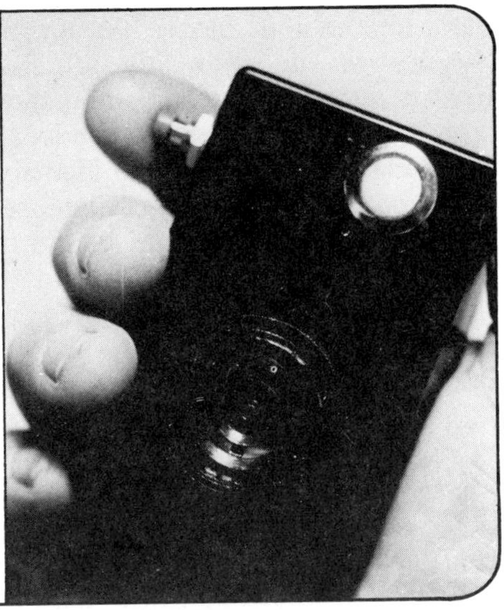

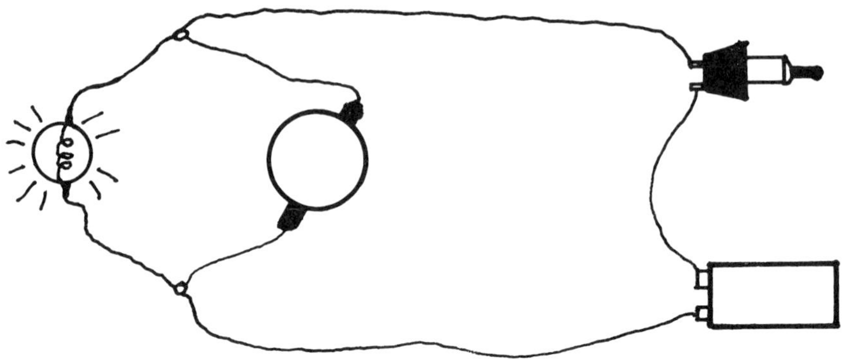
Figure 3: How to wire-up components of sync device.

lights in the store. Instead, I settled on a 6-volt pilot light which worked just fine as it turned out. I also bought a mini-pushbutton switch wire, and a plain black 2- by 3-inch chassis box with a screw-off back. The Sonalert cost $11 and the total cost of all the other components ran to under $3.

I asked a friend to wire the components so that pushing the button completed the circuit of both the Sonalert and the light. The first step is to arrange the components in the chassis to find the best fit (see Figure 1). When you mount the button, decide what finger you will be using to press it and in which hand you plan to hold the device. Since I am right-handed, I prefer to use that hand for my camera and my left hand for the sync device. In our model, we mounted the light and the Sonalert on the same side (see Figure 2), which means that when the light is aimed directly at the camera, the sound is usually aimed away from the mic. This can cause a weaker signal, although the high pitch of the Sonalert is still easy to identify on the editing table. You could improve on our design by putting a semi-globe light at the top of the unit. Since a top-mounted light would be visible from any angle, you could concentrate on aiming the sound at the mic.

When you know where you want the components to go, drill holes for mounting a Sonalert, the light and the push button. Get out your soldering iron and attach one wire from the battery cap to a pole of the mini-switch (see Figure 3). The second battery cap wire attaches to the pilot light and a wire from the light runs to the remaining pole of the mini-switch. Now connect one pole of the Sonalert to the wire running between the pilot light and the mini-switch. The other pole of the Sonalert connects to the wire joining the pilot light and the battery.

Fasten the battery to the back of the chassis, and you're ready.

HOT SPLICER

Cleg Holiman

When I got tired of waiting around for my cement splices to dry, I made a few calls to local electronics parts shops, put in about three hours of work and came up with a hot splicer that cost me only seven dollars. I started with a Bolex, but the idea will work for any cement splicer that has enough room for a resistor to fit under the main clamp plate without interfering with splicing.

An electronics store should be able to supply you with all the parts you need. Ask for a 10-watt, 1500-ohm resistor (85 cents), a 3-amp mini-switch 117vAC ($1.25), a neon pilot light with a resistor 117vAC ($1.30), an AC power cord with female end removed ($1.50), two feet of copper telephone wiring (60 cents), a rubber retaining grommet for the power cord (30 cents) and a kit of two-part epoxy in ¼-ounce tubes ($1.10). The tools I used were a variable speed drill, metal drill parts, center punch, small crescent wrench, soldering gun and solder, screwdriver, metal file and silicone dioxide sandpaper.

On the right end of the Bolex splicer, underneath the base side clamp (see Figure 1, R), mark holes for the neon pilot light and the miniature switch. See Figure 1, #1 and #2 for placement. If your splicer is not a Bolex, take a good look at it to make sure there is enough room to install the pilot light and switch without anything hanging out from under the splicer. On the back of the splicer, centered under the right clamp, set and drill a hole to accept the rubber retaining grommet (Figure 1, #5). Place the switch behind the neon pilot light so that it will be closest to the power source wires. Make sure you leave enough room to

Figure 1: Converted Bolex "hot" splicer.

Figure 2: Underside of "hot" splicer showing placement of parts and wiring.

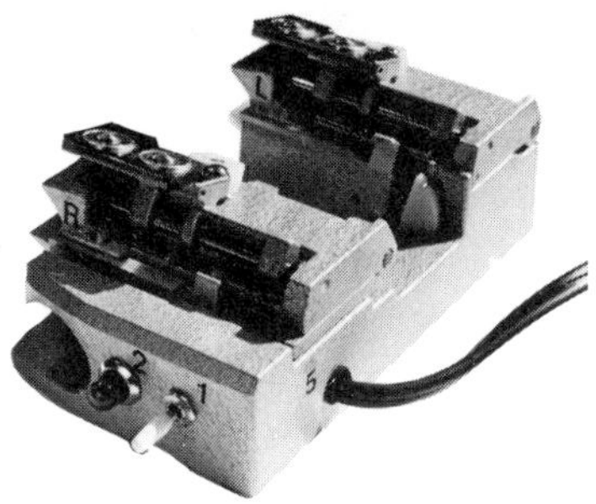

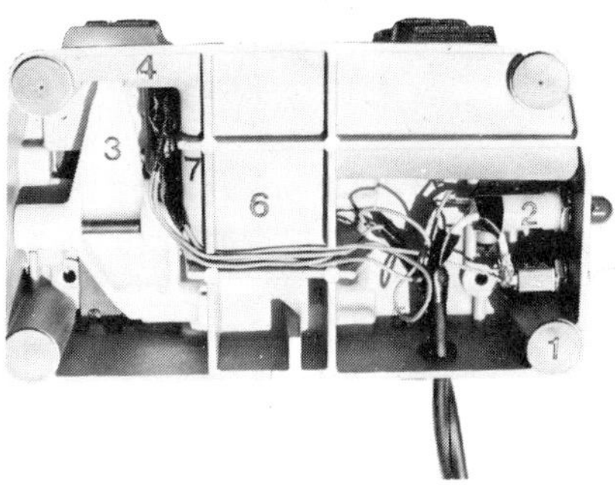

work inside the space that houses the neon light and switch (Figure 2, #1 and #2). Remember that you'll be soldering wires, running leads, making connections, *etc.*, in this space.

Be careful when you drill the holes. Because aluminum is a very soft metal, it's best to drill a "pilot hole" to avoid elliptical, ragged holes. For instance, to drill a 3/8-inch hole, mark the center and drill with a 1/8-inch bit. Then take a ¼-inch bit and drill out the 1/8-inch hole. Finally, drill out the ¼-inch hole with a 3/8-inch bit for a perfectly centered, round 3/8-inch hole. To be safe, use a slow drill speed.

Once the holes are drilled, go over to the left or emulsion side clamp (Figure 1, L) and remove the nylon release key that is fastened by a long screw on the side (Figure 2, #3). File a small notch in this key so that the resistor can sit underneath the clamp plate with a little breathing room between the key and the resistor (Figure 2, #4). You will also have to file away a small portion of the aluminum support ridge (Figure 2, #7) to get the resistor to tuck into the corner. This filing can be a bit tedious, but it's worth it. Next, file two deep notches through the walls of the center compartment (Figure 2, #6) to run wires from the right compartment (switch and pilot) to the left compartment (resistor unit). Make sure the notches are deep enough and wide enough to pass four wires easily. Mount the switch and pilot light in their respective holes and run the power leads through the rubber retaining grommet. Connect one power lead to a switch terminal and the other lead to the closest resistor terminal. The other resistor terminal should be connected to the other switch terminal with a copper telephone wire. Run two leads from the pilot light to the two resistor terminals and you have created a parallel circuit (Figure 3). You cannot connect the circuit in a series because the built-in resistor on the pilot will soak up so much voltage that the heating resistor won't function at all. Don't use a resistor with a different watt or ohm rating or you'll either get no resis-

Figure 3: Follow wiring diagram to create parallel circuit.

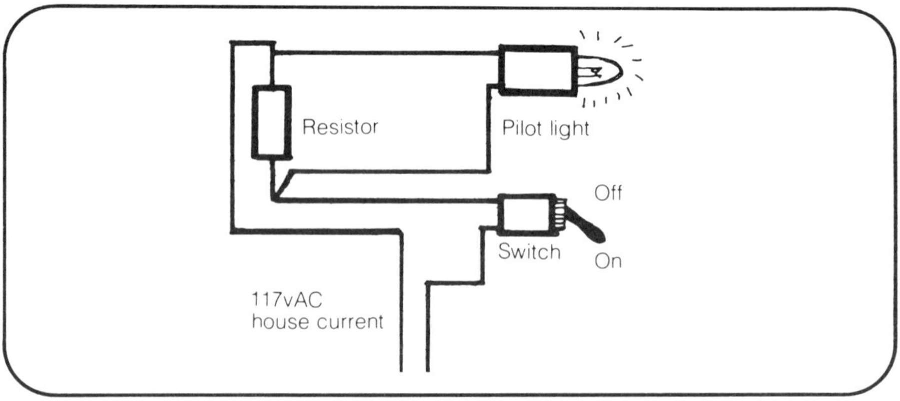

tance, or the voltage will burn up your resistor.

After you've checked your circuitry, epoxy the resistor into place (Figure 2, #4). If you don't want to use epoxy, you can make a screw-type clamp to hold the resistor on. I used epoxy on my machine because it conducts heat very well and very evenly. Remember that the resistor will do a lot of work and it won't burn out for 80 years. Once the epoxy or clamp is set, solder your connections and put the nylon release key (Figure 2, #3) back into place. The nylon is tough and can take any heat it gets from the resistor.

Now you're ready to start splicing. When you flick the switch, the resistor will heat up and dry your cement splices within seconds. The pilot light will tell you when the heat is on. When your splice is dry, turn the heat off right away, so the entire splicer won't heat up and damage your film.

Not only will your hot splicer save time, but the faster your splices dry, the stronger they'll turn out to be.

ANIMATION STAND

Thomas A. Kuster

If your interest is serious animation, you're probably not satisfied with a makeshift tripod set-up. And commercial stands are beyond most of our budgets. Here's a solution—a homemade animation stand that is easy to build and should cost less than $25. The following design is ideal for my Nizo S560 camera—you may have to modify it slightly for your own. The wood used in construction can be obtained cheaply from the scrap box of any lumberyard.

Base and Staging Area

The base of the stand is a 5/8-inch plywood board, 22 inches x 32 inches. Supports for the base are two 1- by 3-inch pieces of oak, 26 inches long. Cut these boards at 63-degree angles along the length of the board (Figure 1). You will need a table saw for these tricky angle

Figure 1: Cut at 63-degree angles along the length of the board. Figure 2: Each base support should extend 4 inches beyond the plywood. Figure 3: The X-dimension is the height of the camera over the staging area. Figure 4: Mount the frame on pine blocks.

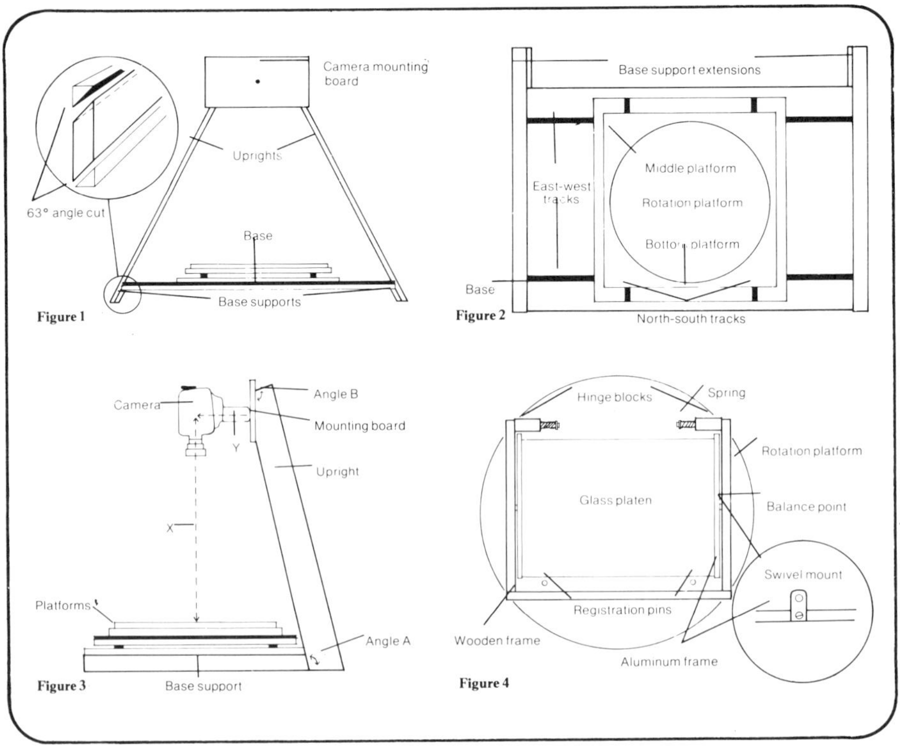

cuts. Lumberyards will charge you extra for cutting. Mount the base supports on the 22-inch sides of the plywood base using 1½-inch screws. Before fastening, apply white glue where the wood surfaces meet. Each base support should extend 4 inches beyond the plywood (Figures 2, 5). These extensions will allow you to attach the camera support uprights.

On top of the base rests the moveable staging area. This consists of three platforms of 5/8-inch plywood. Cut a piece of plywood 19 x 20 inches for the bottom platform. On its underside mount two ¾-inch wood strips parallel to the long length of the board. The strips act as skids and ride in ¾-inch aluminum tracks (Handimetal HM 1285 EA or 1346 EA) which you mount on the base (see east-west tracks, Figure 2). This platform provides east-west movement of artwork. For the middle platform, cut a 17- by 17-inch piece of plywood, and again mount two ¾-inch strips on the underside so they are parallel. These skids run in aluminum tracks mounted on the top of the bottom platform in a north-south direction. Take care in mounting both skids and tracks: make sure they're exactly parallel to prevent jamming. If jamming occurs, work candle wax into the tracks.

The top platform is a circular-cut 5/8-inch plywood board, 16 inches in diameter. This allows rotation of artwork. Drill a hole in the center of this piece and fasten it to the exact center of the middle platform with a single flathead, sunken screw. Felt cloth glued to the platform's underside will provide smooth rotation.

Camera Support Uprights

The uprights which support the camera mounting board are of 1- by 4-inch oak for strength. Their length is determined by finding the X dimension (Figure 3), which is the height of the camera over the staging area. The camera is at the correct height when the camera's zoom lens gives you a 8½- by 11-inch field of view at full wide angle. This field will take in the widest dimensions of the artwork and allow you to zoom in for close-ups of animation subjects. You can find the X dimension by placing an 8½- by 11-inch piece of paper on the rotation platform and holding your camera high enough above it so your wide angle view just takes in the edges of the paper. When you have found the proper height, measure the distance from the surface of the rotation platform to the height of the mounting threads at the base of your camera (Figure 3). The camera should attach to the center of the mounting board at exactly this height to assure full zoom capability. Cut the uprights long enough to support the camera mounting board so its center is at height X.

As you can imagine, cutting the correct angles at the top and base of the uprights is a bit tricky. The object is to center the camera's lens over the rotation platform. On a piece of graph paper, draw a side view of the base and staging area to scale. Draw a line straight up from the center of the rotation platform to represent *X*. Next, find the *Y* dimension (Figure 3) by measuring the distance between the middle of your camera's lens and the camera's base. Draw this dimension on the graph paper at a right angle from the top of *X*. Each upright leans from the base extension to the point where the camera mounting board meets *Y*. Draw an upright in this position. Be sure to leave space on your diagram for the 5/8-inch thickness of the mounting board. Now you can measure (on the graph paper) the precise angle, angle *A* (Figure 3), at which the upright should be cut. Figure angle *B* at the top of the upright so that the camera mounting board, when attached, will be perpendicular to the staging area. Here, once again, you will need to use a table saw to cut exact angles. PLOT THE ANGLES CAREFULLY BEFORE YOU CUT.

Clamp the bottom ends of the uprights onto the base extensions and carefully align before you drill mounting holes. Drill ¼-inch holes and mount the uprights with ¼-inch bolts and wing nuts. These allow easy takedown for storage and travel. The camera mounting board is 5/8-inch plywood, 6 by 12 inches. Drill holes in the mounting board and through the width of the tops of the uprights. Fasten the board to the uprights with ¼-inch bolts and wing nuts. Make sure all the vertical and horizontal lines of the mounting board are as true as possible. Drill a ¼-inch hole for mounting the camera in the center of the mounting board. This hole should be at height *X* above the rotation platform. When you are ready, a ¼- by 1¾-inch squarehead set screw will feed through the hole and into the threads of the camera base. Before feeding the set screw through the hole, thread a wing nut all the way on the screw. The wing nut can then be tightened from the back of the mounting board to pull the camera secure.

Stage With Glass Platen

You need to make a stage on the rotation platform that will hold artwork flat and in place. On this platform, center a sheet of 8½- by 11-inch paper that has been punched with a standard three-holed punch. Mark where the two outer holes lie. In the marks, drill shallow holes barely large enough to fit the narrow ends of two taper pins (Sharon CTP 196 M 4x1 taper pins). Wedge the taper pins tightly into the holes. Make sure that they align correctly with the outer holes of the paper. These serve as registration pins and will engage any tracing paper or transparent animation cels punched with the three-holed punch. Arrange a second set of pins on a table off to one side for preparation of artwork.

A glass platen for holding artwork flat is made from a ¼-inch thick piece of plate glass, 8¼ x 11½ inches. Mount the short ends of the glass in pieces of aluminum storm window frame, available from most glaziers. Next, construct a three-sided wood frame from 1- by 1-inch pine, 14 inches long in the front and 10¾ inches on either side. Mount the frame on 1¼ x 1½ x 1¾-inch pine blocks (Figure 4). Drill holes through the long length of the blocks and attach them to the frame with 5-inch bolts and wing nuts. Then glue the blocks firmly to the rotation platform. Thread springs (Century C-736 cut in two) over the 5-inch bolts and the wing nuts. These create enough friction at the hinges to hold the frame with platen in a raised position.

Fasten the aluminum frame with platen to the wood frame at the balance points with homemade swivel mounts. The swivel mounts (see insert, Figure 4) can be fashioned from small scraps of aluminum. These are firmly screwed to the aluminum frame and loosely bolted to the wood frame so that the platen can swivel freely when it is raised and lowered. Place an 8½- by 11-inch cardboard pad on the surface of the rotation platform under the platen. The glass should press against the pad. Without it, the platen will rest on its aluminum frame and not hold artwork perfectly flat. Be sure the platen is mounted so that the glass, when lowered, just barely clears the registration pins. A coat of flat black paint on all stage parts will reduce unwanted glare.

Adjustable Lighting System

Cut 1- by 1-inch pine strips 48 inches and 33 inches long. Bolt these to each other on either side of the uprights (with the longer strip in the front) using 1/8- by 6-inch bolts with wing nuts. The wing nuts permit vertical adjustment along the uprights. You can attach photo lights with 150-watt bulbs and spring clamps to the adjustable strips. You are now ready for animation.

MINIATURE SETS

Rod Eaton

Do you live in Minnesota and need an establishing shot of the Sahara Desert? Does your script for a sci-fi epic call for a lunar base exterior shot complete with spacecraft departure? Perhaps you want to show a building being blown up, an avalanche covering an Alpine ski lodge, or molten lava inundating a Tahitian fishing village. Or maybe you need to depict the surface of Neptune, the city at the bottom of the sea, or the Great Chicago Fire. Even if you had a multi-million dollar budget, some of these shots would be impossible to get. With my budgets they're *all* impossible. The solution: to build and film miniature sets.

My filmmaking frequently involves the use of miniature sets. I don't think I consciously go out of my way to incorporate miniatures into my films. It just seems to happen. I must be a closet masochist. But, despite the fact that building miniatures requires time, patience and, sometimes, money, they are often the only way to depict your ideas on film. Miniatures can depict what would otherwise be expensive, difficult or even impossible. Several recent feature films have used miniatures effectively, notably *Earthquake* and *The Towering Inferno.*

For the most part, the use and construction of miniatures remain the esoteric secret of a handful of Hollywood special-effects experts. And even though use of miniatures is a fairly common device in commercial cinema, not much has been written about them for the amateur or independent filmmaker, who is left to his own inventiveness. Although it takes a lifetime's skill and experiences, plus boxes full of money, to produce the kind of miniatures used in *Earthquake*, miniatures are definitely not beyond the realm of Super-8 filmmakers. In fact, you don't need any special equipment—just time, patience, and a few guidelines.

Filming Miniature Sets

You have to *build* a miniature set before you film it, but you must consider what you will be filming before you begin to build. I like to sketch the set the way I want to see it on the screen. The sketch helps me visualize the set and decide how I must film it. It also does away with guesswork. What purpose will the set serve in the film? What will it do? Move? Shake? Burn? How will it be lit? What camera angles will be used to film it?

Scale—the measurement of the relationship between your miniature and actual life size—is an important consideration. To some degree, how much you have to show (one house or an entire city), how large an area you have to work in, and how much time and money you can devote to construction are factors you must consider in determining what scale to use. Scale is expressed as a ratio which compares the full-size original (expressed as 1) to your miniature (expressed as a variable number). A scale of 1:24 indicates that the miniature is one-twenty-fourth the size of the full-scale original. Another way to express this would be ½ inch equals 1 foot. The first two columns in Table A list some common model scales and their real-life equivalents. You're free to choose any scale you wish to build in, but before you start to re-create the city of St. Louis on your kitchen table in 1:4,000 scale, there's one more factor you should consider. As scale decreases—that is, the smaller you build your miniature—filming problems increase.

The first problem to be solved is *depth of field.* Depth of field can be defined as the area in front and in back of the subject that appears in acceptably sharp focus for any given focal length. Several factors affect depth of field—the focal length of the lens, the *f*/stop you shoot at, and the lens-to-subject distance. When you shoot with your lens at a short focal length (wide angle) you have a greater depth of field than with a long (telephoto) focal length. Smaller apertures (higher *f*/stops) also produce greater depth. And the farther away the subject that the lens is focused on, the greater the depth of field. A 60mm lens focused at 4 feet and shooting at *f*/1.4 will have an extremely shallow depth of field. A 6mm lens focused at 40 feet and shooting at *f*/22 will have a great depth of field—everything from about 5 feet to infinity will be in focus.

When you look down a street, all the buildings appear in focus; that's the way we see. A camera in the same position will be able to photograph the street in the same way. But, let's say you construct a 1-foot-deep model of the street and try to photograph the same relative view. You will have problems because your proximity to the small model will result in a shallow depth of field. Therefore, you'll be unable

Table A

Frames-Per-Second Increase for Action with Miniatures

Scale	Equivalent	Adjusted fps	
		18 fps	24fps
1:2	6 in. = 1 ft.	25	34
1:4	3 in. = 1 ft.	36	48
1:8	1-1/2 in. = 1 ft.	50	67
1:10	1-1/5 in. = 1 ft.	58	77
1:12	1 in. = 1 ft.	63	84
1:16	3/4 in. = 1 ft.	72	96
1:20	3/5 in. = 1 ft.	81	108
1:24	1/2 in. = 1 ft.	88	118
1:36	1/3 in. = 1 ft.	108	144
1:48	1/4 in. = 1 ft.	126	168
1:64	3/16 in. = 1 ft.	144	192
1:96	1/8 in. = 1 ft.	180	240

Some common model scales and their real-life equivalents.

to render the miniature sharply from front to back. Nothing will give away the true size of a miniature as fast as a shallow depth of field, and working close-up on small models makes it difficult to maintain depth.

You can increase the apparent depth of a set and still maintain focus by *forcing*, or creating the illusion, of perspective. This is simple to do. Build foreground objects relatively large and well-detailed. As you move toward the back of the set, things should become progressively smaller and less detailed. A house near the back of a set may be half as big as one in the front. This way a set may be only 2 feet deep, but to the camera it will look much deeper.

If you plan to incorporate falling objects, explosions, moving water or the like into your set, you will face another problem. To maintain realism in small scale, many actions need to be slowed down by using a faster fps. For example, a real car falling off a real cliff 10 feet high takes X seconds to hit the ground. With a miniature set, however, built to 1:10 scale—making the cliff 1 foot high—a model car falls to the ground in much less time. Gravity won't take direction from anyone, so you'll have to film the falling model in slow motion. To determine how much to slow things down, follow the correct fps in Table A. Consider the same example if the set is built to 1:48 scale—¼ inch equals 1 foot. The proper shooting speed would be 126 fps. Show me a Super-8 camera that will do that! Just remember that by increasing the fps, you're increasing the shutter speed, so you have to open the diaphragm to compensate. This decreases the depth of field, so, in short, when it comes to miniatures, BIG may be best.

Building Miniature Sets

When you're ready to begin construction, you may elect to build in one of the standard model gauges familiar to hobbyists, like 0 (1:48 scale) or HO (1:96). In these scales you can find hundreds of things—

Cardboard boxes are taped to base to provide foundations for ground contours.

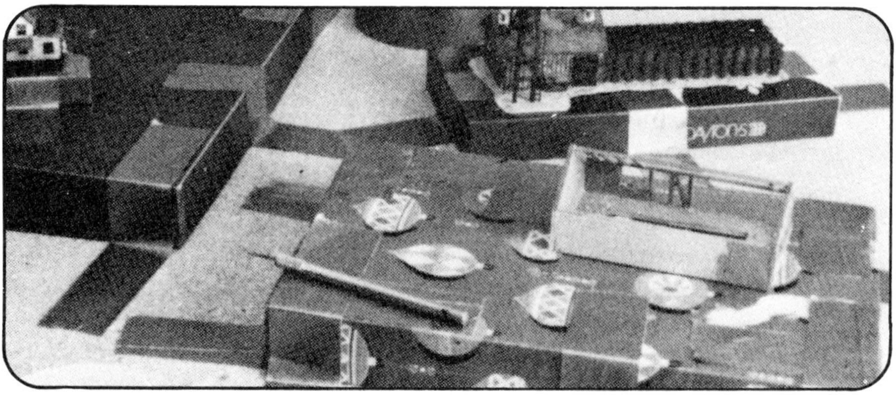

cars, trains, trees, buildings, even grass and stones—at hobby shops, all ready to use.

Sets should be built at a convenient and comfortable height, unless you have no respect for your back. The top of a table is fine, or build a table frame from two-by-fours. Building on the floor may be all right if you want an aerial view. In most cases, however, miniatures should be filmed from eye level, which is easiest with the set at tripod level.

There are any number of ways to construct miniature sets. What you do depends largely on the nature of the set. For a desert, dumping a load of sand on the table may be enough. For a cityscape, more elaborate techniques are needed. Good sources of ideas, materials and building techniques are model railroad publications like *Model Railroader* and *Railroad Model Craftsman*. Even though many of their methods of landscaping can be employed for film miniatures, their basic building materials are generally wood, wire and plaster. Admittedly, plaster sets are sturdy and long-lasting, but they are not requisite for film models.

I usually prefer to use cardboard, tag board, paper towels and aluminum foil. These materials are somewhat cheaper, are easy and fast to work with, and just as important, are easy to get rid of when filming is completed.

I use heavy cardboard for a base and build everything else up from it. The cardboard is easy to tape and staple other things to. The first step is to draw the location of buildings, other structures, terrain detail such as rivers, crests of hills or mountains, and so forth, on the base. If your set is to perform some special function—generate an earthquake, perhaps—you will indicate sections of the set that will move. Do you need a place for an explosive charge? Do you plan to shake a building with a concealed lever? Will a hidden string be used to pull down a tower? Will water run over a part of the set? All of these special

Tag board strips are taped down and woven, basket style, to form skeleton for hills.

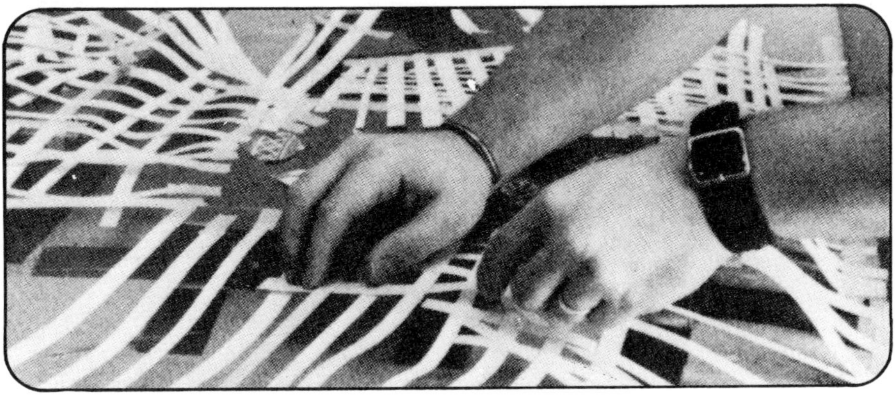

mechanical considerations must be planned at this time.

Next, forms or ribs cut from cardboard are fastened to the heavy cardboard base along the crest lines. To these ribs I tape 1-inch wide strips of tag board to the base, defining the shape of the hills as I go. Other strips can be interwoven basket-style to increase the strength of the form. Over this form I lay sheets of industrial-type brown paper towels which have been soaked in a thinnish flour-and-water paste. One layer of towels is generally enough and will dry quickly into a fairly strong covering that can easily be painted. Sometimes aluminum foil can be laid over a frame allowing quick construction. Foil can be bent and crumpled to represent rocky terrain. One disadvantage of foil is that it will not accept water-base paints.

When constructing your terrain remember you want to convince your viewers that what they see is real, not a miniature shot in your basement. So keep in mind that in reality, land is rarely flat; even "flat" land isn't really flat. There are uneven spots, small rises and depressions. Nature is irregular and uneven; only man-made things tend to be regular, straight and even. Look at life, become observant. Your miniatures will reflect your perceptions.

Dressing the Set: The Finishing Touches

When the basic structure has been completed, the fun begins. The set must be painted and dressed. To begin, paint the set in appropriate colors—greens, browns, reds. Many different kinds of paint will work well for this initial painting. If I'm in a hurry I might use spray paints, but latex or poster paint, tempera, artist's oils or acrylics are all fine. Stay away from paint that will dry glossy, although in most cases, even glossy paints will dry dull on a paper surface. If colors look too bright and shiny when they dry, dull them down a bit with a light spray of flat black or brush them over with a water-diluted wash of earth

Here the set is viewed from camera position.

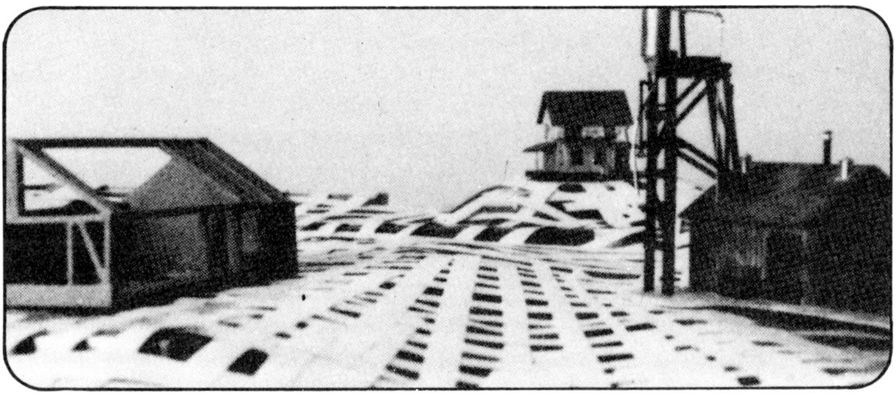

color—raw umber, light to medium brown. Keep all areas of color uneven in shade for a natural look.

If you are using model buildings, cars, and trees purchased from a hobby shop, they will also probably need to be treated to look real. A plastic building looks like a plastic building unless it is aged. Paint with flat colors, and then dull sections with thin washes of paint. Real buildings get dirty, stained, rusty and sooty—and unless one was painted yesterday, it will show the effects of sun, wind and rain.

Hobby shops that cater to model railroaders will have a supply of grass, crushed rock and other kinds of ground coverings. These materials can be sprinkled over appropriate areas of the set or glued down with a water-thinned white glue. If you can get different shades of materials, mix them—grass should contain a lot of yellows, several greens, and some brown. Earth is not all one shade—there are light to dark browns, grays, blacks, reds. If things still look too bright, tone them down with washes. A lot of variety in texture and color looks good in ground coverings. Luckily, almost anything will work. Fine sawdust—dyed to any shade with food colors, clothes dyes, acrylic washes or dry powdered tempera paints—can be used for grass or soil. I have also used salt, sugar, sand, dry coffee grounds—even parsley, sage, rosemary and thyme.

You can buy miniature trees of different types, use pieces of real plants that will look right in miniature, or make your own. It's fairly simple to make a realistic-looking tree by twisting a bundle of light wire and shaping branches off the trunk as you work. This framework is covered with potter's clay which can then be painted. Lichen, available from hobby shops, can then be glued to the branches to create foliage. Small pieces of lichen also make ideal bushes and shrubs. Lichen comes in various colors and, if left in direct sunlight, will fade to realistic shades.

Paper towels soaked in water and flour paste are layered over the tag board strips.

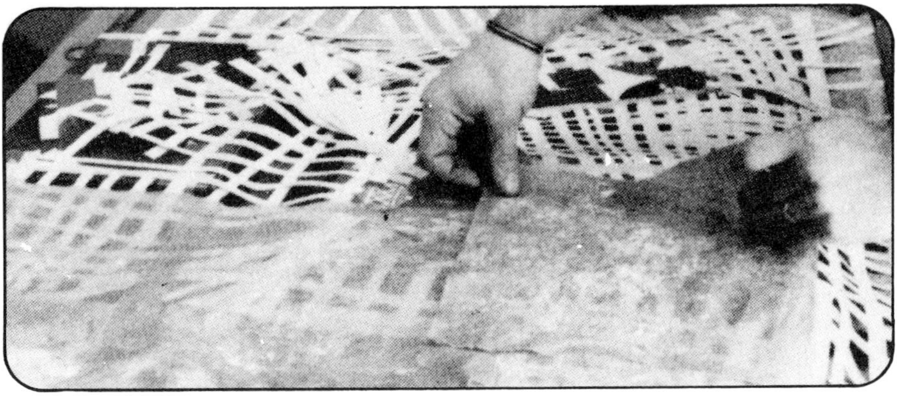

What else does your set need to look finished? How about small rocks (or pieces of cork); weeds made from strands of unbraided twine or theatrical crepe hair (which can be straightened by soaking in water and hanging with a weight at the end); and telephone poles made from balsa wood (or bought ready-made). Look around. What do you see in reality that you can duplicate in miniature? Detail is important—it makes your set come alive.

If your set isn't intended to represent reality—like the surface of an alien planet, for example—you can really let your imagination go. Pieces of broken and crumpled Styrofoam make majestic mountains. Sections of Plexiglas, molded with a propane torch, become jagged outcroppings of ruby-red rock. Twisted cellophane forms frozen florid fountains. Paraffin, melted with colored pieces of crayon, can be poured down slopes, lava from a volcanic eruption eons ago. A cupful of Drano in a sunken pan of water creates a bubbling, foaming pool of liquid hydrogen. Into this barren world your 1:96 spaceship comes, guided by invisible nylon fishing line.

Backgrounds

A suitable background for a miniature set can be painted on a large sheet of paper. You don't really need to be much of an artist to paint white clouds on a blue sky or a distant line of mountains. Things at a distance usually appear soft and indistinct due to the effect of the atmosphere, so you can place backgrounds a bit behind the rear edge of the set and photograph them out of focus. You may have to light the background separately from the set.

Other backgrounds might simply be a piece of colored paper, a large photograph or a poster. To make a night sky, paint a sheet of cardboard black or dark blue and punch a bunch of small holes in it. Lit from behind, these will become stars. To make the stars twinkle, hang

Set is painted with acrylic paint. After the paint dries, grass and earth will be sprinkled on.

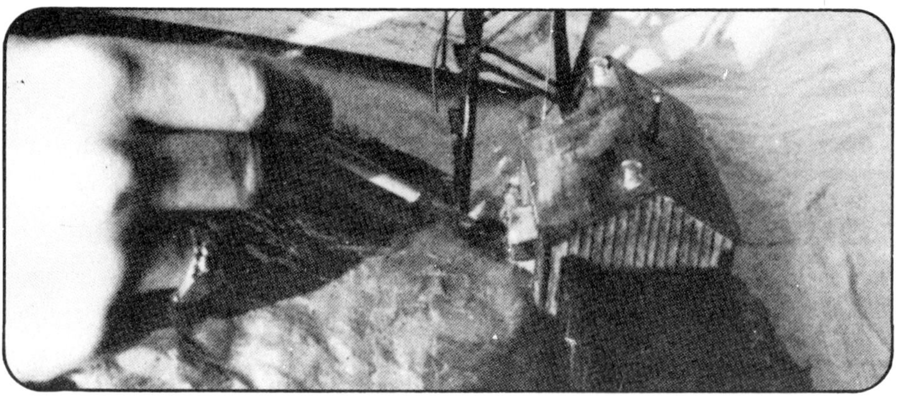

strips of processed film between the backdrop and the light source and blow them around a bit with a fan.

In some cases you can create added depth to your set by positioning a flat—a piece of two-dimensional scenery—just behind the set but in front of the background. A distant mountain range, for example, can be cut from cardboard and be silhouetted by the light on the "sky."

Special Effects: Fires, Explosions, Earthquakes

Fire and water are the two hardest things to deal with in miniature. Regardless of the scale you impose upon them, a flame or a drop of water remain obstinate in their refusal to conform—they stay the same size! Because we are used to seeing these elements and know how they look and behave, they are rarely convincing in small scale. If you need the effect of a fire or flood the best thing to do is build in fairly large scale—perhaps 1:16 (¾ inch equals 1 foot) or larger.

Fire, needless to say, is *dangerous*. If you're not careful, you may start out burning downtown Miami and end up destroying your house. Make sure the areas of the set around the fire will not burn easily. That goes for things around and over the set as well. A miniature fire can quickly get out of hand. If at all possible, shoot a fire scene outside, rather than in the basement (the only other place you might use). Have a fire extinguisher, a hose, or buckets of water handy to put out the fire as soon as the scene is filmed.

To guide the fire on the set you can soak areas and buildings with lighter fluid. Be cautious about fumes from flammable chemicals—keep your filming area *well ventilated*. The sections that are to burn must be constructed in a way that will allow them to burn realistically. Some sections of a real building don't burn easily—metal beams and brick walls, for instance. Use materials for these sections that will not burn too well. You may need to build an interior for a building, since it may

The finished set—a good example of maintaining depth of field and forced perspective.

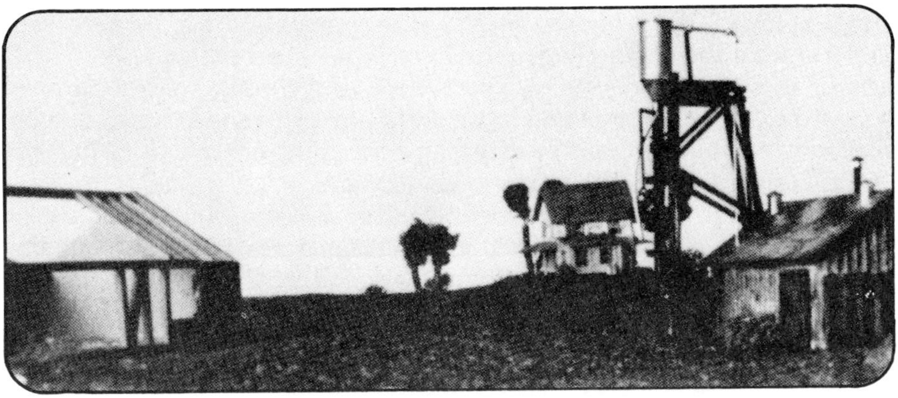

begin to show as the outside burns away. To produce additional smoke you can place smoke bombs (available in magic supply stores) inside the structure. Another method is to put a lot of rubber cement inside—it will smoke as it burns.

Water isn't dangerous to work with—just messy and inconvenient. Areas of the set that must hold water, or have water running over them, will need to be lined with plastic sheeting or aluminum foil. If you're staging a flash flood, buildings and trees that are to be swept away by the raging current will have to be constructed so that they will fall apart. The force of the water may be enough to accomplish this, but hidden strings can be used inside buildings to trip catches that will release walls, roofs and chimneys. Again, it may be necessary to construct interiors.

To create the effect of an earthquake, the camera can be shaken (but not *too* vigorously) or the set can be moved with levers placed under corners. The set could be built in two or more sections, and the seams can be hidden by the covering materials. If the sections are moved individually, cracks will appear, and the earthquake will seem more realistic. Hidden strings or wires can pull down buildings. In addition to the larger sections of the building that fall, you should provide for smaller pieces to fall also—like bricks, glass and other debris. To create dust when large sections hit the ground, blow air into little pockets of sifted flour. Have someone off camera blow through a straw or plastic hose or operate a can of compressed spray air through a plastic hose.

Explosions should be undertaken with the utmost *caution*. Explosions are set up in much the same structural fashion. The buildings to be blown up should be constructed with weak sections. The explosive charge will blow these sections apart inevitably; further destruction can be accomplished with hidden wires. Dust and debris can be blown up from the ground with compressed air to add to the realism.

Firecrackers, which are illegal almost everywhere and difficult but not impossible to get, can be used as the explosive charge. They tend to explode violently, however, and don't produce any smoke or flames. A better choice would be gunpowder in a metal-lid jar. This makes an ideal explosive. A bit of *very careful* experimentation will be necessary to determine the correct amount. Gunpowder can be detonated with a fuse of an electrical device. A short piece of nichrome (nickel/chrome) wire—the stuff that heats up in toasters—can be connected to a good-sized dry-cell battery and inserted into the gunpowder can. When the current is turned on, the powder will explode.

A really first-class explosion involves the use of a number of tricks. A gunpowder charge will blast pre-weakened sections of a building away. The structure is immediately engulfed in flames—lighter fluid ensures it. Compressed air directed into flour simulates dust kicked up by the blast. As various sections of the building crumble and fall away —controlled by wires—dense smoke pours forth.

To film these special-effects scenes will require the help of one or two assistants. The fact that the camera will be running several times faster than normal speed makes it that much more difficult to coordinate the various effects. A good way to do this is to use several cameras, if possible, to film the scene simultaneously. You won't want to redo it—in fact, it may not be possible to re-shoot—and several cameras will give you plenty of footage to edit with.

What other effects do you need? Wind is easy. A good fan will provide anything from a gentle breeze to a hurricane. For the latter, drop dust and assorted junk in front of the fan to blow across the set. Fog can be produced by putting dry ice in pans of water. The pans can be on the set, hidden behind or beneath things, or they can be placed off-camera and the fog can be gently blown onto the set with a fan.

There's no mystery about miniatures, no magic. It's just a matter of pre-planning, gathering your materials, constructing the set, and finishing it off in a realistic way. Obviously, the procedure takes time but the results are well worth it. The extra effort it takes you to construct your set will most likely result in a film that will amaze your viewers with its exciting action and creativity. You don't have to shelve ideas that seemed next-to-impossible; just about anything is possible in miniature. Don't hesitate to take a crack at it. If you've been saving money for the last 17 years to make that film about the day the world ends—take a vacation instead. Then, when you get home, you can construct your miniature sets for a fraction of what the "real" thing would cost—and no one will ever know!

GLOSSARY

A & B rolling: A method of printing from two specially prepared rolls of camera film in order to achieve a spliceless print or to create fades and dissolves and other optical effects.

Aerial image printer: A kind of optical printer used for combining a drawn foreground with background action.

ALC (AGC, AFGC): Automatic level control (automatic gain control, automatic frequency gain control): a feature of some sound cameras allowing automatic adjustment of sound recording level.

Anamorphic lens: (Also called wide-angle lens.) A lens or converter attachment that, in combination with a camera or projector lens, results in a short horizontal and long vertical focal length. Films shot with this attachment must be projected with the conversion in order to achieve a normal image, which will be wider than standard. Films were first commercially distributed with this system in 1953 with the trademark CinemaScope. Many studios adapted the methods under various trade names, and anamorphic lenses are now available for Super-8 use.

Animation: a filmmaking technique wherein inanimate objects or drawings are seemingly made to move, usually achieved by single frame or clusters of 2- or 3-frame shooting.

Answer print: A timed, corrected print submitted by the lab for approval and minute corrections before release prints are made.

Aperture: A flexible, calibrated opening either inside the lens or between the lens and the film in the camera. The opening and closing of the aperture determines how much light reaches the film.

ASA rating: (also ANSI). The exposure index of a film as set by the American National Standards Institute.

Aspect ratio: The relationship of the width to the height of a frame, usually 4 to 3 (1.33:1) for Super-8, 16mm and 35mm. CinemaScope and other wide-angle releases have an aspect ratio of 2.33:1 or 1.85:1.

Available light: Describes a shooting situation using existing light, either sunlight or normal indoor room light with no *special* artificial lighting provided.

Backlight: An illumination from behind the subject, aimed toward the camera.

Backlight control: A feature of many Super-8 cameras that opens the lens about 1 stop to keep the automatic exposure system from being fooled in a backlight situation.

Backwind: A built-in camera mechanism or a manual technique for winding film back on the feed reel or into the feed chamber to allow double exposure, or for adding titles, dissolves or multiple images.

Barn doors: Flat, opaque, hinged objects mounted or clamped in front of lights to control or contain the light. Usually used in pairs or fours.

Barney: A padded soft cover for a camera; reduces the mechanical noise when recording sound while shooting.

Beamsplitter: A device to divert a portion of a light beam in another direction, usually a semi-silvered or two-way mirror or prism. Used in a camera to send some light to the viewfinder and the rest through the aperture to expose the film.

Blimp: Similar to a barney, a rigid, padded housing that totally encloses the camera for noise reduction.

Blow-up: An optical enlargement of the film image to a larger format.

Bounce light: A lighting source aimed at a wall or ceiling or a special reflective screen, allowing reflected light to illuminate a scene.

Cable release: A length of cable attached to the cable release socket on a camera, with a button or plunger at the other end that drives a sheathed wire into the socket to trigger camera action. Used for animation and to eliminate camera shake on a tripod.

Camera angle: The area and viewpoint recorded by the lens, variable according to camera position.

Cartridging: Having the finalized film placed in a cartridge for showing on continuous loop projectors. A service performed by labs, A/V dealers or photo stores.

Cinema verite: (Literally, "film truth.") Both a technique and a style developed primarily by independent filmmakers and strongly influenced by Robert Flaherty's lyrical documentaries. The tenets of cinema verite require as direct and immediate a relationship as possible between subject and camera/filmmaker—no "studio effects."

Clapboard: A chalkboard with a stick hinged on top, so that when clapped together a sharp noise is made to indicate the beginning of a sound take. The number of a take and other identifying notations are chalked onto the board, and when edited, this image is synchronized to the clap sound on the sound track.

Close-up lens: (Macro lens.) Either built-in or an accessory lens, these are capable of allowing continuous focusing from infinity to within several inches of a subject.

Color balance: An adjustment of the sensitivities of the layers and dyes of color film according to the type of light available. Film balanced for indoor light will have a different adjustment than that balanced for sunlight. These adjustments can be adapted further (indoor film used outdoors and vice versa) by the use of selected filters.

Condensor mic: A microphone whose facing conduction surfaces are capable of taking a charge, so that there will be a voltage across the condenser plates. One plate is fixed, the other mobile, making a variable voltage device. Condensor mics require a polarizing voltage, a DC potential from about 50 to 200 volts. The amplifier is generally part of the microphone.

Contrast: The relationship of light and dark colors in exposed film. This relationship is affected by the sensitivity of a particular film emulsion, in both black-and-white and color films. A low contrast emulsion will reflect indistinct color densities, while a high contrast film will have greater distinction in color densities, so that light and dark gray, for instance, may appear to be black and white.

Copying stand: (Animation stand.) There are two basic types, and many brand name makes of animation or copying stands, which provide a method for precisely aligning and registering material to be photographed. Vertical stands have the axis of the camera lens perpendicular to the floor and are commonly used for artwork animation. Horizontal stands have the camera lens axis parallel with the floor, and are most often used for puppet-type animation.

Cookie: A sheet of either opaque or translucent material with a perforated random pattern (leaves, branches, flowers, etc.) that is set to reflect bounce light onto a uniform or monotonous surface in a scene.

Credits: The list of contributors—writer, director, actors, technicians, etc.—to a film; generally included in the filmed "titles."

Crystal sync: A method of synchronizing sound and film by use of a quartz crystal to control the camera and a crystal oscillator to lay an exact 24-frame pulse on the tape.

Cut: An abrupt change from one shot to another. A cut can be made during filming or editing.

Cutaway: A shot that cuts away from the main action to a detail, so that a portion of the main action can be removed without jolting the audience by its removal.

Cut-out animation: Animation of cut-out characters, like hinged paper dolls, placed against a painted or other background.

Day-for-night: Shooting film in daylight underexposed, with house lights and/or car lights on and sometimes a blue filter over the lens, to create the illusion of night.

Depth of field: The range of area remaining in focus both in front of and behind the specific distance for which the focus has been set. The depth of field will alter according to variations in *f*/stop, focal length of the lens and distance of the subject.

Diffusion filter: A type of filter that spreads the light, thereby softening picture quality.

Digital pulse: A sync pulse system for double-system sound recording utilizing one signal per frame.

Diopter: A measure of lens power according to the standards of opticians. In a camera, the diopter finder adjusts the eyepiece to individual (nearsighted, farsighted) specifications.

Diopter lens: A close-up lens attached in front of a regular lens for macro shooting.

Directional mic: Usually called unidirectional or cardioid, this mic has a pickup pattern restricted to the area pretty much in front of the mic in a heart-shaped pattern.

Dissolve: A fading out of one shot superimposed over the fading in of a following shot.

Documentary: A film record of unfictionalized events; a journalistic film investigation.

Dolby: A noise reduction system developed by Dolby Laboratories that reduces tape noise by use of a sophisticated electronic circuit.

Dolly: To shoot with a moving camera; also the name of the device for moving a supported camera.

Double exposure: Exposing the same strip of film twice to two different scenes, for a superimposition of images.

Double Super-8: Roll film (usually 100-foot rolls) 16mm wide, but with the Super-8 format, doubled and side by side. One side is exposed, the roll reversed and the other side exposed. The film is slit in processing, giving 200 feet of 8mm film. For use in specially designed cameras; not interchangeable with Super-8 cartridge-accepting machines.

Dual track: The use of the main and balance stripe in Super-8 films to carry each separate sound track not in stereo.

Dubbing: Mixing sound tracks; laying on a post-recorded track in sync with the filmed image.

Edge numbers: Four- to six-digit serial numbers printed in regular intervals (6 inches or 1 foot) along the edge of processed film. These appear on the original and the workprint and are used to synchronize picture with sound and to conform the cut workprint to the original film.

Emulsion: The light-sensitive coating applied to a celluloid base to create photographic film.

Establishing shot: A long shot at the beginning of a sequence that sets a visual mood or determines the location of subsequent action.

Exposure index: (EI, also ASA and ANSI). A numerical designation of a film's sensitivity to light. A film with EI of 100 requires half the amount of light to form an image as a film with EI 50.

Fade: A gradual disappearance (fade out) or appearance (fade in) of images by increasing or decreasing the exposure of the film. The terms fade up or fade down are used to indicate the emergence or reduction of sound in recording.

Fast lens: Lens speed is determined by the lens' ability to gather light and is measured in *f*/stops. An *f*/1.2 is a fast lens compared to *f*/1.8.

Fast motion: Speeded-up movements of filmed images created by "undercranking," *i.e.*, filming the action at a reduced frame rate and projecting at standard projection speed.

Fill light: Light aimed into and filling the shadows to reduce contrast.

Film chain: A five-bladed film projector and a video camera used in concert to convert motion picture film to video tape.

Filter: A device manufactured in a variety of colors using dyed gelatin or glass; attaches to the camera lens and selectively absorbs or transmits qualities of light in a scene. Absorbed colors will appear darker in the filmed image; transmitted colors will be relatively brighter.

Fine cut: The final, edited version of a film, ready to be either shown or printed.

Flatbed editor: A horizontal editing machine with forward and backward motor drive at variable speeds for editing sound and film in sync.

Focal length: The distance between the film and the optical center of a lens with the lens focused on a far object. The focal length of a camera lens is adjustable and will determine the size of the object filmed: move the lens to long focal lengths (70mm) and the subject becomes larger; move to a shorter focal length and the subject is smaller, but more of it is in view.

Follow focus: To change critical focusing during a shot so that a moving subject remains sharply focused.

Footcandle: A standardized unit of illumination denoting the amount of direct illumination on a square foot of surface that is at every point one foot away from one internationally standardized candle.

Format: A film's physical makeup, i.e., size, perforations, image size and sound track. The specifications of these characteristics are variable according to camera and projector size.

f/stop: A number in a system of numbers used to denote the size of the adjustable opening, or aperture, in the diaphragm within a lens. These numbers are marked on a ring outside the lens and are used to indicate the amount of light passing through the lens. A numerically large *f*/stop equals a small opening or less light.

Fps: Frames per second.

Frame: Each exposed or exposable picture area on a strip of film; used also to describe the outline of the image as seen through a camera's viewfinder.

Frame line: The area between each frame on a strip of film, or the area outlined by the viewfinder.

Freeze frame: An effect created by an optical printer where one frame is printed repeatedly to create an effect of stopped or "frozen" action in the projected film.

Front screen projection: A process where a camera and a projector are aligned, usually with a beamsplitter in front of a high gain screen material the purpose of which is to rephotograph the screened image, most often in combination with live actors in front of the screen. A special effects technique.

Frequency response: The range (in Hertz) of a recording instrument's ability to faithfully record or transmit sound.

Fullcoat: Sprocketed film that is fully coated on one side with a magnetic emulsion for sound recording.

Gaffer's tape: Strong, reusable wide gray adhesive tape that sticks securely to surfaces without marring when removed.

Gauge: A word often interchanged with format, it denotes a measurement of film's width.

Grain: The microscopic particles of silver halides in film's emulsion that are magnified greatly in the projected image and become visible as film grain. Fast films usually require a thicker emulsion and therefore produce more visible grain on the screen.

Grey card: A neutral grey test card with 18 percent reflectance, used as a factory standard for the setting of reflective light meters.

Grease pencil: A wax-based pencil used for marking or writing on film.

Grip: Film production workers whose special province is the physical set-up of equipment—loading, unloading, pushing dollies, moving and setting up walls, etc.

Ground glass: Glass manufactured with light-diffusing qualities.

Handheld: A shot or film made while holding the camera, rather than using a tripod or other support.

Hertz: (Hz.) Unit of measurement of sound waves named for physicist Heinrich Rudolph Hertz. The term is interchangeable with cps, or cycles per second, and refers to the number of "waves" of sound passing a certain point in a given time. 1000 Hz = 1000 cps. The human ear can hear a range of about 20 to 20,000 Hz and is most sensitive to sounds of 2000 to 4000 Hz.

High-speed film: (Also called fast film.) Film stocks that have an exposure index (EI) rating higher than 100. Generally grainier and less sharp than slow film (25 to 60 EI), high-speed films allow shooting in normal indoor (tungsten) lighting and other low-light conditions. There are many brands marketed in color and black-and-white.

Impedance: A measurement of mechanical friction for AC current. The impedance (measured in ohms and written as Z) of a recording device (in-camera or tape recorder) must match the Z of the microphone.

In-camera editing: An editing technique wherein shots are so carefully planned and executed as to require no subsequent (postproduction) editing.

Interlock: Any two or more machines run in synchronization.

Internegative: A negative printed from original camera film to be then printed on positive release stock.

Intersync: A process in video tape editing that locks the video playback machine and the video tape recorder into the same sync pulse.

Interval timer: A timing device, either accessory or built into a camera, that allows time-lapse filming and pixilation.

Jump cut: A break or jump from one setting or action to another from one shot to the next. Can be produced either in-camera or during editing.

Kelvin: A color temperature scale that measures specific changes from red-hot to the blue-white of molten metal. Yellow candlelight is less than 2000 K, an arc light is 5000 to 6000 K. The term is taken from the British physicist, Lord Kelvin. Kodachrome 40 is balanced for 3400 K.

Key light: The dominant light source in a scene.

Lab: The laboratory where film is processed or printed.

Lavalier: A small microphone designed to either hang about the neck or clip to clothing.

Leader: A length of coated or uncoated film attached to the beginning (head) of a reel of film to facilitate threading into the projector. Leaders can be black, white or gray and are sometimes marked with identification numbers.

LED: A light-emitting diode; a feature of some cameras for automatically testing the batteries. A light will appear in the viewfinder when batteries are running low.

Lip sync: A sound track synchronized in coordination with a speaking actor's lips, to within plus or minus one frame accuracy.

Live sync: To film either double or single sync sound as opposed to "dubbing" or recording the sound after the film is processed.

Long shot: (LS) A shot made from a distance that allows the frame to include the entire subject and much of its surroundings. A human figure will occupy less than half the height of the frame.

Loop: A length of film spliced end to end in order to run continuously through a projector usually for the purpose of dubbing a sound track.

Low key light: A lighting style created with dark-colored costumes, a high-intensity lighting ratio and a dimly lit background for a characteristic effect of overall darkness.

Macro filming: Filming with macro or close-up lens.

Macro lens: (Also called close-up lens.) A built-in lens, capable of allowing continuous focusing from infinity to within several inches of a subject.

Mag stripe: The magnetic stripe of iron oxide material applied to a film base for magnetic recording of sound on film.

Manual override: A control device on some cameras having automatic light meters that allows a manual setting of the light meter; similar controls override automatic level control in sound filming.

Master: A piece of equipment (i.e., camera or recorder) is designated "master" if its speed is governed by its own internal speed controls, and is capable of governing the speed of an auxiliary (slave); also, several sound tracks mixed down onto one tape becomes a master sound track.

Matte: An opaque screen or mask, with a cut-out area of various design, mounted in front of the lens or the film to restrict the image to the specific design.

Matte box: A device that will attach to the front of a camera to hold mattes and filters.

Medium shot: A shot made from such a distance so that half the subject is visible. An actor, for instance, would be framed from the waist up.

Mini camera: A line of film cameras by various companies, usually weighing slightly over 1 pound. Advertised as "pocketable."

Mixing: The process of combining several sound sources and controlling intensity and volume by use of an electronic device.

Mixer: An electronic component that will accept a number of different line and mic inputs and combine them into a single output. The relationship (intensity and volume) of a single sound to all the other sounds can be adjusted.

Monopod: A one-footed device for supporting and steadying a camera.

Multitrack: Fullcoat or mag tape with more than one sound-recording channel or track.

NiCad: A nickle-cadmium battery capable of being recharged.

Ohms: Unit of measurement of electrical resistance. Named for German electrician, G. S. Ohm, an ohm equals the resistance of a circuit in which a potential difference of one volt produces a current of one ampere (amp).

Omnidirectional mic: A microphone with a circular pick-up pattern, *i.e.*, it hears equally well in all directions.

Once-per-frame: A system (also known as a digital system) of double-system sync sound recording that utilizes a contact switch or a tone burst to send a signal from camera to tape recorder with each single frame to synchronize sound and picture during editing.

Optical effects: General term for all varieties of unusual visual effects created either in the camera (double exposures, split images), in the printing process (fades, dissolves, superimpositions), or on an optical bench (wipes, flips, freeze frames).

Optical sound track: Sound recording for 16 & 35mm movies utilizing instruments that produce a photographic record of sound on a track, which must be then added to film prints by a lab.

Outtakes: Shots or pieces of shots that have been edited out of the finished film.

Overexposure: Exposing film to more than the recommended amount of light, producing a bleached-out image.

Pan: (Short for panoramic.) A shot made by moving the camera in a horizontal plane from a fixed axis.

PC flash: Derived from Prontor Contact, from the West German company, Prontor, the PC is a specific type of connector in a camera, originally designed to fire a flash for single frame shots (or for still cameras). The system is often used in Super-8 cameras to generate a sync pulse for double system sound.

Pilotone: A type of sync pulse recording system, available in some Super-8 cameras, for double-system sound. The pilotone system uses a continuous sine wave or pulse of 60 Hz (countries outside the U.S. use 50 Hz), generated by the camera and recorded on the sync track in the tape recorder. One frame equals 2½ pulses (2 pulses in the 50 Hz system).

Pixilation: A process of animating live or three-dimensional subjects by single framing.

Polavision: Trade name for Polaroid's Instant movie process, which develops movie film in the cartridge in a matter of minutes, for screening (in the same cartridge) on special viewers.

Polyester base: A film base manufactured from petroleum, it is stronger and thinner than the more common cellulose acetate base.

Postproduction: All work done on a film after the initial footage is shot; i.e., editing, dubbing, printing, etc.

P.O.V.: Point of view; the technique of shooting from the point of view of what someone in the film is seeing.

Pre-striped: Film that has been sound striped in manufacture.

Pressure plate: Also called pressure gate, a plate or flat surface usually as long as several frames that is spring loaded to hold the film against the aperture plate during film advance.

Rear screen projection: Projecting the film image from behind a screen made of special plastic or ground glass. The audience views the image through the screen.

Reflex viewing: A camera design that allows the image to be viewed through the actual taking lens. This gives parallax-free viewing of objects in the field of view.

Regular 8: A version of the 8mm format with sprocket holes comparable to 16 or 35mm film, but with a frame of only 4.27 x 3.28mm as compared to the larger (5.46 x 4.01mm) Super-8 aspect ratio.

Rewinds: (Also called *winds*.) A device (used in pairs) for moving film through the viewer during filming. It is composed of a handle and gears to rotate the spindle on which rolls of film are mounted. Winds may have various handle-to-spindle ratios for controlling the speed of the film traveling through the viewer, and adjustable tension brakes.

Scrim: Wire mesh mounted on a light head to diffuse or reduce light intensity over part of the set area.

Sequence: A series of shots complete in itself that can occur in a single setting or several settings.

Sharpie: A felt tip pen that will write on film.

Shooting ratio: The ratio of film feet shot to the amount of edited footage in the finished film.

Shot: A continuous view filmed by one camera without interruption.

Shotgun mic: (Also called ultradirectional or hypercardioid mic.) A microphone with a relatively narrow pick-up pattern, it can be used at a greater distance from the source, usually as much as 12 feet (some are advertised to pick-up at 60 feet).

Shutter: A rotating disc between the lens and film that determines the length of exposure of each frame. Normal shutters in Super-8 have an opening of about 160 degrees, whereas XL shutters open to 220 degrees.

Shutter opening: A segment (on the order of 180 degrees, or half the disc) of the rotating metal shutter disc. When the shutter opening is rotated into place between the lens and the aperture, light is admitted and an exposure is made.

Single-8: A film product manufactured by Fuji Photo Film. It is actually Super-8 in frame and sprocket size, but packaged in an entirely different cartridge than Super-8 and must be used with a Single-8 camera manufactured only by Fuji. The cartridge resembles a recording tape cassette and allows unlimited backwinding; the film is made of polyester—stronger and thinner than the Super-8 film base of acetate.

Single frame: To expose one frame at a time, as in animation.

Single system: A way of recording synchronized sound directly onto magnetically striped film in the camera.

Slave: A piece of equipment (i.e., camera or recorder) is designated "slave" if its speed is being governed by another piece of equipment (master).

Slow motion: Created by filming at a faster rate of frames per second than is standard, then projecting at standard rate.

S.O.F.: Sound on film.

Sound head: The recording component of a magnetic sound system, the head is basically a circle of iron with a very small gap. Current (sound) passing through the coiled iron creates a field of strong magnetism across the gap. Plastic tape with a magnetic coating drawn evenly past the gap will receive and retain the magnetized particles (sound).

Sound-on-sound: Recording directly on top of a prerecorded track by partially subduing or erasing the original track.

Sound-over-sound: Mixing sound with two monophonic tape recorders by de-activating the erase head while recording. The recording quality will be poor, giving somewhat fuzzy sound.

Sound recording: Acoustical energy collected and converted into electro-magnetic energy (magnetic recording), mechanical energy (disc recording), or photographic energy (optical recording). This energy is stored until required, then transformed again into acoustical energy through sound reproducing equipment.

Sound-with-sound: Making two recordings on two separate tracks that are carried by the same base material.

Sound stripe: A magnetic band or stripe, placed alongside the picture area on movie film to permit magnetic recording.

Splice: To join two pieces of film or tape, either with cement or adhesive splicing tape. The word "splice" is also used to denote the exact line where two pieces of film or tape are joined.

Sprocket holes: Perforations along one or both edges (single or double perf) of film or tape, used to move the film through camera, printer or projector.

Stylus: In terms of recorded sound (disk recordings), there is both a cutting (recording) stylus and a pick-up (reproducing) stylus. Both are small shafts of either sapphire or diamond (sometimes steel) with a carefully designed pointed tip for either cutting or tracing a continuous spiral groove in wax or plastic.

Synchronizer: (Also sync block.) A device that holds 2 or more rolls of film together for frame by frame correspondence while editing.

Telecine projector: A Super-8 projector with a specially constructed shutter that exposes each frame 5 times per second rather than the standard 3 times per second. Used specifically in film-to-video transfer.

Three-D: (Also 3-D.) A process of filmmaking producing an image that allows a fusion of right and left eye images, creating a unique aspect of depth and perspective in the screened image. Three-D movies require specific equipment for both production and viewing.

Through-the-lens metering: A built-in automatic light metering device utilizing a beamsplitter to capture lens light for metering.

Tilt: A camera angle derived by pivoting or tilting the camera either up or down or sideways.

Time exposure: Very long exposures of each frame.

Time lapse: Single frame exposures made at specific intervals, used especially for filming actions that occur too slowly to be normally observed, such as flowers growing.

Transfer: The process of converting the filmed image to video tape or transferring sound from a cassette recorder to a fullcoat recorder.

Tripod: A three-legged, adjustable camera support.

Trucking: Moving a camera along with a moving subject while shooting, usually with a dolly or other mobilized camera support.

Umbrella: A special, silver-surfaced umbrella mounted on a light source for bouncing or reflecting light.

Underexposure: Shooting with too little light, producing darkened images.

UV filter: An ultra-violet (1A) filter, reduces the ultra-violet light reaching the film, thus reducing haze.

Vacuumating: A postproduction film treatment that removes the moisture in newly processed film and replaces it with emulsion hardeners and preservatives.

Variable shutter speed: An option of some cameras allowing the size of the shutter opening to be controlled, thus regulating both exposure and depth of field.

Viewer: A rear screen projection device used for screening film while editing.

Viewfinder: An optical device on a camera that shows the exact area being photographed.

Vignetting: A falling-off in brightness toward the corners of the frame; due to the elliptical shape of taking and projecting lenses. Can be reduced by stopping down the aperture.

Voice-over narration: An unseen narrator's voice describes or annotates the action being viewed.

Wide-angle lens: A lens with a shorter than normal focal length, giving wider than normal field of view.

Wild sound: Sound recorded while shooting or added to the print with no specific aim at synchronization.

Wipe: One shot is gradually pushed off the screen by another shot; produced in optical printing.

Wireless mic: A microphone (a lavalier or easily concealed type) using an FM transmitter to broadcast the signal to the receiver.

Workprint: An inexpensive print (with optional edge numbers) made from all or most of the original footage. It can be roughly handled, cut and recut. When a final edit is decided upon, the original film is carefully match-cut or conformed to the workprint.

Wow & flutter: Distortion in sound reproducing systems caused by speed fluctuations.

XL: (Existing light.) A term used to denote both a camera type and a system of filming. The camera will have a broad (220°) shutter angle and a fast lens (*f*/1.2). The system utilizes an XL camera and fast film and allows filming in extremely low light situations.

AUTHORS' BIOGRAPHIES

Lucien Aigner photographed weddings for several decades and found that his skills as a still photographer helped develop the simplified method he uses for making Super-8 wedding films.

Yvonne Anderson continues her Super-8 work with children at the Yellow Ball Workshop, in addition to teaching a Super-8 course, Filmmaking for the Classroom Teacher, at the University of Massachusetts. She has authored several books on animation and teaches a course in 16mm animation at the Rhode Island School of Design.

Stephen R. E. Aubery was the Senior Motion Picture Sound Technician at Brigham Young University in Utah, and has been connected with Super-8 Concept Films, a Super-8 production facility in Orem, Utah.

Dr. Francis R. Breen, Jr. Director of Clinical Hematology and Oncology for the Mercy Catholic Medical Center, Philadelphia, has produced films for Immaculata College and promotional films for several businesses. He reviews Super-8 commercial prints for two publications, *Film Buff* and *Screen Thrills.*

Mik Derks lives on a farm in Wisconsin. He is author of a book on Super-8 production, *Home Movies the Professional Way*, and is a frequent contributor to *Super-8 Filmaker* magazine.

Don Dohler's sci-fi Super-8 feature, *The Alien Factor*, has recently been bought for worldwide TV syndication and will be released in a Super-8 color/sound version. Dohler manages a production company, Planet Pictures Corp., and is publisher/editor of *Cinemagic* magazine.

Dennis Duggan is an independent Super-8 filmmaker and still photographer, living in San Francisco. He is an editorial consultant for *Super-8 Filmaker* magazine.

Steve Gerber is an amateur filmmaker and a writer of comic book stories for Marvel Comics Group in New York City.

Paul Gray is the director of the Gray Film Atelier, a 2-year intensive Super-8 and 16mm film production school in Hoosick Falls, New York.

Kenneth Gullakson is an amateur filmmaker residing in Glendale, California, where he produced *The Theta Factor.*

James Gustafson is currently working as a producer/writer in the Media Center for the American Hospital Association, where he produces video, film and sound slide programs covering every aspect of health care.

Cleg Holiman has been working in Super-8 since 1974 when he made the prize-winning *Lacuna*. He lives in Colorado and is currently completing a half-hour film, *Circadian.*

Chris Jones, in addition to filming weddings, works as a freelance production assistant on TV commercials in New York City.

Carole Kahn is currently a field film producer with WNBC-TV in New York City, working on "*Buying—Betty Furness*," filmed in 16mm.

Joel Kauffmann is an amateur filmmaker and inventor living in Elkhart, Indiana.

Carl Lamm is a filmmaking instructor at Lawrence Junior High School in Lawrence, New York.

John Lidstone is Professor of Art Education at Queens College and film consultant to the Collegiate School in New York City. He is co-author of *Children as Film Makers*, published by Van Nostrand Reinhold, Inc.

Lenny Lipton has made more than two dozen films, and is presently making stereoscopic films using a system of his own devising. A report on this project will be given in *A Study In Depth*, to be published by the University of California Press. He is the author of *Independent Filmmaking, The Super-8 Book* and *Lipton on Filmmaking*, all published by Simon & Schuster.

Betty McAfee has four Super-8 films currently in distribution. At present she is planning a multi-media presentation of her recent trip to Cuba, using both Super-8 and 35mm slides.

Bernie Michaels is an independent producer and founder of MBM Productions in Victor, New York.

Mark Mikolas served for six years as Super-8 producer, consultant and educator and as a principal of the Super-8 Film Group. He is co-author of the *Handbook of Super-8 Production*, an editorial consultant to *Super-8 Filmaker* magazine, and has published numerous articles. Mikolas has taught Super-8 filmmaking from elementary to graduate school level.

Robert Owen is a freelance filmmaker and writer living in Napa, California. He has worked as a Super-8 stringer cameraperson and reporter for a television station in northern California.

James Percelay has been managing a commercial film studio, Cine Studio, in New York City since his last commissioned Super-8 film, *Drew University. . .A Way of Knowing,* in 1977.

Jim Piper's Super-8 films have won several awards. He is a feature writer for *Super-8 Filmaker* magazine and a film teacher at Fresno State Community College in California.

Tony Plesman is an independent filmmaker living in New York City, and a writer for several periodicals.

Robert Price is a professional photographer and audiovisual consultant. He recently helped a California TV station set up for Super-8 broadcasting.

Raul da Silva has won more than two dozen national and international film awards, including a 1973 Cine Gold Eagle for *The Silent Drum.*

George Siposs has produced several sports training, industrial, teaching and marketing presentation movies in Super-8 and has written on 8mm filmmaking for a variety of periodicals. He is author of *How to Illustrate Publications for Lectures*, in which Super-8 is discussed as an instructional aid for teachers.

Elinor Stecker, a still photographer as well as filmmaker, makes public relations films, mainly in the areas of health and rehabilitation. She writes for a number of publications, and is the author of *The Master Handbook of Still and Movie Tilting for Amateur and Professional.*

J. K. Takahashi is an independent producer of documentary films and videotapes, as well as a teacher in Special Education.

Joe Thompson is an independent film producer and cameraperson and owner of Seavision Productions in San Diego, California. He has worked with underwater explorer Jacques Cousteau aboard the *Calypso,* and has produced documentaries in Super-8 and 16mm.

Karen Thorsen is a freelance writer in New York City. She helped organize the "Carnival Super-8" film festival and has written on Super-8 for various periodicals.

Gerald Vinarcik is a freelance underwater filmmaker who has been filming marine life in the Caribbean.

William C. Wind has been making 8mm films for 20 years and has collected Super-8 commercial prints for almost as long, with over 400 titles in his library. Currently he works as a writer/director of 16mm films.

Jerry Yulsman is the author of *The Complete Book of 8mm Movie Making*, and is currently teaching at the School of Visual Arts in New York City.

Robert and Eileen Zalisk's interests and training are in the natural and social sciences. Eileen is Senior Editor of *Reviews of Modern Physics*, at the American Institute of Physics, and Bob coordinates the University Seminar on Contemporary India at Columbia University and teaches filmmaking at Rutgers University. They are independent producers for WBAI-FM in New York and in 1977 won a Major Armstrong Award in the category of educational documentary.

RESOURCE DIRECTORY

Accessories
Camera Bazaar
2747 E. Atlantic Blvd.
Pompano Beach, Fla. 33062

Camera Mart
625 "B" Street
San Diego, Calif. 92101

Cartoon Colour
9024 Lindblade St.
Culver City, Calif. 90230

Chinon Corp. of America
43 Fadem Rd.
Springfield, N.J. 07081

Halmar Enterprises
Box 793
Niagara Falls, Ontario
Canada L2E 6V6

Animation
Cartoon Colour
9024 Lindblade St.
Culver City, Calif. 90230

Heath Productions
1700 N. Westshore Blvd.
Tampa, Fla. 33607

Ox Products
180 East Prospect Ave.
Mamaroneck, N.Y. 10543

Oxberry & Richmark
180 Broad St.
Carlstadt, N.J. 07072

Batteries
Cine-60
630 Ninth Ave.
New York, N.Y. 10036

Books
Cartoon Colour
9024 Lindblade St.
Culver City, Calif. 90230

Cameras
Bauer-A.I.C. Photo
168 Glen Cove Rd.
Carle Place, N.Y. 11514

Beaulieu
7100 McCormick Rd.
Chicago, Ill. 60645

Bell & Howell/Mamiya
7100 McCormick Rd.
Chicago, Ill. 60645

Bolex (U.S.A.)
250 Community Drive
Great Neck, N.Y. 11020

Canon U.S.A.
10 Nevada Dr.
Lake Success, N.Y. 11040

Carena/Photo America Corp.
7491 N.W. 8th St.
Miami, Fla. 33126

Chinon Corp. of America
43 Fadem Rd.
Springfield, N.J. 07081

Eastman Kodak Co.
343 State St.
Rochester, N.Y. 14650

Elmo Mfg. Co.
70 New Hyde Park Rd.
New Hyde Park, N.Y. 11040

Eumig (U.S.A.)
225 Community Dr.
Great Neck, N.Y. 11020

Fuji Photo Film U.S.A. Inc.
350 Fifth Ave.
New York, N.Y. 10001

Sankyo Seiki (America)
1275 Valley Brook Ave.
Lyndhurst, N.J. 07071

Clapboards
Hollywood Clacker
11166 Gault St.
No. Hollywood, Calif. 91605

Editing Equipment
Cinema Sync Systems
14261 Ave. Mendocino
Irvine, Calif. 92714

Knox Manufacturing Co.
111 Spruce St.
Wooddale, Ill. 60191

Octagon Cinema Equipment
130 Jane St.
New York, NY 10014

SERA
314 Victory Dr.
Herndon, Va. 22070

Victor Duncan
200 E. Ontario St.
Chicago, Ill. 60611

Victor Duncan
32380 Howard St.
Madison Heights, Mich. 48071

Victor Duncan
2659 Fondren Dr.
Dallas, Texas 75206

Film
Fuji Photo Film U.S.A.
350 Fifth Ave.
New York, N.Y. 10001

Leo Diner Films
350 Golden Gate Ave.
San Francisco, Calif. 94102

Film Collecting
Blackhawk Films
1235 West 5th St.
Davenport, Iowa 52808

Columbia Pictures 8mm
711 Fifth Ave.
New York, N.Y. 10022

DeMaio Films
20222 Morristown Circle
Huntington Beach, Calif. 92646

Halco Films
6311 Yucca St., Suite 752
Los Angeles, Calif. 90028

Niles Films
1141 Mishawaka Ave.
South Bend, Ind. 46615

Reel Images
456 Monroe Turnpike
Monroe, Conn. 06468

Select Films
115 W. 31st St.
New York, N.Y. 10001

Universal 8mm Films
445 Park Ave.
New York, N.Y. 10022

Film Preservation & Restoration
Edwal Scientific
12120 S. Peoria
Chicago, Ill. 60643

Filmlife
Div. of American Film Repair Institute
141 Moonachie Rd.
Moonachie, N.J. 07074

Lindau Film Cleaners
P.O. Box 897
Lake Forest, Ill. 60045

Gadget Bags
Knox Manufacturing
111 Spruce St.
Wooddale, Ill. 60191

Ultimate Experience
P.O. Box 2118
Santa Barbara, Calif. 93120

Home Movie Items
Blackhawk Films
1235 West 5th St.
Davenport, Iowa 52808

Chinon Corp. of America
43 Fadem Rd.
Springfield, N.J. 07081

Columbia Pictures 8mm
711 Fifth Ave.
New York, N.Y. 10022

Halmar Enterprises
Box 793
Niagara Falls, Ontario
Canada L2E 6V6

Kem Electronics
24 Vivian Ave.
Hendon, London NW4 3XP
England

Micro Record Processor
487-38 South Ave.
Beacon, N.Y. 12508

Photographic Specialties
Protect-a-Print
11450 Ventura Blvd.
Studio City, Calif. 91604

Lab Services
Cinema Sync Systems
14261 Ave. Mendocino
Irvine, Calif. 92714

Huemark Films
227 E. 44th St.
New York, N.Y. 10017

Kin-O-Lux, Inc.
17 West 45th St.
New York, N.Y. 10036

Leo Diner Films
350 Golden Gate Ave.
San Francisco, Calif. 94102

Newsfilm Labs
516 N. Larchmont Blvd.
Los Angeles, Calif. 90004

Super Cine, Inc.
2218 West Olive Ave.
Burbank, Calif. 91506

Super 8/16 Studios
230 Hyde St.
San Francisco, Calif. 94102

W.A. Palmer Films, Inc.
611 Howard St.
San Francisco, Calif. 94105

Lenses
Chinon Corp. of America
43 Fadem Rd.
Springfield, N.J. 07081

Fuji Photo Film U.S.A.
350 Fifth Ave.
New York, N.Y. 10001

Photo America
7491 N.W. 8th St.
Miami, Fla. 33126

Lighting
Chinon Corp. of America
43 Fadem Rd.
Springfield, N.J. 07081

Lowel-Light Mfg.
421 West 54th St.
New York, N.Y. 10019

Smith-Victor Sales
301 North Colfax St.
Griffith, Ind. 46319

Mail Order Equipment
Berger Bros.
126 Broadway (Rte. 110)
Amityville, L.I., N.Y. 11701

Camera Bazaar
2747 E. Atlantic Blvd.
Pompano Beach, Fla. 33062

Cartoon Colour
9024 Lindblade St.
Culver City, Calif. 90230

Cinema Sync Systems
14261 Ave. Mendocino
Irvine, Calif. 92714

Porter's Camera Store
P.O. Box 628
Cedar Falls, Iowa 50613

Studio-8
246-17 Jamaica Ave.
Bellrose, N.Y. 11426

Microphones

AKG Acoustics
92 McKee Dr.
Mahwah, N.J. 07430

Broadcast Equipment
P.O. Box 3141
Bristol, Tenn. 37620

Chinon Corp. of America
43 Fadem Rd.
Springfield, N.J. 07081

Octagon Cinema Equipment
130 Jane St.
New York, NY 10014

Sennheiser Electrical
10 W. 37th St.
New York, N.Y. 10018

Optical Printing

Newsfilm Labs
516 Larchmont Blvd.
Los Angeles, Calif. 90004

Projection Screens

Da-Lite Screen Co.
Warsaw, Ind. 46580

Knox Manufacturing Co.
111 Spruce St.
Wooddale, Ill. 60191

Projectors

Bauer
A.I.C. Photo
168 Glen Cove Rd.
Carle Place, N.Y. 11514

Beaulieu
7100 McCormich Rd.
Chicago, Ill. 60645

Bell & Howell/Mamiya Co.
7100 McCormick Rd.
Chicago, Ill. 60645

Bolex (U.S.A.)
250 Community Drive
Great Neck, N.Y. 11020

Canon U.S.A.
10 Nevada Dr.
Lake Success, N.Y. 11040

Chinon Corp. of America
43 Fadem Rd.
Springfield, N.J. 07081

Eastman Kodak Co.
343 State St.
Rochester, N.Y. 14650

Elmo Mfg. Co.
70 New Hyde Park Rd.
New Hyde Park, N.Y. 11040

Eumig (U.S.A.)
225 Community Dr.
Great Neck, N.Y. 11020

Fuji Photo Film U.S.A.
350 Fifth Ave.
New York, N.Y. 10001

Octagon Cinema Equipment
130 Jane St.
New York, NY 10014

Photo America
7491 N.W. 8th St.
Miami, Fla. 33126

Sankyo Seiki (America)
1275 Valley Brook Ave.
Lyndhurst, N.J. 07071

Recording Equipment
Cinema Sync Systems
14261 Ave. Mendocino
Irvine, Calif. 92714

Octagon Cinema Equipment
130 Jane St.
New York, NY 10014

Super-8 Sound
95 Harvey St.
Cambridge, Mass. 02140

Victor Duncan
200 E. Ontario St.
Chicago, Ill. 60611

Schools
Columbia College
925 N. La Brea Ave.
Hollywood, Calif. 90038

National Camera
2000 W. Union Ave.
Englewood, Colo. 80110

Sound Effects
BBC Library
Films for the Humanities
P.O. Box 2053
Princeton, N.J. 08540

Thomas J. Valentino
151 West 46th St.
New York, N.Y. 10036

Sound Equipment
Cinema Sync Systems
14261 Ave. Mendocino
Irvine, Calif. 92714

Octagon Cinema Equipment
130 Jane St.
New York, NY 10014

Broadcast Equipment Co.
P.O. Box 3141
Bristol, Tenn. 37620

Special Effects
Camera Bazaar
2747 E. Atlantic Blvd.
Pompano Beach, Fla. 33062

Splicers
Ciro Equipment Corp.
6820 Romaine St.
Hollywood, Calif. 90038

Fuji Photo Film U.S.A.
350 Fifth Ave.
New York, N.Y. 10001

Hudson Photographic Industries
2 S. Buckhout St.
Irvington, N.Y. 10533

Maier-Hancock Industries
13212 Raymer St.
No. Hollywood, Calif. 91325

Metric Splicer & Film Co.
5271 Wendover Rd.
Yorba Linda, Calif. 92686

Striping
Cresta Magnetics, Ltd.
3201 Coral Dr.
Oceanside, Calif. 92054

Magnetone Industries, Ltd.
Magnetone Dr.
Bainsville, Ontario
Canada KOC 1EO

Newsfilm Labs
516 N. Larchmont Blvd.
Los Angeles, Calif. 90004

Octagon Cinema Equipment
130 Jane St.
New York, NY 10014

Rupert Taylor
500 Middle Rd.
Belmont, Calif. 94002

Tape
Magnetone Industries, Ltd.

Magnetone Dr.
Bainsville, Ontario
Canada KOC 1EO

Octagon Cinema Equipment
130 Jane St.
New York, NY 10014

Titles
Presgrip Sign Co.
Winnal Valley Rd.
Winchester
Hampshire, England

Smith-Victor Sales Corp.
301 North Colfax St.
Griffith, Ind. 46319

Transfer Service
Cinema Sync Systems
14621 Ave. Mendocino
Irvine, Calif. 92714

Newsfilms Labs
516 N. Larchmont Blvd.
Los Angeles, Calif. 90004

Tripods & Camera Supports
Miller Professional Equipment
10861 Burbank Blvd.
No. Hollywood, Calif. 90601

P & L Industries
Box 35364
Minneapolis, Minn. 55435

Smith-Victor Sales Corp.
301 North Colfax St.
Griffith, Ind. 46319

Velbon International
2433 Moreton St.
Torrance, Calif. 90505

Underwater Equipment
Fuji Photo Film U.S.A.
350 Fifth Ave.
New York, N.Y. 10001

Ikelite Underwater Systems
3303 N. Illinois St.
Indianapolis, Ind. 46208

Video
Niles Cinema
P.O. Box 1576
South Bend, Ind. 46634

Panasonic
1 Panasonic Way
Secaucus, N.J. 07094

Reel Images
456 Monroe Turnpike
Monroe, Conn. 06468

Video Transfers
Fotomat
Consult White Pages of phone book for nearest location or call toll-free (800) 325-4089, in Missouri (800) 392-3716

Leo Diner Films
332-350 Golden Gate Ave.
San Francisco, Calif. 94102

INDEX

D

E

F

G

H

I

T

U

V

W

X

Z

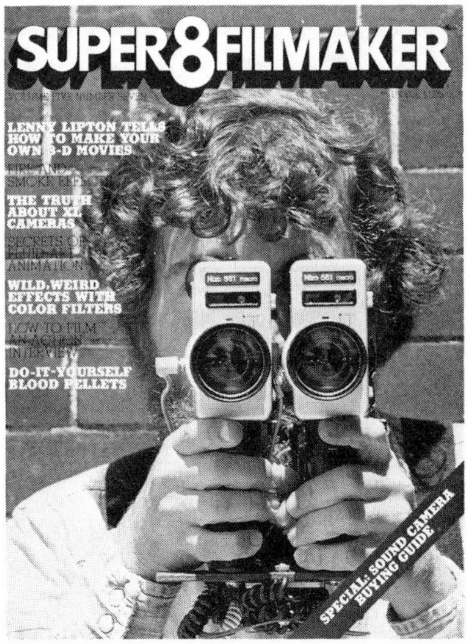

The Filmmaker's Friend

Now that you've read this sampling of great tips and information available in the pages of SUPER-8 FILMAKER magazine, we know you will want to take this opportunity to begin reading SUPER-8 FILMAKER on a regular basis. Write for a sample copy and subscription information to **SUPER-8 FILMAKER, 609 Mission Street, Dept. B, San Francisco, CA 94105.**

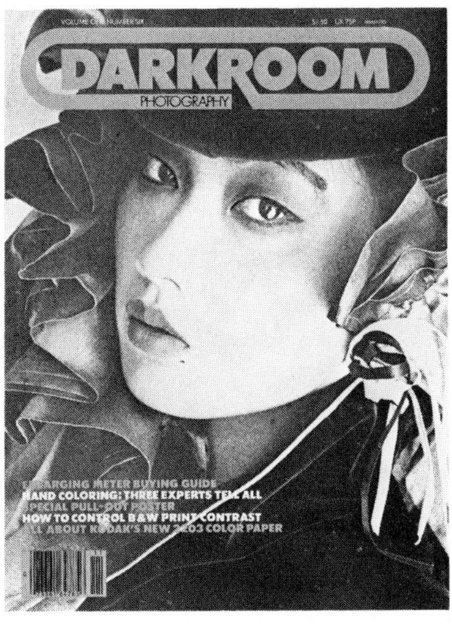

Don't Be Afraid Of The Dark

Are you also interested in still photography? If the answer is yes, then you will want to read SHEPTOW PUBLISHING's newest publication, DARKROOM PHOTOGRAPHY, the magazine that takes over "after you click the shutter." It tells you what you need to know about darkroom techniques, darkroom products and dark room artists. Write for a sample copy and subscription information to **DARKROOM PHOTOGRAPHY, 609 Mission Street. Dept. B, San Francisco, CA 94105.**